Social Work Advocacy

A New Framework for Action

ROBERT L. SCHNEIDER
Virginia Commonwealth University

LORI LESTER

BROOKS/COLE

™

THOMSON LEARNING

Australia • Canada • Mexico • Singapore • Spain • United Kingdom • United States

BROOKS/COLE

™

THOMSON LEARNING

Executive Editor: *Lisa Gebo*
Assistant Editor: *Susan Wilson*
Editorial Assistant: *JoAnne von Zastrow*
Marketing Manager: *Caroline Concilla*
Project Editor: *Pam Suwinsky*
Print Buyer: *Robert King*
Permissions Editor: *Bob Kauser*

Production Service: *Gustafson Graphics*
Copy Editor: *Linda Ireland*
Cover Designer: *Bill Stanton*
Cover Images: *Photodisc, Eyewire*
Cover Printer: *Webcom, Limited*
Compositor: *Gustafson Graphics*
Printer: *Webcom*

Printed in Canada
4 5 6 7 08 07 06

For permission to use material from this text, contact
us by **Web:** http://www.thomsonrights.com
Fax: 1-800-730-2215 **Phone:** 1-800-730-2214

International Headquarters
Thomson Learning
International Division
290 Harbor Drive, 2nd Floor
Stamford, CT 06902-7477
USA

UK/Europe/Middle East/South Africa
Thomson Learning
Berkshire House
168-173 High Holborn
London WC1V 7AA
United Kingdom

Asia
Thomson Learning
60 Albert Street #15-01
Albert Complex
Singapore 189969

Canada
Nelson Thomson Learning
1120 Birchmount Road
Toronto, Ontario M1K 5G4
Canada

For more information, contact
Wadsworth/Thomson Learning
10 Davis Drive
Belmont, CA 94002-3098
USA
http://www.wadsworth.com

Library of Congress Cataloging-in-Publication Data

Schneider, Robert L.
    Social work advocacy: a new framework for action/authors, Robert L. Schneider, Lori Lester.
       p. cm.
    Includes bibliographical references and index.
    ISBN 0-8304-1524-6
       1. Social advocacy—United States.   I. Lester, Lori.

HV95 .S355 2000
361.3'2'0973—dc21

00-042907

Acknowledgments

Our book is indebted to many experiences, resources, and people. We asked for many things and usually received more than we expected or deserved. We are grateful to all, expressing our heartfelt thanks for shared time, knowledge, and ideas.

First, we would like to recognize some important historical figures who not only influenced our own understanding of social work advocacy, but shaped the profession's sensitivities to it as well. While not an exclusive listing, these individuals include: Jane Addams, Lillian Wald, Porter R. Lee, Mary Richmond, Florence Kelly, Julia Lathrop, Sophonisba Breckinridge, Mary Van Kleek, Natalie W. Linderholm, Sidonia Dawson, Mary Simkhovitch, Emily Greene Balch, Frances Perkins, Alexander Johnson, Bertha Reynolds, Samuel Lindsay, Ellen Gates Starr, Graham Taylor, Harry Hopkins, and Charles Faulkner.

Another group of individuals from a more recent time period to whom we are indebted includes: Scott Briar, Nancy Amidei, George Brager, Charles Grosser, Karen Haynes and James Mickelson, Charles Levy, Frances Piven and Richard Cloward, Michael Reisch, Paul Terrell, Leslie Leighninger, Phyllis Day, members of the 1969 NASW Ad Hoc Committee on Advocacy, Harry Specht, Mark Ezell, Arnold Panitch, Jacqueline Mondros and Scott Wilson, Willard Richan, Patrick Riley, Ursula Gerhart, Mary McCormick, Herbert Kutchins and Stuart Kutchins, Marie Weil, Ronald Dear and Rino Patti, Wilbur J. Cohen, Michael Sosin and Sharon Caulum, James Wolk, and Barabara McGowan. Each of these persons has contributed to our understanding of the meaning and role of advocacy with particular insight; they have advanced, we believe, our collective capacity to find solutions through advocacy.

Special thanks go to many colleagues. For Bob, the book would never have been written without the particular support of Dean Frank Baskind, F. Ellen Netting, and Mary Catherine O'Connor, all of the VCU School of Social Work. For Lori, special thanks go to Mindy Loiselle, Beverly Koerin, Jackie Burgeson, Matthias Naleppa, Amy Waldbillig, Jennifer Gray, Barbara Birch, Vicky Fisher, Tony Vadella, and Popular Springs Hospital. Lori and Bob also acknowledge Steve Waldron, who serves as an inspiration to all social workers for his exemplary advocacy on behalf of misrepresented and misunderstood populations.

This book is also significantly indebted to students in the School of Social Work at Virginia Commonwealth University. Thousands of persons in Virginia have been assisted by a few hundred students who have risked becoming advocates over the past ten years. Their enthusiasm and creativity in "advocating" for their clients, causes, agencies, and legislative bills has left an indelible mark on their professor. Some of the testimony and vignettes in this book are based on student advocacy projects. (In some cases, names are disguised.) Many efforts were successful while others were less so, but the spirit of social work advocacy has pervaded them all!

We wish to acknowledge the efforts of the staff of Wadsworth Publishing Company, particularly Lisa Gebo, Susan Wilson, JoAnne von Zastrow, Pam Suwinsky, and Caroline Concilla. Many obstacles were cleared away by their expert and eager assistance.

To our reviewers, we express our appreciation for comments, suggestions, questions, insights, and contributions to the final version of this book. Many thanks to Maria DeGennaro, San Diego State University; Virginia Majewski, California University of Pennsylvania; Sonja Matison, Eastern Washington University; and Carolyn Tice, Ohio University, Athens.

Finally, we recognize those individuals who had to sacrifice the most in order to see this book through to completion, that is, our families. The many days and hours spent with our manuscript meant time away from our spouses, Anita and Marty. We appreciate their patience, prodding, loyalty, and support, and we ask forgiveness for excesses that only a goal like this book could drive us to. We dedicate the book to both of you, hoping you know we still believe in "time together."

To my wife, Anita, a social worker and immigration attorney, who effectively combines advocacy from both professions to help her clients; to my children, Erika and Gabe, young adults now, who are entering the world with a spirit that makes me proud.

—BOB

To my husband, Marty, and my grandmother, Helen, both of whom have been constant pillars of support and love throughout the years. To my daughter, Rene Elizabeth, whose life inspired me into working toward a more humane and just society.

—LORI

Contents

Preface

Our greatest weakness lies in giving up. The most certain way to succeed is to always try just one more time.

THOMAS A. EDISON

The excitement and challenge of social work advocacy often arises from speaking to a colleague or student who has been involved recently in an activity designed to improve conditions for a client or cause. You can read about some of this excitement and hubbub in the "advocates in action" quotes in each chapter. We think you will capture there the adrenaline and yearning that motivates social work advocates who are trying to promote professional values and social change as we enter the 21st century. We also received a letter recently that highlights advocacy for the social work student-author, Keith Gregory, who shared these thoughts with us:

> I went to the all-day conference yesterday on the plight of the Mattaponi Indians who are fighting the proposed reservoir project in King William county (*building a reservoir would seriously damage tribal fishing and inundate sacred grounds*). I went in neutral, but came out mad and embarrassed to be a Virginia "native," knowing that I had to rethink what *that* word really means. . . .

> What I saw today was an arrogant display of indifference to these people, going far beyond economics, cost/benefit analysis, and future water needs. Well, I am angry and ready to roll up my sleeves. I met some of God's most humble creation today being treated as if they did not exist. I immediately felt a kinship and love for these people. I was embarrassed as a fellow Virginian, but Carl Custalow (*tribal chief*) treated me so kindly, inviting me to visit during the spawning of the shad. . . .

> It's not often that I compose a note such as this at this hour of the morning, but I simply have not been able to sleep after witnessing what I did today. . . . Could Pat and I possibly address your current policy class? Would you be willing to meet with us over lunch? Thanks for drilling into me the meaning of social work. It's given me a reason for being out there and I feel I am ready to work now.

Keith Gregory's commitment to advocacy is similar to that of many persons in the profession, and we wrote this book explicitly to *promote the practice and use of advocacy.* We think that advocacy represents all that is best about the profession. In fact, advocacy, social justice, and social reform have been associated with the profession of social work for over 100 years (Gibelman, 1999) (See Chapter 1, Advocacy's Rich and Diverse History.) Our hope is to continue this tradition, improving it if we can, for another 100 years.

As we spent the past two and a half years researching and writing this book, we discovered that, despite the linkage to advocacy, many professionals believe that there is no agreed-upon definition of the term. Indeed, *advocacy* has been used over the decades to describe nearly every conceivable social work role such as broker, facilitator, community organizer, activist, and reformer without any distinguishing and specific characteristics of its own. Consequently, this ambiguity has, in our opinion, weakened the profession's commitment to advocacy because no one knows for sure what advocacy really is, under what conditions one practices it, how obligated social workers are to do it, and what exactly constitutes the practice of advocacy. Ezell (1994) and Pawlak and Flynn (1990) agree with McGowan (1987) that "we know very little about the extent and nature of social workers' advocacy." When questions of efficacy arise, that is, how does one do advocacy well, what works, and what is effective, the authors found no common definition and only limited dimensions by which to evaluate and test it.

We believe that the time has come to clarify again the role that advocacy plays in the social work profession. In order to recognize the work of many others (see the Acknowledgments section), the authors analyzed previous definitions and sorted through the multiple distinctions and dimensions surrounding the term *advocacy*. Then we created our own *new* definition of advocacy (Chapter 2), designed a practice framework (Chapters 3 and 4), and applied advocacy principles to four diverse contexts for practitioners (Chapters 5, 6, 7, and 8). Proposals are recommended for advocacy with clients, causes, legislative issues, and in administrative arenas. Each of these individual chapters can be taught or studied separately from the others, except for the definition and general practice framework chapters. Faculty may use each chapter as a distinct module in order to emphasize advocacy in different settings and roles. The definition and framework remain constant and serve as the basis of the book, reinforcing the unity of advocacy even as it is practiced differently.

We believe that this book now offers the professional social worker a clear, specific, yet limited approach to advocacy that can be investigated and tested, analyzed and compared, taught and studied, and refined into a professional role for all social workers in pursuit of effective advocacy. As Schneider and Netting (1999) stated, social work is the one profession that has maintained a healthy tension between the individual and the larger society decade after decade. Students entering social work educational programs are often unaware of the need to connect the often invisible struggles of individuals with the more public actions of decision makers in powerful positions.

Many have inaccurately assessed the profession as focused largely on individuals. We remind the readers that all social workers are obligated by the National Social Work Association's *Code of Ethics* (1996) to commit themselves to practicing advocacy broadly. *It is not a choice. Advocacy is a requirement as a social worker.*

Given advocacy's importance, one of the primary foci of the book is *effectiveness.* If the profession cannot demonstrate how to actually plan and implement advocacy effectively, its credibility is open to attack. The authors developed the book's guidelines/framework and its principles on as much research data as were available at the time of its writing. Therefore, the new definition and framework are the result of a synthesis of the empirical literature, incorporation of practice wisdom, and analysis of actual advocacy ventures. There are data supporting each major concept and principle.

We also recommend that faculty use current examples of conditions/problems frequently found in the news media as the basis for class discussion, case studies, and analytical assignments. The definition and framework can easily be adapted to these "realistic" situations in which social workers find themselves. The case vignettes found in Chapters 5, 6, 7 and 8 are examples of recent social work advocacy and illustrate several of the principles contained in the practice framework.

With advances in technology and the Internet, advocacy practices will be changing with the times. There are already movements that use websites and networks of communication via e-mail effectively. Current examples are: InterHealth, Alliance for Justice, Amnesty International, Influencing State Policy, Children's Defense Fund, National Coalition for the Homeless, and so on. Listed in Appendix A is a sampling of websites that may be used by students and faculty to serve as resources and examples of advocacy with a high-tech edge. We think the basic principles and definition of advocacy will continue to apply to most social work interventions.

Our desire is for an increasing number of social workers to advocate for their clients and causes. We hope that our attempt to define the concept of advocacy with its specific dimensions contributes to that ideal. If you wish to communicate with us about your ideas, suggestions, and successful or failed advocacy efforts, please send an e-mail to rschneid@saturn.vcu.edu.

Robert L. Schneider, Ph.D.
Lori Lester, MSW
Richmond, VA

REFERENCES

Ezell, M. (1994). Advocacy practice of social workers. *Families in Society: The Journal of Contemporary Human Services, 75*(1), 36–46.

Gibelman, M. (1999). The search for identity: Defining social work—past, present, future. *Social Work, 44*(4), 298–310.

McGowan, B. G. (1987). Advocacy. In *Encyclopedia of Social Work* (18th ed., pp. 89–95). Silver Spring, MD: NASW Press.

National Association of Social Workers. (1996). *Code of Ethics.* Washington, DC: Author.

Pawlak, E. J., & Flynn, J. P. (1990). Executive directors' political activities. *Social Work, 35,* 307–312.

Schneider, R. L., & Netting, E. F. (1999). Influencing social policy in a time of devolution: Upholding social work's great tradition. *Social Work, 44*(4), 349–357.

Advocates in Action

Advocacy is a vitalizing experience! To succeed in advocating for your cause or client is one of life's most satisfying moments. Not only is a victory sweet, but the process of arriving there is usually memorable, filled with special events and friendships. Of course, sometimes advocates only get a partial victory, and other times they lose, only to begin again the next day. But, the joy of advocacy is linked to the knowledge that one's efforts are contributing to the improvement of someone's problems, overcoming an injustice, shaping a life in a small way, and promoting a cause greater than oneself.

Social work students and professionals often express their feelings about being advocates. Throughout the chapters, our "advocates in action" will speak about their advocacy efforts. We believe that these testimonials will encourage the readers to "test out" the steps of social work advocacy, knowing that others, very similar to themselves, have found great satisfaction and challenges entering their lives. The names of the students and professionals are disguised, but the words come from the heart. Look for these inspirational actions in each chapter.

OVERVIEW OF ADVOCACY

Part One introduces the reader to the historical horizon where, for over 100 years, social work advocates have played the role of fighter and champion for many issues and causes. Chapter 1 examines the roots of advocacy in social work and identifies persons who shaped professional practice in its early days. It demonstrates how one person, despite great odds, could make major differences in changing societal conditions. The chapter also points out that developing policies and influential decision makers led to remarkable advances in protecting human rights and individual dignity. Through the many movements in the history of the United States of America, social work activists were involved in pursuing the values of a democratic society. The reader cannot escape the conclusion that the profession of social work is permeated by its historical call to advocacy. Its future is well prepared by a documented past accumulation of knowledge and skills in advocacy.

Chapter 2 continues with a historical approach as it examines how the profession has attempted to define the term *advocacy*. Although the term has been associated clearly with a desire to help others, social workers debated frequently what the nature of this impulse should be. The authors analyzed over 90 attempted definitions of advocacy as found in the literature, dating from the 1960s forward. Through a synthesis of this study, they propose a *new definition* that attempts to capture the essence of social work's commitment to advocacy. New criteria are identified that enable the reader to determine a definition that distinguishes advocacy from other social work functions such as community organizing, brokering, facilitating, and social reform. The authors conclude by proposing a specific definition of advocacy that, if adopted, would provide a common understanding of advocacy for all practitioners. Thus Part One provides the background and primary understanding of advocacy required before the reader encounters the general framework for practicing advocacy in Part Two.

KEY QUESTIONS FOR PART ONE

- When did the social work field emerge in the United States?
- When did the word *advocate* first become a part of the social work vocabulary?
- What part did advocacy play in social work in the late 19th century and early 20th century?
- What role did advocacy play in social work during the 1920s and 1930s? 1940s and 1950s? 1960s and 1970s? 1980s and 1990s?
- What were major events or issues that diverted social work from its original advocacy focus?
- Who are some of the outstanding advocates in social work history?
- What is advocacy?

- What is the authors' new definition of advocacy?
- What is the difference between advocacy and social action? How does advocacy differ from social reform, brokering, problem solving, clinical social work, and community organizing?
- What obligation to practice advocacy do social workers have?
- What values are present in social work advocacy?
- What characteristics are commonly attributed to social work advocates?
- What barriers hold social workers back from doing advocacy?
- Why is it important to define advocacy?

Advocacy's Rich and Diverse History

> *During the historical evolution of the profession, social workers were consistent vocal advocates for social justice—whether the concern was for immigrants during the settlement house movement of the 19th century or the rights of racial or ethnic groups in the United States during the 1960s. "Advocacy is the premise on which the social work profession is founded and an ethical obligation for the practitioner." . . . The time has come for the profession to reaffirm its commitment to social justice both in principle and in practice.*
>
> PAULA ALLEN-MEARES, 1996

OVERVIEW

Throughout social work history, scholars and practitioners have frequently debated the interrelationship of *social work* and *advocacy*. Some believed the two terms were virtually synonymous (Addams, 1912; Devine, 1910a, b, 1911a, b, c; Ehrenreich, 1985; Ezell, 1994; Fisher, 1935; Kahn, 1991; Lee, 1935; Leighninger, 1987; Maslen, 1944; Mayo, 1944; Nees, 1936; Patten, 1907; Richmond, 1907; Spano, 1982) while others believed advocacy emerged during or after the 1960s (Brager, 1967; Craigen, 1972; Dane, 1985; Gilbert & Specht, 1976; Grosser, 1965; Kutchins & Kutchins, 1978; Panitch, 1974; Reid, 1977; Richan, 1973; Riley, 1971; Ross, 1977a). In fact, Wolfensberger (1977) stated that "indeed, the novelty of a clearly conceptualized advocacy approach and component in the human services context is such that the very term 'advocacy' can scarcely be found in the human services literature prior to approximately 1970. I vividly remember the time when most people would stumble over the word trying to pronounce it" (p. 17).

Clearly, research has not yet supported either assertion, due in part to the ambiguous parameters of previously defined and developed advocacy definitions. Through an in-depth review of social work literature, the authors discovered that social work indeed has had a rich and abundant advocacy interrelationship and history. In order to fully understand how advocacy emerged and developed, it is important to know how politics and the profession influenced one another during historical time frames, primarily because advocacy is the culmination of those ideals, beliefs, and value systems prevalent during particular times. A significant amount of this history has not been adequately reflected in social work literature. This chapter will outline and discuss the history of social work advocacy as revealed through the eyes of many practitioners, stakeholders, and historians.

Prelude: When Did the Social Work Field Emerge in the United States?

Social work's ideal of *helping individuals, groups, and populations unable to help themselves* dates back many centuries; it also has many of its roots in Judeo-Christian philosophies, values, and practices. "Social work was an evolutionary phenomenon with roots in social philosophies and ethical values . . . [and used] *to create a means of protecting and helping those individuals adversely affected by changes. . . .*" (Day, 1989, p. 59). In the United States, social work became *organized* in the late 19th century when (1) mass immigration fragmented our nation's social, economic, and political systems; and (2) our country's labor force continued its rapid progression from rural, agrarian settings to urban, industrialized locations.

The National Association of Social Workers (NASW) today considers 1898 as the beginning of *professional* social work because the first formal social work educational program was offered that year by the New York School of Philanthropy (currently Columbia University School of Social Work) (Brieland, 1997). However, the authors believe that 1898 does not accurately reflect *organized* social work's beginnings. Specifically, early literature suggests that organized social work emerged in the 1870s. Bruno (1948) pointed out, in *Trends in Social Work as Reflected in the Proceedings of the National Conference of Social Work, 1874–1946,* that social work began in 1874. In 1922, both Graham Taylor and Julia Lathrop independently wrote to Jane Addams, asking her to run as presidential candidate against Mary Richmond for the 50th National Conference of Social Work. Specifically, Graham Taylor's letter to Jane Addams on June 12, 1922, read that "many others feel that for the 50th Conference the president should not be a leader in a specialized group, however preeminent in the group, but one who is representative of the whole field of social work. Miss Richmond could be elected next year." Based on this letter, social work's earliest history dates back to 1872.

In 1931, Aubrey Williams reported that "in the field . . . there has grown up during the last 50 years the practice of organized social work . . ." (p. 56), placing social work's conception in the early 1880s. Spano (1982) placed organized social work at a time prior to 1898 when he wrote, "by 1890, the Progressive Movement in social work appears as an identifiable entity" (p. 12). Finally, Samuel M. Lindsay, a social work student at the University of Pennsylvania, published *Social Work at the Krupp Factories* in 1892, the first known professional article reflecting the use of the term *social work* (Fox, 1967). Based on these facts, the authors believe social work was *organized* as early as 1872, which supports their assertion that organized professional social work began prior to 1898 in the United States.

ADVOCACY IN EARLY SOCIAL WORK HISTORY

Social science, the precursor to social work, emerged not long after Charles Darwin advanced scientific knowledge with his "survival of adaptation" theory of evolution, better known as "survival of the fittest." Its earliest history was placed in 1865 when the Massachusetts Board initiated a meeting of the "Social

Science League"; other state boards were asked to attend. Its purpose was to discuss common, problematic social issues. The most prevalent topics at that time were (1) public sanitation; (2) relief, employment, and indigent education; (3) revisions to existing criminal laws; (4) prison rehabilitation; and (5) mental health. Following this meeting, the American Social Science Association (ASSA) was founded. Over the next few years, ASSA created four separate departments: (1) jurisprudence; (2) education; (3) social economy; and (4) public health. By 1874, nine state boards were active members, and permanent committees were formed to identify and discuss *critical* social issues. These boards and committees were known as the Conference on Charities (CoC). In 1879, the CoC split from the ASSA and was renamed the National Conference of Charities and Corrections (NCCC) (Pumphrey & Pumphrey, 1961).

The NCCC held annual conferences. Its minutes, discussions, recommendations, and conclusions were recorded in the *Proceedings of the National Conference of Charities and Corrections* (renamed the National Conference of Social Work [NCSW] in 1917, retroactive to the first *Proceedings*) (Henderson, 1899; Johnson, 1923; Trattner, 1994). It was in these official records that the term *advocate* was first discovered. Specifically:

- This board [Commission of Emigration] stands in the way of any proper regulation of immigration, and the legislation *advocated* by Dr. Hoyt will remove the obstacle . . ." (Sanborn, 1887).
- "Indeed, this special work of child saving, which, judiciously accomplished, is more fruitful in its results than the most sanguine *advocates* of the system anticipated, is found to depend largely on its success upon the discretion exercised in placing them in homes . . ." (Smith, 1887).
- "Charity Organization has able *advocates* in Mr. C. S. Loch, of London, Dr. Philip W. Ayres, Professor C. R. Henderson, and others" (Barrows, 1896).
- "Mr. Choate told us that the amendment forbidding labor in prisons . . . was really a reform in constitutional law, an improvement such as all those critics now enthusiastically support, while the very labor leaders who then urgently *advocated* it now seek its repeal . . ." (Lewis, 1898).
- "[I]f a person is a citizen of the United States, he is entitled to be so considered . . . if he has performed his duty *everywhere,* he should be recognized *everywhere.* . . . [I]f a man is liable to be called upon to go to war for the country, he is entitled to some consideration by that same government. . . . [L]et us *advocate* the passage of such laws as will do justice to all . . ." (Lawrence, 1899, p. 165).

Since the National Conference was the only *organized* entity representing social work in the late 19th century, the authors believe that the use of the term *advocacy* in its official records is significant in describing early social work's mission and activities.

It is clear in the five references outlined above that the verb *advocate* was used to "support," "promote," or "influence," and the noun *advocate* identified individuals, groups, or populations that "supported," "promoted," or "influenced." What is not clear through these references is the level and extent of participation by social workers. How active were they? Did they advocate orally or through written documents? Did they advocate in one-on-one situations or in large, defined forums? Clues to the answers to these questions are provided by Sanborn (1887), Lewis (1898), and Lawrence (1899) who outlined *legislation* as advocacy's target effort. In addition, Smith (1887) referred to advocates *of the system,* which probably meant influencing large conventional forums such as municipal, state, or federal government; the court system; or the legislative process.

Alexander Johnson, a 40-year social work veteran and 31-year officer and member of the National Conference, provided insight into many of these questions in his book entitled Adventures in Social Welfare (1923). Johnson explained that state NCSW boards held annual meetings similar to those at the National Conference. When important social welfare issues were reported, discussed, and debated, necessary action was outlined and delegated. Among its multiple responsibilities and duties, "an important function of the Board of State Charities [was] to inform the legislators, and to lead the public opinion of the state, on all matters which [came] within its purview. The board [made] no laws; its function [was] observation; advice; leadership." Johnson went on to explain that "the strongest force in a democratic state is that of public opinion. This influences the legislature; and indeed, without it, most legislation is futile. It is easy to make laws, but without the approval and good will of people, it is difficult, if not impossible, to enforce them" (p. 164). This description of the relationship and duty of the state board to the legislative process is virtually identical to the functions performed by contemporary advocacy organizations nationwide.

To expand further, the following quotation from Sir Charles Stewart Loch identifies his role as an advocate:

> If I were asked why I joined the [Charity Organization] Society I should answer that through its work and growth I hoped that some day there would be formed a large association of persons . . . it could make legislation effective, could see that it was enforced . . . it would open to many a new path for the exercise of personal influence—influence with the churches, the Guardians, the Friendly Societies, the residents of a district, and "the common people." Differing in much, many might unite in this." (Richmond, 1923)

Loch's words and themes duplicate those from Johnson. Specifically, social work advocacy (1) outlined workers' responsibility for and obligation to the legislative process; (2) ensured that legislation was effective and enforceable; and (3) used influence and collective action to impact change. These three dimensions appear to be the critical components for an early definition of social work advocacy.

Precursors to Progressivism

As mentioned earlier, organized social work developed in the late 1870s when multiple social, political, and economic forces were continuously changing and developing social structures in America. Based on the turbulence prevalent at that time, it is not surprising to learn that three separate and distinct social work movements emerged in the last 20 years of the 19th century. Each movement had a different perspective about wealth and poverty as well as the responsibilities each owed to the other and to the developing social systems.

The first movement, represented by the Charity Organization Society (COS), was concerned with the interrelationship of individuals and their communities, particularly the responsibility one had to the other. This movement focused on *community justice*.[1] The second movement, demonstrated specifically in the settlement houses, was concerned about the exploitation, abuse, and oppression thrust on minority and ethnic populations by social systems and their representatives. This movement focused on *social justice*.[2] Table 1.1 outlines the core values of these two movements during their early years. It should be noted that the settlement house movement developed in response to those unmet social needs frequently dismissed by the COS. The third movement, developed by several key academics at the University of Pennsylvania's Wharton School, was concerned with the equitable distribution of excessive and available resources produced by society. This movement focused on *distributive justice*.[3] (See Highlight 1.1 for detailed information about the early development of this movement and Simon Nelson Patten, one of social work's unknown early advocates.) This movement was very important

---

[1]This movement has evolved numerous times though social work history. Although its initial focus was community justice, it moved toward individual casework after the turn of the century, then into psychosocial treatment, and finally to diagnostic and biopsychosocial interventions and treatments.

[2]Of this movement, Bruno (1948) said that "the settlement . . . made no direct contribution to the professional development of social work. . . . [T]he settlement movement chose to remain the conscience of America, the laymen of this country reporting to its citizens on the lot of their forgotten fellows" (p. 119).

[3]Of this movement, Bruno (1948) said that it had "less direct influence on the preparation of the practitioner, but [had a] far-reaching impact on the practice of social work in the twentieth century." Specifically, Patten "advanced what was considered quite an unorthodox theory, that the only sound economic program was to raise the purchasing power of the great body of workers so that they, the bulk of consumers, would be able to buy the goods the machinery was capable of turning out. . . . Patten's findings performed a still greater service to the entire field of the social services by saving it from identification with the conservative classes of society as private social work in Great Britain and France had already done. It preserved the unity of the front between the social services and social reform which was to prove of such great value in the years that followed the first decade of the twentieth century" (pp. 136–137).

TABLE 1.1	IDEOLOGICAL VALUES AND REPRESENTATIONS OF SOCIAL WORK MOVEMENTS IN THE 19TH CENTURY	
	Charity and Poor Relief	**Social Action and Reform**
Representation	Local Charity Organization Societies	Settlement houses
Direct accountability	State boards and National Conference	No formal macro organization or structure*
Primary focus	Individuals adhere to community norms; community assumes responsibility for "worthy" poor	Excluded minority and ethnic populations should be provided with appropriate and equitable living standards
Target of change	Individuals. Problem: lack of appropriate interpersonal skills and/or community knowledge	Local, state, and national government systems. Problem: lack of appropriate social conscience for ethnic and minority tolerance and integration
Responsibility for relief	Private philanthropy; community intervention	Local, state, and national government
Direct interventions	Friendly visiting; community support—almsgiving; relief for "worthy" poor	Artificial community; hold government accountable; ensure appropriate legislation to set boundaries for society
Governance and enforceability	Private citizens, participating on voluntary community boards (voluntarism vs. paid staff issue)	Local, state, and national government

*Note: According to Bruno (1948), the settlement house movement did not form a national association or other formal governing structure until 1911; however, representatives of all the settlement houses met informally at least three times before that date (p. 119).

in those early years and throughout social work's history because it redirected and neutralized the other two movements when they focused their attention inward. All three movements had a strong advocacy focus, and several great social work advocates emerged from them, including Jane Addams, Edward T. Devine, Edith Abbott, Grace Abbott, Sophonisba Breckinridge, Julia Lathrop, Mary E. Richmond, Florence Kelley, Simon Patten, Samuel M. Lindsay, and Francis Perkins, among others.

Three major historic occurrences contributed to the development of these three social work advocacy precursors. First, our country began its rapid progression toward industrialization during the 19th century, and shifted away from a predominantly rural agrarian workforce. In fact, after the Civil War, the United States was increasingly recognized as the leading industrial nation of the world. Those modern, mechanical inventions and factories necessary for industrialization were often located in large cities. Thus, skilled and unskilled workers moved from small towns to large cities to supply the demand. Second,

1.1   *Simon Nelson Patten*
1852–1922
Economist and Social Work Educator

One summer day I took my note-book to a wooded hillside whence I could overlook a rich and beautiful valley. . . . As I seated myself under a chestnut tree a fellow-guest at the hotel came by, and glancing at my memoranda asked if I, like himself, was writing a lecture. He too had come to the woods, he said, to meditate and to be inspired by nature. But his thesis, enthusiastically unfolded, was the opposite to mine. . . . Where I marked the progress of humanity and thrilled with the hope that poverty will soon be banished from the world as it has been from this happy valley, he saw a threatening scene of worldliness where prosperity lulled spiritual alarms to a dangerous moral peace. . . . Yet, in spite of the fundamental differences in our training it seemed strange to me that two men looking at the same picture could agree wholly upon the truths it painted and forthwith interpret them as differently as we did. Looking down into this plentiful valley, one fortified his belief that divine wrath must be invoked upon a region carnal and depraved; while the other joyfully exclaimed, "Here is the basis of a new civilization; here is evidence that economic forces can sweep away poverty, banish misery, and by giving men work bring forth right and enduring character within the race."

PATTEN, 1907, PP. 3–4

Simon Nelson Patten was born on May 1, 1852, to William and Elizabeth Patten in Sandwich, De Kalb County, Illinois. After graduating from Jennings Seminary in 1874, Patten attended Northwestern University for one and a half years, and then attended the University of Halle in Germany where, in 1879, he received his Ph.D. in Political Economy. In 1887, Patten was appointed to the University of Pennsylvania's Wharton School as a Professor of Economics; he remained in that position until 1917 when university trustees forced his retirement because he supported the antiwar movement.

Like others at that time, Patten was concerned about the impact social, economic, and political forces had on the working poor. With his expertise in politics, economics, and sociology, Patten theorized that poverty was an economic phenomenon that should be addressed and abolished, and was convinced that "the state [was] the only social institution with sufficient resources to deal with the complex economic and social forces that create[d] poverty" (Fox, 1968). Patten further theorized that state intervention was necessary to ensure that a fair share of socially produced surplus was

Simon Nelson Patten 1852–1922 Economist and Social Work Educator (continued)

available to the masses. Many great social work advocates studied under Patten, including Frances Perkins, Edward T. Devine,[1] Samuel M. Lindsay, and William H. Allen. Lillian Wald, another social work advocate, was also a strong supporter of his work.

Patten and Lindsay (then an instructor of sociology at Wharton School) interested many students in the emerging field of social work as early as 1893. Jointly Patten and Lindsay developed courses on existing social problems such as labor and currency, public health, marriage and divorce, child welfare, and standards of living. These academics also helped interested students find summer jobs in social service agencies. Based on this foundational work, Patten and Lindsay developed the first formal *two-year* educational social work program, instituted at the Wharton School in 1899. Finally, Patten was the originator of the term *social work* (Kellogg, 1938).

During the turn of the century, an ongoing debate ensued between Patten and Mary Richmond regarding the major focal issues and standards for the transitioning social work field. Issues under debate included, *inter alia*, the role of philanthropy and advocacy; what, if any, influence social workers should have on social change; the distinction and value of professional versus voluntary workers, and position statements about controversial social issues such as prohibition, the cost of living, social insurance, immigration restrictions, and economic conditions.

In 1905, Devine and Lindsay, then academics at (Columbia University's) New York School of Social Work, established the Kennedy Lectureship to enhance students' learning; Patten was constantly invited to speak at these forums. His multiple lectures were subsequently edited and published in *The New Basis of Civilization* in 1907. During these lectures, Patten advocated his platform that social workers should:

1. Initiate and continue a working relationship with existing economic, political, fraternal, and cultural institutions
2. Move beyond their predominant work with individuals and families, and set baseline standards for communities to measure the working poor against the "norm"
3. Become involved in the legislative process and advocate adequate health care and housing, better standards of income, and appropriate working conditions

Simon Nelson Patten 1852–1922 Economist and Social Work Educator (continued)

"Patten's persuasive argument that social workers should 'fix the responsibility of the state in caring for the health and welfare of its citizens' placed him in the vanguard of later American agitation for social legislation" (Fox, 1968, p. xl). During Patten's lifetime, he wrote and published 22 professional books and hundreds of professional articles. He also maintained close and ongoing relationships with many of his former students. Patten died in 1922 when he was 60 years old.

Sources: Devine, E. T. (1939); Everett, J. R. (1982); Fox, D. M. (1967, 1968); Kellogg, P. U. (1938); Patten, S. N. (1907).

[1]Devine was one of only five who received his Ph.D. under Patten at the Wharton School.

immigration increased as many foreign-born emigrated to the United States to take advantage of these new opportunities and to escape oppression. While immigration remained stable in the United States from 1820 through the 1850s, it doubled from the 1860s to the 1870s, and exploded in the 1880s (see Table 1.2). These rapid shifts wreaked havoc on the nation's existing social, economic, and political systems. Third, the Financial Panic of 1893, and its subsequent depression, challenged the traditional COS philosophy and demanded modifications to its values and methodologies. Specifically, for the first time in American history, the federal gold reserve was unable to sustain employment. Thus, the COS could not distinguish between the "worthy" and "unworthy" poor as it tried to accomplish its mission (Chronology, 1884–1894; Ehrenreich, 1985; Katz, 1996).

Prior to and during these changes, American society was not centralized in any large-scale, systemic fashion. Rather, each community had its own unique social structure that included family, education, church, profession, communication, and government. When these social systems worked together, they functioned as autonomous towns and cities. The large-scale social systems necessary to provide structure and balance for the growing industry and population increases were either very weak or nonexistent. Thus, when individuals and families moved to cities, the community spirit that characterized small town living—that is, face-to-face interactions and extended family relationships—suddenly vanished (Ehrenreich, 1985; Spano, 1982). This transition was stressful and alarming for old and new communities. It was also central to the developing COS.

TABLE 1.2	IMMIGRATION IN THE 1800S	
	Decade	**Number**
	1820–1830	128,393
	1830–1840	539,391
	1840–1850	1,423,337
	1850–1860	2,799,423
	1860–1870	1,964,061
	1870–1880	2,834,040
	1880–1890	**5,246,613**

Source: Hoyt (1893).

Scientific knowledge also progressed during the latter half of the 19th century. Not long after Charles Darwin proposed his scientific theory of evolution, commonly known as "survival of the fittest," other professions adopted this methodology. In the 1870s Herbert Spencer proposed "Social Darwinism," a combination of Darwin's scientific theory of evolution and the accepted Protestant work ethic. The foundation and ideology of Social Darwinism theorized that ethnic minorities were genetically inferior, economically unfit, and morally degenerate, with no rightful place in society. According to Day (1989), Social Darwinism was an intellectual rationalization that allowed the wealthier classes to ignore the conditions of the poor; it encouraged the philosophy that "a better world could be created by 'containing' people afflicted with problems such as poverty; mental, emotional, or physical disabilities; or not being white" (p. 219). Based on the values associated with this theory, indigents were classified, under the auspices of "scientific charity," as products of misconduct or misfortune. Table 1.3 outlines the distinction between these categories, their corollary indicators, and recognized causes. It was from these categorizations that indigents were classified as "worthy" or "unworthy," and thus allowed or denied relief assistance (Axinn & Levin, 1997; Day, 1989; Trattner, 1994; Warner, 1894). This value system was enmeshed in the developing community justice movement.

Proponents of social justice were concerned with society's neglect and exploitation of the working poor, most of whom were from ethnic and minority populations. Of course, many of these factors were the result of the constant influx of immigrants and laborers, which obviously created new problems for existing social systems. For example, housing was needed for shelter. Because the demand for housing was great, unsafe and flimsy buildings (i.e., tenements) were built rapidly. Even with this continuous development, overcrowding was

TABLE 1.3	CLASSIFICATION OF INDIGENTS	

Relief Classifications	Causes of Poverty
Misconduct 1. Drink 2. Immorality 3. Shiftlessness and inefficiency 4. Crime and dishonesty 5. Roving disposition	**Subjective characteristics** 1. Undervitalization and indolence 2. Lubricity 3. Specific disease 4. Lack of judgment 5. Unhealthy appetites

Misfortune
1. Lack of normal support
  a. imprisonment of breadwinner
  b. orphans and abandoned
    children
  c. neglect by relatives
  d. no male support
2. Matters of employment
  a. lack of employment
  b. insufficient employment
  c. poorly paid employment
  d. unhealthy and dangerous
    employment
3. Matters of personal capacity
  a. ignorance of English
  b. accident
  c. sickness or death in family
  d. physical defects
  e. insanity
  f. old age
	Habits producing and produced by the above
	1. Shiftlessness
	2. Self-abuse and sexual excess
	3. Abuse of stimulants and narcotics
	4. Unhealthy diet
	5. Disregard of family ties
	
	Objective
	1. Inadequate natural resources
	2. Bad climate conditions
	3. Defective sanitation, etc.
	4. Evil associations and surroundings
	5. Defective *legislation* and defective
	  judicial and punitive machinery
	6. Misdirected or inadequate
	  education
	7. Bad industrial conditions
	  a. variations in value of money
	  b. changes in trade
	  c. excessive or ill-managed taxation
	  d. emergencies unprovided for
	  e. undue power of class over class
	  f. immobility of labor
	8. Unwise philanthropy

Source: Warner (1894, 1889).

the norm because of the high rents that were charged, which created unsanitary conditions. Lack of running water and appropriate toilet facilities made tenement life unsanitary, while horses (the primary mode of transportation) filled the streets with urine, manure, and cadavers. Epidemics spread rampantly, leaving many seriously ill, and often resulting in death (Day, 1989; Ehrenreich, 1985).

Working conditions were harsh for industrial workers. Because compensation was minimal, every member of the family needed to work for survival. Immigrants, women, and children were exploited in those environments, and working conditions were unsafe, unregulated, uncomfortable, and unsanitary. Workdays and workweeks were long, often requiring 12 to 16 hours per day each and every day of the week. Holidays and vacations were unheard of at that time. These and other conditions led to organized labor strikes (Pullman, Haymarket, Homestead, Pittsburgh) that were often violent and punitive, and sometimes resulted in death. Some early settlement house leaders were advocates in many of these strikes (Axinn & Levin, 1997; Chronology, 1884–1894; Ehrenreich, 1985; Trattner, 1994). (For detailed information about advocacy efforts during this time and in the subsequent Progressive Era, see Highlight 1.2.)

Many other factors shaped the development of the three movements. For example, "robber barons" made the rich richer and the poor poorer, often with little regard for human suffering or resulting consequences. Corporations grew and monopolized; many were owned by millionaires like J. P. Morgan, Andrew Carnegie, and John D. Rockefeller. These philanthropists contributed a portion of their wealth to "deserving" causes, which perpetuated and widened the gap between the rich and the poor. Transportation became an

1.2   *Laura Jane Addams*
1860–1935
Social Work Advocate

> *One man or group of men sometimes reveal to their contemporaries a higher conscience by simply incorporating into the deed what has been before but a philosophic proposition. By this deed the common code of ethics is stretched to a higher point.*
>
> JANE ADDAMS, 1895

Laura Jane Addams was born on September 6, 1860, in Cedarville, Illinois, to John Huay and Sarah Weber Addams. After graduating from Rockford Female Seminary in 1881, Addams attended the Woman's Medical College of Pennsylvania, although she was required to leave within the first year for medical reasons. In June 1882, Addams was one of the first women to receive an A.B. degree from her alma mater. During her lifetime, Addams received 14 honorary degrees: 10 LL.D.s (University of Wisconsin [1904]; Smith College [1910]; Lincoln Memorial University [1920]; Illinois Woman's College [1928]; Lombard College [1928]; University of Chicago [1930]; Swarthmore College [1932]; Knox College [1934]; Holyoke College [1935]; and University of California, Berkeley [1935]); one A.M. (Yale University [1910]); and three L.H.D.s (Tufts University [1926]; Northwestern University [1929]; and Rollins College [1932]).

Laura Jane Addams 1860–1935
Social Work Advocate (continued)

Addams is best known for her founding role and settlement house work at Hull House in Chicago, Illinois. However, little is known about her active and passionate role in politics, or her strong legislative, peace, and women's suffrage advocacy work. For example:

- In 1893, Addams actively (a) lobbied for the creation of a factory inspector's office in Illinois, and (b) participated in six social welfare congresses at the World's Columbian Exposition in Chicago.
- In 1894, Addams was appointed to the Civic Federation of Chicago Arbitration Committee in Illinois. She subsequently testified, in 1895, before the United States Strike Commission regarding the Pullman strike.
- In 1895, Addams was appointed as a garbage inspector in the 19th ward of Chicago after she lobbied for this position.
- From 1895 until 1900, Addams campaigned against Chicago Alderman John Powers (when women were not even allowed to vote).
- In 1899, Addams (a) lobbied for the establishment of a juvenile court in Cook County, Illinois, and (b) spoke before the Central Anti-Imperialist League in Chicago.
- In 1903, Addams (a) advocated for the Illinois Child Labor Law, and (b) served on the Arbitration Committee for the Ladies' Garment Workers Union.
- In 1904, Addams was appointed to the National Child Labor Committee.
- In 1909, Addams (a) spoke at the Second American Peace Conference in Chicago, (b) advocated the Juvenile Protection Association in Chicago, and (c) was elected the first women president of the National Conference of Charities and Corrections.
- In 1910, Addams (a) was the first women elected to the Chicago Association of Commerce, and (b) served as a mediator in the Hart, Shaffner, and Marx strike in Chicago.
- In 1911, Addams was elected the first vice-president of the National American Woman Suffrage Association.
- In 1912, Addams (a) seconded Theodore Roosevelt's nomination to the Progressive Party, (b) was appointed to the Progressive National Committee, and to the Illinois and Cook County Progressive Committees, (c) was appointed to the Progressive National Service as the chair of the Social Industrial Justice Department, and (d) served on the Legislative Reference Bureau.

Laura Jane Addams 1860–1935
Social Work Advocate (continued)

- In 1913, Addams spoke at the 7th Congress of International Alliance of Women for Suffrage and Equal Citizenship in Budapest, Hungary.
- From 1914 until 1918, Addams actively opposed U.S. involvement in World War I for humanitarian reasons.
- In 1915, Addams (a) helped organize and was elected chair of the Woman's Peace Party, (b) was elected president of the International Committee of Women for Permanent Peace, and (c) served as representative of the International Congress of Women.
- In 1919, Addams was elected president of the Women's International League for Peace and Freedom.
- In 1929, Addams received the honorary president for life position at the Women's International League for Peace and Freedom.

In addition to these positions, Addams presided over a number of women's international peace conferences from 1915 through 1929 and received numerous awards, to include the Nobel Peace prize. In addition to hundreds of articles, speeches, and endorsements, Addams wrote 11 books.

Addams was highly respected by her friends and colleagues. Emily Greene Balch—cofounder of the Denison Settlement House in Boston, social work educator at Wellesley College, coadvocate in the peace effort, and corecipient of the 1939 Nobel Peace prize—said when Addams died, "I think her greatness has been veiled by her goodness" (Lasch, 1965). Immediately following her death, Lurie (1935) wrote: "To the social workers of the predepression years, Jane Addams stood out magnificently as an example of what humanitarian zeal and sincere devotion could achieve in advancing social welfare programs. . . . Her sincerity and her personality attracted a group of students, intellectuals, and liberal philanthropists to aid her in the welfare projects in which she was engaging single-handed. . . . In her various activities Jane Addams stood out as the symbol—the successful social worker, improving the conditions of the poor by her power to influence persons of wealth and position. . . . The unsolved social problems of our time growing more rather than less acute will have need of the rare personal qualities which were embodied in Jane Addams" (pp. 17–18). Addams died in 1935 at the age of 75.

Source: The Jane Addams Collection, University of Illinois at Chicago, Illinois.

important issue as products and supplies were moved from city to city, which required technical sophistication and long-term absences of workers from families and communities. Moreover, manufacture, industry, and transportation made information readily available to larger populations. Table 1.4 outlines many influential writings that greatly impacted the country's social development at that time (Chronology, 1884–1894; Chronology, 1895–1904; Ehrenreich, 1985).

TABLE
1.4   **INFLUENTIAL WRITINGS**

		Title	Author
Year:	1872	*The Dangerous Classes of New York and Twenty Years' Work Among Them*	Rev. Charles Loring Brace
Description:		Autobiography of author's work with the homeless, and vagrant children. He referred to these children as "menaces to society."	
Year:	1888	*Looking Backward, 2000–1887*	Edward Bellamy
Description:		Described a utopian society where citizens' social and economic needs are provided by the government.	
Year:	1889	*The Gospel of Wealth*	Andrew Carnegie
Description:		Article set forth author's theory of philanthropy, and further defended capitalism. The article also urged the business community to donate wealth to deserving issues and causes.	
Year:	1890	*How the Other Half Lives*	Jacob A. Riis
Description:		Photographic account and written documentary of the housing conditions in New York City. Two years earlier George Eastman perfected the Kodak hand camera, which made amateur photography possible. The descriptive photographs in this book enhanced its effectiveness in intiating housing reform efforts.	
Year:	1890	*The Principles of Psychology*	William James
Description:		First American writing regarding individual treatment in experimental psychology.	
Year:	1894	*American Charities*	Amos G. Warner
Description:		Social work classic; the first source to describe U.S. charities in detail, and to delineate principles of relief.	
Year:	1899	*The Man with the Hoe*	Edward Markham
Description:		Social protest poem published in the *San Francisco Examiner.* Within its first week of publication, it appeared in a large number of newspapers across the country.	
Year:	1899	*Friendly Visiting Among the Poor*	Mary E. Richmond
Description:		Set forth as a charity worker handbook.	

Source: Brace (1872); Chronology 1884–1894 (1968); Chronology 1895–1904 (1968).

Finally, the Financial Panic of 1893 played a significant role in the development of all three movements. Specifically, on April 21st the U.S. gold reserve fell below the acceptable and safe minimum of $100 million. A number of factors contributed to this financial decline; the most important were the enactment of the Dependent Pension Act on June 27, 1890, and the McKinley Tariff on October 1, 1890. The Dependent Pension Act authorized funding for the Union's Civil War veterans and their families. Within the first few years of this act, government payments increased from $90 million to $150 million. The McKinley Tariff raised duties to approximately 50% to protect industry. By the end of 1893, the gold reserve fell to $80 million, and in 1894 the federal budget experienced its first deficit since the Civil War—$61 million. Many businesses failed, railroads went bankrupt, unemployment increased to approximately 18% (estimated at 2.5 million people), and a depression ensued that remained until 1897 (Chronology, 1884–1894; Katz, 1996).

The magnitude of this depression overwhelmed traditional relief work, particularly since its agents could no longer use scientific methodology to distinguish between the worthy and unworthy poor. Private industry was unable, at that time, to provide sufficient employment opportunities. Therefore, relief responsibility shifted to the local, state, and national governments. Charitable contributions were streamlined to the government to alleviate financial distress (Katz, 1996). The ideology of COS slowly shifted, and those individuals and populations needing relief became genuine "social work" constituencies. The distributive justice movement developed in response to society's obvious economic and resource needs. Hence, the stage was set for social work advocacy activities headed by early settlement house leaders and other colleagues.

THE PROGRESSIVE ERA: MID-1890S TO WORLD WAR I

The social worker at his best is an indefatigable crusader for specific reform or reforms, one who combines a knowledge of facts with a zeal for action; who agitates ceaselessly for the cause, whether others are interested or not; who cheerfully accepts the hostility of any who profit from the evils to be eradicated, but seeks to make friends of all who can be brought to enlist in the righteous cause; who builds his program on the basis of experience—that is to say, the actual experience of the victims of injustice or hardships—rather than on the illusions, the easy generalizations and the prejudices absorbed in casual contacts.

EDWARD T. DEVINE, 1939

The Progressive Era was a significant period in social work history. It was a time when community unrest and organized agitation were directed at industry and government. Those activities provided the momentum for numerous social reforms. Social workers participated in reform efforts, and their tangible accomplishments were best evidenced through effective legislation and developing community programs. Social workers also dedicated significant time, energy, and talent to eradicating poverty and its accompanying misery. The Progressive Era was also significant because it revolutionized and altered traditional American politics and their affiliated social systems. For the first, and maybe the last time in its history, social work advocacy was purely altruistic (Bremner, 1967; Bruno, 1948; Pacey, 1950).

Early settlement house workers were "movers and shakers." This should not be surprising. After all, the settlement house movement emerged when the classes and masses, or the rich and the poor, were geographically and ideologically segregated from one another. According to Addams (1892), "the settlement was a protest against this division" (pp. 10–11), although settlement workers sought harmony rather than conflict between the two classes. Their efforts were successful because they were directly involved in all aspects of community life. Furthermore, because settlement workers provided a variety of services such as nursing, education, nursery schools, child care, libraries, boys' and girls' clubs, men's and women's clubs, playgrounds, homemaking skills, industrial workshops, recreation, and vocational guidance, they had the direct and constant access to understand routine and seasonal constituent stressors. This firsthand knowledge allowed them to become effective and accomplished advocates for the poor and displaced populations. The issues and causes represented throughout the Progressive Era are numerous; the best known included homelessness, compulsory education, labor organization, emergency relief, child protection, legal aid, inadequate and unsafe housing, public health, women and children, exploitation, immigration, standards of living, wages, safe working conditions, discrimination, and institutionalization (Bremner, 1967; Bruno, 1948; Pacey, 1950).

So many advocates emerged and developed during this time that it is difficult to encapsulate them into this brief history chapter; each addressed a myriad of social welfare issues and causes. Their individual and cumulative contributions were significant because they forced government and society to take a more responsible role in the well-being of *all* its citizens—an ideal referred to as *social justice.* In addition to the examples provided in the highlights, early advocacy examples were represented through the work of Jane Addams, Julia Lathrop, and Florence Kelley who, in partnership with labor unions, advocated a woman's eight-hour labor law in Illinois, as well as the Act Concerning the Education of Children and the Child Labor Law, which removed children who lived in the West Side of Chicago from factory work and put them into schools (Lenroot, 1935). Further, Jane Addams and Julia Lathrop advocated the first juvenile court, located in Cook County, Illinois, passed in 1899 through An Act to Regulate the Treatment and Control of Dependent, Neglected, and Delinquent Children. The juvenile court system was designed to reeducate youth rather than punish them (Trattner, 1994). In many instances, one successful advocacy action built a foundation for another, which then built a foundation for another. A great example of this "building-block" effect is reflected in "A Class Advocacy Act" (Highlight 1.3).

1.3   *A Class Advocacy Act*

One morning in 1906, Lillian Wald and Florence Kelley, two early social work advocates, were eating breakfast together when Wald noticed in the newspaper that the president's cabinet called a special session to investigate the threat of boll weevils on the cotton crop. Astonished, Wald turned to Kelley and said, "This is interesting. Nothing in the interest of children could or would bring about a special Cabinet meeting, or fix the attention of our legislators. We count the boll weevil, or the lobster, or a fish, or a pig as more important than a child." (Bruno, 1948). The two talked about how they wished the federal government would put as much energy into threats facing children as it did into the cotton crop; perhaps someday it would establish a children's bureau. Not long after, Kelley talked with Edward T. Devine about this idea; Devine promptly sent a telegram to President Roosevelt highlighting their discussion. The president wired back, "It's a bully idea. Come to Washington and let's see" (Bruno, 1948).

Wald and Devine traveled to Washington, DC, to discuss this matter with President Roosevelt. After soliciting congressional leaders, Senator Murray Crane of Massachusetts drafted and submitted a bill authorizing the federal children's bureau. Hearings were held across the nation, and in 1909 the president convened the White House Conference on Child Welfare. A resolution supporting the bureau was passed at that conference, and the authorizing legislation was signed into law on April 9, 1912. However, this six-year advocacy effort did not escape without significant opposition. During the intervening period, Homer Folks and others argued that a children's bureau would be (1) fruitless, (2) expensive to taxpayers, (3) destructive to the current form of government, and (4) unconstitutional. Despite years of opposition, the authorizing legislation was, indeed, passed.

The origination of the U.S. Children's Bureau was the first time the federal government assumed responsibility for a social issue outside public health and education. The Bureau's objective was to investigate conditions that adversely affected children from *all* classes, and to report on those findings. Under the leadership of Julia C. Lathrop, another early social work advocate, the U.S. Children's Bureau:

A Class Advocacy Act (continued)

- Initiated and advocated that children's births be registered in all states
- Investigated infant mortality rates—the results suggested a definite correlation between infant deaths for children under the age of 2 and their families' economic status
- Established guidelines for the prenatal and postnatal care of unwed mothers and their children
- Set standards for biological fathers' responsibilities to their children
- Initiated and advocated the Child Labor Law, which forbid the interstate transfer of goods manufactured by child labor.

Under the subsequent leadership of Grace Abbott, another early social work advocate, the Sheppard-Towner Act was initiated and advocated. It was passed in November 1921, and offered grants-in-aid for states to establish maternal and infant services in rural areas if they established standards of care as specified by the U.S. Children's Bureau. By the middle of 1922, 42 states passed legislation that conformed to these specifications.

The U.S. Children's Bureau has been actively involved in *all* matters that impact children, to include, among others, foster care, juvenile justice, public assistance and welfare, compulsory education, and day care issues.

Source: Bruno (1948); Chambers (1963); Costin (1983); Taylor (1932).

The growth and development of advocacy practice and principles can be found in the *Proceedings of the National Conference of Charities and Corrections* as early as 1900. The focus of advocacy on social justice was presented through the conference's presidential addresses. To highlight a few points:

- In 1900, Charles E. Faulkner set the stage with his presidential address *Twentieth Century Alignments for the Promotion of Social Order.* As Faulkner closed his address, he encouraged social workers to place "more earnest effort" on preventing those causes that led to oppression (p. 9).
- In 1906, with Edward T. Devine at the mast of the National Conference, the pulse of social action and advocacy were pushed beyond their conventional limits. Specifically, Devine asked, "[I]s it not time to recognize that practically all the other forms of degeneracy and dependence require at some stage or other a conjunction of some inherited or acquired weakness in the individual and an overt

temptation or an unfavorable condition external to him which would ordinarily not be presented at all if it were not to the advantage, apparently, of another party to the transaction? *The most profitable task of modern philanthropy is to find this other party and to deal by radical methods with him*" (p. 9).

- In 1911, Homer Folks' presidential address *The Rate of Progress* highlighted the National Conference's successful and powerful advocacy efforts. However, Folks went further, indicating that social workers had not done enough, when he said, "[O]ur section of last year and of this, on Standards of Living and Labor, is indeed a courageous attempt to make our contribution to industrial progress, and social workers certainly have contributed very largely to the present movement. . . . [A]s we now look at the matter, however, is not the cause for wonder not that we have entered upon this field, but that our entry was so long delayed? Even with the notable recent interest in these subjects, and with many praiseworthy efforts at legislation, are we not still, in labor legislation, in workingmen's insurance, in compensation for accidents, and in kindred lines, far behind other countries supposedly less democratic, less prosperous, less progressive than our own?" (pp. 6–7).

- In 1912, the Honorable Julian W. Mack completely redirected social work's early focus from charity to justice in his presidential address *Social Progress*. Mack eloquently remarked that "true social justice implies love, compassion, and personal service. It demands . . . that society in its organized capacity shall secure each individual in the full enjoyment of all those fundamental rights without which no human being can fulfill his God-given destiny" (pp. 6–7).

- Finally, in 1913 social work advocacy reached its climax with Frank Tucker's presidential address *Social Justice*. An outline of this inspiring oration is provided in this text (see Highlight 1.4).

The momentum of social work advocacy was also reflected through the National Conference's constantly emerging and developing committees. Specifically, in 1900 the new Standing Committee of Politics in Charitable and Correctional Affairs set forth to "deal with two questions, first . . . the evil results arising from the defects of political machinery, and, second . . . how these defects may be overcome" (Blackmar, 1900). In 1901, the Committee on Legislation emerged to "arouse and lead public sentiment—to create a soil and an atmosphere in which legislative projects may generate and develop spontaneously" (Folwell, 1901, p. 112). This committee further suggested that its primary role should be "the collection, interpretation, and publication of statistics" (p. 115). A third new committee developed that year to discuss the division of work between private and public charities.

1.4   *Social Justice*

On July 5, 1913, Frank Tucker, president of the National Conference of Charities and Corrections, addressed the Fortieth Annual Session, held that year in Seattle, Washington. This presidential address, entitled "Social Justice," exemplified the culmination of work over those 40 years.

According to Tucker (1913), social justice:

- Is a "state of existence, brought upon by individual, family and community acts, based on ideals of honesty, efficiency and service. . . . [T]o obtain it means coordinating and standardizing all social effort" (p. 6).
- Is a "state of community life which is in equilibrium maintained by rules of conduct called law" (p. 6).
- Demands a minimum of (1) a living wage, (2) reasonable working hours and conditions of work, (3) education, (4) housing, (5) food, (6) clothes, (7) health, (8) recreation, (9) security of life and economic status through social insurance, (10) transportation, heat, and light, and (11) government (pp. 6–11).

With respect to the role of government, Tucker (1913) stated:

> What progress are we making toward Social Justice through Government! Never before in our history has such a mass of legislation, most of it ill thought out and badly drafted, been offered for the benefit of the people. It is the inevitable response to the cry for Social Justice offered by the fake reformer and the incompetent legislator, and with our national tendency to search for panaceas that will stop the pain and cure the disease at once, we are storing up for ourselves economic and social diseases that will become painfully apparent when the legislative narcotic has failed to work. *Let me beg of the social workers of the country never to suggest or support a legislative bill until its language has been made exact and its effects have been studied to their minutest ramifications* [emphasis added]. We are insane for the act of legislation; we are feeble minded in failing to realize that only the broadest legislation on human relations and conduct can be enforced and to demand that the multifarious details of human relations and conduct shall be adjusted and carried on according to individual and community character and standards.
>
> We cannot have Social Justice if the billions of money we are spending for community property is wasted or stolen. The burden of community waste and dishonesty falls heaviest upon the man of minimum earning capacity who, Social Justice demands, shall have items in his budget for recreation, health, preservation, insurance and savings.
>
> We cannot have Social Justice if the personnel of Government, the men and women whom we hire to do the community work, are wasteful, dishonest

Social Justice (continued)

and inefficient; if they conduct our work for their personal gain and are not inspired with the spirit of professional and community service. Community employees will be just what community character and standards demand they shall be. If we think of the Mayor as the community business manager; of the superintendent of schools as the guardian of educational efficiency; of the city engineer as the promoter of a pure water supply, adequate sewage and garbage disposal, substantial paving, economic lighting; of the health officer as the guardian of community health; of the comptroller as the watchdog of the treasury and the producer of the fiscal facts of government; and demand that they be technically efficient and inspired with ideals of service we shall get them. And until we get them we cannot have Social Justice.

Men are not born free and equal. They never have been and they never will be. No one is free. In community life we are all interdependent. It is easy for that interdependence to sink into economic slavery if the powerful, the rich and the unscrupulous are permitted to manipulate government, to exploit labor, physical and economic necessities, weaknesses of character, and ignorance. Men are not equal one with the other either in physical or mental strength, training or knowledge. Education will prevent extremes but it will never produce equality in physique or knowledge. Community standards embodied in wise law will help to give equality of opportunity.

Social Justice demands a sense of social stewardship on the part of those of larger knowledge and power and calls upon them to lead the fight against the selfish financial purposes of those economically powerful and those socially destructive.

Social Justice demands that workers, of every class, grade and occupation shall be honest, sincere and faithful; efficient as workers and as community members.

Can we hope for a social equilibrium here in America which embodies and is built on social justice? Yes, if we deal with the problems of industry and finance with wisdom; yes, if we have an enlightened attitude towards government; yes, if community character is the resultant of individual and family character and ideals; yes, if there is a sense of social stewardship on the part of those of larger knowledge and power for those of restricted life. (pp. 11–13)

The year 1906 reflected the full integration of advocacy into the National Conference's pulse. With Edward T. Devine as president, advocacy was pushed beyond its conventional limits when he challenged social workers to identify and contest the organized corruption, greed, and injustices responsible for perpetuating poverty and hardship for disadvantaged populations. This year was also important because it reflected, for the first time, the need for effective legislation and corresponding advocacy activity in virtually *all* working committees. Specifically, a very active and vocal Committee on Statistics emerged from the Committee on Legislation, explaining that "the collecting of statistics means the gathering of facts; the preservation of accurate data; the compilation of definite information regarding the individuals, localities and conditions with which those engaged in the wide range of philanthropy have to deal. Without definite knowledge no scientific consideration of a subject is possible" (Butler, 1906). In 1911, working committees were refined to address all matters related to populations, issues, and practice areas. Furthermore, two new committees developed: first, the Committee on Standards of Living and Labor; and second, the Committee on Housing, Health & Recreation. The emergence, development, and work of all these committees were indicative of social work advocacy's development through the progressive years.

In 1908, the Committee on Press and Publicity emerged to discuss how social workers could educate the public on its mission and constituent needs. Methods identified included: (1) published reports; (2) circulars and pamphlets; (3) books; (4) magazines; (5) newspapers, to include news stories, paid advertisements, and editorials; (6) public addresses and debates; (7) lectures, stereopticon shows, and exhibits; (8) billboards and posters; and (9) streetcar advertising (Steele, 1908). Considerable attention highlighted the use and effectiveness of publicity, and many discussions outlined its need and potential impact in multiple practice areas. It is important to note that throughout the previous year, a study of publicity's use and effectiveness was conducted by members of this committee in 68 cities; the results were reported at the National Conference and supported the information outlined in that session (Steele, 1908).

In 1909, the Committee on Press and Publicity provided more sophisticated information to the Conference attendees. Those topics discussed were (1) The Opportunity of the Publicist in Relation to Efforts for Social Betterment; (2) Symposium: What Constitutes Right Publicity?; and (3) Social Photography: How the Camera May Help in the Social Uplift (*Proceedings of the National Conference,* 1908). It was overtly implied that if social workers used these methods, they could successfully broaden their base of support outside the boundaries of their field and immediate constituency. Much of this work set the foundation for *The Survey,* which became "social work's 'semi-official' journal and a stalwart reporter of social ills and the policies and programs designed to improve or eliminate them"

(Steinwall, 1986); Paul U. Kellogg, another social work advocate, was its founder and editor-in-chief.

A number of writings used the terms *advocate* and *advocacy* during the progressive years. In addition to using them to support, promote, and influence *legislation* (see Patten, 1907; Devine, 1911a) and *systems* (see Richmond, 1906; Patten, 1907; Devine, 1910b), the terms now included *issues* (see Richmond, 1906, 1907a, 1907b; Devine, 1912; Addams, 1912) and *ideals* (see Patten, 1907; Richmond, 1907b; Devine, 1910b, 1911b; Addams 1912). In one article, Devine (1911b) stated that "for as long as I can remember I have been an *advocate*, even though a more or less inarticulate *advocate* of the suffrage movement" (p. 74). This was the first social worker to self-report an advocacy role. Finally, Kaufman (1912) stated, in his letter to Jane Addams, "[Y]our womanly *advocacy* of the most just and worthy platform of the new party, will so enhance your influence across the nation. . . ." This statement is unique because it was used to describe the advocacy work from one individual directly to another. Needless to say, the use and meaning of *advocate* and *advocacy* matured and expanded during the progressive years.

Social workers from all movements and ideologies joined together to collaboratively advocate social reform during the progressive years. Mary Richmond's statement in 1910 from *The Interrelationship of Social Movements* is an example of the collaborative relationships between the various social work factions:

> It is only to be expected, perhaps, that a new worker in a new movement embodying a newly discovered principle of social action should be impatient of the adjustments necessary with older but equally true principles. . . . [T]hese separate social movements should, as time goes on and our social work becomes even more highly specialized than it is now, build up a social synthesis, a technique of interrelations, involving more careful preparation of the ground for both our legislative and our field operations, and then a generous making way for one another, a hearty lending a hand to one another for the sake of the harvest. (pp. 289–291)

WORLD WAR I AND THE POSTWAR YEARS: 1914–1919

The events surrounding World War I played a significant role not only in the developing social work field, but in its ongoing advocacy practice as well. During the war's early years, the United States remained neutral despite provocation from German hostility. Such hostile actions included the controversial German torpedo attack on the passenger ship *Lusitania*, which resulted in 1,198 civilian fatalities; 128 were American citizens. In April 1917, three years after the war began, the United States joined the other allied nations by declaring war on Germany. However, this decision was not unanimous; 6 senators and 50 congresspersons voted against this war declaration. Congresswoman Jeanette

Rankin, a social worker and lifelong pacifist, cast one of the dissenting votes (Chronology, 1905–1915; Funk & Wagnalls, 1994; Kennedy, 1991).

There were many reasons why the United States remained neutral through those early years, but the primary reason focused on the number of European immigrants living in the United States at that time. Specifically, the 1910 census identified one out of every three residents, or approximately 32 million, as a first- or second-generation immigrant. From that population, approximately 10 million were descendants of Germany or Austria-Hungary, the two aggressor, enemy nations. With this strong domestic European influence, the U.S. government was unsure where loyalties would fall if it joined in the war. "Knowing this, the Wilson administration undertook an extraordinary propaganda campaign aimed at shaping American public opinion favorable to the war and mobilization efforts" (Kennedy, 1991). It was under these conditions, as well as the heightened social justice momentum, that many social work advocates pushed for humanitarianism and international peace, and specifically opposed United States involvement in the war. This opposition was consistent throughout all four war years.

While the best-known peace advocate was Jane Addams, many others were equally dynamic and active during that time. There were those who, in 1914, were concerned that the war would damage the interethnic relations previously established. These advocates, including Lillian Wald, Paul U. Kellogg, and Emily Greene Balch (in addition to Jane Addams), organized the American Union Against Militarism (AUAM) (Alonso, 1995). In addition, many others actively organized the Woman's Peace Party, which was "organized to exert considerable influence upon . . . Americans, men as well as women, to receive the commendation of President Wilson and other statesmen for its plan of international reconstruction" (Degen, 1972). Grace Abbott, Sophonisba Breckinridge, Lillian Wald, Emily Greene Balch, Mary Simkhovitch, and Florence Kelley were among the many representatives in the U.S. delegation (Costin, 1983; Degen, 1972).

During this time, Addams frequently advocated humanitarianism and international peace. One example is seen in the following request from Rector William H. Talmage of the Flandreau, South Dakota, Social Service Commission on October 18, 1915:

> There is a matter now before the Government for consideration which is vital to the program of the Woman's Peace Party. Your Committee on NATIONAL LEGISLATION should become concerned at once. . . . Kindly let me know if your organization cares to have a share in the *advocacy* of this fundamental peace reform, if so I would be glad indeed to suggest some ways by which you could do so. . . . (Talmage, October 18, 1915).

Further, in partnership with others Addams actively advocated the development of an international commission to arbitrate world peace. This grassroots effort was promoted through the "Continuous Mediation Without Armistice" manifesto which was printed and distributed across the nation. This was the first document that provided a conceptual advocacy framework in early social work history. Specifically, the manifesto stated:

> If the course of action which we have outlined is indeed the reasonable one to follow, if it contains any promise of help, direct or indirect, immediate or future, to the cause of peace, then the natural thing for the individual to do is to *advocate* that course in season and out of season, *by personal propaganda, through the press, through public meetings, by resolutions of societies, through appeal to persons in authority. . . . [T]he task is a definite one. It is the task of persuading to immediate action those individuals and groups, official, semi-official, or unofficial, who have power, direct or indirect, to bring about the establishment of an international commission.* (Wales, 1915, p. 12)

At first glance, we see embedded in this quotation from the manifesto those advocacy components identified in the late 19th century, specifically responsibility for and obligation to a legislative process necessary to achieve systems-change and to ensure effectiveness and enforceability. In addition, influence and collective action were used as the vehicles to effectuate change. Finally, this quotation highlights those methodologies necessary to establish a broad base of support.

Based on Addams's international peace work and lifelong humanitarianism, she was awarded the Nobel Peace Prize in 1931. But Addams was not the only social worker to receive this distinguished award; her colleague, Emily Greene Balch, "social worker, economist, and peace advocate," also received the Nobel Peace Prize in 1946 for her lifelong international peace work (Bicha, 1986).

In conjunction with these peace efforts, other social workers advocated important legislation at home. For example, the National Consumers' League (NCL), headed by Florence Kelley, and the Women's Trade Union League (WTUL), headed by Margaret Robins, continued to advocate women's industrial reform. The National Child Labor Committee (NCLC), headed by Samuel M. Lindsay, continued to advocate child labor regulation and legislation, as well as continued and inclusive compulsory education (Chambers, 1963). The Chicago Immigrant's Protective League, headed by Sophonisba Breckinridge and the Abbott sisters, continued to advocate immigrant acculturation in American society (Costin, 1983). Finally, in partnership with Julia Lathrop and others, Judge Julian Mack advocated the Soldiers' and Sailors' Insurance Law of 1917. This important legislation provided disability benefits to *all* enlisted men (to include African Americans), and their families, injured during the war. Disability benefits included lifetime medical care, financial compensation, vocational reeducation, and low-cost life insurance (Bruno, 1948; Spano, 1982).

However, many of the events surrounding the war had an adverse effect on mainstream society. You may recall that those decades preceding the war focused primarily on social justice issues, or basic human rights for oppressed groups; the most prevalent group was immigrants. Class struggles were focal issues of reform, and labor disputes and remedies took significant time, money, and energy. Consequently, the United States delayed entry into the war despite constant provocation from external forces because of the strong foreign influence in our country. In other words, political decisions affecting Americans were made based on how they would be interpreted by immigrants. Even national security decisions were made based on perceived immigrant perceptions, which often placed civilian lives abroad in great danger. Thus, by the time the United States allied in the war, this decision was both welcomed and supported by middle-class America. Many social workers advocating international peace and humanitarianism during and following those years were identified as traitors and treated with hostility (Ehrenreich, 1985; Kennedy, 1991). For example, Jane Addams was ostracized by the social work profession, and Emily Green Balch was fired from Wellesley, for vocalizing their pacifistic attitudes (Alonso, 1996).

Finally, the anticommunist movement (better known as the Red Scare) predominated 1919 and 1920 and set the stage for American self-protection and -absorption in the following decade. Specifically, once the Bolshevik Communist Party overthrew the Russian imperial government earlier that decade, Americans affiliated with socialist and communist factions were seen as a threat to democracy. Nativism was embraced, and social reforms were identified as anti-American. "Social experimentation and proposals for social reform became dangerous. The very idea of the government being responsible for public welfare was branded 'communistic'" (Ehrenreich, 1985). This was a time wrought with racism, labor strikes, minority emancipation, continued immigration, lynchings, fear of revolution, urban riots, and rural migration. Based on the swell of emotions related to external forces and foreign influences, the subsequent decade focused exclusively on middle-class America. Those values were reflected in the social work field as well as in American society (Chronology, 1916–1928; DeLong, 1991; Ehrenreich, 1985; Kennedy, 1991).

AMERICAN SOCIETY AND SOCIAL WORK INTERNALIZE: 1920–1929

The decade following World War I was a time marked by political isolation, cultural egocentrism, and individual hedonism. It was significant because middle-class America focused exclusively on *self* rather than *other*. This should not be surprising when considering what we already know. Those decades preceding this era targeted social reform, that is, interethnic integration, humanitarianism and social equity, class and labor remediation, and indigent relief. This social justice effort placed a great burden on the middle-class because, in many respects, it "picked up the tab" for social reform without reaping any benefits. As such, the day had finally arrived for this group to internalize and self-nurture. Clark Chambers, an early social work historian, succinctly and accurately summed up this decade when he said that "America seemed more excited by the contemplation of the internal landscape of the person . . . than the external landscape of society" (Spano, 1982).

As previously mentioned, political isolation was predominant during the 1920s. On the heels of World War I and the Bolshevik revolution, Americans learned how devastating political and governmental intervention could be for large-scale society, particularly when it was misguided or misdirected. In the years following World War I, mainstream America decided it was easier to close its political doors than it was to resume social reform. Coincidentally, at that same time the U.S. economy had grown stronger than ever. National income rose approximately 44%, manufactured products increased by 34%, and stock dividends grew to 110%. This financial security provided the gateway to "consumerism." As such, credit was promoted and provided by private businesses to micro and macro communities. This higher standard of living was welcomed by constituents, even when financial stability was unable to support it (Ehrenreich, 1985; Spano, 1982). The natural reaction was cultural egocentrism, and society became intolerant of class and ethnic integration.

Technology and industry continued to advance well into the 1920s. Automobiles, an early 20th-century invention, were mass produced and readily available to consumers. Through credit, individuals could easily purchase this luxury, which in turn provided the middle class with significant mobility. Many individuals and families thus moved away from the cities, into the suburbs. Furthermore, new home appliances were designed, developed, and manufactured, and commercially produced foods were readily available to the general public. These home conveniences emancipated middle-class women from traditional homemaker roles. However, most household incomes required supplementation so that housewives could afford these luxuries. As such, many women joined the professional world, which drastically altered traditional family life. Several of these factors also opened the door to sexual promiscuity. Separation and divorce took precedence. And, where personal lifestyles became upwardly mobile, so too did professional careers. Social legitimization was often attained through one's professional status (Ehrenreich, 1985; Spano, 1982). As you can see, this cycle fed upon itself. It was the predominant backdrop of American society during the 1920s, one that had a direct impact on social work practice and service intervention.

According to Kurzman (1974), "social workers, like almost everyone else, were influenced deeply by the events and mood of the decade; they were optimistic, little oriented toward social action, and generally pleased with the tenor of laissez-faire" (p. 163). While this widespread internalization and egocentrism did spill over, the profession had been moving slowly in that direction for many years. Take, for example, the fact that early social work operated with the manpower and expertise of a voluntary workforce. Specialized organizations and governmental institutions were by-products of social reform, and paid staff was necessary to effectively operate those entities. Thus, social work slowly transformed from a voluntary, altruistic mission to a highly regulated and accountable bureaucracy. Examples of such organizations included the Child Welfare League, the Children's Aid Society, the Family Welfare Association of America, the Association for Improving the Conditions of the Poor, the American Association for Organizing Family Social Work, the Juvenile Protective Association, and the International Migration Service. Of course, women emancipated from homemaker roles filled most of the administrative and clerical positions. As these organizations continued to grow in size, operation, manpower, and revenue, they became increasingly difficult forums to serve *and observe* more than a small percentage of human service clientele on an ongoing basis. This bureaucratization also made it difficult for social work practitioners to impact or influence others or large-scale change efforts.

The social work profession was not immune from organizing as a bureaucracy. On May 17, 1915, Abraham Flexner, the assistant secretary of the New York City General Education Board, challenged social workers in his address *Is Social Work a Profession?* Of the multiple components required of a profession, Flexner stated that the most important was an adherence to professional standards. Not long after this challenge, several professional social work organizations emerged and developed; the most important was the National Social Workers Exchange (NSWE), formed in 1917. In 1921 the NSWE was renamed the American Association of Social Workers (AASW) (it merged in 1955 to become the National Association of Social Workers [NASW]). It was this organization that guided the social work profession through the next few decades (Brieland, 1997; Flexner, 1915).

As you can imagine, the primary objective of the AASW was to (1) define professional social work standards and (2) ensure these standards were implemented and subsequently enforced. Through this work, the AASW established both responsibilities *and* rights for all social workers, whether public or private employees. As those professional standards were developed and defined, the AASW insisted that social workers had the right to participate in policy making, and to ensure those policies were effected. In 1921, the AASW represented approximately 750 members; by 1926, membership grew to 3,512 (Chambers, 1963; Leighninger, 1987). Subsequent growth also demonstrated the effectiveness of this type of organization; in 1930, the AASW had 4,657 members, and that number grew to 8,016 by 1934 (Ehrenreich, 1985).

In conjunction with this increasing bureaucratization, social work practice settings also evolved as they specialized and then diversified. For example, social workers could be found practicing in multiple professional environments, including medical and mental hospitals, schools, private family welfare agencies, child guidance clinics, children's aid societies, and mental hygiene clinics. Social work specializations were further refined into three broad practice areas: community organization, casework, and group work. Based on the widespread fragmentation, diversification, and specialization in this field, it was impossible for social workers to present themselves to larger populations with any uniformity. It was equally difficult for them to take consistent ideological or philosophical positions on causes or issues, as had the early social work reformers (Chambers, 1963; Ehrenreich, 1985; Leighninger, 1987).

Although these factors explain how and why social work dynamics changed to coincide with mainstream society's ideologies during the 1920s, they do not explain how advocacy practice was affected, particularly since it was so well developed in the previous decades. The strongest adverse influence on advocacy was the development and inclusion of psychology in social casework techniques. Sigmund Freud's psychoanalytic theory was the most common psychological theory discussed and debated during that time. You may also recall that William James wrote *The Principles of Psychology* in 1890, the very first identified and recorded psychological accounting in the United States. As such, social workers were eager to incorporate the principles and theories of psychology into its practices.

Most contemporary social workers credit Mary Richmond and her two timely works, *Social Diagnosis* (1917) and *What Is Social Casework?* (1922), for the profession's intense interest and attraction to psychology. Although Richmond's works did play a significant role in defining casework during the 1920s, her ideology was actually minimized at that time. It turns out that Richmond's work was a balanced approach of service *and* action. Psychology, however, focused exclusively on individuals, particularly their inadequacies, which made practitioners aware of the complex and intrinsic problems that individuals faced on a daily basis. Psychology "portrayed man as moved less by rational considerations than earlier generations had believed; it seemed to deny the existence of will and consciousness, reason, and moral values" (Chambers, 1963). To reflect on history's perpetuation, social workers embraced psychology in the 1920s just as they embraced Social Darwinism in the 1870s. In many respects, psychology was an extension of Social Darwinism because it placed the blame for poverty and hardship on the individual rather than the larger forces of society (Kurzman, 1974).

The decline of social work advocacy was best evidenced by the way Julia Lathrop was treated at the 1923 National Conference of Social Work. That year, when she brought a series of peace resolutions and legislative agendas on prisoner enforcement, minimum wage, and child labor to the forum, she received applause, devotion, and respect. However, the conference chair upheld a previous decision to disallow consideration of social policy resolutions. The conference, therefore, moved to other agenda items and issues. As Chambers (1963) noted:

> The climate of the 1920s was just not hospitable to the extension of reform measures . . . with a few exceptions, legislative proposals . . . were met with indifference, disinterest, or hostility, whether in national or state government. To social reformers, the strategy was perfectly clear—keep on the firing line, study and agitate and propagandize, beat tactical retreats when necessary, engage in flank attacks, never for a moment surrender the initiative, and wait for the breaks. This line of action was not as clear to social workers, and most of them returned to careers of professional welfare service, leaving for odd moments the task of reconstruction. (p. 89)

THE GREAT DEPRESSION AND ADVOCACY'S RESURGENCE: 1931–1939

The "Roaring 20s," which were carefree years, came to a sharp halt in October 1929 when the stock market crashed. Americans were completely unprepared for the swift, harsh, and disastrous depression that followed, which had a direct impact on every facet of society. For example, between 1929 and 1933 manufacturing decreased by 40%, the gross national product dropped 25%, and for those individuals fortunate enough to have jobs, the average weekly income declined by 35%. Where corporations had aggregate profits of $8.7 billion in mid-1929, these profits dropped to <$2.7 billion> in 1933. Approximately 4,000 banks dissolved during those years. But there were many warnings prior to the crash. High unemployment, insufficient consumer purchasing, loss of homes and farms due to unmet mortgage payments, and strikes and riots (when financial support was unavailable to adults and families) were only a few of the multiple warning signs. To illustrate the long-term devastation, one month after the stock market crashed, 3 million Americans were unemployed. By the end of 1930, approximately 5 million were unemployed; by March 1932, that number doubled to 10 million; and by 1933, more than 13 million were out of work. For the first time in history, poverty could not be attributed to personal failure because it affected *everyone* regardless of class, gender, occupation, or professional status. Poverty thus resulted from a poorly functioning society. But this time, government intervention would have to specialize and integrate to ensure adequate safety nets in the future years (Day, 1989; DeLong, 1991; Ehrenreich, 1985; Kurzman, 1974; Spano, 1982).

President Herbert Hoover was the first to point fingers as he blamed the overproduction of goods and commodities for the stock market crash. He urged businesses to counter the early damage by retaining employees and maintaining production at predepression levels. Despite multiple congressional efforts to enact direct federal relief legislation, within the first two years Hoover vetoed all legislation intended to provide federal funding for relief assistance. Finally, on February 3, 1931, Hoover made the following statement with respect to his policies on the national economic situation, which stated in part:

> This is not an issue as to whether people shall go hungry or cold in the United States. It is solely a question of the best method by which hunger and cold shall be prevented. It is a question as to whether the American people on the one hand will maintain the spirit of charity and mutual self-help through voluntary giving and the responsibility of the local government as distinguished, on the other hand, from appropriating out of the Federal Treasury for such purposes. My own conviction is strongly that if we break down this sense of responsibility of individual generosity to individual and mutual self-help in the country in times of national difficulty and if we start appropriations of this character we have not only impaired something infinitely valuable in the life of the American people but have struck at the root of self-government. (Kurzman, 1974)

Of course, the depression did not subside; instead, it got worse. And by 1932, with presidential elections underway, Hoover enacted the Emergency Relief and Construction Act, making $300 million in federal loans available to states for direct and/or work relief, repayable at 3% per annum (Kurzman, 1974). It was under these conditions that the "rank and file" movement emerged. This movement comprised those social workers who worked directly in the field; many did not possess the education and criteria mandated by the AASW to be considered "professional social workers."

As you can imagine, the depression's economic calamity had a drastic adverse effect in the field. Caseloads increased, agency resources were depleted, and private philanthropy disappeared. Further, wages were slashed, and working conditions were unbearable. Because mass unemployment was so high, individual counseling and psychotherapy were abolished because services were unaffordable. Instead, relief work predominated. Under all these variables, social workers were unable to effectively serve their clients. In fact, many social workers were worse off financially than most of their clients. Because of this firsthand experience in the field and in their own personal life, rank and file workers identified with clients and the need for organized labor protests. Many were quick to participate in organized activities (Ehrenreich, 1985; Spano, 1982). It is within the documents and journals of the rank and file social workers that we found the strongest evidence of advocacy practice, as many social workers fought for economic equity and social justice for their clients *and* for themselves.

Rank and file social workers advocated for appropriate and sufficient economic relief. They challenged the controversial Temporary Emergency Relief Administration (TERA) enacted by President Roosevelt; they further advocated for a *permanent* federal relief administration—the Federal Emergency Relief Administration (FERA)—subsequently headed by social worker Harry

Hopkins. They challenged the partisan politics responsible for the ineffective public relief measures shaping the labor force. The rank and file movement was so strong that in 1935, it comprised 8,200 members compared with the 8,600 members in the AASW (Fisher, 1935). Rank and filers held monthly meetings in major cities across the nation to address the full range of issues and measures that sustained poverty. Further, they held annual conferences each year. The First National Convention of Rank and File Groups in Social Work held in 1935 proposed that the following relief agenda be advocated by its members:

1. Support of the Workers Bill for Unemployment Insurance
2. Support of an improved relief program as an interim measure, with federal responsibility, adequate relief standards, no discrimination, recognition of the right of the unemployed to organize and to petition for redress of grievance without intimidation or police interference, prompt investigation of need, and financial support out of steeply graded income and inheritance taxes
3. Support of an extended and improved work program
4. Adequate maintenance with federal aid of other social services
5. Cooperative action with other groups of workers and with professional organizations in their demands for adequate relief and security measures
6. Support of measures to guarantee freedom of organization and collective bargaining for both industrial and professional workers either in private or governmental employ
7. Support of national measures to guarantee civil liberties (Fisher, 1935)

(See Highlight 1.5.) The issue of employers' responsibility to employees, particularly with respect to advocacy policy and practice, was embedded in this movement's development. The best example of this issue occurred in 1934 when Sidonia Dawson, a supervisory aide at the Home Relief Bureau of New York, promoted and participated in a labor protest with and on behalf of her clients.

Dawson was not a professional social worker, although as an officer in a public relief protective organization she was considered a social worker. Many of Dawson's clients worked in overcrowded, badly lit, and poorly ventilated environments. These conditions often induced fatigue and hysteria. One day, as many clients filed grievances with local administrators, the police inappropriately intervened. Dawson then called a public meeting and urged her clients to picket the bureau offices. She also took part in these protests. Based on Dawson's actions, she was fired. The reasons cited were insubordination, inefficiency, and disloyalty. Although this matter was mediated through the AASW and other professional associations, it was most significant because this was the first time social work advocacy practice was directly challenged as a legitimate role and function within an agency (Leighninger, 1987; Spano, 1982).

1.5 *National Coordinating Committee of Rank and File Groups in Social Work*

Office of Chairman
Six East 46th Street
New York
A Letter to the Social Workers of America

After a week's discussion of technical and social problems you are about to leave Montreal and the 62nd National Conference of Social Work. Within a few days you will be back on the job in the cities, towns and rural committees of the United States and Canada.

Through the Conference you have been stirred and given food for reflection, you know how easy it is, once back home, to slip again into the old routine; into the old habits of thinking and action.

Mary van Kleeck told you Tuesday evening that social workers should be "outposts in defense of human liberties against the forces of reaction" wherever they find themselves. She called attention in the splendid history of the profession which has played a stirring role in protesting social ills. She appealed to you, now that these ills press so overwhelmingly upon us, to become articulate once more against their perpetuation. Not that social workers alone can change the course of history. For it should be clear to us now, in the light of recent events, that the sources of power for the social welfare program we must espouse reside in labor alone, labor gathering around it such allies as it can, including of course social workers.

For the rank and file the Conference has proven an extremely clarifying experience. The courage of some of the speakers, our own discussions, have made us surer of ourselves, of our purposes, of our methods. We will go home to build our organizations, to set up more organizations, which will stand for a decent standard of living for employes [*sic*] of social agencies; which will *advocate* genuine social insurance for the present unemployed, and a completely adequate social welfare program which will in many ways show that they more and more fully recognize that their place is in a broad labor movement.

But we appeal not only to the rank and file in this letter, but to all social workers who value their professional integrity and who seek, above all, to have it grounded in the welfare of the American and Canadian peoples. There are tasks which you cannot shirk, tasks for all social workers

National Coordinating Committee of Rank and File Groups in Social Work (continued)

inside and outside the rank and file movement who cannot accept a program of reduction in the standard of living of the people of Canada and America; who stand fast against attacks on civil liberties; against racial discrimination; against all devices leading to fascism in America, whether open or disguised.

There are organizations through which you can play an important role, the American Association of Social Workers, state and local conferences, the various other professional groups in the field of social work. You can do much to align these organizations in a common front with us against the forces of reaction and despair. The need for unity on our common issues is very great.

Another employee termination shaped a subsequent social work advocacy practice policy. During the last quarter of 1935, the County Relief Commission in the state of Michigan demoted a social worker for participating in organized labor protests. A week later, another employee protested this demotion and was fired. Several hearings and internal protests materialized, but the matter was not resolved. Thereafter, the Michigan Conference for the Protection of Civil Rights submitted a list of questions to the State Relief Administration, Division of Social Services, to clarify policies and procedures around these issues. Two specific questions regarding social work advocacy were addressed:

Questions 2 and 3
Do caseworkers and Federal employees have the right to *advocate* the organization of welfare clients, and have they the right to participate in such organizational work?

Answer to questions 2 and 3
These are abstract rights only; practically, for caseworkers to *advocate* or participate in such organization of clients is quite inconsistent with their responsibility as employees of the Relief Commission. A worker who accepts a position with the Relief Commission assumes an obligation to carry out the policies and regulations adopted by the Commission or imposed upon it by act of Congress or the Legislature. This responsibility cannot be consistently fulfilled if he also actively encourages or participates in the organization of clients for the purpose of changing those regulations and policies. (Nees, 1936)

It is clear from this example that advocacy was an unacceptable practice for those social workers employed in public agencies. The emergence of such restrictive policies was further evidence of the rapid decline of advocacy practice in social work history.

The term *social action*, which many practitioners correlated with advocacy, was not a new concept in professional social work. In 1935, Porter R. Lee defined and developed the term, and placed a conceptual framework around it during his address *The Social Worker and Social Action*. Lee (1935) stated that "participation in social action may be analyzed as presenting two types of activity. Leadership or *advocacy* on the one hand and support on the other" (pp. 260–261). Moreover, Lee identified the following components of social action, and thus advocacy:

(1) promoting an idea as part of a public obligation;
(2) supporting a political party's agenda if its success would benefit a greater social welfare program;
(3) organizing special interest groups intended to shift the control of economic power in class conflicts;
(4) participating in legislative action to achieve social security or child labor abolition; and
(5) promoting safety campaigns and cooperative movements. (p. 259)

According to Lee, advocacy must demonstrate technical competence before it could be considered an authentic and direct professional activity, or a legitimate social work role. Further, technical competence could only be achieved through professional training and experience; without it, the profession's status and programs would be at great risk. Lee also reported that social work advocacy was accomplished through political participation and legislative activity, and social action was an obligation and responsibility of the social work profession (Lee, 1935).

Needless to say, social work advocacy developed and matured into a legitimate and accepted function and practice area during the 1930s. Unfortunately, the triangulated relationship of agencies, social workers, and clients led to increasing restrictions for social work practitioners, which made them ineffective advocates for their constituent clients. In that regard, advocacy practice disappeared as rapidly as it arrived. However, many social workers continued to practice advocacy when opportunities arose in subsequent years.

DECADES OF CHANGE: 1940s AND 1950s

Our profession will be judged by what we are, what we say, what we do. Its capacity will be measured by our competence, its integrity tested by the ethics of our conduct, by our respect for the rights of others, our loyalty to our associates, to our standards, and to the organizations we represent. Its sincerity will be the sincerity of our fighting faith in the creed we live by. The reputation and the future of the profession we honor are ours to make or mar.

NATALIE W. LINDERHOLM, 1945

The first few years of the 1940s concentrated on World War II. Men were sent abroad to fight for freedom while women and children worked domestically to support the war effort. Once hostilities ceased in 1945, men returned home to their families and picked up where they left off. For the remaining decade, and throughout the 1950s, social workers helped clients obtain decent housing, appropriate employment, adequate education, good health, equal opportunity, and legal protection. Large-scale social issues were concerned about the equitable distribution of goods and services, the establishment of necessary social programs, and the elimination of ignorance, prejudice, and discrimination. Social work practitioners were required to perform (1) in client-worker contexts, (2) within agencies, (3) directly with the social work profession, and (4) through those organized forces responsible for social change within micro, mezzo, and macro communities (Mayo, 1944, 1948; Pray, 1945). Hence, the social work field continued to expand and diversify during those years.

With a few exceptions, the word *advocacy* virtually disappeared from social work literature. However, while the term was not prevalent in form, it was in spirit. Lively discussions and debates highlighting advocacy's previously defined and developed framework and practice parameters continued in the social work literature, although the term *social action* was used in its place (see Altmeyer, 1955; Benjamin, 1945; Blackburn, 1954; Clague, 1946; Cohen, 1954; Danstedt, 1958; Hathway, 1944; Hoey, 1944; Howard, 1952; Kaiser, 1952; Kingsley, 1954; Lane, 1946; Larcom, 1953; Leader, 1957; Maslen, 1944; Mayo, 1944, 1948; Meyer, 1956; Ostertag, 1946; Pray, 1945; Schottland, 1953; Shiffman, 1958). When the term did emerge, it was used in conjunction with other social change terminology and concepts. For example, Maslen (1944) associated advocacy with "lobbying," as outlined below:

> Different procedure is called for in *advocating* or sponsoring a bill, as compared with supporting or opposing a bill that has been sponsored by another organization. In order to sponsor a bill, it is essential that an organization have one individual who can develop a cordial relationship with the legislators, who understands the legislative processes, who can appraise a situation and judge what appropriate steps should be taken. This function is commonly called 'lobbying.' . . . (p. 273)

It should be noted that scholars, academics, and practitioners tried to convince social workers of their responsibility for, and obligation to, advocacy and social action. However, those pleas and directives fell on deaf ears.

Following World War II, many questions arose with respect to social change methodologies. For example, scholars asked if professionals could engage in social action as effectively as they practiced family intervention, permanency planning, and collective leadership; and academics asked if it was appropriate to prepare aspiring social workers for the dual responsibilities of service *and* action

(Hathway, 1944; Mayo, 1944). The biggest obstacle for social action in large-scale environments, however, was the threat of external influences, particularly communism. Mayo (1948) noted that while "the period following the first World War was characterized by disillusionment, the era following the second World War [was] one of frustration and desperate fear" (p. 30).

America had reason to be afraid. After all, World War II demonstrated first-hand the devastation associated with atomic energy. While America was the first to use this power, other countries (particularly the Soviet Union) had it available in their arsenal. Furthermore, the Holocaust and its aftermath remained alive for many, many years. It took more than a decade for Americans to calm from the hysteria associated with World War II (Mayo, 1948; Wirth, 1949).

During these years, the concept of *advocacy* vis-à-vis *social action* was referred to by many other names in various contexts. For example, Mayo (1944) stated that social action would better be described as "statesmanlike organization for social change" (p. 32). Hathway (1944) reported that "a course in community organization [was] a course in social action" (p. 369). Bouterse (1948) associated social action and community organization with "citizen participation" (p. 153). Reid (1955) introduced the formal concept of social change (pp. 75–85). Also, Dunham (1948) stated that "the roles of community organization workers would probably run the whole gamut from fact-finder, analyst, planner, catalyst, interpreter, educator, conferee, negotiator, mediator, and consultant to organizer, agent, executive aide, *advocate,* promoter, social actionist, and militant leader" (p. 169). Needless to say, the role and function of advocacy took on many shapes and forms during the middle of the 20th century; its concepts and practice methodologies did not disappear, but simply changed names.

An important advocacy forum developed during this era that piggybacked the events of the previous decade. You may recall the fragmentation and diversification of social work settings and practice areas during the 1930s, as well as the emergence of professional organizations. During the 1940s, and continuing into the 1950s, social workers began to channel strength and energy into national networks with specialized interests. The American Association of Social Workers and the National Social Work Council were two such organizations. Those networks provided forums to express concerns, discuss solutions, and provide collective action; they grew in size, number, and popularity following World War II. Of this effort, Mayo (1944) stated:

> As a profession . . . we must work with and through many and diverse groups in the community. If we are wise, however, we will not identify ourselves with any one political party or any one group to the exclusion of others. Our great strength as a profession lies and will continue to lie in our freedom to throw our influence in the direction of what ever responsible and reputable groups or parties in the community or nation are moving in the interest of basic human need. (p. 32)

This intradisciplinary network of professional social work associations became stronger and stronger through the years. It also set the stage for those advocacy organizations prevalent in the second half of the century.

THE WAR ON POVERTY REENGAGES
THE SOCIAL WORK PROFESSION: 1960S

By the 1960s, very different social problems and social issues were prevalent in our society. First were those associated with the working and nonworking poor; single women with children made up its largest population. Second, widespread minority discrimination predominated the business sector and the government, particularly with regard to hiring, firing, and promotion practices. Finally, factors associated with inner-city life—insufficient schools, crime, malnutrition, inadequate housing, physical and mental disabilities, and poor health—made it difficult for indigents to integrate into mainstream society. As those issues developed, anthropologist Oscar Lewis identified the "culture of poverty" theory, which speculated that long-term indigence was responsible for marital instability, poor health, community and individual apathy, helplessness, inadequate education, dysfunctional behaviors, skewed value systems, and a loss of self-esteem. This theory further hypothesized that such characteristics stymied efforts meant to improve individual circumstances. In addition, Michael Harrington (1962) argued that a "cycle of poverty" was perpetuated from one generation to another based on these and other biopsychosocial factors (Ehrenreich, 1985).

Poverty and its corresponding social issues held the attention of the media. Thus, President Lyndon B. Johnson initiated an antipoverty campaign designed to stimulate the economy. The campaign created new welfare organizations and thus new jobs, and further developed equal opportunity laws, training programs, and health services. Referred to as the "Great Society," its planners developed programs to change indigent opportunities through expanded social systems and structures. Numerous community action programs were initiated through the Economic Opportunity Act of 1965 intended to ameliorate poverty. Among them were the Job Corps, the Youth Corps, Head Start, VISTA, family planning services, neighborhood legal services, and community health centers (Ehrenreich, 1985). The groundwork for these social policies was the catalyst for social work's renewed interest in advocacy practice.

Specifically, in 1961 two professors from Columbia University's School of Social Work, Cloward and Ohlin, argued that society's economic structure was responsible for poverty, not individual deficits. Based on their work, Cloward and Ohlin were invited to help the Ford Foundation develop and initiate the Mobilization for Youth program; its goal was to reduce delinquency and crime through consolidated, coordinated, and integrated service programs that included education, casework, and on-the-job training. This campaign also provided the framework for those programs sponsored through the Economic Opportunity Act of 1965. In fact, it was the community-based legal services provided within these programs that renewed social workers' interest in advocacy practice (Kutchins & Kutchins, 1978).

Professional attention and focus continued once these programs were developed. For example, Charles Grosser (1965) provided the first extensive outline of an advocate's role. While he reported that advocacy was "co-opted from the field of law" (p. 18), he further stated that an advocate *should not be* an "enabler, broker, expert, consultant, guide, or social therapist" but *should be* "a partisan in a social conflict." Grosser also said that social workers should provide the expertise necessary to serve the clients' best and exclusive interests (p. 18). Briar (1968) addressed micro advocacy practice when he pointed out that caseworkers were labeled deviant when they practiced advocacy, or were recognized as innovators; unfortunately they were not provided the necessary support for their professional endeavors. He went on to say that if social work continued to state its primary goal was to ensure its clients' welfare, it must develop and expand its functions, obligations, and practice techniques. He further stated that advocacy should be included in those expanded efforts (pp. 7–8). It was Briar's work that first placed social work advocacy in casework methodologies.

In 1969 this renewed interest prompted the NASW to appoint an Ad Hoc Committee on Advocacy; its purpose was to develop this practice area within the profession. The committee's first task was to define the term *advocacy*. It began with two dictionary definitions; the first outlined an advocate as "one who pleads the cause of another" (Ad Hoc Committee on Advocacy, 1969, p. 17). This definition was meant to reflect the lawyer-advocate role as "his client's supporter, his advisor, his champion, and, if need be, his representative in his dealings with the court, the police, the social agency, and other organizations that [affect] his well being" (p. 17). The second definition outlined an advocate as "one who argues for, defends, maintains, or recommends a cause or proposal" (p. 17). Its intent was to maintain advocacy practice in the political environment. Based on the social unrest and war focus in America at that time, the committee emphasized the need for social workers to immediately engage in advocacy practice. In that regard, the committee recommended that the NASW:

1. Urge social workers to exercise actively and diligently, in the conduct of their practice, their professional responsibility to give first priority to the rights and needs of their clients.
2. Assist social workers—by providing information and other resources—in their effort to exercise this responsibility.
3. Protect social workers against the reprisals, some of them inevitable, that they will incur in the course of acting as advocates for the rights of their clients.

Certain assumptions were implicit in these program objectives, namely:

- That the social worker has an obligation under the *Code of Ethics* to be an advocate.
- That this obligation requires more than mere "urging."
- That under certain circumstances . . . the obligation is enforceable under the *Code of Ethics*.

- That the *moral* obligation to be an advocate is not limited to one's own clients, although this cannot be enforced in the same way.
- That encouragement of advocacy and provision of certain kinds of assistance to *advocates* need not be limited to members of the professional association. (p. 21)

According to the Ad Hoc Committee, advocacy was both an obligation and responsibility of social workers. It recommended that the NASW support individual advocacy efforts above and beyond the individuals' responsibility to agencies, or agency needs.

Brager (1969) was the first to discuss in any depth the multiple problems associated with advocacy practice. While trying to maintain advocacy in the political environment, Brager identified its primary objective as the redistribution of community resources (i.e., power, programs, and policies) within disadvantaged populations. This advocacy concept set the stage for "empowerment" practice. However, Brager understood the multiple barriers that confronted effective advocacy actions, which included (1) social workers' responsibility and obligation to agencies, (2) societal competition for available resources, and (3) individual, societal, and professional values. Brager did, however, specify that while "advocacy *may* be found in any professional interaction in which a client's interest is opposed by some other person or institution, it *must* be part of a worker's armamentarium when environmental change is the objective" (p. 111).

Funding for and management of the federal programs initiated by the Great Society were allocated through federal grants. This new source of financial aid was developed so that government could exercise exclusive control over those social policy programs initially targeted as "entitlements." For example, where entitlements could be monetarily expanded through inflation and population growth, federal grants required explicit authorization to effectuate program and funding changes. Federal grants were also time-limited (Danziger & Weinberg, 1994; Kalas, 1987). The significance of this change from private philanthropy and foundational giving to a third-party form of government is evidenced in the following quotation from Kalas (1987).

> In the 1960s and early 1970s, politically based criticisms . . . centered on grants that appeared to result in "social manipulation" based on then-current theories of social change. A good example is the criticism levelled [sic] at the Ford Foundation for supporting New York's Mobilization for Youth, because it overtly sought fundamental social reform by empowering individuals and groups that were marginal in society both with respect to political power and wealth. Other foundations . . . were supporting organizations seeking racial justice, particularly in the South. One school of thought . . . suggests that the 1969 tax law regarding foundations was enacted to limit the advocacy for social change. . . . (p. 25)

As you can see, new barriers severely limited social workers' ability to perform the intended mission of social work—to protect and help individuals adversely affected by change.

ANALYSIS, APATHY, OR PROFESSIONAL DESPERATION: 1970s

Activism was the strongest force in the United States during the 1970s. Unrest predominated as activists fought to (1) end the Vietnam War and (2) promote women's liberation and civil rights. Social policy agenda items advocated women's rights (social equality and equity) and environmental issues. However, Richard M. Nixon was in the White House for part of the 1970s and was opposed to continuing the social reform programs initiated by the Great Society. In fact, Nixon was the *first* official proponent of welfare reform, and he engaged his cabinet and Congress in this battle. His administration reduced the number of social programs nationwide, and further mandated that social agencies and urban programs *compete* for available federal funding. Finally, Nixon placed multiple restrictions and limitations on social policies and advocacy practices (Day, 1989; Ehrenreich, 1985). This era was accurately described by many as "a period of 'benign neglect' of social problems" (Ehrenreich, 1985).

During the 1970s social workers disengaged from advocacy practice. Reasons identified for this disengagement included (1) intense financial competition for existing social programs, and (2) strict limitations on programs funded through federal grants. Moreover, the social work profession was under increasing scrutiny as it became the *target* of social change. In that regard, many practitioners formed alliances with activists and external organizations that worked to effect social service change. Other practitioners were embarrassed that nonsocial work professionals developed the necessary expertise to effectuate social work's original mission; they were thus apathetic to advocacy practice. Finally, many professional organizations such as the National Organization for Women, National Welfare Rights Organization, the Family Service Association of America, and Social Welfare Workers Movement assumed responsibility for governmental and societal advocacy practices (Ehrenreich, 1985; Riley, 1971). For the first time in the history of social work, social workers received much of their support *outside* their profession. In addition, scholars were outspoken about social workers' need to join forces with other groups and professionals to accomplish social work's intended mission (Dumont, 1970; McCormick, 1970; Riley, 1971).

Despite the fact that social work advocacy was not universally practiced throughout the United States during the 1970s, it was actively discussed, debated, and analyzed in the professional literature. Was this intense interest a desperate effort to engage social workers in advocacy practice? Or did it occur because scholars were presented with an intellectual dilemma that required resolution—that is, just what is social work advocacy? In either event, research outlined in this literature did not accurately reflect social work history. These scholars were only concerned with clarifying advocacy practice.

However, advocacy was outlined and analyzed in virtually every social work setting and practice area. It was further applied in some capacity to each and every social issue and concern identified with the social work profession. It was in this material that the authors found social work advocacy's increasing fragmentation, which created chaos for professionals hoping to practice it.

McCormick (1970) referred to advocacy as a form of interference, and stated that the decision to engage in professional advocacy was a personal choice, thus negating the NASW's position statement. Riley (1971) identified family advocacy as "service designed to improve life conditions for people by harnessing direct and expert knowledge with the commitment to action and the application of skills to produce community change. It deals with institutional systems rather than individuals" (p. 374). As such, Riley implied that advocacy could be broken down into specialized practice areas, yet he presented it as a broad spectrum of community actions. Richan (1973) described advocacy as action taken on behalf of aggrieved persons or groups, and further stated that its definition was contingent upon the definition of individual rights. In that regard, Richan implied that the advocacy definition must continually change as societal needs change. Why did advocacy not maintain its historic ideology of *protecting* social needs, as it had in the past? Further, Richan was the first to identify paternalism as a component of advocacy practice.

Craigen (1972) identified advocacy as a form of direct service when he said "advocacy is increasingly being practiced with families, in planning at the macro level, and through technical assistance to community groups and paraprofessionals. However, this activity is still infrequent, and it creates an uncomfortable societal role for some clinicians" (p. 154). As you can see, advocacy was once again refined to encompass the needs of society rather than continuing with the historic social change approach. Furthermore, Craigen confused the terms *activism* and *advocacy* by implying that the two were synonymous. To add insult to injury, Panitch (1974) incorrectly stated that "prior to 1965 limited information was available in the social work literature about the concept of advocacy" (p. 326). Based on the information presented in this chapter, we know this is not a true statement. He continued to explain that advocacy was regarded as a combative practice, an unnatural role for social work professionals. As such, Panitch specifically stated that social workers could not be effective advocates because they lacked the required orientation and technical skills to engage in combative techniques. But since when was "influence" synonymous with "combat"? Influence implies discussion and negotiation; combat is an authoritative and omnipotent approach. Surprisingly, Kutchins and Kutchins (1978) reported that advocacy "has been confused with social action, social change, and social reform" (p. 24). Although this is a true statement, it can only be considered as valid during the 1960s and 1970s.

Finally, Holmes (1976) outlined advocacy as one of two social work strategies used to service rape victims. Gilbert and Specht (1976) challenged the social work profession when they asked why "the image of the ethical social worker [was] so unappealing that it must be clothed in the guise of advocacy to attract the profession's attention" (p. 291). Reid (1977) identified advocacy as one of many social work methodologies, but further reported that social workers were unable to combine and apply it to action to alleviate social problems. Ross (1977a) associated social work advocacy with urban planning; and McGowan (1978) and Takanishi (1978) outlined historical information about advocacy's role in the children's welfare movement. While this is not a comprehensive assessment of the literature analyzing social work advocacy during the 1970s, it is a good representation of the content and context of the literature during that time.

As you can see, social work advocacy broadened and expanded its functions and roles during the 1970s. Based on the information presented here, can you answer the following questions: Was social work advocacy analytical and apathetic in professional practice during the 1970s? Or was it a desperate attempt to engage professionals in its practice? The authors believe the first question best answers this dilemma, and are further inclined to believe that this analysis was directly responsible for its fragmentation and ambiguous practice parameters.

REAGAN'S LEGACY—NEW FEDERALISM: 1980S

During the 1980s, the federal government revealed an unusually cruel side once Ronald Reagan was elected to presidential office. Within his first year, Reagan set his primary political objectives in motion, which were to (1) reduce the federal deficit and balance the nation's budget (provided military appropriations increased or remained the same), and (2) significantly reduce or eliminate burdensome social welfare programs. With respect to the second objective, Reagan and his administration fought hard to shift poverty's financial and programming responsibilities back to the charitable sector by targeting private philanthropy and voluntary service. Politically, this objective was accomplished through legislation, regulation, and deficit reductions. Of particular importance was the Gramm-Rudman Balanced Budget and Emergency Deficit Control Act of 1985, which mandated significant reductions in almost every low-income entitlement program across the nation. Of course, most Americans knew that social welfare programs were scapegoats for escalating military defense spending and federal income tax reductions. Unfortunately, little could be done once Reagan's policy agenda was set in motion (Day, 1989; Demone & Gibelman, 1984; Haynes & Mickelson, 1991).

There were two important components to Reagan's New Federalism. The first was "reprivatization," which required that the private sector assume sole responsibility for personal indigence and hardship. This was redirected through individual donations, ecumenical involvement, and nonprofit intervention. The second component "devolved" the financial and programming responsibilities for federal entitlement programs, such as Aid to Families with Dependent Children, Supplemental Security Income, and food stamps, directly to state governments. Responsibility for Medicaid would remain shared with the federal government (Day, 1989; Haynes & Mickelson, 1991). These policy changes had a significant impact on social work's direct service delivery system.

Consider, for a moment, those community-based programs developed during the 1960s meant to alleviate poverty. Initiated by Johnson and his Great Society planners, program accountability, development, and service delivery were implemented and monitored by social work practitioners. Then the Reagan administration cut or eliminated many of those same programs during the 1980s, leaving social workers as ineffective public servants. Based on this reduced funding, individuals with mental illness were served in communities rather than institutions. These new issues grew in both size and dimension; specifically, homelessness, substance abuse, and HIV/AIDS (Stern & Gibelman, 1990). "The desire to incorporate new programs that are responsive to emerging needs, while continuing traditional services, poses resource and priority dilemmas for social agencies" (Stern & Gibelman, 1990, p. 14).

A third-party form of government continued to develop and placed multiple restrictions on private practitioners and not-for-profit agencies. Specifically, competition for funding increased, third-party service contracts were implemented, and managed care developed. Reprivatization created several social crises; the most predominant was deinstitutionalization. Suddenly individuals with severe mental illness previously treated by institutions were discharged into the community. Most of these individuals did not have independent or work-related skills. With nowhere to go, these deinstitutionalized persons became part of the increasingly growing homeless population. Based on these external limitations and variables, the social work profession was again precluded from accomplishing its original mission of protecting and helping individuals adversely affected by change. What were social workers to do?

Advocacy emerged as a viable answer. During the 1980s, social workers were ready and willing to engage in their historic advocacy practice. There was only one problem—few could uniformly agree on its definition (see Chapter 2, Advocacy: A New Definition, for a complete discussion). In response to this dilemma, social workers from every practice area tried to define and expand on this term. They were, however, unable to uniformly outline a generally acceptable framework, or concrete practice parameters, to everyone's satisfaction. Once again, the professional literature demonstrated increased fragmentation with respect to advocacy's function and domain (see Beecher, 1983; Brown, 1981; Browning, Thorin, & Rhoades, 1984; Fabricant & Epstein, 1984; Fandetti & Goldmeier, 1988; Favero, 1987; Frost, 1983; Henk, 1989; Higgins, 1983). Advocacy further diversified into multiple practice settings such as casework, legislation, policy, systems, administration, populations, and causes. Terms and concepts such as *internal advocacy, external advocacy,* and *self-advocacy* emerged as well.

In response to community and societal needs, grassroots efforts and voluntary organizations grew in size and proportion. While most grassroots efforts developed to initiate changes within local and regional jurisdictions (Edwards, 1991), voluntary organizations developed reflecting society's specific needs, conditions, and values. In particular, these voluntary organizations functioned as "agents of social control and social change" (Stern & Gibelman, 1990). According to Fisher (1984), grassroots efforts and voluntary organizations sought to "address community problems, empower citizens at the community level through self-help projects, and demonstrate the chronic need for more public funding. Their aim was to meet community needs and to attract more people to a politics and vision of social, economic, and political democracy, one that will challenge the prerogatives and processes of corporate and political elites" (p. 179). These trends continued into and throughout the 1990s; in most instances they became powerful forces, particularly in political arenas. It is important to note, however, that these efforts were usually led by individuals outside the social work profession.

COUNTDOWN TO THE MILLENNIUM: 1990S

During the 1990s, the word *advocacy* became the buzzword in professional social work. Textbooks and journal articles from this decade almost always contain the word *advocacy* somewhere in the text. While some literature simply used the word to either describe an activity or induce a specific outcome (Bailey & Koney, 1996; Coulton, 1996; Gutierrez, Alvarez, Nemon, & Lewis, 1996; Halter, 1996; Hoechstetter, 1996; Jansson & Smith, 1996; Kamerman, 1996; Kim, Garfinkel, & Meyer, 1996; Mills, 1996; Weil, 1996), other authors attempted to define and apply it to multiple practice areas and settings (Bentley & Walsh, 1996; Cole, 1995; Compton & Galaway, 1994; DuBois & Miley, 1996; Eriksen, 1997; Friesen & Poertner, 1995; Gerhart, 1990; Hardcastle, Wenocur, & Powers, 1997b; Hepworth & Larsen, 1993; Jansson, 1994; Kirst-Ashman & Hull, 1993; Northen, 1995; O'Connor & Ammen, 1997; Peled & Edelson, 1994). It is interesting to note that, despite advocacy's long-standing history, practitioners were still unable to accept a universal definition, or practice parameters, for the term.

Over the course of the decade, many social workers recognized the need to advocate for and on behalf of clients, and attempted to do so using the various definitions and frameworks provided within the profession. In the interim, millions of individuals and families were directly impacted by the residual effects of federal and state policy initiatives. Of particular importance, entitlement programs crucial to the survival of vulnerable, displaced, and at-risk populations were devolved to state governments via block grants. Although block grants were not new to the 1990s, their specific aim was to decentralize the federal government's role and authority within existing social welfare programs while simultaneously reducing the federal government's budget (Bailey & Koney, 1996; Hoechstetter, 1996). According to Weil (1996), many politicians intentionally used block grant methodologies to transfer decision-making power for social welfare programs and related services directly to state and local governments (p. 481).

The most egregious authorizing legislation enacted during the 1990s was the Personal Responsibility and Work Opportunity Reconciliation Act of 1996 (PRWORA) (P.L. 104-193), better known as "welfare reform." Its intent was to tighten government's grip on programs serving the poor, specifically Aid to Families with Dependent Children (AFDC), General Assistance (GA), Supplemental Security Income (SSI), and food stamp eligibility and distribution. In addition to restricting access to funding entitlements, PRWORA also placed numerous limitations on consumer availability and accessibility, to include circumstances and situations reflecting time and reproduction (Ozawa & Kirk, 1996; Poole, 1996). It was well known that PRWORA was introduced and enacted because "our nation [was] threatened by women who join[ed] the welfare rolls instead of the labor force" (Ozawa & Kirk, 1996, p. 93). Single mothers, the primary target population, were blamed for their indigent status through continuous media exposure; they were also blamed for the moral deterioration of their children and youth.

These two stigmas presented a unique paradox. First, welfare recipients were admonished for their role as unproductive members of society. On the other hand, when employed outside the home, single mothers were blamed because they failed to meet domestic responsibilities to their children and home. It is interesting to note that only a small percentage of the federal budget was allocated to "welfare" programs at that time. Despite this fact, many politicians set forth a widely accepted ideology that our country was unable to effectively compete in the global market because single mothers were unwilling to enter the workforce (Edwards, Cooke, & Reid, 1996; Ozawa & Kirk, 1996). "Welfare bashing" became a prevailing theme in our society. In its worst form, it continued to emphasize and reinforce these and other destructive stigmas.

Another policy initiative with deep and long-lasting ramifications was Medicaid managed care. Perloff (1996) stated that "Medicaid managed care [sought] to bring increasing numbers of recipients into health care delivery systems . . . subject to 'the new economics of managed care' . . . based on the fact that care [was] provided to a defined number of enrollees at a fixed rate per member per month" (p. 418). Along with Medicaid managed care's practice parameters sprang terms and concepts such as *gatekeeping, capitation, preferred provider organizations, primary care physicians, health maintenance organizations, service bundling, carveouts,* and *cost-efficiency* (Poole, 1996; Shera, 1996). While higher quality health care services were available to indigent, disenfranchised, displaced, and at-risk populations, the number of available health care providers within the Medicaid managed care system was extremely limited.

In response to these and other large-scale crises, in 1996 the NASW implemented a revised *Code of Ethics*. Among other things, it not only renewed social workers' commitment to advocacy, it placed a greater emphasis on its practice as well. The Preamble states, in part:

> Social workers promote social justice and social change with and on behalf of clients. . . . Social workers are sensitive to cultural and ethnic diversity and strive to end discrimination, oppression, poverty, and other forms of social injustice. These activities may be in the form of direct practice, community organizing, supervision, consultation, administration, *advocacy*, social and political action, policy development and implementation, education, and research and evaluation.

Outlined below are additional advocacy references identified throughout the revised *Code of Ethics:*

> 3.07. Administration
> (a) Social work administrators should *advocate* within and outside their agencies for adequate resources to meet clients' needs.
> (b) Social workers should *advocate* for resource allocation procedures that are open and fair.
>
> 6.01 Social Welfare
> Social workers should promote the general welfare of society, from local to global levels, and the development of people, their communities, and their environments. Social workers should *advocate* for living conditions conducive to the fulfillment of basic human needs and should promote social, economic, political, and cultural values and institutions that are compatible with the realization of social justice.
>
> 6.04 Social and Political Action
> (a) Social workers should engage in social and political action that seeks to ensure that all people have equal access to the resources, employment, services, and opportunities they require to meet their basic human needs and to develop fully. Social workers should be aware of the impact of the political arena on practice and should *advocate* for changes in policy and legislation to improve social conditions in order to meet basic human needs and promote social justice.
> (c) Social workers should promote conditions that encourage respect for cultural and social diversity within the United States and globally. Social workers should promote policies and practices that demonstrate respect for difference, support the expansion of cultural knowledge and resources, *advocate* for programs and institutions that demonstrate cultural competence, and promote policies that safeguard the rights of and confirm equity and social justice for all people.

As can be seen from these excerpts, although the NASW revised *Code of Ethics* made numerous references to social workers' need to advocate on behalf of clients as well as to the capacities and practice areas of social work, the term was once again not well defined.

SUMMARY

Organized social work and its constituent advocacy practice emerged and developed in approximately 1872 with the development of Social Darwinism. The term and concept *advocacy* was first evidenced in the *Proceedings of the National Conference of Charities and Corrections.* Within this literature, advocacy was defined as an obligation of social workers to the legislative process. In that regard, social workers were responsible for ensuring that social legislation was effective and enforceable. Advocacy used influence and collective action to impact social change. Social work advocacy was at its height during the Progressive years (late 1890s until 1914). It was during this era that the strongest social work advocates fought for basic human rights and social justice for oppressed, vulnerable, and displaced populations, including immigrants, women, children, and minorities. Jane Addams, Edward T. Devine, Edith Abbott, Grace Abbott, Sophonisba Breckinridge, Julia Lathrop, Florence Kelley, Simon Nelson Patten, Samuel M. Lindsay, and Francis Perkins were considered social workers' greatest advocates during this time period.

World War I and the postwar years presented a unique challenge to advocacy practice as anticommunism and political neutrality took precedence. However, these influences did not deter many social workers from advocating on behalf of humanitarianism and international peace. As a result of their international peace work, two social work advocates received the Nobel Peace Prize— Jane Addams in 1931 and Emily Greene Balch in 1946. Advocacy practice virtually disappeared during the 1920s as carefree social attitudes and societal self-absorption changed the dynamics of our society. Nevertheless, following the stock market crash in October 1929, advocacy reemerged with a vengeance. During the Great Depression, economic relief legislation and measures such as the Temporary Emergency Relief Administration (TERA), Federal Emergency Relief Administration (FERA), and other social service programs were advocated and established. Social workers also advocated for unemployment insurance, improved and extended relief programs, cooperative action between groups of workers, the freedom to organize and use collective-bargaining, and national support for civil liberties. During this era, advocacy roles and functions were expanded to include political participation and legislative action; advocacy also became an obligation and responsibility of the social work profession.

Advocacy did not reemerge again until the 1960s following widespread social problems and media attention to their corresponding issues. After numerous successful interventions and programs were developed by the Great Society, advocacy was once again in the spotlight. However, there was a great deal of dissension between scholars and practitioners regarding advocacy's definition, framework, and specific practice parameters. Following several decades of debate and contention, advocacy practice diversified into social work's multiple practice areas.

DISCUSSION QUESTIONS

1. Discuss how the social work field emerged in the United States as well as differences of historical accounts identified from other professional sources.
2. How did the concept of advocacy emerge in early social work history, and what were the specific components related to its development?
3. Identify and discuss early social work advocates and their contributions to historical events and practice outcomes.
4. How did World War I and World War II impact social work advocacy's momentum during and after those wars?
5. When did a concrete advocacy definition emerge, and what were the specific characteristics associated with its practice parameters?
6. When was advocacy first embraced by professional social work, and how was it idealized and presented to practitioners? How did this change in subsequent years?
7. Discuss how the social work profession expanded through the years and how this expansion impacted advocacy practice.
8. When and why did advocacy diminish during the second half of the 20th century, and how did it reemerge? How did its practice parameters change?
9. What function did advocacy serve during the 1980s? Who or what benefited from advocacy practice?
10. Under what time period was advocacy most effective? How can we take this cumulative knowledge and make advocacy more effective to social work clients today?

RECOMMENDED READINGS

Axinn, J., & Levin, H. (1997). *Social welfare: A history of the American response to need* (4th ed.). White Plains, NY: Longman.

Day, P. J. (1989). *A new history of social welfare.* Englewood Cliffs, NJ: Prentice-Hall.

Ehrenreich, J. H. (1985). *The altruistic imagination: A history of social work and social policy in the United States.* Ithaca, NY: Cornell University Press.

Leighninger, L. (1987). *Social work: Search for identity.* New York: Greenwood Press.

Spano, R. (1982). *The rank and file movement in social work.* Washington, DC: The University Press.

Trattner, W. I. (1994). *From poor law to welfare state: A history of social welfare in America* (5th ed.). New York: Free Press.

Advocacy: A New Definition

In a world where there is so much to be done, I felt strongly impressed that there must be something for me to do.

DORTHEA DIX

This chapter attempts to provide a fuller explanation of the term *advocacy*, how it has been used in recent literature, how it is different from other social work interventions, which special dimensions and barriers affect social workers, and finally, how the authors developed a new definition of advocacy that will enhance social workers' effectiveness with their clients.

WHAT IS ADVOCACY?

"Advocacy is one of the activities that may distinguish social work from other helping professions" (Kaminski & Walmsley, 1995); but in order for social workers to evaluate their work as advocates, they must understand what is meant by the term. Advocacy is associated with exciting changes that benefit vulnerable groups. Although the profession of social work has long been associated with advocacy, Blakely (1991) suggests that a clear definition of advocacy seems to have eluded the profession. "The role of the advocate seems to be practically synonymous with about all social work roles, and it is presented in such broad strokes, that it cannot be systematically studied or described" (Sosin & Caulum, 1983, p. 12).

Kutchins and Kutchins (1978) also state that *advocacy* is essentially an undefined term that is used to refer to all kinds of social action. In 1976, Gilbert and Specht observed that the word *advocacy* was used to describe consumer education, civil rights and social protest actions, referral and brokerage activities, and a Big Brother program for the developmentally disabled. The advocate is often viewed as synonymous with social work roles such as broker, advisor, champion, representative, and enabler. Some view advocacy only from an individual perspective while others believe advocacy is related to a group or class of people. Bull (1989) argues that advocacy is easier to practice than it is to define or justify. O'Brien et al. (1989) describe advocacy as a "conceptual disaster area." So, who is right? Isn't advocacy simply "speaking up"?

As the reader will see in this chapter, there are multiple definitions and dimensions of advocacy, many of which produce confusion, not clarity. In the following paragraphs, the authors created a typology based on an analysis of over 90 definitions of advocacy in order to: (1) illustrate the number and range of concepts included historically in the term *advocacy*; (2) compare the different emphases in definitions used by social work scholars; and (3) evaluate critically how these dimensions may influence the readers' own personal definition of social work advocacy as they practice it in today's society.

The authors believe that much personal and professional benefit will accrue to the readers as they examine these varied definitions. This assessment will lead the readers, as it did the authors, to search for and develop a definition of advocacy that is personally relevant and meaningful.

Key Dimensions

In Figure 2.1, we have summarized key dimensions of advocacy derived from our analysis of over 90 definitions of the term found in the research literature. We present a brief explanation of each dimension and illustrate it by using examples.

Pleading or Speaking on Behalf of Advocacy is frequently defined in terms of "pleading" or "speaking on behalf of another." In the *Oxford English Dictionary* (1989), an advocate is one who "pleads, intercedes, or speaks for or on behalf of another" (p. 194). Barnhart and Barnhart (1991) state that advocacy is the "act of speaking or writing in favor of something; public recommendation; support" (p. 32). In the 1996 *Webster's New World College Dictionary*, an advocate is a "person who pleads another's cause . . . or speaks

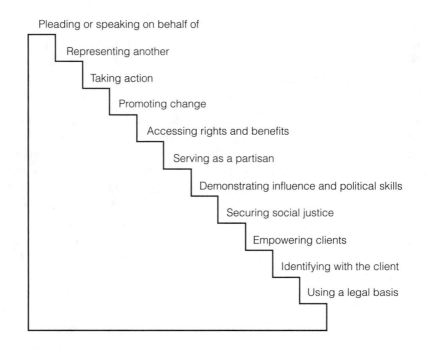

FIGURE **2.1**

Summary of key dimensions of advocacy from an analysis of over 90 definitions.

or writes in support of something" (p. 20). When the Ad Hoc Committee on Advocacy (1969) of the National Association of Social Workers published its definition of advocacy, one of its major emphases was the advocate as "one that pleads the cause of another" (p. 20). Amidei (1991) said that advocacy "just means to speak up, to plead the case of another, or to champion a cause" (p. 12). Freddolino (1990) suggested that advocacy means "speaking on behalf of a person or issue" (p. 381). Miller et al. (1990) noted that the "advocate speaks in the name of and in the interest of a population . . ." (p. 360).

Representing Another   Another key dimension used to define advocacy is representation of oneself or another individual or group before decision makers or authorities. Horn (1991) referred to advocacy as "representing the interests and welfare of a person as if they were your own" (p. 1). Briar (1967) described the caseworker-advocate as "his client's supporter, his adviser, his champion, and, if need be, his representative in his dealings with the court, the police, the social agency, and other organizations that affect his well-being" (p. 28). Brager (1968) viewed the advocate-reformer's primary responsibility to be "the tough-minded and partisan representation of [clients'] interests . . ." (p. 6). Checkoway (1995) described public advocacy as "the process of representing group interests in legislative, administrative or other established institutional arenas" (p. 10). Active representation closely resembles the concept of advocacy, according to Henderson (1978). Matson and Mulick (1991) state, "Advocacy is . . . the representation of the rights and interests of oneself or others in an effort to bring about change" (p. 24). Barker (1995, p. 11), in the third edition of *The Social Work Dictionary,* and Litzelfelner and Petr (1997, p. 393) state that "advocacy is the act of directly representing or defending others."

Taking Action   Advocacy is associated with action in many definitions. Its usual meaning is related to doing, taking steps, acting, responding, moving ahead, initiating, and doing deeds. Richan (1973) stated that "advocacy is action in behalf of an aggrieved individual, group or class of individuals" (p. 220). Similarly, Woodside and Legg (1990) proposed that advocacy is "the actions of individuals or groups to defend the rights of less powerful others" (p. 41). The Association of Retarded Citizens (ARC; 1991) viewed advocacy as meaning "acting and communicating in support of a policy, idea or concern" (p. 1). According to Mickelson (1995), quoting *The Social Work Dictionary,* second edition, advocacy is "action that empowers individuals or communities" (p. 95). Klein and Cnaan (1995) proposed advocacy as "an action-oriented response to issues generated by the objective conditions of clients" (p. 204). Lourie (1975) believed that advocacy "means actions in support of one's beliefs in a cause . . ." (p. 72).

Promoting Change   Many definitions of advocacy include references to "changing" conditions in society or a community on behalf of a client or a group. Its usual meaning often refers to modifying, altering, resolving, improving, and transforming. Woodside and Legg (1990) stated that the "primary focus of an advocate is to promote change in the environment for the best interest of the other" (p. 41). According to Young (1992), "advocacy organizations attempt to change the status quo" (p. 4). Payne and Pezzoli (1977) viewed advocacy as attempts to "ameliorate the condition of individuals or groups rendered disadvantaged and relatively powerless by prejudice, injustice, and social institutions" (p. 154). Davis (1993) said that advocacy is fundamentally a process designed to promote systems change" (p. 4). "An effort to bring about change" is presented in Matson and Mulick's (1991, p. 24) definition of advocacy. Litzelfelner and Petr (1997) defined social advocacy as working to "effect changes in policies, practices, and laws that affect all people in a specific class or group" (p. 393).

Accessing Rights and Benefits   Several definitions characterize advocacy as promoting client access to services, entitlements, benefits, and rights to which they have a legitimate claim. Johnson (1995) and Teare and McPheeters (1970) identified the advocate role as helping clients obtain services in situations where they may be rejected or helping expand services to persons in a particular need. Holmes (1981) noted that the basic function of the advocate is to "make sure the system is responsive to . . . needs and ensure consumers receive all benefits to which they are entitled" (p. 34). Panitch (1974) quoted Wineman's (1968) belief that advocacy meant controlling the unchecked violations of civility and institutional authority vested in agency settings (p. 328). Davis (1993) spoke of advocacy as "deliberate efforts aimed at advancing the rights, interests and cause of some specific group of individuals" (p. 4). The NASW Ad Hoc Committee on Advocacy (1969) urged social workers to "give their first priority to the rights and needs of their clients" (p. 21). McGowan (1987) offered the following outcomes for advocacy: "(1) to secure or enhance a needed service, resource or entitlement; (2) to develop new ones; and (3) to prevent or limit client involvement with a dysfunctional system" (p. 92). Ambrosino (1979) described advocacy as helping clients obtain necessary assistance from community resources (p. 581). Sheafor et al. (1994) stated that advocacy was "to secure services that the client is entitled to, but unable to obtain on his or her own" (p. 104). Kirst-Ashman and Hull (1993) noted that social workers used their positions and skills to exercise leverage for needed services on behalf of clients (p. 466). Lourie (1975) viewed advocacy as a system of delivering human services focusing on ease of access at local neighborhood levels (p. 81).

Serving as a Partisan   There are some definitions of advocacy that highlight the role of the advocate as a "partisan," zealous champion, or supporter of an individual or group. Brager (1968) viewed the advocate-reformer's primary responsibility as the "tough-minded and partisan representation of [clients'] interests, superseding his fealty to others" (p. 6). Panitch (1974) referred to advocacy as the techniques of "taking a stand in favor of" human-ization of services (p. 331). According to McGowan (1987), advocacy is "parti-san intervention on behalf of an individual client . . . to secure or enhance a needed service" (p. 92). Grosser (1965) noted that the social work advocate must become a "partisan in social conflict whose expertise is available exclu-sively to serve his clients' interests" (p. 18). Miller (1968) eloquently stated: "Let us become their allies and champion their cause" (p. 33). Northen (1995) viewed case advocacy "as partisan intervention on behalf of . . . clients with one or more secondary institutions" (p. 295).

Demonstrating Influence and Political Skills   Several authors describe advocacy and its relationship to political processes or attempts to influence authorities and decision makers. Brager (1969) stated that the advocate's role "inevitably requires that the practitioner function as a political tactician" (p. 102). Sosin and Caulum (1983) described advocacy as "an attempt, with a greater than zero probability of success, by an individual or group, to influence another individual or group to make a decision . . ." (p. 13). According to Ezell (1994), advocacy activities are "those purposive efforts which attempt to impact a specific decision, law, policy or practice on behalf of a client" (p. 38). Ward (1995) concluded that one function of advocacy is to "apply pressure at a decision point necessary to counteract inertia" (p. 624). Cohen (1971) defined advocacy as "a political process aimed at reshaping entrenched atti-tudes that rule economic, political and social decisions so as to ultimately bring about social change in our institutions" (p. 807).

Securing Social Justice   References to social justice or injustice are often found among the definitions of advocacy. Mickelson (1995) defined advocacy as "the act of directly defending . . . a course of action . . . with the goal of securing or retaining social justice" (p. 95). Payne and Pezzoli (1977) stated that advocacy was an attempt to "ameliorate the conditions of individuals or groups rendered disadvantaged and relatively powerless by prejudice, injus-tice and social institutions" (p. 154). Hollis (1964) viewed advocacy as "attempts to secure for clients rights and benefits . . . which they are unjustly denied . . ." (p. 84). Claxton (1981) urged all practitioners of advocacy to make "a new commitment to social justice and avoid any move towards social con-trol" (p. 44). Lourie (1975) proposed advocacy as a "device for increasing pres-sure against social structures to achieve social equity and justice" (p. 69). Frost, Higgins, and Beecher (1983) stated, "[A]dvocacy is pleading the cause of justice in meeting human service needs in our society" (p. 53).

Empowering Clients   In the advocacy literature, empowerment and self-expression emerge as very key concepts for many advocates. Empowerment was usually presented in the context of encouraging individuals or groups to assume control of their destinies. In some cases, empowerment was viewed as the primary outcome. Self-expression was promoted as a logical outcome of an advocate's efforts to encourage individuals and groups toward empowerment. Mickelson (1995) defined advocacy as "action that empowers individuals or communities" (p. 95). Riley (1971), in discussing planning and implementation of advocacy, stated that leadership and decision making for the advocacy action should be transferred to the consumer groups (p. 374). Moxley and Freddolino (1994) viewed advocacy as "a means of improving the well-being of people . . . through a process of skill development and support, leading ideally to empowerment" (p. 95). Barker (1995) noted that advocacy is "the championing of the rights of individuals or communities through direct intervention or through empowerment" (p. 11). Petr and Spano (1990) urged a "redefinition of advocacy that emphasized helping others speak on behalf of themselves" (p. 233). Dubler (1992) noted that advocacy meant providing for the client's interests and needs as the client defines them. Freddolino and Moxley (1992) urged mental health advocates to "act on those needs, issues, and goals that clients desire to achieve for themselves" (p. 340).

Identifying with the Client Some authors suggest that, for advocates to act truly on behalf of another, they must identify clearly and purposively with their clients. Such identity goes beyond "partisanship," which fosters an exclusive and singular focus on the client. It refers to "putting oneself in the footsteps" of the client and experiencing life from this perspective. Johnson (1995) described the advocate as the professional who identifies with the victims of social problems. Similarly, Brager (1968) saw the advocate-reformer as one "who identifies with the plight of the disadvantaged" (p. 6). Miller (1968) exhorted advocates to "let our clients use us to argue their cause, to maneuver, to obtain their rights and their justice, to move the immovable bureaucrats" (p. 33).

Using a Legal Basis Compton and Galaway (1994) argued that advocacy is borrowed from the legal profession. The Latin term *advocatus* (i.e., someone called in to help) is used in Roman law to designate a professional who defended someone's interest in court (*Family Word Finder,* 1975, p. 28). The Ad Hoc Committee on Advocacy (1969) of the NASW used two dictionary definitions of advocacy, one of which was the "traditional caseworker-advocate, who is his client's supporter, adviser, champion, and, if need be, his representative in his dealings . . ." (p. 17). Levy (1974) stated that many terms such as "the act of pleading, supporting, recommending active espousal, defending, vouching, interceding in the cause of another" all seem appropriate in both legal and social work terms (p. 40).

Definitions of advocacy refer often to laws that may be unjust or difficult to apply to an individual or group. Raider (1982) asked if advocacy meant protecting the substantive rights of the clients, thereby requiring the social worker to involve legal processes. Advocacy is also directed, according to Compton and Galaway (1994), toward securing benefits to which the client is legally entitled. Ezell (1991) pointed out that advocacy activities are "attempts to impact a specific decision, law, policy or practice on behalf of a client or group of clients" (p. 5). Hepworth, Rooney, and Larsen (1997) concluded that advocacy works to "effect changes in policies, practices, and laws that affect all people in a specific class or group" (p. 468).

This typology highlights two opposing elements, breadth and specificity. Faced with such a wide array of concepts, can the reader identify readily the specific elements of the practice of advocacy? On what basis could a social worker determine how to undertake advocacy? How would you choose your definition of advocacy? This dilemma represents the unseen controversy about the role of advocacy in the profession: Can advocacy be unlimited in its dimensions, or should it be understood in specific, measurable, and identifiable terms and concepts?

New Definition of Advocacy

Throughout its history, the profession of social work has been propelled by an impulse to assist others, to change the order of things, to overcome injustice, to prioritize human needs and rights, to reduce suffering, and to promote the fullest, actual potential of each person. This desire remains equally strong today among current practitioners and students who are entering the social work profession. The authors believe that this book, with its new definition of advocacy and a defined set of applied principles to guide the social worker–as–advocate, will contribute to further clarity about the term.

Criteria for New Definition

In order to overcome some of the shortcomings of previous attempts to define advocacy, the authors have developed a new definition of advocacy using the following criteria.

Clarity   The authors use uncomplicated words and concepts that are understandable, jargon-free, distinct, and easy to remember.

Measurable   This definition has distinct, observable dimensions. Elements and activities are present that are identifiable and can be empirically verified.

Limited   Our definition disallows the application of the term *advocacy* to every activity undertaken by a social worker because advocacy can be distinguished from other activities such as social action, brokering, problem solving, and community organizing.

Action-Oriented   Action is a fundamental basis for advocacy. While "actions" may constitute many different activities, the essential elements of initiative, taking steps, participation, engagement, expending energy involvement must be present.

Focus on Activity, Not Roles or Outcomes of Advocacy Although outcomes of advocacy—for example, gaining access to services, overcoming racist ordinances, or increasing benefits—are very important, our definition does not use them to determine the meaning of advocacy. Our definition concentrates on *what one does as an advocate,* not what one achieves or intends to produce. Although social workers may play the roles of tactician, adviser, champion, defender of the poor, or partisan, our definition depicts the *actual activity of advocacy itself,* not a particular portrayal of a certain role.

Comprehensive Our definition can be applied to the full range of advocacy opportunities in social work practice, that is, client, cause, legislative, and administrative advocacies. Social workers are employed in a myriad of practice settings and must practice advocacy within their own unique environment, each with its various constraints, policies, emphases, priorities, and service delivery system. This means that some workers will practice advocacy primarily in a legislative setting, some in a family agency, and some in a for-profit corporation. Our basic definition and principles will guide social workers to practice as advocates in every setting in which they find themselves.

New Definition

The authors propose the following new definition: *Social work advocacy is the exclusive and mutual representation of a client(s) or a cause in a forum, attempting to systematically influence decision making in an unjust or unresponsive system(s).*

Explanation of Terms

Exclusive This term is used to describe the relationship between the client and the advocate as singular, unique, focused solely on the client, primarily responsible to the client, and centered on client needs. It means that the client's needs are the sole priority for the advocate, and all activities, strategies, and tactics are specifically designed to address the concerns of the client.

Mutual This term is used to describe the relationship between the client and the advocate as reciprocal, interdependent, equal, joint, sharing the same level of the relationship with each other, exchanging ideas and plans jointly, and having a commonality between each other. A "mutual" relationship means that the advocate does not dominate or set the agenda for the client because the client's needs are the exclusive focus. The advocate collaborates with the client, and together, they proceed in an agreed-upon direction.

Included in the term *mutual* is also the notion of empowerment, a key social work value. Even though clients with problems may be overburdened or feel they are powerless, advocates need to pursue activities that support clients and encourage them to take charge of situations in which they have been powerless (Johnson, 1995; Taylor, 1987). Empowerment means not only enabling the clients to carry out an activity, but also motivating them and teaching skills required to interact with their environment.

Representation   This term is action-oriented and describes the activity of an advocate as speaking, writing, or acting on behalf of another; communicating or expressing the concerns of a client; setting forth or stating the ideas or desires of another; standing up for another person or group; pleading the case of a client; and serving as an agent or proxy for another. An advocate who truly represents a client must take some identifiable action that expresses the concerns of someone.

Client(s)   In social work advocacy, a client(s) engages a social worker to act on his or her behalf as described in "representation" mentioned above. The client(s) may be an individual person, small or large groups, a community association, an ethnic population, individuals with common concerns or characteristics, or other loosely or tightly knit organizations. Sometimes an advocate, initially representing an individual, will be asked to act on behalf of a group with the same or similar concerns as the individual. The "client(s)" is not restricted *a priori* to certain sizes or numbers. The advocate can work with all clients, from one person to large associations to community groups.

Cause   A cause is usually a single issue, condition, or problem that a number of people are interested in and support. According to Kotler (1972), there are three types of causes: (1) *helping* causes where advocates try to provide aid, comfort, or education to victims of social maladies such as a shelter for abused women or protecting the elderly from fraud; (2) *protest* causes where advocates try to reform institutions that contribute to a social problem, asking for new behaviors to improve conditions, for example, asking the city to rehabilitate a slum or demanding the state reallocate funds for community-based mental health services; and (3) *revolutionary* causes where advocates hope to eliminate institutions or parties that promote unjust conditions or suffering. This last option is not dedicated to violent means to achieve its goals, but recognizes that as long as the offending institution exists, no solution for victims will ever be found.

Forum   A forum is any assembly that is designated to discuss issues, laws, regulations, rules, public matters, differing opinions, or the settlement of disputes. Social work advocates often use a forum in order to represent or act on behalf of a client. Commonly known forums are public hearings, legislative committees or subcommittees, special commissions, blue-ribbon task forces, courthouses, administrative hearings, agency policy committees, board meetings, supervisory meetings, agency staff meetings, citizen's tribunals, and so on. Although there are variations among these forums, two features are usually present: (1) a set of specific procedures to guide the conduct of the participants, and (2) a decision-making mechanism (Kutchins & Kutchins, 1987). The social work advocate attempts to use existing forums or develop new ones in order to address the concerns of a client(s).

Systematically   "Systematic" advocacy is an application of knowledge and skills in a planned, orderly manner. Decisions are not based upon intuition alone even though such insight is often necessary. Rather, the advocate will apply a set of guiding principles to a situation and skillfully analyze the circumstances and conditions before deciding how to proceed mutually with the client. Although there is limited empirical data available about the effectiveness of advocacy guidelines, the authors believe that there is sufficient knowledge derived from practice wisdom and empirical study to warrant a careful application of such guidelines. The framework found in this book (see Part Two) is one such set of principles to follow in a methodical and logical way.

Influence   The term *influence* is the other fundamental activity of our definition, describing what advocates *qua* advocates attempt to do. It is a tangible activity that can be identified specifically even though it has many different expressions. To "influence" means to modify, change, affect, act on, or alter decisions that impinge upon a client(s). It is an attempt to persuade or sway another person or group who has authority or power over resources or policy making. The means by which an advocate can influence are varied and are chosen usually with respect to the circumstances or current issues of the situation. Some "influential" activities are: organizing client groups, forming coalitions, educating the public, persuading administrators and supervisors, contacting public officials and legislators, gathering data from studies, giving testimony, appealing to review boards, using the media, developing petitions, and/or initiating legal action (Hepworth, et al., 1997).

Decision Making   This term refers to the object of the effort to "influence" in the definition. Primarily, advocates want to change or alter the conclusions or judgments of those who are authorized to allow the allocation of resources, definition of benefits, determination of eligibility, access to services, grievance adjudications, appeals, and/or policy making for a state or agency. Decision makers can be elected officials, civil servants, not-for-profit agency administrators, supervisors, board members, influential leaders in the community, church leaders, coalitions, collective associations, judges, civic leaders, and more. Some decision making is very formalized, that is, it follows established or mandated rules and procedures, while some is informal, that is, it depends on personal connections, ties to the community, family status, and wealth.

Unjust   This term characterizes an action, stance, institution, regulation, procedure, or decision as not being in accord with the law or with the principles of justice. "Unjust" indicates that fairness, equity, lawfulness, justice, and righteousness are absent to some degree. As a result, there are injuries to certain persons, whose moral, civil, or constitutional rights may be violated, or who may suffer a grievance due to inequity and lack of justice.

Unresponsive   This term is typically applied to persons or institutions that fail to reply to, acknowledge, correspond about, or answer inquiries, requests, petitions, demands, questions, letters, communiqués, or requests for appointments in a timely fashion, if at all.

System(s)   In a social work context, the word *system(s)* refers usually to organized agencies that have been designed and authorized to provide services to eligible persons, distribute resources, enforce laws and judgments, and be responsible for key areas of a society's interactions and resources. Hence, one hears frequently about the criminal justice system, the mental health system, the legislative system, the welfare system, the health care system, and the transportation system. Each of these systems is organized and mandated to provide access, resources, and services in an equitable manner. Organized structures such as hospitals, state and local agencies, community service agencies, judicial districts and courts, social service departments, and legislative committees are arranged with the intent of delivering an appropriate service effectively. Large, bureaucratic organizations frequently fail to be responsive to individual needs despite their good intentions.

A Note to the Reader

This new definition of advocacy and these interpretations of each term will be the basis of all future discussion and analysis throughout the remainder of the book. Readers must familiarize themselves with the specific dimensions of the definition and no longer globally use the term *advocacy* to refer to any worthwhile activity undertaken to improve the lives of clients. Advocacy is now conceived as a specific activity with defined dimensions.

HOW ADVOCACY DIFFERS FROM OTHER SOCIAL ACTION

What is the difference between advocacy and social action? Social reform? Brokering? Problem solving? Clinical social work? Community organizing?

Since *advocacy* is a specific term that the NASW *Code of Ethics* uses to describe a social worker's role and responsibilities, we believe that knowing what advocacy is and how advocacy is different from other actions will promote a clearer recognition of what is expected of the social worker-as-advocate. Many times, the generic word *advocacy* is used interchangeably with other terms such as *social action, social reform, brokering, problem solving, community organizing,* and *clinical social work.* Do they all mean the same thing? No! Is it important to know what the differences are among them all? Yes!

Of course, these different terms are related to each other in the study of social intervention and change, and often have similar nuances in their meaning and use; but they should not be thought of as interchangeable. It is important to clarify the meaning of the terms so that when we speak with one another, we will use words with a common meaning understood by all social workers in the same way.

Brokering Versus Advocacy

According to Johnson (1995), the social worker-as-broker "helps a person or family get needed services. This includes assessing the situation, knowing the alternative resources, preparing and counseling the person, contacting the appropriate service, and assuring that the client gets to the help and uses it" (p. 316). Wilensky and Lebeaux (1958) spoke of social work-brokering as "an example, par excellence, of the liaison function, a large part of its total activity being devoted to putting people in touch with community resources they need, but can hardly name, let alone locate" (p. 286). The major emphasis is to expedite the client linkage to the needed resource in the community. It involves giving adequate information and support and teaching clients how to use resources. Johnson (1995) suggests that there may be some negotiation with the agency to which the client is referred, but only if the brokering role is ineffective does the social worker use a more forceful "advocacy" role that includes other specified activities such as representing, influencing, using a forum, and so on.

Social Reform Versus Advocacy

Social reformers are concerned chiefly with the development and improvement of large-scale social problems. Within the history of social work, we frequently refer to the early pioneers such as Jane Addams, Jeannette Rankin, and Florence Kelly as "social reformers" who fought extensive problems related to immigration and the impact of urbanization and industrialization (Kirst-Ashman & Hull, 1993). In the Progressive Era, 1895 to 1915, they relied frequently on the "social conscience" of the community to support and implement their changes (McCormick, 1970). The reform efforts of these early group workers were focused on environmental modifications, including workplace conditions, education, protection of children, and the quality of housing (McGowan, 1987). Social workers-as-reformers helped to develop vocational education, hot-lunch programs, neighborhood playgrounds, and community housing codes. George Brager (1969) used the term *reform* to describe efforts to impact social problems by influencing change in organizations and institutions (p. 111).

Social reformers generally hope to modify predominant conditions of society that seriously threaten the well-being of citizens or prevent them from developing their potential (Kirst-Ashman & Hull, 1993). Social reform differs from advocacy mostly in terms of scale. An advocate can be a reformer and vice versa. But while the reformer's vision is primarily a large vision about correcting a societal ill, the advocate's perspective will be highly focused on clients' identifiable needs, influencing decision makers in particular forums through systematic application of advocacy practice principles.

Clinical Social Work Versus Advocacy

In 1987, the Board of Directors of NASW, the Board of the National Registry of Health Care Providers, and the American Board of Examiners in Clinical Social Work voted to accept the following definition of *clinical social work:*

> Clinical social work practice is the professional application of social work theory and methods to the treatment and prevention of psychosocial dysfunction, disability or impairment, including emotional and mental disorders. It is based on knowledge and theory of psychosocial development, behavior, psychopathology, unconscious motivation, interpersonal relations, environmental stress, social systems, and cultural diversity with particular attention to person-in-environment. It shares with all social work practice the goal of enhancement and maintenance of psychosocial functioning of individuals, families and small groups. (Northen, 1995, pp. 7–8)

Clinical social work includes but is not limited to individual, marital, family, and group psychotherapy. Clinical social work services usually consist of assessment, diagnosis, treatment (including psychotherapy and counseling), client-centered advocacy, consultation, and evaluation.

Many view this type of definition as heavily indebted to psychotherapy and psychoanalytic psychotherapy in particular (Briar, 1967), as overemphasizing psychosocial adaptation, and as a very minimal and narrow view of the social and environmental aspects of social work practice. Lieberman (1982) attempted to correct this view by stating that, in clinical social work, psychotherapy is always directed toward the interactions and transactions within the social orbit in addition to addressing the internal life of the client. The maladaptive behavior of clients as well as malignant elements within the clients' environment become the focus of treatment as indicated (Northen, 1995, p. 8).

Compared to clinical social work, advocacy has a much broader domain, including a focus on "unjust and unresponsive" systems, influencing decision makers, and use of forums.

Problem Solving Versus Advocacy

Research on problem-solving capacity indicates that social workers encounter many clients whose problem-solving skills and coping capacities are inadequate (Hepworth et al., 1997). Social workers frequently decide that clients will benefit from mastering problem-solving skills and employing them in situations where their own coping efforts have previously failed to produce a remedy. By learning such skills, it is hoped that the client can transfer effective principles from one type of situation to another.

The steps of the problem-solving process, according to Hepworth et al. (1997), are:

1. Acknowledgment of the problem
2. Analysis of the problem and identification of the needs of the participants
3. Brainstorming and generating new solutions
4. Evaluation of each option while considering the needs of participants
5. Implementation of the option selected
6. Evaluation of the outcome of the problem-solving efforts (p. 415)

The social worker guides clients through these six steps, assisting them to transfer their problem-solving skills to different situations confronting them. The social worker will "teach" clients, provide opportunities for them to refine their skills, and eventually intervene less frequently, giving less direction as the client demonstrates increased mastery of the process. The ultimate success is reached when the clients are able to function effectively without the social worker's services.

Advocacy is not a form of problem solving using the standard model illustrated above. The primary concern of problem solving is teaching an orderly method of analysis of problems and being supportive to the client(s) as time progresses. Advocacy is very specific and requires particular actions such as representation, influencing, and use of a forum, actions beyond those used in the problem-solving model.

Social Action Versus Advocacy

According to Thursz (1971), social action encompasses individual or group activity designed to influence a change in social policy. It represents the responsibility and privilege of each person to attempt to mold the environment in terms of his or her values. According to Woods and Hollis (1992), social action refers to a general attempt to bring about changes in policies or practices that adversely affect a whole group of clients or others in the community. Paull (1971) states that social action refers to those organized and planned activities that attempt to influence the social distribution of status, power, and resources. Kinduka and Coughlin (1975) argue that social action is a strategy to obtain limited social change at the intermediate or macro levels of society. Social action, according to Figueira-McDonough (1993), stands for redistribution of resources and reduction of inequalities and is, by definition, communitarian. Its success is measured not by fervor, but by outcomes that accrue resources to the deprived community.

Kutchins and Kutchins (1978) argue that advocacy is a form of social action, and we would agree. Advocacy incorporates most of the important elements of the concept of social action such as influence, systems-level change, systematic application, and issues of power and justice. However, advocacy specifically represents a client(s) in a forum within an exclusive and mutual relationship. Advocacy, as a form of social action, further guides the actions of social workers in assisting a client(s) within the overall framework of the notion of social action and its purpose.

Community Organization Versus Advocacy

Community organization aims to build permanent community structures that can address and advance the needs of citizens or particular groups. Although Weil and Gamble (1995) believe that community organizing, that is, building groups, has a dual focus of capacity building and task accomplishment, Kahn (1995) notes that community organizing is a tool used in all societies to redress the classic imbalance between the powerless and the powerful. Within community organizing, a saying exists: "Organizers organize organizations." According to Kahn (1995), the critical challenge for community organizers today is to reach, teach, and organize people in ways that transform their understanding and their relationship to *power.*

Weil and Gamble (1995) state that the objectives of community practice are to:

- Develop the organizing skills and abilities of citizens and citizen groups
- Make social planning more accessible and inclusive in a community
- Connect social and economic investments to grassroots community groups
- Advocate for broad coalitions in solving community problems and
- Infuse the social planning process with a concern for social justice

Martinez-Brawley (1995) describes traditional models of community organizing as having three modalities for purposeful intervention. Rothman et al. (1995) developed these three orientations in the mid-1970s and further refined them in the 1980s and 1990s. *Locality developers* emphasize community building and a grassroots perspective, strengthening the capacities of individuals and organizations to improve social and economic conditions preferably with the participation of the entire community. *Social planners* use information management systems, data collection, rational analysis and technical expertise to develop, expand, and coordinate social services and make better use of resources. Public hearings are frequently conducted to ensure citizen participation. *Social actionists* often challenge the existing power structures, inequalities, and unjust decisions, and focus primarily on basic social changes or redistribution of power, resources, and decision making. Organizing large numbers of people, capacity building, targeting elected or corporate officials, developing media relations, doing investigative research, advocacy, and community educating are tactics used by social actionists.

When compared to the authors' definition of advocacy, Rothman et al.'s broad notion of community organizing reflects parallel dimensions such as injustice, forums, systematic methods, mutuality, systems that abuse power, and influence. However, we believe that community organizing is primarily an organizing and capacity-building function, with an emphasis on producing collective support and channeling group energy through education and participation toward addressing common concerns. Rothman et al.'s description of "social action" under a community-organizing rubric seems forced, since social action can exist without developing permanent structures or geographical or grassroots structures usually implied in community organizing. Advocacy, as noted before, is a form of social action, a social work practice requiring specific dimensions that can be used in community organization.

OBLIGATION OF SOCIAL WORKERS TO DO ADVOCACY

What obligation to practice advocacy do social workers have? Why do social workers become involved in advocacy?

Social work's mission combines concern for both the individual and the social environment surrounding the individual. Litzelfelner and Petr (1997) state unequivocally that "the social work profession considers client advocacy an ethical responsibility and a primary function of social work practice . . . and few in the social work profession question their role as client advocates" (p. 393). The following questions of behavior and obligation arise: Does a strict responsibility exist for social workers to practice as an advocate? *Is it an obligation or an option?* How can we identify more specifically what the foundation for advocacy is in social work practice? What leads a social worker to become an advocate? The following resources respond to these questions.

National Association of Social Workers (NASW) Code of Ethics

As of August 15, 1996, NASW's Delegate Assembly approved a revised version of the profession's *Code of Ethics* and promulgated these standards to all members to be effective January 1, 1997. An analysis of the new text reveals a very prominent place for advocacy in the role of a practicing social worker. In the Preamble, the *Code* states:

> An historic and defining feature of social work is the profession's focus on individual well-being in a social context and the well-being of society. Fundamental to social work is attention to the environmental forces that create, contribute to, and address problems in living at local, state, national and international levels. Social workers promote social justice and social change with and on behalf of clients. . . . [They] are sensitive to cultural and ethnic diversity and strive to end discrimination, oppression, poverty, and other forms of social injustice. These activities may be in the form of direct practice, community organizing, consultation, administration, *advocacy,* social and political action, policy development and implementation, education, and research and evaluation.

Under "Ethical Principles and Values," the *Code* states that "social workers' primary goal is to help people in need and to address social problems." The *Code* also states that "social workers challenge social injustice" and "pursue social change, particularly with and on behalf of vulnerable and oppressed individuals and groups of people." Under "Value of Dignity and Worth of the Person," the text reads, "[S]ocial workers are cognizant of their dual responsibility to clients and to the broader society." Hence arises the obligation of social workers to undertake advocacy.

In the *Code* section on "Ethical Standards," under "Social Workers' Ethical Responsibility in Practice Settings" [section 3.07(a)], the text reads "[S]ocial work administrators should *advocate* within and outside their agencies for adequate resources to meet clients' needs"; and in section 3.07(b), the text states, "[S]ocial workers should *advocate* for resource allocation procedures that are open and fair."

In section 6, "Social Workers' Ethical Responsibilities to the Broader Society," the *Code* notes:

> [S]ocial workers should promote the general welfare of society, from local to global levels, and the development of people, their communities, and their environments. Social workers should *advocate* for living conditions conducive to the fulfillment of basic human needs and should promote social, economic, political, and cultural values and institutions that are compatible with the realization of social justice. (section 6.01)

Further, section 6.04(a) states, "Social workers should be aware of the impact of the political arena on practice and should *advocate* for changes in policy and legislation to improve social conditions in order to meet basic human needs and promote social justice." And section 6.04(d) reads, "Social workers . . . should *advocate* for programs and institutions that demonstrate cultural competence, and promote policies that safeguard the rights of and confirm equity and social justice for all people."

Clearly, the obligation of social workers to commit themselves to advocacy flows directly from our *Code of Ethics.* It is not an option; it is an obligation.

Social Work's Understanding of the Person-in-Environment

The social work profession's unique approach to assisting people grows out of its belief that the circumstances or social environment surrounding individuals affects their well-being directly (Kirst-Ashman & Hull, 1993). It follows that, in order to assist individuals with problems flowing from the community, state, national, or international levels, social workers must be able to intervene effectively at levels beyond the one-to-one relationships so frequently encountered. Commitment to change only at the individual level would be insufficient. As social workers assess all of the factors that impinge on clients' lives and problems, it is only logical and reasonable to include *advocacy* and social change strategies at the policy and systems levels in the skill repertoire of each social worker.

Historical Position of Advocacy in Social Work

Historically, advocacy was in the forefront of social work practice. Amidei (1991) notes that advocacy represents traditional social work practice, agreeing with Reisch (1986, p. 20) and the NASW Ad Hoc Committee on Advocacy (1969) that many advocacy organizations can "trace their roots as far back as the reformist and radical efforts of the Progressive Era." Jane Addams, for example, embodied what social work is all about, and her life was a summary of the "person-in-environment" perspective. According to Amidei (1991), Addams worked to nurture the body and the spirit, but also was keenly aware of the environment in which her Hull House neighbors lived. She did not refrain from involvement in politics and policy making. Along with others of the era such as Florence Kelly, Jeannette Rankin, and the Abbott sisters, Addams used the following tactics that present-day advocates also employ:

- Creation of coalitions that bridge class status and issues
- Fact finding and research
- Use of *moral* issues and an appeal to "traditional values"
- Focus on specific "populations-at-risk," such as children, immigrants, or widows
- Introduction of legislation
- Emphasis on public education
- Creation of political coalitions
- Use of preexisting groups as organizational building blocks
- Connection of specific social policies to broader social causes
- The use of service centers as focal points for political organizing (Reisch, 1986).

Societal Sanction of Advocacy

Dean (1977) argued that modern society has declared social work to be the professional discipline to serve individuals and groups in our disjointed development as industrial, urban, and technological communities. As religion has declined in our era, social work is asked to ensure the wholeness and uniqueness of the individual. Society has determined social workers to intervene in those situations that call for a nontechnical, human-to-human approach to problem solving.

Personal Reasons for Becoming an Advocate

In a 1990 study, Mondros and Wilson examined the reasons why community organizers entered the field of organizing; among the sample were social workers and social science degree holders. Although we believe that the definitions of *organizing* and *advocacy* are not identical, we believe that the two fields are sufficiently related that one can learn about the motivations of persons who want to produce social change. Here is a sample of themes that motivated the study's subjects to pursue a job with social change as a large component:

1. Frustration with jobs viewed as non–change-oriented
2. A family background in activism
3. Personal background in volunteering and activism
4. Personal experience under oppression
5. Readings on social change influenced them
6. The evolution of a personal ideology reflecting belief in change

In addition to these personal reasons, Hardcastle et al. (1997) remind us that "social workers whose *indignation* as well as *compassion* quotients run high are primed for professional advocacy" (p. 347). These two characteristics are part of the cornerstones of social work according to Saleebey (1990, p. 37). A sense of compassion drives social workers to try to right wrongs and to secure remedies for clients, from children without housing to the elderly person abused by a relative. A sense of indignation or injustice also moves social workers to intervene in situations lacking social justice and simple fairness. This is a visceral experience, not a utopian striving alone (Kutchins & Kutchins, 1978). These factors and sentiments often motivate social workers to become involved in advocacy that not only helps the individual in the here and now, but also seeks solutions that must come from the community, agency boards, or state legislatures.

Influence of Agency-Based Social Work Practice

Social workers are employed in some agencies or organizations where advocacy is highlighted. The agency's function may be primarily to plead the cause of children, victims of domestic violence, and elderly nursing home residents, or the agency may advocate indirectly for and with them. It may use a variety of methods to advocate, such as promotion of certain legislation, support of particular politicians, demonstrations, argumentation, representation at hearings, and protests. If a social worker is employed by an agency that, as a matter of agency policy and function, engages in advocacy, then advocacy is not only legitimated, it is required (Levy, 1974).

The extent and level of involvement in which the social worker will advocate in an agency will be limited by his or her job description and assigned work responsibilities. That the social worker should engage in advocacy is not questioned at all. According to Levy (1974), social workers "defend and represent clients within agencies, including their own, and outside of them to the extent that agencies and others do not give clients their due" (p. 42). They also defend and represent clients when agencies and others are guided by policies and practices that are not in the best interests of their clients.

VALUES PRESENT IN SOCIAL WORK ADVOCACY

"Values" represent the significant beliefs, important dimensions, or vital issues held by an individual person or by a group such as a religious congregation, an ethnic population, or a professional association like the National Association of Social Workers. An analysis of "social work advocacy" reveals several values that the profession and its practitioners hold in very high esteem and consider fundamental to the basic nature of the profession. This analysis illustrates that the social worker–as–advocate clearly represents many of the profession's core values and beliefs.

Depending on the particular advocacy effort, there may be potential conflicts among the values, but no true incompatibility exists between advocacy and traditional social work values. With knowledge about the value base of social work advocacy, professional social workers can proceed with certainty and confidence that they are practicing appropriately and advancing the mission of the profession.

Value Base of Social Work Advocacy

Dignity and Rights of the Individual   Implied in the notion of advocacy is the basic social work value of infinite respect for each individual person by virtue of being human, and the social or human rights that derive from the special uniqueness of every single human being (Lourie, 1975). The dignity of each person is found throughout the thought of Western civilization and is the original foundation for the democratic ideal projected for the United States of America (Miller, 1968). Liberty, justice, and equity are all rights that flow from this belief. The business of social work is with people and "above all, our business is with dignity" (Miller, 1968).

Giving Voice to the Powerless   Social workers traditionally have attempted to address injustices, abuse of power, and neglect of legal or moral rights by voicing concerns on behalf of those who cannot or do not speak. Among the earliest efforts to change social conditions was a focus on poor children and labor laws at the time of the Industrial Revolution. Other groups with limited voices speaking on their own behalf are mentally ill individuals, refugees, orphans, persons with HIV, the homeless, and low-income families.

Self-Determination   Moxley and Freddolino (1994) stated that "the value of self-determination means that clients must understand their own needs and define what action they want to take to fulfill them" (p. 96). The social worker–advocate facilitates the identification and definition of problems from the client's perspective (Moxley & Freddolino, 1994). While the professional social worker should exercise caution not to usurp the individual client's prerogative of determining his or her priorities or making decisions, social work advocacy emphasizes helping others speak on behalf of themselves (Petr & Spano, 1990).

Compassion and the Relief of Suffering   Relieving the distress and suffering of particular individuals and groups has been a constant value in social work. One early example was the work on behalf of the institutionalized mentally ill who were warehoused in filthy and pitiable conditions. Social workers now work to provide community-based services to mentally ill individuals and their families. Children who are physically or mentally abused by parents or others are frequently key targets of social work compassion and intervention. Immigrants and refugees, often confused, poor, victims of fraud, and unaware of their legal rights, are yet another example of suffering. Compassion for victims of the AIDS virus and the developmentally disabled are current examples.

Empowerment and Strengths Perspective   Empowerment means that "the advocacy process involves direct action by clients to resolve their problems or to fulfill their desires" (Moxley & Freddolino, 1994). Social work advocacy is not a passive activity in which the social worker takes action on behalf of clients. Empowerment occurs when clients successfully confront and overcome the issues or barriers preventing them from achieving what they want for themselves (Moxley & Freddolino, 1990). This value is based on the belief that individuals have strengths to acquire knowledge, become assertive, and develop skills, and that these strengths can be set in motion.

Social Justice   In its first attempt to define "advocacy," NASW (Ad Hoc Committee, 1969) stated that social work must commit itself to defending the rights of those who are treated unjustly. The 1996 *Code of Ethics* of NASW clearly notes in the Preamble that "social workers . . . strive to end discrimination, oppression, poverty and other forms of social injustice . . . by activities in the form of direct practice . . . *advocacy,* social and political action, policy development, etc." In section 6.01 of the *Code,* social workers are called upon to "promote social, economic, political and cultural values and institutions that are compatible with the realization of social justice."

These values reflect the very heart of the social work profession and provide a firm basis for the practice of advocacy. While values represent core beliefs, they also serve to inspire and motivate us. Remembering the values associated with social work advocacy will not only guide, but also reinforce our commitment as social workers.

CHARACTERISTICS ATTRIBUTED TO SOCIAL WORK ADVOCATES

The authors believe that a summary of those characteristics, qualities, skills, behaviors, and attitudes commonly attributed to social work advocates is useful as a means of introducing the reader to the social work advocacy role. However, this summary is neither exhaustive nor universally accepted. Nevertheless, an effective social work advocate can be described as follows.

Summary of Characteristics

Action-Oriented   Advocacy requires social workers to take action or steps to bring about a change. Advocacy is not merely an attitude or belief. Social workers take the initiative. They conduct research, organize coalitions, mobilize groups and communities, participate in planning and strategizing, influence decision makers, do outreach, and propose alternative policies. A social work advocate is a "catalyst" who launches activities and events. Jane Addams once said that action was the one medium humans had for appropriating and expressing the truth (Lourie, 1975).

Opposed to Injustice   Social work advocates are involved frequently in pleading the cause of justice in meeting human needs. They will argue, speak out, organize, and combat injustices when clients' rights are at risk or inequities are found in society. As Freddolino (1990) points out, advocacy involves the distribution of power, authority, and resources, none of which people give up willingly. The Preamble of the NASW *Code of Ethics* states that social workers strive to end discrimination and "other forms of *social injustice*" in the form of advocacy, social or political action, and so on. The *Code* further describes social workers as those "who should advocate for changes in policy and legislation . . . in order to meet basic human needs and promote *social justice*" (section 6.04).

Not Neutral   In the face of injustice, inequity, oppression, discrimination, and poverty, social workers do not remain neutral regarding the complexity of forces facing a client. The values of the profession compel the social worker to side with those who are disadvantaged, vulnerable, voiceless, and at-risk. The primary mission of social work is to enhance human well-being and help meet the basic human needs of all people. Freire (1990) states that "in that sense, the social worker is not a neutral agent, either in practice or in action" (p. 5). Advocacy, with its unreserved commitment to the plight of the disadvantaged, stands out in bold relief to neutrality, according to McCormick (1970).

Links Policy to Practice   Davis (1993) said that "social work advocacy requires a dual policy and practice orientation." Since the lives of clients and professional social workers themselves are affected daily and directly by agency or governmental policies, social work advocacy must include interventions that will address changes at the policy level as well as at the individual client level. Societal or community conditions impacting a client are usually discovered by clinical social workers, since they are "on the frontline." Meeting the immediate need of the client will remain insufficient as long as the broader social conditions causing this need are unaddressed. (See also Schneider & Netting, 1999.)

Patient and Hopeful   Freire (1990) described social work advocacy in terms of "impatient patience." Neither patience nor impatience is sufficient to achieve the goals of meeting human need. If we are simply patient, the time for action may never arrive; if we are always impatient, we may ignore the realities of history and the world about what is possible. Social work advocates must maintain this attitude of "impatient patience" because it offers a strategy that has greater potential for success in our complex world. It also offers a realistic "hope" to both the client and the social worker. In its desire to be relevant to current problems, social work cannot afford to stray far from the pursuit of problem resolution. Social workers give hope to their clients in both short- and long-term situations by demonstrating a steady activism.

Empowering   Social work advocacy usually includes a dimension far beyond the paternalistic notion of helping determine what is in a client's best interests. Social work advocates transfer leadership of the problem-solving effort to the client as soon as possible. They teach, mentor, persuade, and encourage personal participation in order to provide their clients with a sense of competence. The advocate encourages clients to speak up for themselves as much as possible. Pearlman and Edwards (1982) described the advocate as one who respects, supports, uses, and preserves participant initiative and group autonomy.

BARRIERS THAT HOLD SOCIAL WORKERS BACK FROM DOING ADVOCACY

Many social workers who are professionally trained and performing their duties competently do not perceive themselves as advocates, or they view advocacy as an "extra" option available to them on an "as needed" basis. Why does this perception exist? Has it always been this way? Why do many social workers not feel obligated to practice advocacy? Why are some social workers uncomfortable with an activist role?

Historical and Professional Issues

The authors have identified certain historical and professional issues that have a bearing on social workers' identity as advocates. A fuller explanation of each factor is beyond the scope of this book, but this introduction to these issues will help the reader understand better some of the basic pressures prevailing upon today's social workers.

Preoccupation with Service Role In the social work profession, there has been a historical preference and preoccupation with the direct service role. Rather than influencing external public policies, social work agencies and their staff often devote most of their energies to direct service programs (O'Connell, 1978).

Managerial Considerations Due to budget allocations by agencies, daily work procedures, organizational norms, politics, and excessive cutbacks, much of social work practice is dictated *de facto* by managerial, not professional considerations. Efficiency is valued over effectiveness (Reisch, 1986).

Lack of Professional Norms and Standards Advocacy has not been well delineated, and definitions, as noted in this chapter, have multiple and confusing dimensions. There are few visible and legitimate professional norms or standards by which one can determine whether or not an activity is advocacy (Blakely, 1991; Connaway, 1975). The word *advocacy* means something different to each person using it.

Employment Setting The employment setting of social workers often restricts them from acting as advocates (Blakely, 1991). Social workers may work in host settings where the rules are made by the medical profession, which by law, in many states, is the legal authority with respect to the majority of decisions. In these settings, social workers have limited capacity to initiate advocacy independently (Connaway, 1975). There may also be competing loyalties for the workers between the client and the agency's priorities (Richan, 1973).

Perception of Advocacy as Confrontation   Advocacy may be perceived as a "confrontation," and therefore filled with risks such as ruining relationships with other professionals and agencies or losing one's job (Sheafor et al., 1994). There is a tendency to equate social action and advocacy exclusively with contest strategies, norm-testing, and norm-violating strategies (Khinduka & Coughlin, 1975). This type of combative stance, an essential part of a partisan or advocacy alignment, is not viewed as "natural or comfortable" (Holmes, 1981; Panitch, 1974).

Uncertainty About Clients' Needs   Uncertainty about the client's situation often leaves social workers reluctant to employ advocacy. Client distortions, omissions, provocative behavior, and use of unclear facts may "set up" a social worker and lead to potentially embarrassing consequences (Hepworth et al., 1997). It is difficult to discern or to clarify important issues involving some clients' needs.

Concern with Professionalism   Historically, social workers have sought recognition and the rewards of "professionalism" (Reisch, 1986). This desire has had a conservatizing effect on the actions of social workers who do not want to be seen as behaving outside the status norms of "respectable" professions.

Fear of Losing Status   Because many of their clientele, such as the homeless, unmarried teenage mothers, mentally retarded individuals, AIDS victims, and juvenile offenders, have low status in our society, some social workers are reluctant to advocate for them for fear of becoming equally low in status.

Other Fears   Fear prevents some social workers from pursuing an advocate's role. Some individuals stand in awe of politicians and prefer to refrain from "dirty" politics, while others fear the media and exposure to public review (Riley, 1971). Others fear the legal-judicial system that is frequently necessary to use (Holmes, 1981). There is also timidity about community or collegial pressures about "bucking the system" (O'Connell, 1978; Richan, 1973). Agency administrators may fear that conservative board members will move to dismiss them (Riley, 1971).

Lack of Training or Education   Specific instruction in advocacy and the technical expertise needed for advocacy has been minimized in social work education (Blakely, 1991; Richan, 1973; Wolk, 1981). There has been little commitment by social work educational programs to teaching the practice of advocacy (Blakely, 1991). Professional social work education and practice have tended to make a *consensus* orientation legitimate and to oppose an *adversarial* one. Political content in social work courses is minimal, reflecting a bias toward direct service methods of intervention (Kaminski & Walmsley, 1995). Even now, many do not believe that all social workers require a combination of both micro and macro skills (Mickelson, 1995). Some have even suggested that social workers were trained by professional schools to acquiesce to the authority of others in order to prepare them to submit to the bureaucratic authority of employers (Piven & Cloward, 1975).

Unpopularity of Intervention Strategies   Another barrier today is the unpopularity of state intervention in social problem areas (Reisch, 1986). Many citizens believe that welfare policies are a ripoff, and there exists a natural antipathy among practical politicians to social reform, social welfare, and the redistribution of income.

Misunderstanding About the Nature of Advocacy   Often there is a basic misunderstanding of the nature of advocacy. It is an activity requiring patience, tenacity, long-term commitment, energy, broad bases of support, research, political skills, knowledge of government, and capacity to analyze. Sometimes one must compromise. Advocacy is rarely a quick fix. The skills are not beyond the abilities of most social workers.

Overcoming the Barriers

These barriers confront social workers daily in their decisions to undertake advocacy. With renewed emphasis on professional obligation and values, proper education, and commitment, social workers can overcome these barriers and move ahead in serving as advocates.

IMPORTANCE OF DEFINING ADVOCACY

The authors have written many words about the term *advocacy* in this chapter, based on the rationale that it is important to understand clearly what is meant by the term. They believe this clarification is significant for the following reasons:

1. If *advocacy* has multiple meanings, it becomes a useless term because no one has a common understanding of the word. No one will know which meaning is being considered when the word is used.
2. With no agreed-upon definition of *advocacy*, practitioners and researchers will have no common language to use in order to plan, implement, and evaluate advocacy activities. Research questions cannot be composed, and respondents are unable to reply if the term is not well defined and commonly accepted.
3. Students cannot be taught to be advocates because (a) faculty do not agree upon a definition; (b) faculty may not have been educated well themselves about advocacy; and (c) faculty may not teach about

advocacy due to the fuzzy concepts in the literature. Ambiguity discourages use (Mailick & Ashley, 1981).

4. Current and future generations of social workers will muddle along "doing advocacy," avoiding the present conceptual confusion, and miss opportunities to define and limit the term and thereby sharpen effectiveness skills.

5. In the case of social workers who continue to believe that advocacy is working actively to meet client needs by arranging services, Herbert and Mould (1992) suggest that such professionals are commingling two roles, that is, service delivery and advocacy. Advocacy is a frankly partisan intervention, assuring availability and relevance of services, not just providing services.

6. Even though the NASW *Code of Ethics* (Preamble and section 6.01) requires all social workers to be advocates, many will not understand their obligation or the conditions under which they should act without a clear definition of *advocacy*.

SUMMARY

The reader now possesses a "new" definition of *social work advocacy*, derived from analysis and practice data. Care must be taken to use this term consciously throughout the remainder of the book, since *advocacy* now refers to specific dimensions and skills. All social workers are obligated to practice advocacy and usually find key social work values at the heart of their advocacy efforts. Advocacy is a form of social action—not community organizing, as some would claim. Barriers and fears about doing advocacy are present in the social work profession, but can be overcome with persistent education.

DISCUSSION QUESTIONS

1. How does the authors' new definition of *advocacy* differ from previous definitions?
2. Are the barriers to doing advocacy too risky to someone who wants a career in social work?
3. How would you differentiate between advocacy and other social work methods and techniques?
4. How possible is it for every social worker to practice advocacy according to the authors' new definition?
5. Why do social workers overlook the role that advocacy plays in the NASW *Code of Ethics*?

6. What contradictions exist among the values of social work and the practice of advocacy?
7. How much advocacy should every social worker undertake?
8. Why should a definition of advocacy focus on the activity itself, and not on the role a social worker plays or the outcomes of the advocacy effort?
9. How do we know when to use advocacy?
10. Discuss how advocacy differs from brokering, community organizing, and problem solving. Use some current examples from practice.

RECOMMENDED READINGS

Ezell, M. (1994). Advocacy practice of social workers. *Families in Society: The Journal of Contemporary Human Services, 75,* 36–46.

Freire, P. (1990). A critical understanding of social work (M. Moch, Trans.). *Journal of Progressive Human Services, 1,* 3–9.

Grosser, C. F. (1965). Community development programs serving the urban poor. *Social Work, 10,* 15–21.

Hardcastle, D. A., Wenocur, S., & Powers, P. R. (1997). Using the advocacy spectrum. In *Community practice: Theories and skills for social workers,* (pp. 346–388). New York: Oxford University Press.

Kutchins, H., & Kutchins, S. (1978). Social work advocacy. In G. Weber & G. McCall (Eds.), *Advocacy and the social sciences* (pp. 13–48). Beverly Hills, CA: Sage.

Levy, C. S. (1974). Advocacy and the injustice of justice. *Social Service Review, 48,* 39–50.

Lourie, N. V. (1975). The many faces of advocacy. In I. N. Berlin (Ed.), *Advocacy for child mental illness* (pp. 68–80). New York: Brunner & Mazels.

McCormick, M. J. (1970). Social advocacy: A new dimension in social work. *Social Casework, 51,* 3–11.

National Association of Social Workers. (1969). The social worker as advocate: Champion of social victims. *Social Work, 14,* 16–22.

Richan, W. C. (1973). Dilemmas of the social work advocate. *Child Welfare, 52,* 220–226.

Sosin, M., & Caulum, S. (1983). Advocacy: A conceptualization for social work practice. *Social Work, 28,* 12–17.

GENERAL PRACTICE FRAMEWORK FOR ADVOCACY

She didn't know it couldn't be done, so she went ahead and did it.

MARY'S ALMANAC

Part Two offers a comprehensive guideline for using the new definition of advocacy in a systematic way in social work practice. The authors elaborate briefly on the necessity for social workers to undertake advocacy using a pragmatic and planful method to achieve their own and their clients' goals. They also examine the basis of advocacy and its efficacy. Finally, they present evidence supporting successful advocacy efforts by social workers based on research findings, practice wisdom, and many case examples of effective advocacy.

Part Two then highlights the two skills that macro and clinical social workers must demonstrate in order to be effective advocates: the abilities to (1) represent a client(s) or a cause, and (2) influence decision makers. Both of these skills have multiple dimensions and principles of action that must be understood and mastered. Chapter 3 presents the essential knowledge and skill areas for *representing*, while Chapter 4 provides the same for *influencing*. Later, in Part Three of the text, the focus will shift to social work within specialized practice contexts: client advocacy, cause advocacy, legislative advocacy, and/or administrative advocacy.

KEY QUESTIONS FOR PART TWO

- Why use a guideline for studying and practicing advocacy?
- Are the guidelines for advocacy supported by research or empirical data?
- Can we apply these guidelines to both clinical and macro social work?

WHY USE A GUIDELINE FOR STUDYING AND PRACTICING ADVOCACY?

There is a saying that "nothing is as practical as a good theory." This admonition is necessary to counter the many individuals who believe that theories are abstract, irrelevant, pie-in-the-sky, inapplicable in the "real" world, and devised by ivory-towered academics to torture students. In much the same way, terms like *comprehensive guidelines, conceptual framework*, or *practice framework* are often dismissed by professionals and students who only want down-to-earth, nuts-and-bolts techniques to help them provide services to clients. Unfortunately, they believe that "conceptual" ideas and principles are too remote from actual situations and therefore are not worthy of study, let alone using them in one's practice.

The authors are convinced that just the opposite is true, that is, that a guideline or conceptual framework is a very useful tool in general, and when applied to social work advocacy, it is exceedingly valuable to practitioners who want to improve conditions for their clients. The authors define a guideline or conceptual framework as a structure holding concepts or ideas together in a basic or systematic arrangement. It is an attempt to develop an overall perspective on a topic and to arrange clearly the most important knowledge we possess about it. We should understand the topic better as a result. The following section outlines several positive reasons why practitioners and students should consider using a "guideline" to their advantage.

Advantages of Using a Conceptual Framework or Practice Guideline

Systematic, Rational, and Comprehensive Application of Knowledge

A framework consists of an explicit number of carefully determined principles and components that should be considered by social workers each and every time they practice advocacy. This rational method of inquiry uses tested knowledge, experience, and practice wisdom, not mere guesswork. Rather than relying on individuals' independent judgment on a case-by case basis, experts identify key factors that are likely to apply to most situations calling for advocacy. Compiling these important factors into an organized framework and explaining their interrelationships toward advocacy is essential. Once all the major factors are identified, this framework offers a unified and comprehensive understanding of advocacy. Practitioners can then proceed in advocating knowing that, by adhering to these significant issues, principles, and/or facts, they increase their likelihood for mastery and success.

In other arenas, we find the same attempts. Kubler-Ross (1969) developed a framework for understanding death and dying consisting of five stages: denial and isolation, anger, bargaining, depression, and acceptance. Maslow's (1954) framework for understanding human growth and development consists of meeting five basic needs: physiological, safety, love and belongingness, esteem, and self-actualization. These authors have each constructed a framework for use by practitioners in dealing with death (Kubler-Ross) and understanding human behavior (Maslow).

A disciplined analysis using a framework is more likely to lead to a "professional" judgment, away from personal biases. Applying advocacy principles in a systematic way not only permits one to understand better a situation or condition, but also guides the decisions and actions of the practitioner in an informed way. Practitioners should consider *all* of the framework's principles or factors in order to avoid overlooking an important dynamic or element. Picking and choosing among the principles to study and apply would make the process subjective and arbitrary.

Recognition of Complexity   Most situations requiring advocacy are complex due to personal or environmental factors. By applying an entire framework with its multidimensional principles to a situation, social workers take into account the confusing nature of advocating for a change. Decisions will not be made in a vacuum without consideration of the many variables, facts, pressures, and conditions present in a particular advocacy effort.

Common Base of Knowledge   A framework organizes the substantive knowledge base and skills required for effective advocacy (Carroll, 1977), thus providing a succinct and limited set of terms and guidelines that all social workers can use in discussing or doing advocacy. This common base of knowledge provides a professional identity for social workers. It leads social workers to be disciplined in their use of the word *advocacy,* applying it in a limited and restricted fashion, and not referring to every social work effort to help someone as some form of "advocacy" (see Briar, 1977).

Evaluation of Effectiveness   Social workers who use an advocacy definition and framework consistently over time can gain new knowledge from the application of the framework to different advocacy situations. They can evaluate the efficacy of the framework by identifying the outcomes achieved and the processes used. This continual testing of the framework constitutes a research-based approach to professional practice demanded by funding sources as well as imperatives for accountability. Such a framework can also be used to compare practices of advocacy in other countries or by other professions (Carroll, 1977).

Clarity for Student Learning   With a well-organized framework, students find it easier to memorize the substantive principles and recall them in practice situations. Often professional social workers participate in groups or committees that are deciding whether or not to take action in order to improve a client's circumstance. If social workers have a framework or a set of principles on advocacy at their fingertips, they will be able to (1) analyze the discussion and recognize what issues or factors are present, and (2) offer to the group a coherent plan of study or action based upon their specific knowledge of social work advocacy. This allows the social worker to assume a leadership role and presents an opportunity to introduce professional-level interventions into discussions and decision making.

ARE THE GUIDELINES FOR ADVOCACY SUPPORTED BY RESEARCH OR EMPIRICAL DATA?

Ezell (1994) and Pawlak and Flynn (1990) agree with McGowan (1987) that "we know very little about the extent and nature of social worker's advocacy." Reisch (1986) notes that research findings on advocacy were found "scantily" in the literature, and states that "since 'street wisdom' seems to be more accurate than the practice [empirical] literature, social workers need to do more careful research on subjects like advocacy" (p. 23). McGowan (1987) stated that the only reported study of methods of case advocacy in the previous 12 years was one she conducted in 1974. Our review of the advocacy research literature, however, reveals five distinct areas of studies and data: (1) writings in the 1960s that were exhortative and polemical in nature (Ad Hoc Committee on Advocacy, 1969; Brager, 1968; Briar, 1967; Grosser, 1965; Terrell, 1967); (2) studies that examine the extent to which social workers consider advocacy a part of their professional duties (Epstein, 1968; Ezell, 1994; Herbert & Mould, 1992; Pawlak & Flynn, 1990); (3) reputational studies about various organizations or associations' effectiveness as advocates (Gormley, 1981; Reisch, 1990; Ross, 1992); (4) case studies (Hyman, 1983; Mayster et al., 1993; Olley & Ogloff, 1995; Tefft, 1987); and (5) empirical studies producing data that attempt to measure the effectiveness of an advocacy intervention (Bridgman, 1992; Freddolino & Moxley, 1992; McGowan, 1974; Reisch, 1986).

How do these sources support the guidelines for this book? Is the practice of advocacy just an admirable attitude, or is it based on a systematic, empirical approach to social work practice? What works, and under what conditions? After careful analysis, the authors have developed the guidelines and the principles in this book on the research available at the time of its writing. The definition and framework are the result of a synthesis of the empirical literature, incorporation of practice wisdom, and analysis of successful advocacy ventures. There are data supporting every major concept and principle.

While there is clearly a need for additional studies and support, this framework now offers the professional social worker a clear, specific, and data-based approach to advocacy that can be studied and tested, analyzed and compared, and refined into a professional role for all social workers in pursuit of effective advocacy. We hope that future students and practitioners will produce more and more convincing data that will support the development of guidelines, much as we have attempted to do here.

CAN WE APPLY THESE GUIDELINES TO BOTH CLINICAL AND MACRO SOCIAL WORK?

There should be no reason that advocacy, as defined and outlined in this book, is not a central part of every social worker's practice. Since *all* social workers are bound to advocate, the authors have designed a *universal* set of guidelines to assist both macro and clinical practitioners. In other words, social workers can apply the definition and guidelines to practice advocacy in clinical settings, community agencies, state-level policy issues, or other situations where it is called for. The basic knowledge and skills required for advocacy can be taught in programs of social work education in core courses required of all students. Continuing education for experienced practitioners can also provide learning opportunities.

There are special dimensions to remember. Although the definition and guidelines apply universally to clinical as well as macro settings, there are shifts in emphasis depending upon what is called for. For example, in one-to-one or client advocacy, there may be more emphasis on influencing immediate supervisors or changing indifferent agency procedures. In legislative advocacy, there may be more emphasis on long-range policy changes and political tactics. Cause advocacy may stress coalition building more so than client advocacy. Administrators and internal advocates may work behind the scenes to alter policies and practices. The essential point is this: whether you are a clinical or a macro social worker, you will be called upon to advocate. The definition and guidelines in this book can be applied differentially to most advocacy opportunities. They are useful to any practitioner who wants to improve conditions for clients or a cause. As a consequence, the authors predict there will be an increase in social work advocacy activity because every practitioner will view himself or herself as capable of initiating and carrying out advocacy when it is demanded.

REPRESENTATION

You don't get a second chance to make a first impression.

OLD SAYING

OVERVIEW

Representation is one of the two fundamental skills required by social work advocates. In Chapter 2, we characterized *representation* as a term that is action-oriented and describes an advocate as communicating or expressing the concerns of a client; speaking, writing, or acting on behalf of another; setting forth or stating the ideas or desires of another; standing up for another person or group; pleading the case of a client; and/or serving as an agent or proxy for another. An advocate who truly represents a client must take some identifiable action communicating the concerns of that client to another. (See also Schneider & Sharon, 1982.)

The authors also view *communication* as central to the activities undertaken to represent a client. Social work advocates attempt to inform others about the concerns or problems of their clients, usually employing the two basic forms of communication, *speaking* and *writing*. Successful communication takes place when what was meant by the speaker or writer is actually understood as such by the receiver of the message. It follows that social workers should be skilled in these two methods of communication because, as Drucker (1967) suggests, effectiveness depends on your ability to reach others through the spoken or written word. Of course, effective verbal or written communication is challenging in most circumstances, requiring frequent repetition or clarification.

KEY CHARACTERISTICS

Before examining some methods of effective communication, the authors present three other dimensions of representation always present in social work advocacy. These dimensions are *exclusivity, mutuality,* and *use of a forum.* When social workers act as advocates in representing a client or a cause, they must demonstrate clearly that: (1) they are doing so exclusively on behalf of their client; (2) the client is engaged mutually in the advocacy effort; and (3) the concerns are represented in a forum or place where decision makers discuss and finalize issues and concerns. If any of these elements are absent, then the activity is not considered true social work advocacy.

Exclusivity

Exclusivity is used to describe the relationship between the client and the advocate as singular, unique, focused solely on the client, primarily responsible to the client, and centered on client needs. It means that the client's needs are the sole priority for the advocate, and all activities, strategies, tactics, and so on are specifically designed to address the concerns of the client.

To represent a client *exclusively,* social workers must view themselves as a strong source of support to their clients (Moxley & Freddolino, 1994). According to Levy (1974), advocacy and affective neutrality do not mix; an advocate cannot remain in the middle or stay neutral when a client's interests are at stake. The client's interests are the primary consideration.

Social workers also represent clients energetically within agencies, including their own, and outside, when agencies and others are guided by policies and practices that are not in their clients' best interests. Briar (1967) noted that commitment for his own clients took precedence over all other commitments. Likewise, Brager (1968) viewed social work advocacy as "tough minded and partisan representation of clients' interests, superseding his fealty to others" (p. 6). Grosser (1965) described the advocate as one whose expertise was available *exclusively* to serve client interests. Hardcastle et al. (1997) state that to represent someone is to take that person's view.

Mutuality

Mutuality describes the relationship between the client and the advocate as reciprocal, interdependent, equal, joint, with the same level of relationship between each other, exchanging ideas and plans jointly, and possessing a commonality between them. A *mutual* relationship means that the advocate does not dominate or set the agenda for the client. The advocate collaborates with the client, and together, they proceed in an agreed-upon direction.

Representation-as-mutuality is related to one of social work's most distinguished values, *self-determination.* The 1996 NASW *Code of Ethics* states that social workers must "respect and promote the rights of clients to self-determination and assist clients in their efforts to identify and clarify their goals" (section 1.02). Moxley and Freddolino (1994) note that advocacy is not a paternalistic activity in which the advocate identifies barriers and then takes action on behalf of clients. The role of the social worker is to facilitate the identification and definition of the problem as viewed from the client's perspective.

Richan (1973) warns of advocates taking over too much responsibility and making clients dependent on the social worker. If the client's decision-making power is displaced by paternalistic social workers, there will be no empowerment and an almost certain failure of mutual representation. Advocates must guard against taking from clients the right to help themselves. Social workers must demonstrate their readiness to stand with the client and to go the distance together in mutual respect and understanding. Representation between the client and the social worker must maintain this balance of respect in order to promote true social work advocacy.

Use of a Forum

Successful representation of a client or a cause includes the use of a *forum*, that is, an assembly, meeting, session, or council where issues, concerns, and viewpoints can be brought and expressed. The target of the advocacy effort may be an individual, a group, a corporation, an agency, or formal or informal organizations. According to Kutchins and Kutchins (1987), advocacy is practiced in an adversarial context with one of the important elements being the use of a forum to resolve conflict and reach decisions. Lawyers practice legal advocacy within legislative, administrative, and court forums (Fiedler & Antonak, 1991). Social workers also use many types of forums: public hearings, committee meetings, budget hearings, staff meetings, supervisory meetings, councils, board meetings, legislative hearings, courts, local and state government meetings, civic association meetings, town hall meetings, and so on. Through these forums, social work advocates can effectively represent the concerns of a client or cause.

We include as forums not only the large, public, well-attended meetings or councils, but also smaller forums such as scheduled staff meetings, supervisor-supervisee sessions, internal agency committees, and small task force subcommittees. Most forums have the following features: (1) opportunity to raise awareness; (2) capacity to make decisions or recommendations to decision makers; and (3) use of a specific set of procedures (Kutchins & Kutchins, 1987). Advocates learn how to address each as these features as follows:

Opportunity to Raise Awareness   Education of an audience about the importance of a client issue is one of the primary functions of a forum. In such a setting, advocates have the opportunity to highlight the facts or issues surrounding their cause or client and to bring to light new information, hidden agendas, different points of view, and the concerns of those without easy access to decision makers. A California Task Force provided testimony and funding requests along with press releases at budget hearings in order to raise public awareness about the problems of the medically indigent (Mayster et al., 1993). During a regular monthly staff meeting, a social worker may call attention to an agency policy that fails to address the needs of certain clients; for example, there may not be adequate evening hours for working clients to receive services. State child welfare policies may favor keeping families together at great risk to the safety of children. A supervisor may be unaware of how some agency personnel are inadvertently insulting immigrant clients. A social work advocate can use large or small forums as opportunities to educate colleagues or agency personnel about the impact of particular policies or practices.

Capacity to Make Decisions or Recommendations to Decision Makers Decision makers may be elected officials of a state legislature, city council, board of supervisors, or school board; county officials; or court judges. Nonelected persons are also given authority to make decisions or recommendations about policies. Appointed board members of public or private agencies, government agency executives and department heads, committees of voluntary agencies such as United Way, civic associations, community task forces, statewide commissions appointed by the governor, and long-range planning agencies or councils are a few examples. On an agency level, there are owners, administrators, supervisors, managers, coordinators, and senior staff with authority to decide or recommend policy changes. All of these persons have formal or informal authority to make policies or recommendations about policies.

Most forums are also designed to assist policy makers in making decisions about resource allocations, program development, policy changes, and other issues that impact clients or citizens. Hearings, committee meetings, staff sessions, and other mechanisms are conducted so that those who are decision makers can hear from others about a policy under consideration, what its impact might be, how it will promote or diminish certain values, who will win and who will lose, and other relevant information. Usually, members of a forum are required to make the final decisions (Kutchins & Kutchins, 1987), but not always. Advisory groups may not have formal authority, but do have political clout. Social work advocates who hope to change policies or conditions know that influence and change take place effectively *through decisions made in forums* favorable toward their clients.

Use of a Specific Set of Procedures A third feature of a forum is the presence and use of specific procedures that guide the participants in conducting their business and fulfilling their responsibilities to make final decisions or recommendations. It is very important that social work advocates representing clients know what the procedures are and if they have been promulgated. Social service departments, public housing authorities, courts, legislative bodies, and commissions have adopted specific rules and procedures for resolving conflict and disputes; making decisions; accepting evidence, public input, or testimony from clients or citizens; and so on. "Advocates have frequently achieved victory simply by getting agencies to promulgate procedures. Once this is accomplished, the agency is committed to follow its rules and often yields without further struggle over an individual problem" (Kutchins & Kutchins, 1987, p. 123).

Procedures vary depending on the agency or nature of the forum. Some small forums are conducted very informally without extensive rules. Regular biweekly meetings between a supervisor and supervisee may well be conducted on an informal basis with each individual raising issues, discussing them freely and flexibly, and deciding almost consensually about the next step to take on behalf of a client. However, giving testimony before a legislative committee may (and usually does) require that a speaker notify the clerk of the committee, register in advance, limit the presentation to 10 minutes or less, and leave a written copy of one's remarks that includes the name and address of the organization one is representing. A grievance subcommittee of a Human Rights Commission may require that formal notification of all parties be issued 14 days in advance of a scheduled meeting and that each side be allowed 20 minutes for presentation and 5 minutes for rebuttal. It may also make its final decision behind closed doors and notify the parties by mail within 10 working days.

Social work advocates need to be aware of the specific rules and procedures for each forum in which they want to participate. Effective representation includes this knowledge and the ability to use it.

COMMUNICATION

This project to improve communications was a personal success. I took a concern and issue that affects many and I did something about it rather than just complain.

—TANYA

The importance of effective communication was noted earlier in this chapter. Suffice it to say that, without skills in representation, that is, speaking and writing, advocates will be not be able to stand up for their causes or clients. Following are detailed directives about developing competent skills in speaking and writing.

Speaking

"Speaking up" is an essential part of representation. "The purpose of a speech is to move people to action" (Bobo et al., 1996, p. 105), or, as Blankenship (1966) says, "The end of public speaking is persuasion" (p. 163). Social work advocates speak frequently in order to communicate with others, to educate or influence them, and to recommend activities that will accomplish a desired change. As defined before, these speaking opportunities often take place in a forum, be it large or small. It may be testimony before a legislative hearing, a brief report to a community coalition, a comment delivered before an agency staff, or remarks in a supervisory session designed to influence a change in policy that will benefit a client.

Speaking requires skills that most persons can acquire. It requires planning and practice as well as style and substance. There are entire books and volumes devoted to rhetoric, public speaking, speech making, and how-to-be-a-good speaker. This book is not intended to substitute for them in any way. In this chapter, we present some basic elements for speaking in a forum. We believe that all of these elements are important and encourage students to learn and practice them regularly.

The eight elements of effective communication through speaking are: the speaker, audience, place, time, purpose, content, style, and delivery. Here are some basic dimensions and descriptions of each of them.

Speaker   In every oral communication, someone is doing the speaking. This person has his or her own character, particular personality, background, experiences, and reputation. What the person says and how he or she says it often depend largely on such characteristics. While an audience may or may not know about the integrity, intelligence, and goodwill of the speaker, a dynamic relationship between the speaker and the audience is always flowing.

Speakers make themselves known to their audience by what they bring to a speech (character and reputation) and by what they say in their speeches (judgments, commitments, facts, opinions, and values) (Blankenship, 1966). On the one hand, speakers must know what they value, what they prefer, what they can tolerate, what attitudes they possess, and what positions they hold on various issues. To be effective, speakers must determine that their point of view is meaningful. Distinguished speakers rarely speak on subjects to which they are indifferent.

On the other hand, prior to making a speech, speakers may or may not be known to their audiences. Even if they are known, there may be a variety of ways in which speakers are perceived by different members of the audience. Acceptance of their speeches, of course, will be based on many factors, but trust in the speaker is one important element. In the introduction of unknown speakers, the audience is usually reminded of their professional credentials, experiences, achievements, expertise, and current status. This recitation helps to establish integrity and credibility. Then, each word uttered by the speaker is a request to trust and is a public commitment that represents what the speaker truly believes.

Audience   Audiences come in all shapes and sizes. They differ according to educational level, age, sex, economic and social group, political ideology, religion, race or ethnicity, and other special interests and variables. Some audiences will be informed on your topic, and others will be uninformed. There will be audiences with high involvement in the topic and those with low involvement. Speakers will encounter friendly and hostile audiences. Sometimes, the audience may be only one or two persons, and other times, hundreds. As speakers prepare to address any given audience, they must *research the audience* (Bobo et al., 1996) in order to connect their message successfully to the individuals listening to them.

Knowing about the audience affects several decisions that speakers need to make: What is appropriate language and vocabulary with this particular audience? What type of humor can be used? Can one use statistics or anecdotes? What levels of knowledge does the audience have? What types of recommendations can be made? How committed to action is the audience? Is there a primary and secondary audience? It is also helpful to determine the reasons why persons are coming to this speech, what their expectations are, and what are their moods. Armed with this information, social work advocates can adjust their messages to an audience more effectively.

Place   The place or location where a speaker addresses his or her audience is another important variable because it may become part of the message the speaker is attempting to deliver. Speakers may consciously choose a setting that has an emotional or historical significance, thus wrapping their words in a symbolic context and increasing the power to influence the audience. A traveling group of individuals who were attempting to combat current racism, stopped for two days in Richmond, Virginia, in 1998. Together with the mayor, the group chose to walk arm-in-arm on the old pathway from the docks of the city on the James River (where former slaves were led from the ships) to the jail and auction area. Both the leader of the group and the mayor then spoke to an audience of 200 from the site where these enchained slaves were auctioned off to plantation owners in Virginia. They decried racism and the mayor apologized for the past and promised to help the city look forward to a prejudice-free future. This "place" provided the speakers with great symbolism and dramatically increased the power of their messages.

Frequently, social work advocates do not have a choice about location, but must deliver their words in a setting that is prearranged by others. They may have to speak to legislators at public hearings that are held in conference rooms of the state capitol. They may share their concerns with staff colleagues in the staid meeting rooms of their agencies. They may be asked to speak on the spur of the moment to a rally or to members of a community council. Despite the lack of control over the location, the importance of the place where one will speak is not lessened at all. It means that social work advocates must continue to be highly aware of the place where they will speak.

Each site also demands certain respect and appropriate behavior. One dresses in formal attire when speaking to a panel of legislators in the Senate conference room. Why? Because this setting requires respect for the office of the Senate and recognition of the significance of the Senate's role in determining the direction of policy in the state. Effective advocates will wisely use such a setting to reinforce their arguments, calling upon previous Senate decisions in this room to support their current request.

Speakers should view the place where they provide their comments as an ally that most likely can be used to improve their message. Echoing sentiments related to the setting usually produces a receptive audience, and without forcing the parallels, advocates may be able to advance their client's goal or cause by conscious reference to the site. From history, we remember these examples: President Lincoln delivering the Gettysburg Address from the cemetery there; President Washington giving his farewell address to his troops on a battlefield; Martin Luther King, Jr. speaking about freedom from the steps of the nation's capitol; East and West Berliners pulling down the Berlin Wall while seeking escape from communism; Nelson Mandela addressing the parliament in South Africa for the first time as president; Geraldine Ferraro on the podium receiving the Democratic nomination for vice president; and the list could go on.

Time Every speech is delivered at a certain hour, and timing is important for the success of the message. Delays in responding to crises or to proposals might well ensure that few, if any, appropriate actions will be considered. When social work advocates failed to respond to recent state social service proposals regarding declassifying social work positions, many jobs were reclassified as not requiring formal social work education. Eventual speeches and proposals came too little and too late.

Likewise, prompt responses often initiate support for a proposal because they may preempt opposing viewpoints and set the agenda for decision making. Mental health advocates had already developed proposed policies and programs when the governor of the state unexpectedly made mental health services a priority of her administration. These advocates quickly made a series of proposals that were well suited to meeting the needs of community and institutional-based clients.

Timing is also an important element in the actual speech given on an issue. Here it refers not to a calendar day, as described above, but to a stage in the development of a policy agenda, process of problem solving, or progress on resolving an issue. By referring to the timing or sequence of events, the speaker is able to inform the audience about the larger context of the issue. This may in turn be very useful to listeners who can then understand better where the process of change has been and may be headed.

The speaker may be calling for immediate action or for patience from the audience. In either case, the speaker can refer to time and use it to advantage. One speaker who had helped in the establishment of an agency assisting the poor elderly for over 20 years called for immediate help when government actions were initiated to close this agency down. Another advocate reminded her audience that patience and persistence were required to change legislation on abortion rights. She told them that their current proposal may receive the same fate as those of the past decade, but they would eventually succeed in finding a formula for legislation acceptable to the legislature and the governor. This conscious use of "time" is an effective tool in speaking about an issue because it can persuade the listener to act with greater knowledge about the life of the issue.

Purpose Clarity about the purpose of a speech may seem obvious, but speakers may not take the time to specify even to themselves exactly what they hope to accomplish by speaking to a particular audience. Because the purpose of the speech is central to other decisions about content, style, and proposed action, it is very important that the speaker know the reason(s) for addressing the audience. Usually, the purpose of a speech can be written in one sentence that summarizes what the speaker hopes to achieve. It is good practice to write this sentence out as one begins to prepare the speech. This activity will ensure that the speakers know clearly why they are speaking and will assist them in constructing as persuasive an account as possible.

Let us examine a few examples of *purpose statements*: (1) To encourage the state mental health department to create an independent ombudsman program for community-based service delivery; (2) To counter the arguments that welfare recipients would rather stay on benefits than seek a paid position of employment; (3) To persuade the audience to organize local councils that would attempt to reduce the number of drug-related arrests among 14 to 20 year olds; (4) To provide direction for the audience to establish education programs for the fathers of illegitimate children; and (5) To convince a supervisor that current agency restrictions on petty cash prevent workers from assisting clients in emergency situations. Because the speakers in these five examples are clear about their purposes, they will surely speak with persuasive effect (Blankenship, 1966).

Content The substance of a speech is highly relevant to the ultimate success sought by the speaker. Later, we will examine the role that style and delivery play in making a successful speech, but here our focus is on the actual message that will be composed and spoken to an audience. Speakers are obliged to be accurate and well versed on their topics.

First, the speaker must research the topic well by reading professional literature, examining current events, interviewing experts, and obtaining documents with relevant information in them. While it is true that most speeches will only focus on two or three essential elements, it is important that the speaker know considerably more than these two or three points. Without a broader understanding of the topic, the speaker may be unable to analyze the topic properly and gain a level of certainty about which elements are important and which are unimportant (Bobo et al., 1996). Speakers are responsible for each statement they make, for the supporting facts and evidence, and for the conclusions they draw (Blankenship, 1966).

Speakers must also keep in mind that, while they are familiar with the topic and what they will be saying, the audience is coming in cold. What may be perfectly clear to the speaker may not initially be evident to the listeners.

Here speakers should attempt to provide their audiences with a limited, succinct, well-organized presentation, using concrete examples to illustrate their points and the meaning of them to the audience (Richan, 1996).

Bobo et al. (1996) points out that every speech has a beginning, middle, and end. The content of each section should be planned and written separately. This follows the adage that journalists have developed: *tell the audience what you are going to tell them; tell it to them; and remind them of what you just told them.* The *beginning* or introduction is really a summary of the speech, stating the problem or issue and informing the audience of what will be expected of them. The *middle* of the speech adds details and richness to your message, often using specific facts, stories that illustrate your point(s), previous efforts to address the topic, successful outcomes elsewhere, and whatever else might add realism to your speech. The *ending* moves the listeners closer to understanding what action may be required of them and summarizes the steps that they need to take. The ending pulls together your major thoughts, giving a charge or lift to the audience or a call to action (Richan, 1996).

Style   The style of a speaker is determined, not by any lucky choice of words, but by the decision of the speaker not only about what to say, but also how to say it. According to Blankenship (1966), effective style means that a communication is: (1) clear; (2) appropriate; and (3) vivid or impressive. The speaker's choice of words are *clear* when they are accurate, concrete, and familiar to the listener. *Accuracy* means that the word used actually conveys the meaning intended by the speaker. Great care must be given to finding the "best" word to support your meaning. Speakers must constantly be on guard not to use ambiguous terms. Does *old* refer to someone over 65 years of age? Over 85? Over 62? Over 55? Are there such categories as "young-old" and "old-old"? How can a speaker use the term *old* accurately?

Words that are *concrete,* very observable, or perceived through the senses are usually better understood than more abstract terms. A policy may be "harmful," but it is better understood when the listener hears that the "policy unfortunately permits foster teen children to be moved from a foster family without explanation and a period of transition."

Words that are *familiar* to the audience are preferable because, if a word is unfamiliar to the listener, it will have no meaning at all. Using very complex, sophisticated, or highly technical terms is risky because listeners may get an impression from the speaker that he or she only wants to impress them, not communicate with them. Such negativity will turn the listener away from the speaker's message. It may also show disrespect for the audience, indicating that the speaker did not investigate the audience and determine what vocabulary would fit best with them.

Style also must be *appropriate* to the speaker, the audience, the topic, and the occasion. Presidents of universities use formal language in many of their speeches because of the importance of the occasion, for example, award ceremonies, announcements of research findings, or presentations to community leaders about the mission of the university. Speaking to a legislative session also requires more formal language due to the nature of such sessions. Informal language may be appropriate to smaller groups or with fellow staff members, but one must be certain to be respectful to the audience above all else.

One's speaking style should also be *vivid or impressive.* Vivid language means speakers can give more "clues" to their audiences about exactly what they mean. Usually, vivid terms contribute to specific images or precise pictures, not general ideas or abstract actions. In referring to an advocate who "started" a movement, it might be more concrete to say, who "created, launched, or initiated" a movement. Rather than refer to a report as "nicely" written, one could say "exactly, critically, admirably, or accurately" written and be more effective.

Imagery is also used to make the listeners respond with their human senses. Such images often enhance the idea the speaker is trying to explain. The senses of vision, hearing, smell, taste, touch, and movement are used frequently to capture an image. Consider the following images: "bitter struggle for freedom; dark path of deception; a dash across the aisle; soaring through the speech; fiery words flashing from her lips; serene, but unwavering confidence; mellow mood of the group"; and so on. By evoking images, the speaker reinforces the message in an active and unforgettable manner.

Metaphors and similes can also be used to create a vivid impression. A metaphor emphasizes the interaction between two ideas such as "jump on the bandwagon, tied up in knots, cutting-edge technology, power vacuum, politics of the oppressed, two is company and three is a crowd," and so on. A simile is also a comparison directly expressed as in "simple like a fox, a voice like an angel, speeding like a bullet, red as a beet, busy as a bee, good as gold, trusty like a sister," and so on. These impressions allow the listener to understand more exactly what the speaker intends to convey.

Delivery   The delivery of a communication is the culmination of all of the work done beforehand. The main point, of course, is to convey the speaker's idea effectively to the listener, and anything that impedes this process is a barrier. If speakers mumble, speak in a low, monotone voice, talk too quickly, mispronounce words, appear bored or dull about the topic, have poor eye contact, move or gesture awkwardly, are very nervous or tense, apologize for themselves, use "ah, er, um" excessively, have trouble reading from notes, and so on, their actions will surely detract from their message. One rule to follow is: if the listener is conscious of the delivery itself—whether good or bad—the listener is not paying complete attention to the speaker's message (Blankenship, 1966).

Here are several techniques that can improve a speaker's delivery:

1. Use an outline of your speech; avoid memorizing the complete text; and refer to the outline to jog your memory about the important points.
2. Practice! Use a tape recorder and listen to the timing, articulation, emphases, long sentences, and volume. Practice in front of a mirror and see how your gestures come across, if you ever smile, and if you have good eye contact.
3. Dress slightly more formally than the group you are addressing. It is a sign of respect, and you want them to remember what you said, not what you wore (Bobo et al., 1996).
4. Consider your speech as a conversation and a dialogue. You will not feel separate from the audience, but will be speaking *with* them.
5. Believe in what you are going to say. There is no substitute for it. When your beliefs are strong and clearly defined, when you are confident in them, you will convey your feelings and attitudes dynamically to the audience.
6. Establish eye contact with at least some members of the audience. In conversation, we normally look at the persons we are speaking with in order to share an idea or thought. This simply tells them that we are interested in them, we are concentrating on them, and we want to communicate directly to them.
7. Use notes to ensure confidence, accuracy, and completeness of facts or opinion. Beware of speaking to your notes, not the audience. Practice with your notes. Type them, and use colored highlights to distinguish different ideas.
8. Listen to the members of your audience and judge how they are responding. If you have lost them (lots of coughing, chair movement, small talk, looking around), you must bring them back. Check your speed and volume. Slip in a joke. Maybe you need to make a change in mid-speech. This may be a good time to ask the audience a question or play the role of devil's advocate.
9. Be prepared! Research your topic, assemble the information, and make a draft of your important points. Be sure your speech has a beginning, middle, and ending. Always write a second draft and ask yourself: Can I say this better? Look for the best words and illustrations. Preparation also reduces nervousness and gives the speaker confidence.

Writing

Writing is the second keystone of representation and communication. In addition to speaking, advocates must be able to compose informational sheets, documents, letters, reports, memoranda, and so on, in order to communicate effectively what the concerns and issues of clients or a cause are. As Sherman and Johnson (1975) noted to social workers: "Writing will be a part of your work . . . and skill in writing must be regarded as a professional tool to be ranked on a par with the other knowledge and skills that will comprise your professional qualifications" (p. 3). If a social worker writes poorly, this weakness will obscure the possible contributions he or she might be able to make or will require embarrassing corrections from supervisors or bosses. If a person writes well, he or she will receive credit and recognition for his or her efforts and be in a position to influence decisions that will be made about changes or events. This advocacy book places equal emphasis on representation and influence; writing, along with speaking, becomes a key aspect of advocacy.

Again, there are hundreds of textbooks, self-improvement books, and guidelines about writing effectively. This chapter is not intended to replace them, and the authors encourage the readers to consult other books about learning how to write well. In fact, as Strunk and White (1959) pointed out long ago, "There are no infallible guides to good writing, no assurance that a person who thinks clearly will be able to write clearly, no key that unlocks the door, and no inflexible rules by which the young writer may shape his or her course" (p. 52). Many who must write have also been "brainwashed into thinking that writing competence is a function mostly of grammar, punctuation, syntax, and the like" (Ewing, 1974). Such is not the case. In the following pages, the authors have selected several basic guidelines for effective writing. Much could be added, and many will disagree with our emphases, but we believe all advocates will be well served by incorporating these basic propositions into their written work.

In the authors' opinions, Ewing's (1974) "writer's wheel" reflects the essential elements of the writer's task (see Figure 3.1). We believe it provides students of advocacy with a visible tool to improve their writing. Each *spoke* in the wheel as well as the *rim* and the *hub* are explained briefly in the following text.

Writing is a means to an end. For social work advocates, it usually means that they want to convey written ideas, facts, messages, and arguments to others so that a client's condition or situation will improve or a cause will be served. The *hub* of the wheel represents the message and the motivation that ultimately inspires the writer to proceed. Once the hub is known, the advocate then decides how to use each of the different spokes in the wheel advantageously.

Every form of communication is intended for an audience. It is incompatible to write, to speak, or to produce a radio, television, Internet, or e-mail message without hoping to influence a group or set of individuals. If we did such random planning, the impact of our messages would most likely be very confusing. In the writer's wheel, the *rim* represents the *impact* on the readers, individuals, or groups whom social work advocates hope to persuade. Knowledge of the desired impact plays a major role in deciding how advocates use the spokes of the wheel in devising strategies for writing.

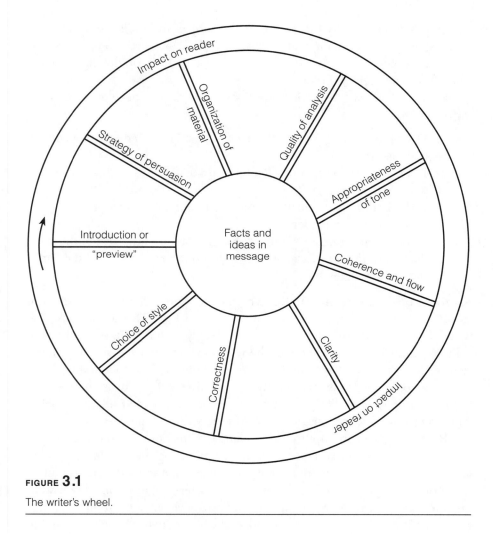

FIGURE 3.1

The writer's wheel.

In the construction of a wheel, the *spokes* connect the hub to the rim. They serve essential roles without which the wheel could not function properly. In the writer's wheel by Ewing (1974), there are nine spokes: introduction or preview; strategy of persuasion; organization of materials; quality of analysis; appropriateness of tone; coherence and flow; clarity; correctness; and choice of style. In the following text, the authors explain briefly how each of these spokes connects the message and ideas of the advocate (hub) to the desired impact on intended readers (rim).

Introduction or Preview Many readers will put a document aside if the initial message is confusing, misleading, or abrupt, or they do not perceive quickly what the writer wants to communicate. Opening sentences and paragraphs should clarify the nature of the subject to be discussed, attempt to engage the reader, comment briefly on conclusions or recommendations in the document, and give the reader a general idea of the direction in which the document will flow.

Ewing (1974) suggests four questions to guide the development of an introduction:

1. Does the opening paragraph specify the subject matter of the writer's document?
2. Does the introduction telegraph the principal message that the writer will emphasize?
3. Is the reason made clear why the document and its content are important to the reader?
4. Does the introduction outline the organization of the rest of the document in order to allow the reader to follow easily and efficiently the logic of the writer?

Strategy of Persuasion Writers who seeks to persuade must make a set of careful judgments about their readers (Ewing, 1974). This author asks the writer to decide whether the readers are: deeply or mildly interested in the subject; familiar or unfamiliar with the writer's views; knowledgeable or ignorant of the writer's authority on the subject; committed or uncommitted to a particular opinion; likely or unlikely to find the writer's ideas threatening; prejudiced or unprejudiced about the topic; and associated or unassociated with groups or organizations involved with the writer's topic.

Persuasion is an attempt to make clear to the reader why your proposal or new idea makes sense. Hence, the relationship among the writer, the reader, and the message is the fundamental focus of persuasion. It is important to know or to analyze this relationship well as writers begin to decide on what ideas to include, which arguments to emphasize, which facts are most important, what level of credibility is needed, and what sequence should be used to communicate their proposals effectively.

Ewing (1974) offers another set of questions and principles to assist a writer in preparing a persuasively written document:

1. How much background about the subject is required for a particular audience of readers? How resistant to change or how threatening is the subject? How familiar are readers with the subject?
2. Is the writer credible with the readers? What do the readers have in common with the writer? Credibility comes from several sources: position, reputation, associations with groups or individuals, or the message itself. Often, writers identify themselves with the goals and interests of the readers.

3. If the readers most likely will disagree with the writer's ideas or will be uncertain about them, the writer should present all sides of the argument. This approach suggests that the writer is objective, treats the reader with respect, and is helpful by organizing the pros and cons clearly.
4. Put the recommendations, fact, or arguments the writer wants the reader to remember *first* or *last*. Ideas stated first or last have a better chance of being remembered than ideas stated in the middle of your proposal.
5. Cite materials and opinions from groups or associations to which your readers most likely belong. People's attitudes and opinions are strongly influenced by the churches, synagogues, clubs, ethnic groups, and professional associations to which they belong.
6. Be cautious in using "sensational" or "bizarre" facts, claims, or examples to support the message. We can raise suspicions and distrust by using extreme or exaggerated positions. By using the real world as a tool toward objectivity, writers will gain the confidence and cooperation of their readers.
7. What evidence can advocates produce that demonstrates their methods will actually get the desired results (Sherman & Johnson, 1975)? Can writers illustrate how their proposals are better than any others?

Organization of Materials Advocates must decide what facts, figures, and ideas to use; how to put them together; what order to choose; and how to make them "fit" or "flow" in an unboring, nontedious manner. Writers typically establish meaningful relationships among ideas, concepts, propositions, and facts, hoping that their readers understand them properly. The facts and ideas must be linked and associated with each other because leaving these relationships to random organization would ensure that no reader would ever understand them.

The following principles should assist the advocate in deciding how to organize a document or proposal:

1. Remember that writing is ultimately a teaching process (Sherman & Johnson, 1975). The writer is trying to give information to the reader (who does not have such information), and the reader is attempting to learn what the writer has to say.
2. Most persons can retain in their short-term memory only five to nine items. This research finding illustrates the limitations of the human mind, and there should seldom be more than five main points in a written proposal (Sherman & Johnson, 1975).

3. Writers should alert the readers to their organizational plan with devices such as headings, subheadings, and cue-words like first, second, furthermore, on the one hand, and so on.

4. Creating a draft outline forces the advocate to clarify his or her thinking and settle questions about relationships before going further. Mental notes are not enough; writers should make draft notes on paper or computer.

5. Once writers know the material, it is then possible to decide how to organize it. Writers should arrange the different pieces of information, facts, findings, and opinion into categories. Bunch the main topics together.

6. As writers continuously think about the topic and the reader, they will decide upon the main points of the outline. Each point should be ranked according to its importance.

7. Arrangement of the material is the result of a conscious decision, not left to chance. It may be in chronological order, order of increasing difficulty, or order of logical progression. This sequencing is also subject to the strategies of persuasion mentioned above, and a final organizational decision considers these elements very seriously.

Quality of Analysis   Sherman and Johnson (1975) suggest that an *analysis* examines parts of something either separately or in relationship to the whole. An advocate may want to examine the eligibility policy of a disability entitlement program. Ewing (1974) calls for the writer to evaluate evidence, test assumptions, and consider alternatives to proposals by using methods based on objectivity and relevance. Guidelines include the following principles:

1. The writer should be aware of who will read the finished document and why. This information will help determine what data or level of interpretation will be required.

2. The writer should not confuse his or her own personal conclusions with a presentation of the objective facts.

3. Writers should point out assumptions made in their analyses. Whatever the writer takes for granted should be noted. Phrases like "assuming such-and-such to be true," "if this trend continues," or "without additional evidence" are examples.

4. Writers should use care to avoid nonsequiturs, attributing simple causality to complex issues, and overconfident inferences.

5. Expert testimony, research findings, and data must all be confirmed as coming from qualified sources. If inaccurate facts or data are exposed, readers will lose confidence in the entire proposal.

6. In analyzing, the advocate should try to follow these steps:

   • Define the key problem—the most important one.
   • Describe the significant dimensions of the key problem.

- Identify the cause or causes of the key problem.
- Enumerate alternative ways of coping with the causes of the problem.
- Outline the solution and course of action the writer considers most effective (Ewing, 1974).

Appropriateness of Tone   Words and phrases often connote meanings that can be friendly or hostile, and writers strive to use those that advance their intended meaning. "You will be happy to know" and "I wish to advise you" may be similar in meaning, but are very different in tone. There are many different tones that the writer may seek to achieve: friendliness, warmth, formality, respect for authority, awareness of delicate situations, desire to maintain goodwill, empathy, anger, familiarity, and so on. Key words can be used to accentuate each of these tones.

Coherence and Flow   If writing is to be clear, every sentence must be coherent, that is, it must hold together. The reader should be able to grasp readily the relationship between the thoughts expressed. Here are several rules that will improve the coherency of written proposals:

1. When the writer begins a paragraph, he or she should set forth the main topic in the first sentence. The reader will expect the rest of the paragraph to explain this main thought.
2. Use parallel constructions to emphasize important themes or patterns of facts.
3. The writer should be sure to include transitional words or sentences when leaving one topic and introducing another. Such transitions keep the reader on track.
4. Revise and rewrite the text several times. Awkward expressions, lack of transitional words or phrases, and illogical thoughts are always present in a first draft, and revisions will reduce them for the final text.

Clarity   Strunk and White (1959) state that since "writing is communication, clarity can only be a virtue" (p. 65). Clearness results from choosing our words intelligently; writing sentences of suitable length; being concise, direct, and simple; and using the English language correctly and accurately (Sherman & Johnson, 1975).

Enumeration, and the use of numerals and letters to serialize several facts, ideas, or issues, helps to clarify a series of points, giving them more visibility in the reader's mind. Examples of enumerations are: 1, 2, 3; A, B, C; I, II, III; and (a), (b), (c). *Headings and subheadings* allow the reader to see which ideas are important and which are subordinate to other ideas. They help the writer and reader keep their thoughts organized while drafting or reviewing.

Correctness   Writing correctly and accurately seems to be obvious advice. However, it is worth reminding readers of the reasons for expressing oneself correctly:

1. A messy-looking document creates a negative impression even before the reader starts to pour over it.
2. Carelessness and poor use of grammar, syntax, and spelling communicate a disrespect to the reader.
3. Errors and inaccuracies are distracting because every time one occurs, it interrupts the attention of the reader.
4. Grammatical mistakes, spelling errors, insufficient data, and untruthful or inaccurate information all contribute to a loss of clarity.
5. Multiple errors contribute to a loss of confidence by the reader in the accuracy of the writer's overall message.

Style   "Style is not a stage in the writing process," according to Ewing (1974), and it concerns not what writers say but how they say it. Strunk and White (1959) also point out that there is "no satisfactory explanation of style." References abound in writing handbooks to "legal style," "academic style," "journalistic style," "abstract style," "analytical style," "flowery or pompous style," or "straightforward style." It is beyond the scope of this chapter to define each style, and the authors refer readers to other classical resources on style such as *The Elements of Style* by Strunk and White (1959) for fuller discussion of the topic.

Social work advocates will use combinations of writing styles to represent their clients or causes. Regardless of the style, advocates hope to achieve clearness and readability as the end result. Effective style is usually achieved, not by resorting to tricks, devices, flamboyance, or affectation, but by approaching it with plainness, simplicity, orderliness, and sincerity (Strunk & White, 1959). Below are listed several principles that will assist writers in developing their styles:

1. Use the active voice. The active voice is usually more direct, definite, and vigorous than the passive voice according to Strunk and White (1959). "I will never forget my only visit to the detention center" is better than "My only visit to a detention center will never be forgotten by me." These authors suggest that using the active voice produces a more forcible, straightforward, bold writing. They also point out that when a sentence is made shorter, it is usually made stronger.
2. Omit needless words. The writer should learn how to trim out every word that can be spared without sacrificing precision and readability (Sherman & Johnson, 1975). Some of the main causes of wordiness are repetition, wordy phases ("due to the fact that," "the question as

to whether," "has proved itself to be"), and using general rather than specific words ("made contact with her by e-mail" rather than *e-mailed*; "gave his ideas by oral communication" rather than *spoke*). Revising and cutting superfluous words are essential to good writing, and it is not a sign of weakness to reread, revise, and rewrite documents and papers. These steps are intended to produce an impact on the reader that will assist the advocate in achieving a desired goal.

3. Avoid excessively long sentences. Shorter sentences frequently contribute to clearer expressions that are easy for the reader to follow. Long sentences usually become very complex and involved, and readers may lose the main point. Ewing (1974) suggests that writers vary the structure and length of their sentences. Short, choppy sentences are not pleasant to read in the same way that long sentences are too confusing.

4. Use nouns and verbs. Sherman and Johnson (1975) recommend that writers use verbs that say what the writer really wants to say about a subject and use subjects (nouns) that show what the writer's sentences actually concern. Using nouns and verbs gives color and toughness to writing: "In the legislative chamber, voices rumbled along the aisle" or "The mother hurled the stubs of food stamp coupons." Adjectives and adverbs are also indispensable, but strength in writing comes from the use of the right nouns and verbs.

Style will always remain a personal expression, and there are no universal rules that guarantee effectiveness. But, writers should concentrate on clearness and readability. With practice, all advocates can improve their style and impact.

SUMMARY

Chapter 3 provides the social work advocate with knowledge and skill development in one of the primary tasks of an advocate, that is, representation of a client or a cause. "Speaking up" must also reflect professional attitudes of exclusivity, mutual decision making, and thorough knowledge of various forums where decisions are discussed and decided. Communication forms the basis of representation, attempting to clarify and persuade another of one's point of view. Finally, the importance of speaking and writing effectively are underscored. Without these skills, advocates will be unable to represent clients and causes effectively.

DISCUSSION QUESTIONS

1. What are the two action dimensions of the "new" definition and conceptual framework for advocacy? Define them and use examples.
2. Give three reasons for using "guidelines" in the practice of advocacy.
3. Why is advocacy expected from both clinical and macro social workers?
4. What important distinction is made by defining advocacy by its "activities" (what you do) versus its outcomes (goals and hopes)?
5. How important are communication skills in representing a client?
6. Why is a forum required in order to do advocacy?
7. What are the eight elements of communication to consider when speaking?
8. Explain why you agree or disagree with this statement: "Skill in writing must be regarded as a professional (social work) tool to be ranked on a par with the other knowledge and skills that will comprise your professional qualifications."
9. Which is worse: having inaccurate facts and information in a document you wrote, or having multiple grammar, spelling, or syntax errors?
10. What is the best way to overcome nervousness before public speaking?

RECOMMENDED READINGS

Bobo, K., Kendall, J., & Max, S. (1996). *Organizing for social change: A manual for activists in the 90s* (2d ed.). Santa Ana, CA: Seven Locks Press.

Ewing, D. W. (1974). *Writing for results.* New York: Wiley.

Flynn, J. P. (1985). Frameworks and models for policy analysis. In J. P. Flynn, *Social agency policy: Analysis and presentation for community practice* (pp. 33–53). Chicago: Nelson-Hall.

Richan, W. C. (1996). *Lobbying for social change* (2d ed.). Binghamton, NY: Haworth Press.

Strunk, W., & White, E. B. (1959). *The elements of style.* New York: Macmillan.

INFLUENCE

(S)he who waits to do a great deal of good at once will never do anything.

CHINESE PROVERB

OVERVIEW

Influencing is the second of two fundamental activities required by our definition and framework for social work advocacy. To *influence* means to modify, change, affect, act on, or alter decisions that intrude upon a client(s). It may be an attempt to persuade or sway another person or group who has authority or power over resources and policy making. Influence has been described as a variety of tangible, identifiable activities: forming coalitions, educating the public, contacting public officials and legislators, gathering data from studies, giving testimony, appealing to review boards, developing petitions, organizing client groups and demonstrations, using the media, and/or initiating legal action (Hepworth, et al., 1997). Influencing one person or several persons derives from the same goal: changing an opinion and altering a behavior.

We have identified eight practice principles for influencing that are associated with successful social work advocacy. Each of the principles has been selected because of a connection to empirical research literature, practice wisdom, and/or case studies. While the principles discussed in this chapter are in a sequential order, we alert the reader that these principles are dynamic, often used simultaneously, and cannot be ranked in order of importance. In reality, the principles interact with each other. As the reader may recall, one of the advantages of using a guideline is to consider systematically all important variables when deciding how to proceed as an advocate. Each of the principles discussed here deserves the careful scrutiny of social work advocates.

IDENTIFY THE ISSUES AND SET GOALS

Although my efforts at advocacy were largely unsuccessful, I learned that I must respond to the needs of the community that I serve. When I attempted to pursue the project according to my agenda, the response was negative. When I responded positively to the needs expressed by the children, they took on the responsibility of advocating for themselves.

—MICHAEL

Identify the Issues

After an hour of spirited discussion during a strategy session about a client's problem, someone usually asks the following questions: "What is the issue here? What are we really talking about? Can someone clarify what we are trying to do?" It surprises some people who gather together to address a client concern that everyone does not understand the concern in the same way. They discover that there are multiple ways of interpreting the same circumstances. Of course, whenever there is an opportunity to interpret an event or problem individually, there will be competing opinions. People see things differently for many reasons.

Consider this example: *Should district court judges appoint sheriffs as guardians of last resort for incompetent wards?* Some *advocates* believe that the sheriff is the last person who should serve as a guardian because of the law enforcement and punishment image that a sheriff represents. How can an incompetent person receive respect and at least some dignity while under the supervision of a sheriff? *Sheriffs*, on the other hand, oppose this arrangement because they resent the extra time it takes away from their normal duties. "We are trained to be law enforcement officers, not social workers," they add. Then, *judges* view this appointment favorably because, when there is absolutely no other person or relative to serve as guardian (which happens frequently), the judge knows that the sheriff will perform the duties of guardian, and the ward will not be abandoned or fall through the cracks of the adult protective services. Judges want to preserve the safety of citizens and believe that the sheriff is in a key position to protect vulnerable persons.

What are the issues here? How is the problem defined by each group? Who is correct? Which interpretation of the problem is the most valid? These are the types of day-to-day problems advocates must face.

Let us begin with a definition of the word *issue.* An issue is the substantive matter in dispute (Kutchins & Kutchins, 1987). It is a matter of critical importance (Tefft, 1987) or a problem that affects a significant number of people (Amidei, 1991). In the previous example, there are several issues: safety of vulnerable persons; job overload; training; the dignity of a person; courtroom efficiency; and fear of negligence. Advocates recognize this basic dilemma all too well. Which issue is the most important here? Why? Without agreement on the issue, it is impossible to create a solution.

This principle requires effort on the part of all participants to identify and clarify the issues facing clients. There will always be competing individual interpretations. But the advocate must try to advance the discussion to a point where all of the issues are identified and participants can begin to decide which of them are more or less important. The advocate can assist in identifying if there is agreement or disagreement, how strongly held are participants' convictions, and how different perspectives on the issue can be combined. Through this clarification and educational process, the advocacy effort becomes more specific and limited rather than broader and less focused.

This process is not always popular with persons who want to act immediately and forcefully. They will warn the group about the "paralysis of analysis."

But effective advocacy is based on as clear an understanding of the issues as possible, and this clarification stage must be undertaken. Although the discussions will take time and require patience on the part of all, they are crucial to the entire advocacy effort. The final resolution of the concern depends upon how the issue is defined in the first place.

What exactly can a social work advocate do to analyze a client's concern or community problem and assist in identifying the issues? How can one clarify the issue(s)? There is no set formula that will guarantee that discussion or analysis will produce clarity and agreement. Following are several key questions that will guide the social work advocate in identifying the important issues for deeper discussion and understanding. Readers should apply these questions to the problems, concerns, and issues for which they wish to advocate.

Questions: How to Identify Issues   Is the issue specific, and does it address a definite need (Claxton, 1981; Kutchins & Kutchins, 1987; Lurie, 1983; Pearl & Barr, 1976; Tefft, 1987)? Broad issues like human suffering or improving mental health services are real, but they must be turned into specific issues. Examples might be: lack of medical equipment for handicapped infants, failure to provide funding for community-based medication services, human rights violations in facilities, and parental abuse of immigrant children.

What are the causes and history of this issue (Altman et al., 1994; Friedman et al., 1989)? Advocates often learn more about an issue once they learn about its background, previous programs or policies designed to address it, community conditions, historical factors, and key events or persons participating in resolving the issue.

How many are affected by the issue (Altman et al., 1994; Bobo et al., 1996; Dluhy, 1981)? Without knowing the dimensions of the issue and how many persons are affected by it, advocates will understand only superficially the nature of the issue. How many handicapped children need special equipment? How many diabetics need insurance for insulin treatment? How many teenaged girls are made pregnant by males over the age of 21?

What are the consequences of the issue (Altman et al., 1994; Tefft, 1987)? Advocates can find out what the impact of an issue is by conducting studies; examining existing research, archives, newspapers, and records; speaking to clients and community leaders; and conducting focus groups. With well-documented evidence about outcomes, advocates can impress on others the need to address an issue.

What is the economic impact of the issue (Altman et al., 1994)? Most discussion of issues revolves around costs and competing priorities for funding. Advocates can demonstrate the high cost of doing nothing or the value of each dollar invested in solving the issue in order to highlight the economic dimension of an issue. Costs and benefits need to be provided.

Can the issue be framed to have both a rational and an emotional appeal (Bersani, 1996; Bobo et al., 1996; Reisch, 1990; Tefft, 1987; Tourigny et al., 1993; Tropman et al., 1977; Wallach, 1994)? Combining the facts with existing values and beliefs changes an audience from passive recipients to active participants in understanding the issue. The civil rights movement, originally cast as "the Negro problem," was reframed as national evidence of stubborn prejudice. "Sheriffs as guardians of last resort" was reframed from a work overload issue to an issue of protecting the vulnerable and helpless.

Symbols and images, for example, a telephone for runaway children, hungry faces, songs of freedom, and so on, often produce emotional reactions to the issue. If an issue is perceived as a crisis and not some chronic year-after-year need, it often adds an emotional element. When the issue is framed to resonate or strike a chord with the audience, it gives the message higher and more effective impact.

What are the barriers for addressing the issue (Altman et al., 1994)? Advocates can identify the forces, persons, conditions, and values that prevent the issue from being resolved. There are always barriers present, and an examination of them usually provides a clearer understanding of the task of moving forward.

Who has the power to address these issues (Friedman et al., 1989)? Power represents the capacity to make others change their behavior. Advocates must learn who the key influential persons in the community, state, or agency are before attempting to design solutions. Future decisions usually include strategies to work collaboratively with influential persons or to devise activities to oppose them. In either case, it is important to know who has a significant amount of power.

What are the resources for addressing the issue (Altman et al., 1994; Dluhy, 1981)? Resources are always finite, and need is always infinite. Advocates can learn what resources are available in a community by a knowledge of agency policies, programs, and personnel. Resources may be funding, in-kind resources such as building space, partial assignment of a worker, or extra supplies, equipment, transportation, utilities, and volunteers. Keen insight into obtaining resources enhances the options for addressing an issue.

What are the chances for success in settling this issue (Bobo et al., 1996; Friedman et al., 1989; Lurie, 1983)? From the start, advocates should identify issues where there is a reasonable likelihood of achieving a successful solution. If the odds are very overwhelming, it is advisable to shift to another issue. Participants in advocacy must be able to see there is a chance of winning or they will soon become demoralized. There should also be a realistic time frame within which a goal is achievable.

Set Goals

Once the issue is well understood or accepted by participants, it is very important to set goals (Amidei, 1992; Bevis, 1989; Bobo et al., 1996; Hallman, 1987; Lurie, 1983; Olley & Ogloff, 1995; Reisch, 1990; Ross, 1992). Amidei (1991) suggests that a *goal* is what you hope to accomplish and the end toward which your advocacy efforts are directed. Hallman (1987) calls a *goal* a "clear specification of the desired change." Netting et al. (1998) describe a *goal* as a statement of hopes and expectations.

Examples of goals might be: (1) the appointment of a patient ombudsman inside a community mental health facility; (2) the allocation of $50,000 by the state health department for AIDS protease inhibitors; (3) the prevention of public social services eligibility workers' jobs from being transferred to private companies; and (4) the requirement for insurance companies to cover insulin and equipment that measures blood-sugar levels for all of the state's diabetics. In each of these goal statements, the reader can identify what the advocate hopes to achieve in relatively specific, but not measurable, terms. Without this level of focus, it is difficult to promote clarity of purpose, identify next steps, find resources, organize people to help, and create strategies and symbols for change.

Reisch (1990) states that effective advocacy organizations are more likely to have a structured goal-setting process. This process takes place in a mutual context where social work advocates are very aware that they must consult with those whom they represent and speak on behalf of. It requires great sensitivity to represent or speak for others, especially those unable to speak for themselves such as mentally retarded children, incompetent older persons, victims of trauma, and so on. This process must be carefully planned in advance and carried out consciously by the advocate.

Another method of using goals to improve the effectiveness of advocacy efforts is to designate short-term, intermediate, and long-term goals (Bobo et al., 1996; Lurie, 1983; Reisch, 1990; Ross, 1992). Using the previous definitions of a *goal*, the reader can refine the desired change into temporal segments and further specify the desired outcomes according to a dynamic, time-related process.

Long-Term Goals   A long-term goal would be the ultimate or eventual change or outcome that an advocacy group desires. An AIDS advocacy group may want the state to allocate annually a progressively greater share of the budget for protease inhibitors and make them available free of charge to any citizen.

Intermediate Goals   An intermediate goal would be an outcome or change that an advocacy group desires during a specific campaign. It will not accomplish everything that the group desires (i.e., the long-term goal), but it is a step in that direction. So, an AIDS advocacy group may have intermediate goals of winning the support of key legislators on the budget committees of the legislature and the passage of a $50,000 budget allocation for the present fiscal year.

Short-Term Goals   A short-term goal would be a step on the way toward achieving the intermediate goal(s). Short-term goals are specific actions or outcomes that will permit two necessary conditions: (1) small victories during the campaign that are important for morale among participants, and (2) time for the group to build up a power base. These short-term goals are very concrete, down-to-earth, and tangible outcomes with which people can readily identify. For the AIDS advocacy group, short-term goals might be getting an appointment with the chairperson of one of the legislative budget committees or finding a sponsor for a budget amendment for the coming session.

Without the setting of goals, most advocacy efforts are unable to focus clearly on how to proceed and identify the resources or strategies required for success. Goal setting through a participatory and mutual process provides the structure and support needed for gaining agreement and consensus on next steps.

GET THE FACTS

In order to influence community leaders, legislators, agency staff, supervisors, funding sources, bureaucrats, or other key persons, social work advocates must use *facts* to demonstrate the need for change or to support the rationale for addressing an issue (Altman et al., 1994; Amidei, 1991; Gormley, 1981; Hallman, 1987; Kaminski & Walmsley, 1995; Mayster et al., 1993; Schlager, 1995; Taylor, 1987; Van Gheluwe & Barber, 1986). Advocates need to be expert on the issue(s) under consideration or have experts available to them. Armed with this knowledge, advocates are in a strong position to present the issue to others, the media, and the opposition, and they can suggest strategies and tactics based on a realistic understanding of the issues.

It must also be said that nothing can "sink an advocacy group faster than being caught with its facts wrong or incomplete" (Altman et al., 1994; Amidei, 1991). Advocates must use solid facts and evidence, not guesswork, hunches, anecdotes, or only what they have heard or read in the media. Opponents ask questions that may stump the advocate in order to prevent the issue from being viewed favorably. Advocates must prepare themselves to anticipate hard questions and have factual information ready. If advocates fail to answer these questions factually and correctly, the credibility of the entire effort will be seriously impaired.

Although advocates do research in order to produce facts and quantifiable justification for an issue, they know that facts, in and of themselves, do not guarantee that listeners or readers will be convinced to change their minds. Persons whom we wish to influence frequently are subject to other pressures such as electoral politics, funding sources, personal ambitions, superiors, rival-ries, power struggles, historical events, and personality quirks. These pressures modify the impression that an advocate's message makes in the recipient's mind, altering the meaning of facts and figures. Nevertheless, it is unthinkable to pursue social work advocacy without gathering the best data and facts avail-able regarding the issue. Advocates must always undertake this task, hoping that correct data will eventually serve their efforts effectively.

Methods for Gathering Facts

Each issue requires research and fact finding from a variety of sources. Advocates must try to imagine the hardest questions that opponents will pose and strive to prepare answers. Sound and well-reasoned arguments and pre-sentations are critical for successful advocacy.

Types of Information   *Broader trends in society or a community.* These trends may serve as background to an issue: cultural diversity, global econom-ics, issues of social justice, information technology, rising educational levels, demographic data such as aging populations, the breakdown of the family, health care restructuring, indifference to politics, women in the workforce, and so on. A careful search for how trends affect an issue usually strengthens an argument and indicates how well advocates understand the challenges and future ahead.

Specific information on an issue. Advocates attempt to assemble facts, tables, charts, statements, cases, examples, precedents, research studies, needs assessments, reports, statistical data, financial reports, survey results, and any other documents that are related to the issue under consideration. Gathering specific information frequently will result in finding more information than one can use, but a careful search often yields informational gems and key data that will allow advocates to present a strong defense of their issue(s). Although conducting one's own surveys or questionnaire will produce specific informa-tion on an issue, there already exists an enormous amount of information avail-able to the public. While the former is usually time-consuming and expensive, the latter is free as long as one is willing to search for it.

Questions: Deciding Which Information to Pursue   Who is affected by the issue? How many persons? What is the profile of a person affected by an issue? What are the consequences of the issue? What are the dimensions of loss? Suffering? How widespread is the problem? What is the economic impact of the issue? What existing resources are known? What barriers are present in addressing the issue? What is the history of this issue? What were the results of previous efforts to resolve the issue? How has anyone success-fully addressed this issue? How do community leaders feel about the issue? How do clients feel about it?

Sources Easily Available to Research an Issue(s)   Among the places to search for facts and documents are the following: government agencies at federal, state, and local levels; research libraries and social science databases; the Internet; national associations and their local affiliates; universities and professors with expertise about the issue; state and local United Way offices; planning departments of cities and counties; U.S. Census Bureau data; law enforcement records, health and human service agency records, court records, and existing surveys conducted by agencies or associations; reports published annually for certain groups; newsletters or minutes of organizations; the local media; international organizations like the United Nations; and so on. While collecting facts, it is very important that advocates *document* and *reference* exactly which sources they used to produce their own reports or remarks. This process adds to the advocate's credibility and assists others who wish to pursue additional information about the issue.

PLAN STRATEGIES AND TACTICS

Effective advocates select appropriate strategies and tactics in order to achieve their goals (Altman et al., 1994; Amidei, 1991; Bobo et al., 1996; Davidson & Rapp, 1976; Flynn, 1989; Hallman, 1987; Kaminski & Walmsley, 1995; Khinduka & Coughlin, 1975; Lurie, 1983; Mayster et al., 1993; Netting et al., 1998; Reisch, 1990; Schlager, 1995; Simons, 1982; Sosin & Caulum, 1983; Taylor, 1987; Tropman et al., 1977; Van Gheluwe & Barber, 1986). After deciding what the issue(s) is and learning what facts are available, advocates must determine how they will achieve what they desire. The group or individual advocate must decide how they intend to persuade others to change their minds, to support or modify a legislative policy, or to alter a community regulation. Eventually, advocates and their groups must agree upon what actions they will take and on how they will carry out the difficult task of getting others to change their behaviors, values, attitudes, or positions.

Most advocates make a distinction between a strategy and a tactic. Netting et al. (1998) describe a *strategy* as the overall plan or general conceptual approach (Sosin & Caulum, 1983) that will be used to pursue a proposed change. Altman et al. (1994) state that a strategy provides advocates with a broad blueprint to achieve their objectives. Kotler (1972) states that a strategy is a basic mode of influence such as education, persuasion, or coercion. Some refer to strategies as the long-range linking of tactical activities needed to achieve a desired goal (Brager & Holloway, 1978). *Tactics* are the nitty-gritty steps taken to carry out the overall strategy (Bobo et al., 1996). Tactics are reflected in day-to-day, short-term activities; they are the specific techniques and behaviors designed to increase the probability that the proposed change will be adopted (Netting et al., 1998). Together, strategies and tactics integrate considerations of *what to do* (goal) with *how to go about it.* The key task, of course, is selecting strategies and tactics that will produce the desired changes.

Strategies

In order to accomplish any goal, individuals or a group must have an overall plan to guide them in deciding what direction or steps to take. Because change is so complex, uncoordinated activities and random, impulsive planning may do little in reaching a desired goal. A group may have a rally one day on the capitol steps, invite the media to cover clients struggling to get services the next week, and spend much of their cash resources on computer systems in the office. If there is no coherent, overall plan guiding these efforts, change is unlikely and valuable energy is lost. To achieve desired changes, advocates must realize that serious time and energy must be given to planning an over-all approach (strategies) as well as the specific activities or tasks (tactics).

Advocacy strategies are based on assumptions about human behavior and beliefs about why persons modify or change their previous positions and reach a new understanding. The psychology of persuasion and changing another's behavior is very complex and beyond the scope of this book, but it is central to the development and selection of strategies.

There have been several attempts to formulate model strategies that will increase the probability that proposed changes can be achieved (Chin & Benne, 1976; Flynn, 1989; Khinduka & Coughlin, 1975; Kotler, 1972; Mayster, et al., 1993; Netting et al., 1998; Simons, 1982; Sosin & Caulum, 1983; Tropman et al., 1977; Warren, 1971). However, there is no definitive consensus about which model is the most effective. *Most often, choosing a strategy depends upon what the opposing forces are like, what resources are available, and to what extent opponents favor a change or not.* Variables are likely to be different in every advocacy situation, and the identification of firm, conclusive, "it-always-works" strategies is very difficult. Nevertheless, the authors believe that choosing a strategy in every attempt to do social work advocacy is imperative and useful.

Because it is crucial to choose a strategy that fits the particular circumstances (Altman et al., 1994), *where does one start?* First, we recommend that advocates analyze the people, issues, and environment in order to determine the nature of the opposition. Who opposes what the advocate desires? Why? How strong is the opposition? Perhaps opponents greatly respect some members of your group or they seem philosophically in accord with your purposes. Some may lack important information, while others are simply indifferent to your cause. Maybe they are half in agreement with you. Perhaps a few are highly politicized or a few are downright hostile. One group may be clearly in disagreement with your aims and resistant to any change you propose.

Advocates must first assess the individuals or groups who may be opposing them in order to decide upon a broad strategy that will ultimately influence these particular persons to change their minds.

The authors, along with others (Kaminski & Walmsley, 1995; Khinduka & Coughlin, 1975; Sosin & Caulum, 1983; Warren, 1971), propose three categories of individuals or groups who may be potential opposing forces. Although these general distinctions are not all-inclusive, they are useful in distinguishing among opponents typically faced by advocates. The *three categories of individuals or groups who may oppose an advocacy effort* are:

1. Individuals or groups who may need more knowledge, who may lack information, who may be uninformed or ignorant about an issue, who may share basic values with the advocates, who probably agree with the advocate on many concerns, or who are usually cooperative on similar issues

2. Individuals or groups who are neutral, indifferent, or apathetic about an issue; who may share only a few sentiments in common with the advocate; who probably disagree more than they agree with the advocate; who have a "show me" attitude; who have little invested in the outcome; or who may have competed with the advocate before

3. Individuals or groups who are clearly in disagreement on the issue(s); who are hostile, unwilling to listen, and nonsupportive; who share little if any common ground or understanding with the advocate; who are unwilling to share power; who are protecting vested interests; or who may be in open conflict with the advocate

After analyzing the opposition, advocates can usually place them in one of these three categories or in combined categories. *It is now, and only now, that advocates should determine the choice of a strategy.* Following are three strategies (Warren, 1971) illustrating broad-based, overall planning directions for advocates. Day-to-day tactics will be decided later. But first, advocates must decide on which strategy will be most effective against the opposition as they now understand them.

Collaborative Strategies   These strategies of influence are most likely to succeed with opponents in category 1 above. The level of opposition is diffused and not highly intense, parity in power may exist, and there are common bonds between the advocate and the opponent. Advocates seek to share information and educate the opponent with rational or empirical data. Communication between the two groups is open and candid. Problem solving is undertaken jointly and tasks shared equitably. Committees or task forces can be formed for mutually beneficial purposes. In a spirit of collaboration, the advocate and the opponent usually compromise and negotiate solutions to major differences. After a period of joint effort, an accommodation acceptable to both sides is usually reached.

Campaign Strategies   These strategies are used effectively with opponents in category 2 above. The level of opposition reflects greater disagreements, less shared values, differences in attitudes, and distant, cooler relationships. Advocates can appeal to the natural interests of the opposition and demonstrate that proposed changes will serve these interests well. Campaign strategies rely on persuading and convincing the opposition through appeals to logic, emotion, and self-interest. This strategy tries to modify attitudes and values less than to evoke already existing ones held by the opposition. Advocates point out how the change will only enhance those closely held beliefs. A campaign strategy relies on education, but not a strictly rational and empirical one. Advocates frequently negotiate, bargain, and use political maneuvering to influence this level of opposition.

Contest Strategies   These strategies are effective with opponents in category 3 above. The level of opposition is clearly very high, nonsupportive, with little if any common connections, and frequently demonstrating hostility. Advocates hope to change behaviors, not beliefs or values. They will apply pressure from political or grassroots sources, rely on public confrontation with the opposition's stance, force compliance with existing laws, and exert partisan power. At times, advocates become noncooperative, initiate harassment, use boycotts or sanctions, violate normative behavior, or violate legal norms. Some contest strategies contain risks for the social worker and clients, and there must be informed agreement between the advocates and clients before pursuing such high-risk strategies. At no time do the authors recommend behavior that is contrary to the NASW *Code of Ethics.*

At this point, social work advocates have now analyzed the opposition and matched them with a strategic category. There will never be a perfect matchup, but the selection of a strategy provides much of the overall approach required to influence this or that particular opponent.

Focus of Strategies   Before describing some of the tactics available to advocates, there is one other model of setting strategies that should be considered. Netting et al. (1998) recommend selecting a strategy based on five approaches to change that focus on the following: policy, program, project, personnel, and/or practice. Netting et al. propose that advocates, after analysis of all of the participants, their openness to change, and with knowledge of available resources, select a change strategy with a specific focus.

Policy. Advocates can try to change or influence the *policies* of a government, agency, or association in order to produce the desired outcome. Existing policies may be too restrictive and need to be modified. A new policy may be needed to address recent circumstances. Because policies represent the formal guidelines used by decision makers to implement action and use resources, a shift in policy may be the best strategy to use to produce a desired change. A state policy that caps the number of persons with AIDS who can be treated with protease inhibitors may be the target of a policy change strategy.

Program. Advocates often try to change *programs* sponsored by service providers because the program is poorly administered, insensitive to client needs, wastes resources, is inaccessible to certain clients, or fails to achieve its stated goals. A new program is often proposed to meet changing conditions. Advocates may decide to intervene at the program level because the policy of the agency is acceptable, but programmatic issues need attention. Employment programs for low-income persons may be jeopardized if there is no transportation to suburban-located jobs.

Project. Advocates suggest that a *time-limited effort or project* be implemented to address a client problem rather than create a large-scale program that may be expensive or controversial or both. Because a project is more flexible and experimental, adjustments can be monitored and changes reviewed before additional resources are committed to it. The project serves as a pilot or trial effort that may lead to a more favorable outcome. Some agencies have established a community-based teenage pregnancy prevention project for a one year period.

Personnel. Advocates may conclude that a change in *personnel* is needed in order to produce a desired outcome. Some employees are conflict-prone, poorly organized, lack training, or are deficient in some key skill, and it would seem to improve the program or project by removing them. Social work advocates should be very careful about getting involved in deposing an unpopular administrator because of the risks to themselves, clients, and colleagues. Hiring a grant writer to assist the program director may improve the agency's ability to procure funding.

Practice. Advocates often want to change the way an agency does business. *Practices* are not policies; they are procedures and regulations that usually are about service delivery or interactions with clients. Perhaps clients must wait in a stark, forbidding room for hours. Maybe the agency car is unavailable to the worker on a regular basis. Changes to these practices are important and often are accomplished by calling attention to them in staff meetings or supervisory sessions.

Advocates can incorporate Netting et al.'s (1998) strategic approach above and integrate it with their judgments and choices about collaborative, campaign, or contest strategies described earlier. Now let us examine tactics.

Tactics

Tactics are the actual steps taken to carry out an overall strategy (Bobo et al., 1996). Tactics are day-to-day behaviors and refer to particular tools, techniques, and responses designed to increase the probability that a proposed change will be adopted (Netting et al., 1998). Certain tactics are more useful for collaboration than for contesting. While a good tactic will often make a demand on the power structure, it remains within the experience and comfort level of the group (Bobo et al., 1996). Advocates can create their own tactics and modify others as long as they contribute to achieving the agreed-upon strategy.

The authors have divided the tactics described in the following text into three broad categories that correspond with the three strategies described earlier. Each category highlights specific actions ranging from cooperative to increasingly competitive (see Figure 4.1). Advocates are free to choose among them. However, it is advised to use only those tactics that directly support the strategy chosen and to follow the principle of parsimony, that is, use the most modest or least confrontive tactic that will accomplish the job. Using more coercive or powerful tactics than necessary requires more energy, may satisfy only the psychic needs of the advocate, and often makes one appear unreasonable or irresponsible.

Tactics Supportive of Collaboration Strategies *Conduct research and study the issue.* Advocates can review existing research data, professional literature, community studies, and local, state, and national statistics and to share these data with the opposition, thus strengthening a mutual bond. If resources permit, doing applied research on the conditions or problems at hand is also very useful. Data can be gathered on public opinion by using focus groups. Complaints about services can be documented and evidence of benefits can be demonstrated with data.

Develop fact sheets and alternative proposals. In order to educate the opposition quickly, advocates can assemble fact sheets about the issue and about their group. A one-page fact sheet with all pertinent data and evidence clearly organized is an effective tool to distribute during meetings, rallies, and hearings. Preparing alternative proposals and solutions to problems in the form of a position paper also promotes understanding and creative thinking. With a clearly constructed solution written out in a persuasive manner, advocates usually gain the respect of the opposition and encourage deeper discussion of the issue.

Create task forces or subcommittees. Advocates can suggest forming a task force or subcommittee between their members and those from the opposition. The purpose of these small groups is to focus on working together in order to solve problems or clarify issues. The spirit among the members is intended to be collaborative, not competitive.

Conduct workshops. Advocates can be effective through the use of workshops. The advantages of a workshop (Pearl & Barr, 1976) are: (1) it brings together people from a variety of constituencies to consider a particular problem; (2) when covered by the media, it heightens community awareness of the issue; and (3) it may become the starting point for a group to take action. A workshop

Strategy   **Tactics**

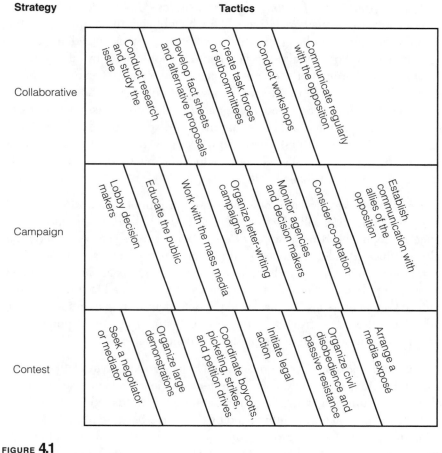

Conduct research and study the issue

Collaborative

Campaign

Contest

FIGURE 4.1

Specific tactics that can be used within the three categories of strategies.

may be the first step in addressing an issue, and with proper planning, it can go beyond being a one-time event. Careful preparation of an agenda, speakers, location, announcements, and arrangements for the meeting is essential.

Communicate regularly with the opposition. In order to increase collaboration and head off confrontation, it is useful to establish consistent channels of communication with opposition groups and leaders. Written correspondence and e-mail networks are examples that can be used to inform opposition leaders about the activities of the advocacy group. A quarterly or semiannually scheduled meeting with the head of a department is useful in keeping communication lines open. Information from these sources also gives the advocate ideas about the opposition's positions and helps in planning strategies and tactics.

Tactics Supportive of Campaign Strategies *Lobby decision makers.*
Advocates try to persuade decision makers by lobbying them into supporting
a proposed change. Lobbying can be described as a "special pleading" according to Richan (1996). The most direct method of lobbying is by talking in person or in a small group to the decision makers or their staff. Personal visits and
phone calls are essential to effective lobbying. Lobbying is also an exchange:
the advocate wants action and help, and the decision maker wants to be
reelected or reappointed or knows that the lobbyist has useful information to
pass on. Netting et al. (1998) advise lobbyists to always be factual and honest,
straightforward and data-based, and include estimates of costs and social
impacts of a proposed change.

Educate the public. Advocates must often establish public support for an issue
before the opposition will take them seriously. Using the data and information
collected about the issue, a series of educational events can be planned that
will introduce a wider audience to the importance of an issue. Community
conferences can be sponsored; group members can speak at churches, associations, and public hearings; and teach-ins can be organized to inform participants of the major issues. Media participation is helpful at generating publicity
and shows others the strength of the group. Testimony given at public hearings provides information to the public and policy makers.

Work with the mass media. There are many sources of media available to advocates: television, radio, newspapers, letters to the editor, talk shows, press
releases, the Internet, magazines, newsletters, billboards, and news conferences. Decision makers are influenced by the media because of their desire to
maintain a positive public profile; consequently, they strive to listen to public
opinion. It is crucial for advocates to learn what is considered "newsworthy" by
local media reporters and editors. Likewise, it is very helpful to know reporters
personally who cover the group's issues. It is wise to send news releases to
them on a regular basis and to be willing to serve as an expert reference on
various topics. People love to see themselves on television and in print; such
exposure often promotes motivation and strength to a group's members.

Organize letter-writing campaigns. Most elected officials or their staff actually read and answer letters they receive. Individual, handwritten letters are
most effective rather than a form or a preprinted letter. Personal explanations
about an issue can be very powerful in a letter because the content is heartfelt
and based on an individual's experience. It takes fewer letters than one imag-
ines to have an impact on the decision maker. It is said that 10 personal letters
on the same issue constitutes an avalanche of support that cannot be ignored.
If advocates organize a letter-writing group, the group should be able to
respond within a few days. If an important meeting is planned with a significant decision maker, be sure to have as many letters arrive as possible *before*

the meeting. It is also a good idea to write complimentary letters and letters of appreciation when they are earned.

Monitor agencies and decision makers. Advocates make their presence felt by assuming the role of watchdog. Members can attend most meetings, hearings, and public events and keep track of how issues are faring. The mere presence of a monitor reminds office holders and decision makers that they are accountable to someone for the actions they take or fail to take. Many public meetings are on television, and their minutes are usually public record, available to any citizen for the asking. The Freedom of Information Act also permits access to nearly all public documents and legislation. The Internet contains tremendous resources about issues, government agencies, policies, late-breaking news, and specialized information. "Consumer audit groups" is another name for groups that perform this function.

Consider co-optation. Advocates who wish to minimize conflict often try to invite a prominent member of the opposition to participate in problem-solving meetings and help make decisions about new proposals. As Netting et al. (1998) state, once someone takes part in planning a change, that person begins to feel ownership for it. It is also a good idea for advocates to try to participate in the opposition's decision making by volunteering or "getting invited" to attend meetings. This process usually avoids public disagreement and controversy because issues can be explored quietly and potential solutions proposed without the glare of a public spotlight.

Establish communication with allies of the opposition. Advocates can establish alliances or linkages with traditional allies of the opposition and gain greater access to resources and expert insight. Such alliances also tend to strengthen the advocate's position vis-à-vis the opposition because traditional allies will not want to offend each other by causing harm to one of their other friends. If a central city opposes a program to assist the homeless, engaging the help of key business leaders or companies may be effective.

Tactics Supportive of Contest Strategies   *Seek a negotiator or mediator.* When advocates believe that there is great alienation between the opposition and themselves with little likelihood of productive outcomes, it may be useful to seek out a mediator or negotiator who can assist both sides in reaching an agreement. These individuals arrange meetings and begin to negotiate with both sides about the status of the issues and possible solutions. This tactic demonstrates a willingness to be reasonable and a commitment to resolving conflict.

Organize large demonstrations. In order to gain broad, public exposure and support for an issue, advocates organize mass demonstrations, rallies, marches, street theater, or assemblies that may include hundreds of persons. Peaceful demonstrations are legal, but there are usually permits needed to hold them, so it is important to be sure legal requirements are met. Demonstrations require a considerable amount of work and organization, but if the event is successful, the advocacy group's reputation will be enhanced for a long time. The target of the demonstration should be a specific, not a global or utopian issue. An added benefit from demonstrations is an increase in solidarity and commitment of the group's members. Banners, brightly colored buttons, flyers, placards, posters, songs, slogans, and speakers are needed. Inviting the media is imperative. It is also important to have a plan of action ready after the demonstration.

Coordinate boycotts, picketing, strikes, and petition drives. Advocates sometimes reach an impasse with the opposition and the level of conflict rises. Nonviolent confrontation is an option that is used to highlight the differences between the opposing groups. Boycotts depend upon large numbers of persons refusing to use a service or a product in order to get the attention of the provider. Picketing requires committed individuals to spend many hours carrying placards and posters in front of a targeted agency. Strikes demand that employees walk off the job in unison in order to protest policies or conditions unacceptable to them or their clients. Petition drives require the collection of thousands of names to be attached to a letter to the opposition. These tactics increase broad public awareness of a group and its issue, especially if the media provides coverage.

Initiate legal action. Legal action is usually a last resort after advocates have determined that the opposition will never negotiate or search for an acceptable solution. Class-action lawsuits apply to an entire group of people such as the homeless, victims of domestic violence, or incompetent wards. Filing a formal complaint or grievance may be done to address injustice or unresponsiveness on the part of agencies. Legal action is usually expensive, and it requires an attorney and complainants who are willing to speak out publicly. These actions put the issue on the public record, and even the mere threat of legal action may lead to a settlement. If successful, these cases can set precedent for future issues.

Organize civil disobedience and passive resistance. Civil disobedience and passive resistance are also acts of last resort. While they may frighten people and make recruiting difficult, these tactics are not ends in themselves but ways of moving an issue forward. After careful consideration of the situation and the group's constituency, advocates may decide to refuse to comply with laws, regulations, or policies that they believe are unjust. Mahatma Gandhi and Martin Luther King, Jr. are the great teachers of this tactic. Participants must be aware that they may be arrested and jailed, that the public will perceive them negatively, that resources may be used up in legal actions, that it may require a long period before there is any impact, and that there is a possibility of failure. However, this option may be necessary when informal and legitimate efforts to produce change have completely stalemated. Social work advocates also believe that physical violence and terrorism cannot be condoned in professional interventions in a civilized society (Netting et al., 1998).

Arrange a media exposé. When the opposition hardens its stand, it may be necessary to embarrass them by arranging for the media to provide coverage of improper conduct, mismanagement, and improprieties. This is a tactic of last resort and has several perils in it. If there is anything inaccurate in such allegations, the advocates may find themselves in court being sued for libel or slander. It is not certain that such exposes will soften the opposition for change. The opposition will most certainly investigate the advocacy group, which should be sure that it can survive an energetic hunt for controversy. The main issue may also get lost in this scuffle. However, this tactic is a quick way to get public attention and secure the interest of the media.

Summary of Tactics Used by the Opposition   Altman et al. (1994) warn that opponents resist calls for reform and change, and advocates should never underrate them. To increase an advocacy group's effectiveness, the authors identify the following typical responses given by opponents in order to obstruct and block actions.

Deflect. When criticized, it is natural to sidestep the attack and try to shift the focus of attention elsewhere. Opponents often try to "pass the buck" to persons with little or no authority in order to frustrate the advocate's efforts.

Delay. Opponents often postpone addressing an issue and hope to remove it from the public eye. "Study commissions" are used regularly for this purpose.

Deny. Often opponents will deny the validity of an advocate's claim or approach to a solution. The decision makers are "unavailable" for meetings or say, "My hands are tied, even though I would like to help you."

Discount. Opponents frequently minimize the importance of an issue by downplaying it and questioning the legitimacy of the advocacy group, even resorting to labeling such groups as extremist, radical, socialist, and so on.

Deceive. Clever deceptions to confuse, distract, knock off balance, or mislead advocates are used by the opposition when they wish to appear sympathetic, but have no intention of engaging in a meaningful dialogue.

Divide. Opponents try to divide the unity of an advocacy group by planting dissension, offering insignificant concessions, pitting moderate members against more aggressive ones, offering rewards for leaders, and causing general discord whenever possible.

Dulcify. Opponents often try to mollify or pacify their adversaries by giving short-term benefits, services, jobs, or other concrete resources to ward off harsh criticism and prevent long-term solutions from being considered.

Discredit. Advocates may be described as agitators, radicals, or unrepresentative of the community in public hearings or in the media. Opponents will try to cast doubt on the motives, methods, and values of the advocacy group.

Destroy. If the stakes are high enough, opponents may try to eliminate the advocacy group by threatening lawsuits, using discovery procedures prior to formal proceedings, deposing group members, and posing economic threats, job losses, evictions, or curtailment of credit to clients and group members.

Deal. Opponents may want to avoid conflict and offer to strike a deal with the advocacy group. If both sides collaborate and work harmoniously, mutual understanding and improved decisions usually emerge. Be careful of compromising your original goals.

Surrender. Rarely do opponents simply give in and give the advocacy group everything they requested. If it happens, advocates are warned to be sure that promises are followed up and the actual terms are implemented. Get it in writing.

Supply Leadership

Effective advocacy requires leadership (Altman et al., 1994; Amidei, 1982; Bobo et al., 1996; Mayster et al., 1993; Moxley & Freddolino, 1990; Reisch, 1986, 1990; Roberts-DeGennaro, 1986b; Tefft, 1987). Leadership is defined differently depending upon whom one speaks with. There are countless books on the subject of leadership and decades-long research on attempts to discover what actually constitutes effective leadership. This section does not resolve these issues. Rather, the authors attempt to define leadership in basic terms, describe leadership in advocacy situations, and make recommendations about learning how to become an effective leader.

According to *Webster's New World College Dictionary* (1996), *leadership* is the "ability to lead . . . to be a leader, to be a person who directs, organizes, or guides a group or activity." Social work advocates demonstrate leadership when they organize task groups to seek more funding for community mental health services. Advocates act as leaders when they form a coalition to persuade the city council to allocate revenue-sharing funds for services instead of buildings. Persons who can plan and run a meeting of concerned citizens or clients are acting as leaders. Leadership is frequently associated with initiative and a willingness to speak up and ask questions. Testimony before a legislative committee or a juvenile court advisory board constitutes leadership activity. Moxley and Freddolino (1990) refer to leadership in terms of "engagement," that is, a proactive, reaching-out linkage with clients instead of passively waiting for the client to report a need or violation of rights.

Leadership often flows from the first person to articulate a vision about what needs to be done or how desperate clients have become without certain services. A leader might also emerge from a group *after* a discussion and preliminary investigation of a community crisis. Leadership may also be shared among members of a group. It might also be left to the initiative of *any* member of the group depending on the issue, need for expertise, linkages to other groups or leaders, and comfort level of the person (Altman et al., 1994).

A social worker who speaks up at staff meetings about agency policies that affect clients negatively is leading. Administrators may lead collective responses among agencies to community concerns. Mayster et al. (1993) reported that an advocacy task force helped organize a broad community coalition to oppose a takeover of a hospital by a for-profit corporation that was unwilling to ensure continuing access for publicly insured or uninsured patients. While these examples introduce the reader to a few illustrations of leadership, there is an infinite number of examples of social work advocates serving as leaders.

Steps to Providing Leadership

The following principles reflect several basic steps to providing leadership, summarizing for readers specific skills and knowledge to be learned.

Be able to articulate a vision. Guiding a group requires a focus and a capacity to motivate that encourages participants to commit time and energy needed to achieve a desired change. Successful leaders are able to prevent groups from wandering from issue to issue and to outline a vision of what the group can accomplish. This vision is usually found in the basic rationale for the existence of the group. Why are people gathering together? What do they share in common?

A vision statement usually contains the following: (1) an ideal state ("women free from abuse"); (2) conditions that should be changed ("victims' failure to report abuse"); (3) remedy to a shared problem ("police, not abused women, must initiate charges"); (4) personal responsibility ("it could be our sister"); and (5) hope and the possibility of success ("Delegate Hall would support a bill") (Altman et al., 1994). A vision statement becomes an excellent tool for reminding and motivating participants to cooperate and search for ways to continue to plan and pursue their desired goals.

Remember that all leaders require followers. Leaders must pay attention to the concerns of the members of a group advocacy effort. Social work advocacy includes the concept of mutuality. If a person is a leader, but no one is following her or him, is the person truly leading? The answer is usually "no." A leader must pay attention to the fine line between pushing members to advance and take risks and letting mutual-based opinions rule the group. Certainly, leaders must express their point of view as persuasively as possible, but they must also recognize when the other participants do not agree with the content of the leader's opinion. If the members are not "on board" after hearing from the leader, there is little likelihood they will support a proposal even if it is passed in order to please the leader. Mutuality, compromise, and keen listening to the members' advice and opinion will enable the leader to continue to progress toward the desired vision.

Balance task and maintenance leadership skills. In the life of any group, it is important to "keep people happy" and to "get the job done." Effective leaders are aware of this dual role and consciously plan steps to promote both goals. On the one hand, *task-oriented activities* include: preparing a meeting agenda; guiding discussions with time limits; using Robert's Rules of Order to run a meeting; recording minutes of meetings; posing key questions and delaying discussions on other ones; starting and finishing on time; proposing alternative plans; summarizing information and clarifying discussions; passing out key information before discussions; organizing subcommittees; and so on. On the other hand, *maintenance activities* include: welcoming and introducing members; actively listening to people's ideas and advice; assuring everyone they can participate; seeking out shy and quiet people and asking them for an opinion; giving positive feedback to speakers; thanking people for their contributions; recognizing successful efforts and contributions; providing food or drink at meetings; making sure rooms are clean and suitable for conversation; and planning small victories for boosting participants' morale.

Be active and assertive. Leadership is not necessarily loud and noisy, but it is not usually associated with being a wallflower either. Taking a small risk by offering a perspective or proposal should not be viewed as a serious threat to one's well-being. People who are courteous and respectful may fear being considered aggressive and pushy. However, as advocates watch others dominate or control the discussion, ignoring key information, or manipulating the agenda, it should become clear that unless advocates participate actively, they will play only a marginal role in guiding the direction of the effort.

In studying group behavior, one frequently finds that persons who assert opinions early in a conversation receive more serious consideration and acceptance than if they had waited until late in the discussion. As leaders, we do not wish to dominate the conversation; rather, we want to encourage others to participate freely. Nevertheless, if questions arise during debate or planning, leaders can usually help the group advance if they actively insert an opinion or clarification. If the comment is off base, the group will ultimately ignore it anyway.

GET TO KNOW DECISION MAKERS AND THEIR STAFF

Effective advocates cultivate relationships with and get to know decision makers and their staff members (Amidei, 1991; Berger, 1977; Bobo et al., 1996; Dluhy, 1981; Kleinkauf, 1988; Lurie, 1983; Mayster et al., 1993; Ross, 1992). Since decision makers usually have formal responsibility for allowing or disallowing proposals from advocacy groups or individuals, communication with these power holders is very important. By establishing a dialogue, advocates improve access to decision makers and learn what needs they have and what information is important to them. This effort requires considerable time, but it is usually time well spent.

In getting acquainted with decision makers, it is important to know background information about them such as political affiliations, community or civic associations to which they belong, causes they favor, colleagues and close associates, educational background, voting records if they hold public office, issues close to their heart, family members with any particular qualities or issues they may have such as a handicap or an illnesses, personal achievements, occupation, and so on. This knowledge often leads an advocate to identify issues or strategies that a particular decision maker would be effective in promoting and also makes casual conversation easier. It is wise to establish contact with decision makers who are opponents. Such contact allows resolution of disagreements before they become public, prevents misunderstandings, allows one's group to learn what the opposing issues are, and reduces tension.

Advocates believe that it is equally important to know the staff members of decision makers because they may well be more influential than their bosses. Staff members often control access to decision-makers, dictating who may speak or meet with them. Because the decision makers are frequently pressured by heavy demands and circumstances beyond their control, they simply do not have the time to study and understand fully what an issue is all about. Instead, they rely on their staff and aides to become knowledgeable about the issue and to advise them on an appropriate position to take or how to vote. Staff attend hearings, draft proposals and report to the boss, and will always protect their boss's interests.

Advocates are advised to consider contact with a staff member as equal to contact with the decision maker in most cases. Normally, it is not inordinately difficult to get to know a decision maker and his or her staff. Once advocates have decided on establishing contact, a phone call or letter asking for an appointment usually suffices. Other methods are also effective such as introducing oneself before or after meetings, inviting a decision maker to lunch, asking someone to give a speech to a group, volunteering to help out with a project sponsored by the decision maker, having a friend or colleague introduce you, and so on. Assertive behavior is called for, and it usually works.

Once advocates have established contact with a decision maker, they must decide how to make their position on an issue clear. Dhuly (1981) recommends two strategies: (1) analyze the person's decision-making style, and (2) find out what the informational needs of the decision maker are.

There are three typical decision-making styles used by persons who are responsible for deciding outcomes among proposals:

1. *Rational/deliberative.* This individual values highly information that has been collected, analyzed, and interpreted using specific methods and analytical procedures. This approach is as scientific as possible, using facts, research data and findings, and technical interpretations.

2. *Pragmatic/incremental.* This individual values getting things done, moving ahead, and keeping the momentum alive. Scientific data do not drive this person's decision making as much as political and personal preferences. If the data is not perfect, an adjustment can be made as long as something is getting done.
3. *Emotional/ideological.* This individual clearly is committed to action. It is not necessary to wait for the next research study. If there are compelling problems, this decision maker will try to be persuasive and convincing based on values and emotional bases. Data and study are secondary to making a convincing argument.

Social work advocates can analyze decision makers and classify them into one of these three styles or a combination of them. This requires learning about the decision maker through observation, reputation, and experience.

Once advocates have determined the decision-making style, they can provide appropriate types of information to the individual. Here are the basic characteristics of the information to be passed on to each style:

1. *Rational/deliberative.* Documents that are concise, based clearly on scientific methodology, and carefully researched, analyzed, and interpreted. This would include charts, tables, statistical summaries, fact sheets, research findings, and results of analyses or surveys.
2. *Pragmatic/incremental.* Available data, even if not fully valid, are acceptable; instructive documents on how to get something done; and documents highlighting the political context of the issue are deemed most important here. Included here would be strategic plans, political analyses, environmental scans, evaluations of the opposition, tactics needed to achieve the goals, poll data, and identification of key players and power sources.
3. *Emotional/ideological.* Documents with persuasive, convincing arguments are highly sought after; action-oriented recommendations or options are preferred; and data and feasibility are clearly secondary. Advocates would include here personal testimonies, written vignettes highlighting an issue, audiovisual resources, examples of previous efforts to succeed, copies of speeches with emotional content, and colorful stories about special people or events.

Finally, advocates must be good at saying "thank you" as well as "please." Decision makers receive hundreds of requests, and when a proposal is passed or acted upon, advocates must not forget to acknowledge the importance of their support. It also reinforces the notion that while advocates are watching an issue carefully, they are also very appreciative of assistance.

BROADEN THE BASE OF SUPPORT

Effective advocates usually participate in coalition building and ally with others who share common values and goals (Altman et al., 1994; Amidei, 1982; Bobo et al., 1996; Bridgman, 1992; Dluhy, 1981; Gormley, 1981; Hallman, 1987; Haynes & Mickelson, 1997; Pearl & Barr, 1976; Reisch, 1990; Ross, 1992; Schlager, 1995; Tefft, 1987; Tourigney et al., 1993; Tropman et al., 1977). Schlager (1995) points out that a single-issue group is almost never powerful enough to achieve its desired goals. The limitations of being a soloist are: insufficient staffing and analytical resources; limitations in addressing issues from different angles; competition among diverse groups for media attention; and appearing as the only voice on an issue. Often, the best way for advocates to make their voices heard is to unite with others who have similar concerns.

Bobo et al. (1996) define a coalition as "an organization of organizations working together for a common goal" (p. 70). Most coalitions are formed to build up the power needed to do something that one organization cannot do by itself. There are a variety of coalitions: ad hoc or temporary, permanent, limited to certain constituencies like women's issues or child abuse, geographically defined like the Midwest Coalition for Incest Survivors, single- or multi-issue, and loosely connected or federated.

Although we typically refer to coalition building in community or legislative settings, the authors also affirm its usefulness in advocating for clients and in one-to-one situations. An advocate will often seek support among colleagues on an issue before a biweekly staff meeting where it will be discussed. The same dynamics apply in smaller settings.

Advantages of a Coalition

What are the advantages to belonging to a coalition? In fact, coalitions will help in the following ways.

Maximize the number of organizations and people involved in an issue. A coalition consolidates the concerns of specific groups and multiplies their effectiveness in making social change. Large numbers will bring optimal forces to bear on the opposition.

Avoid circumstances where similar agencies make contradictory statements before decision makers. Nothing will undercut the efficacy of an advocacy effort more quickly than having groups disagree publicly on the causes, effects, scope, costs, or solutions to a problem.

Represent more than one aspect or angle of an issue. If a variety of agencies and experts form a coalition, deeper insight into the issue usually is gained. Knowledge of laws and regulations, how the legislature works, what the impact on practitioners and clients is, and how technical resources can assist are a few examples of the benefits. This broadened perspective may even open up state or national issues that make the work more meaningful and exciting.

Share the workload of collecting and analyzing data or legislation about an issue. Responding to demands for information or correcting misinformation is beyond the resources of most small groups. Tracking several issues simultaneously can be done if more people are participating. A division of labor can produce all-important analyses and data needed to convince skeptical decision makers.

Coordinate grassroots activities rather than relying on a helter-skelter approach. A coalition is able to harness and focus the energy of constituents. With access to high levels of "person-power," it is important to use this resource effectively, concentrating its energy on particular actions.

Expand limited resources in pursuit of a common goal. Resources such as staff time, supplies, meeting space, transportation, full- or part-time salaries for coalition staff, communication costs, postage, and cash outlays can be consolidated for greater impact.

Increase the visibility and respectability of the issue and the individual advocacy group. A coalition can clarify the rationale and value base to the larger public and, by so doing, enhance its credibility. Coalitions also represent a powerful image to the community. An individual agency can be perceived as a leader in the community and its reputation for cooperation is improved.

Build an ongoing power base. Because human service advocacy groups usually collaborate with relatively vulnerable persons or associations, such individual organizations have little capacity for exerting political influence. A coalition provides an enduring voice and requisite resources needed to sustain change overtime.

Make individual organizations feel safer advocating as part of a large group. "Safety in numbers" frequently permits individuals or groups to take a stand on an issue they might remain silent on if they were alone. Agency boards must be informed and approve of coalition stances before staff move ahead. From time to time, an agency may also want to be more confrontational or assume a different position than the coalition.

Disadvantages of a Coalition

What are the disadvantages of being a member of a coalition? Coalitions can be hindrances in the following ways.

Most organizations only commit a minimal amount of resources to interorganizational collaboration (Roberts-DeGennaro, 1986b). An agency calculates the overall cost to itself for being a member of a coalition, and if the payoff or benefit is uneconomic (i.e., very small), the agency will not be very active. Calculating staff time or workload constraints often leads to decisions that affect the amount of effort that will be allocated to the coalition.

If the coalition's issue(s) is not your agency's main issue, it can divert your time and energy. When the advocate's original reason for joining the coalition is subverted or ignored, there is no pragmatic reason to remain active.

Sometimes weak members of the coalition cannot deliver on their commitments, which leads to frustration on the part of other members. If the range of resources, power, and personnel among member agencies is too unequal, this creates internal problems such as resentment, decision-making power going to the "wealthiest" agency, poor performance, and diversion from the issue(s).

The greater the diversity among the cooperating agencies, the more possible the coalition could be splintered. If a crucial issue or change opportunity arises and divides the coalition, it will not be able to present a unified front and affect the decisions made about the issue. Too many compromises might be demanded or members might refuse to support a certain position. Most decision makers dismiss groups who cannot agree among themselves.

Making a Coalition More Effective

If it is advantageous for an advocate to join or form a broad-based coalition, what else can be done to ensure the emergence of a sound coalition? First, member organizations must *believe* that by acting collectively to change policies or conditions, they will each be better off. There should be a positive payoff for the amount of energy expended by each of the organizations.

Second, a moral concern for the plight of others is often the primary motivating factor, such as "speaking on behalf of those who cannot speak for themselves." Members of the coalition usually share beliefs in certain global values and altruistic community service.

Third, effectiveness is significantly related to the availability of resources such as staff time, background research, capacity for communication, leadership, outside funding, volunteers, and so on. Hope for future resources or materials is also a key factor.

Fourth, successful coalitions are able to enlist the support and endorsement of other organizations and individuals, broadening the awareness and understanding of the issue. Celebrity figures, community leaders, key institutions, business leaders, and churches are engaged for their support and ability to communicate to wider audiences.

Fifth, coalitions also use the public media to increase public awareness and create pressure. Journalists, newspaper columnists, and television and radio reporters are frequently able to bring attention to a coalition's issue. Advocates distribute news releases and factual information to them regularly.

Sixth, member organizations of effective coalitions are kept as informed about current issues as possible. Coalitions employ methods for frequently monitoring and reporting on events in order to maintain the interest of their members. E-mail networks serve this function well.

Seventh, coalitions often combine advocates who work *inside the system* with independent advocates outside of the system. Together they collaborate on achieving solutions to problems and issues. Government employees often assist coalitions by providing information, technical assistance, and political advice.

Eighth, a successful coalition has strong leadership usually consisting of a small, inner circle of leaders who manage the affairs of the coalition. Participation levels among members may be low due to limited resources, time, and varied levels of commitment. Without consistent and effective leadership, however, most coalitions fall apart.

Finally, there is a cohesion among members of effective coalitions that reflects unity of purpose and approach. No divisions or divisiveness are aired in public forums or before decision makers. Members gain strength knowing they are not alone.

BE PERSISTENT

I feel that I have started something here that I will continue to be involved with for a long time. I feel that I am making a difference that cannot be compared to writing out a donation check. I look forward to seeing the women at the shelter and talking with them about their concerns. Through this advocacy adventure, I not only feel that I've made a difference, I can see it every time I walk through the shelter doors.

—MIRA

One quality separates effective advocates from others: *persistence* (Amidei, 1991; Berger, 1977; Gormley, 1981; Hallman, 1987; Herbert & Mould, 1992; Reisch, 1986, 1990; Ross, 1992; Tefft, 1987; Van Gheluwe & Barber, 1986; Yep, 1992). Whether trying to influence one's supervisor, an agency administrator, city hall, the state legislature, the school board, Main Street, Congress, or professional associations, advocates must decide to persevere in their efforts. External conditions such as recessions, tax cuts, political battles, personality feuds, and short-term crises often interfere with the fate of an advocate's proposed change, sometimes leaving him or her with little control over the situation. The choice becomes: to give up or to go on.

Failure to persist in advocating for a cause or client often results in the loss of long-term gains or benefits. Short-term pain may produce shortsightedness unless advocates know that persistence is a fundamental virtue of success. Success on behalf of one client often improves the lives of many other clients in similar situations. Initial setbacks in introducing legislation or proposals to administrators/supervisors are discouraging. But, there are countless examples of successful advocacy after, *and only after,* three, five, seven, or more years of repeated attempts to change a policy or law.

In the 1980s, a bill on expanded Medicaid coverage in Mississippi was passed, and advocates thought the war was over. Soon it was learned that severe budget shortages would delay implementation of the bill for the next two years. By working with legislators and offering compromise alternatives, advocates secured funding for a similar program that began one year later (Van Gheluwe & Barber, 1986). In the 1970s, it took a citizen's coalition seven years of perseverance to force Nestle's multinational corporation to change the way it advertised and distributed baby formula in developing countries (Hallman, 1987).

Yep (1992) urges advocates not to lose hope even if the first effort fails. He suggests that raising the public's awareness about an issue should be seen as a victory. If the governor does not sign the bill a group supported, advocates should begin working with legislators on the bill for the next session. If a supervisor rejects a proposal submitted on behalf of a client, an advocate can rethink the strategy and determine how to present another proposal the next month. Reisch (1986, 1990) documents that continuity of effort is a significant contributing factor to effective advocacy. Amidei (1991) compares advocates to marathon runners, the types who pace themselves and never give up. Tefft (1987) also believes that "small wins" is an important strategy and holds great promise for promoting organizational endurance so critical to achieving permanent change.

EVALUATE YOUR ADVOCACY EFFORT

Effective social work advocacy includes regular evaluations of the usefulness and accomplishments of an advocacy effort (Altman et al., 1994; Bersani, 1996; Bridgman, 1992; Davidson & Rapp, 1976; Moxley & Freddolino, 1994; Olley & Ogloff, 1995; Pearlman & Edwards, 1982; Taylor, 1987; Tefft, 1987). Chief among the reasons for assessing an advocacy program are to determine what has been accomplished and how well the advocacy process has worked. Are there indicators of success? Did advocates actually do what they said they would do? Can advocates learn anything from their efforts? Did individuals in the effort get along well or were there factions and dissatisfaction? Were clients satisfied? Answers to these and similar questions form the rationale for explicit evaluations of advocacy activities.

Reasons for Evaluation

First, let us examine in more detail why conducting evaluative studies of social work advocacy is important.

Evaluation provides accountability. Without systematic and careful study, it is difficult to provide accurate data to funding sources supporting advocacy programs and policies. Feedback from structured evaluations, complete with randomly selected control and comparison groups, will provide conclusions important to those who examine what happens to dollars earmarked for advocacy.

Evaluation provides perspective on the managerial effectiveness of the organization. Insights into the processes of managing an advocacy program can lead to improvements and efficiencies of services. The planning process often experiences delays, uncertainty about tasks, disruptive individuals, or inequitable workload problems. Through evaluation, boards of directors and administrative staff can assess the quality and quantity of the advocacy effort and make needed changes.

Evaluation enables the staff to review past efforts in order to plan for the future. Findings may be used by administrators to develop staffing plans, new goals, or different directions for the coming year. Such an assessment will assist the agency in making projections about the use of resources like vehicles, volunteers, part- or full-time staff, and cash or in-kind contributions.

Evaluation results are frequently shared with funding sources. Such data are used to justify renewal of funding and to account for expenditures of past funding allocations. Evaluative capability is also perceived positively by funding sources in applications for new funds.

Evaluative information can be used effectively for testimony at various forums. Indicators of success can be highlighted before policy makers or administrators. Positive impact statements describing the advocacy effort's benefits for clients or causes can support a reasoned plan for enacting or modifying policies or decisions.

Evaluative information can be used to educate the board, staff, volunteers, and key informants in the community. Internal agency inservice programs and public education are important because new knowledge can provide justification for advocacy programs and keep persons informed about results or positive outcomes. Data from evaluative studies add specific knowledge to understanding problems or conditions.

Evaluation of advocacy efforts allows for assessment of client satisfaction. Since social work advocacy is a *mutual* and *exclusive* undertaking, evaluations reinforce the clients' status as a partners, respecting their status as decision makers, and reminding the advocates of the centrality of the client in social work advocacy (Moxley & Freddolino, 1994).

Where to Begin?

In the following pages, the authors describe different levels or types of evaluations that can be used by social work advocates. However, a plan to evaluate must begin with a decision about what one wants to measure. Usually, these decisions are made at the beginning of a project, and measurable objectives are developed that can be assessed during and after the advocacy effort.

   Taylor (1987) has developed a comprehensive model of evaluating advocacy programs (see Figure 4.2). (Using the model, the reader uses a clockwise
circular motion in order to follow each step.) She notes that the advocacy program's base is rooted in the overall goals and objectives established by an
agency. These overarching goals and objectives are derived from the mission,
charter, or purpose of the agency (step 1). The advocacy program's goals and
objectives flow from the agency's mission, goals, and objectives (step 2). The
evaluation process begins by looking (step 3) at the advocacy program's goals
and objectives (what you hoped to accomplish) and, at some point, reviews
how well or poorly the work was done (step 4), and to what extent the goals
and objectives were met (step 5).

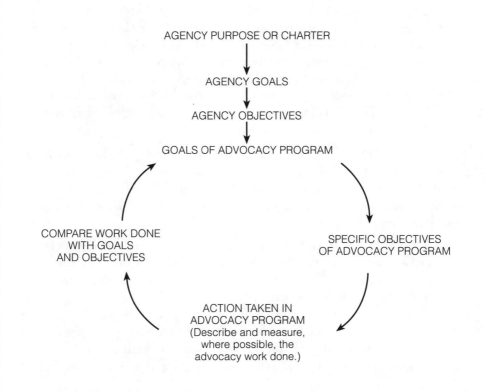

FIGURE 4.2

The process of advocacy

Source: Taylor, E. D. (1987). From issue to action: An advocacy program model (p. 125). Lancaster,
PA: Family Service.

According to Altman et al. (1994), there are three types of evaluation that can be used by social work advocates to assess objectives: process measures, outcome measures, and impact measures.

Process Measures   Objectives that focus on *process* are concerned with information about how well the advocacy effort operated. Did it run smoothly? Were there enough staff? Were there sufficient resources? Was communication effective? Was it supported by the community? Was leadership adequate? Did other groups give in-kind support? Were members satisfied with the group process? What happened during a critical event(s)?

Outcome Measures   Objectives that focus on *outcomes* are concerned with information about specific accomplishments or results that the advocacy program achieved. These are usually concrete, quantifiable measures such as:

- *Types or frequency of services provided.* How many meetings were held? How many classes? What new service is now available?
- *Community or group activities.* How many rallies? How many people participating in forums? How many meetings with key leaders?
- *Changes in programs.* Were there policy changes at city hall? At the legislature? Were new services initiated? Any small victories?
- *Access to services.* Were more clients served? What were the barriers?
- *Number of objectives met over time.* Review the program objectives that are met and record the progress.

Impact Measures   Objectives that focus on *impact* provide information about the ultimate effectiveness or actual changes an advocacy program produced. Measuring such results depends on initial baseline data gathered before the program started. Successful intervention by an advocacy program may be measured by:

- *Behavioral measures.* Have persons' behaviors actually changed? Is there more or less of certain types of behavior? For example: Are teens smoking less? Are more individuals using a shelter? Are fewer middle-school kids dropping out of school?
- *Community-level indicators.* Are there certain changes in the community as a result of your program? Have statistics gone up or down? For example: Are there fewer abandoned cars in the area? Are there cleaner alleyways? Are police getting more calls for helping seniors?

Information Base   It is important for advocacy projects to develop an informational base linked to the proposed evaluation activities. How does one keep track of specific information, data, research, and other studies? This chapter is not a substitute for the many texts on research methods and program evaluation, and readers are urged to refer to them for more extensive knowledge and skill-building. Summarized below are methods and sources that contribute to building an informational base from which evaluations can be designed:

- Minutes of meetings, logs of activities, sign-in sheets
- Data sheets containing information on specific activities such as staff time, client appointments, and so on. These can be daily, weekly, monthly, quarterly, or annual documents.
- Evaluation ratings by consumers and staff
- Agency mission, goals, and objectives statements
- Newspaper column inches, newsletters, and radio/TV coverage in minutes
- Grants, contracts, in-kind services, or donations received
- Interviews of key persons during special events or activities
- Data from federal, state, and local agencies related to the advocacy topic
- Surveys conducted by agency staff or other community associations/agencies

SUMMARY

Chapter 4 provides the social work advocate with knowledge of the second fundamental skill of the general practice framework: influencing. The capacity to alter another person's behavior, to modify a decision, or to change an opinion each signify this essential skill of influencing that advocates must possess in order to advocate effectively. There are eight principles of influencing that offer direct application for the advocate: (1) Identify the issues and set goals; (2) Get the facts; (3) Plan strategies and tactics; (4) Supply leadership; (5) Get to know decision makers and their staff; (6) Broaden your base of support; (7) Be persistent; and (8) Evaluate your advocacy effort. Together with representation, the other essential skill of advocacy, social workers can use this practice framework as they pursue the goals of their clients, implementing the values of social justice, and fulfilling the mission of their profession.

DISCUSSION QUESTIONS

1. What is the difference between a strategy and a tactic?
2. How important are "facts" in influencing powerful people?
3. Can a person be taught to be a leader?
4. On what basis can an advocate analyze the opposition?
5. Some tactics are confrontational. Do they always work? If not, when do they work?

6. Some would say that persistence is the most important characteristic of an advocate. Would you agree?
7. How do opponents resist proposed changes made by advocates?
8. Why do many people fail to approach decision makers?
9. Discuss the advantages and disadvantages of belonging to a coalition.
10. How much effort and money should be allocated for evaluation of an advocacy program?

RECOMMENDED READINGS

Altman, D. G., Balcazar, F. E., Fawcett, S. B., Seekins, T., & Young, T. Q. (1994). *Public health advocacy: Creating community change to improve health.* Palo Alto, CA: Stanford Center for Research in Disease Prevention.

Bobo, K., Kendall, J., & Max, S. (1996). *Organizing for social change: A manual for activists in the 90s* (2d ed.). Santa Ana, CA: Seven Locks Press.

Checkoway, B. (1995). Six strategies of community change. *Community Development Journal, 30,* 2–20.

Eriksen, K. (1997). *Making an impact: A handbook on counselor advocacy.* Washington, DC: Accelerated Development.

Richan, W. C. (1996). *Lobbying for social change* (2d ed.). Binghamton, NY: Haworth Press.

Taylor, E. D. (1987). *From issue to action: An advocacy program model.* Lancaster, PA: Family Service.

SOCIAL WORK ADVOCACY CONTEXTS

Part Three builds directly on the definition of advocacy in Chapter 2 and Part Two, the general practice framework in Chapters 3 and 4. In fact, the contents of Part Three cannot be taught or learned apart from these chapters.

Part Three consists of four separate chapters that address social work advocacy in four interconnected, but differing contexts for practitioners. Chapter 5 uses client advocacy as its focus, suggesting how clinical social workers working primarily one to one with clients can advocate effectively. Chapter 6 concentrates on cause advocacy, that is, when individual concerns turn out to also be issues for a larger group. Chapter 7 demonstrates how social work advocates can serve their clients and causes in the legislative domain. Chapter 8 provides advocacy insights and strategies for administrators of agencies and internal advocates.

Each chapter is organized in a parallel fashion with the general practice framework in Chapters 3 and 4. *The reader is expected to already be familiar with the contents of the framework and the general application of the guidelines and principles for effective social work advocacy.*

In each of the four chapters, the authors provide in-depth, specialized knowledge and skills for a particular focus of social work advocacy, that is, client advocacy, legislative advocacy, cause advocacy, or adminstrative advocacy. The reader continues to apply the general framework of Chapters 3 and 4, but now can also learn new insights into one particular arena of advocacy. The chapter on client advocacy, for example, provides specific information on representation and influencing on behalf of single clients and families, empowering clients to act, working with decision makers and supervisors, and broadening the base of support for client proposals. The chapter on cause advocacy provides specific information on representation and influencing at the community level, how to build coalitions, use of the media, and evaluation of an advocacy effort.

Each chapter is written so that it is free-standing. Each is independent of the others and can be read individually. The only caveat for the readers is to remember that each chapter is based on a familiarization with the new definition and the general practice framework in Parts One and Two. This content should support the reading of Part Three's chapters; otherwise, there may be only a limited understanding of the specialized materials.

CLIENT ADVOCACY[1]

---

[1]Note to readers: This chapter reflects a change in terminology from the traditional *case advocacy* identification to a contemporary *client advocacy* identification. This is simply a semantic versus a substantive change.

> *It is unreasonable to focus therapy on superficial problems . . . our clinical inter-*
> *ventions must be provided in context so they make sense to the families we seek to*
> *serve, and so they aggressively pursue necessary resources. The narrow definition*
> *of "therapist" needs to be broadened to include the concept of advocacy and provi-*
> *sion of concrete services. In order to be effective advocates, we must interact with*
> *our communities; give voice to our concerns through policies and legislation; and*
> *commit a percentage of our time, however we see fit, to social and political concerns.*
>
> ELIANA GIL, 1996

OVERVIEW

According to a report by Gibelman and Schervish (1997), 65.5% of social workers with BSW degrees, 71.7% with MSW degrees, and 40.4% with Ph.D. or DSW degrees practice in clinical or direct service settings (p. 114). Ezell (1994) further reported that approximately 90% of social workers studied "engaged in advocacy activities as part of their job"; of that number, approximately 75% practiced *client advocacy* (p. 39). Based on these statistics, you should not be surprised to learn that client advocacy is an extremely important social work practice area. Consequently, it is where social workers can have the loudest voice and greatest impact for those who truly need help.

Client advocacy is built upon a philosophy that seeks to protect, enforce, and ensure clients' *rights, entitlements, resources, services,* and *benefits* (see Compton & Galaway, 1994; DuBois & Miley, 1996; Gerhart, 1990; Hardcastle, Wenocur, & Powers, 1997b; Jansson, 1994; Kirst-Ashman & Hull, 1993; McGowan, 1987; Northen, 1995; Peled & Edleson, 1994; Sheafor, Horejsi, & Horejsi, 1994; & Stroul, 1995). Sheafor, Horejsi, and Horejsi (1994) advised that "when the social worker performs as a client advocate, he or she speaks, argues, manipulates, bargains, and negotiates on behalf of the client. At the direct service level, an advocacy stance may be necessary . . . to secure bene-fits or services that the client is entitled to but, for one reason or another, is unable to obtain" (p. 404). *Of particular importance, client advocacy's primary mission is to ensure that services provided to clients are both relevant to the problem and available within the community;* its primary concern is *not* to provide those services (Herbert & Mould, 1992).

Before discussing the specifics of client advocacy, let us look at how these terms are identified and defined within the profession:

1. *Rights.* According to Kirst-Ashman and Hull (1993), "[r]ights are those protections and guarantees to which people . . . have a just claim and cannot, in American society, be denied without due process of law" (p. 474). A right is often determined by its purpose and objective. Hardcastle et al. (1997b) reported that rights fall into three broad categories: (1) due process or procedural rights, (2) substantive rights, and (3) basic human rights. Figure 5.1 outlines those rights most frequently evidenced in direct social work practice.

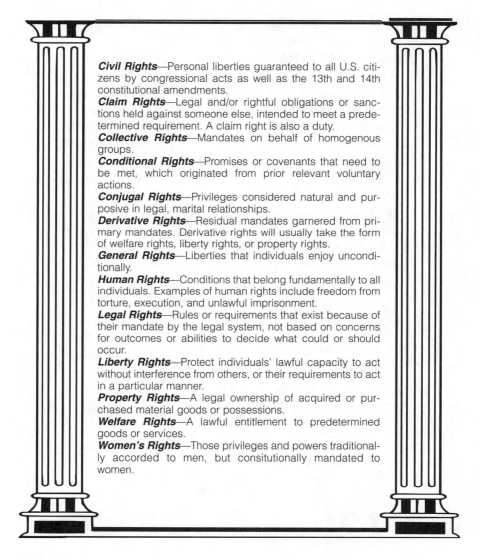

Civil Rights—Personal liberties guaranteed to all U.S. citizens by congressional acts as well as the 13th and 14th constitutional amendments.

Claim Rights—Legal and/or rightful obligations or sanctions held against someone else, intended to meet a predetermined requirement. A claim right is also a duty.

Collective Rights—Mandates on behalf of homogenous groups.

Conditional Rights—Promises or covenants that need to be met, which originated from prior relevant voluntary actions.

Conjugal Rights—Privileges considered natural and purposive in legal, marital relationships.

Derivative Rights—Residual mandates garnered from primary mandates. Derivative rights will usually take the form of welfare rights, liberty rights, or property rights.

General Rights—Liberties that individuals enjoy unconditionally.

Human Rights—Conditions that belong fundamentally to all individuals. Examples of human rights include freedom from torture, execution, and unlawful imprisonment.

Legal Rights—Rules or requirements that exist because of their mandate by the legal system, not based on concerns for outcomes or abilities to decide what could or should occur.

Liberty Rights—Protect individuals' lawful capacity to act without interference from others, or their requirements to act in a particular manner.

Property Rights—A legal ownership of acquired or purchased material goods or possessions.

Welfare Rights—A lawful entitlement to predetermined goods or services.

Women's Rights—Those privileges and powers traditionally accorded to men, but consitutionally mandated to women.

FIGURE 5.1

Legal and social rights guaranteed in the United States.

Source: Jacobs, (1993); Merriam-Webster, (1994).

2. *Entitlements.* Barker (1995) identified entitlements as "services, goods, or money *due to an individual by virtue of a specific status*" (p. 121). Entitlements fall into three broad categories: (1) "those established by law"; (2) "those based on organizational policy"; and (3) "those based upon an interpretation of organizational policy" (Kirst-Ashman & Hull,

1993). Figure 5.2 outlines several *federal* entitlement policies signed into law *over the past 10 years* that directly impact the social work delivery system and, correspondingly, its clients.

3. *Resources.* Barker (1995) defines resources as "any existing service or commodity . . . to help take care of a need . . . and typically includes other social agencies, government programs . . . professional or volunteer personnel, self-help groups, natural helpers, and individuals in the community who possess the qualities and motivations that can help the client" (p. 324). (See Table 5.1.) Resources include commitment, money, prestige, power, authority, and other mechanisms necessary to help reach the intended goal (Kirst-Ashman & Hull, 1993).

4. *Services* and *Benefits.* According to Merriam-Webster (1994), a service promotes the welfare of others (see Figure 5.3), while benefits provide financial assistance during sickness, old age, or unemployment.

P.L. 105-89, the Adoption and Safe Families Act of 1997
P.L. 105-33, the State Children's Health Insurance Program
P.L. 104-204, the Mental Health Parity Act of 1996
P.L. 104-193, the Personal Responsibility and Work Opportunity
    Reconciliation Act of 1996
P.L. 104-91, the Health Insurance Reform Act
P.L. 103-259, the Freedom of Access to Clinic Entrances Act
P.L. 103-322, the Violent Crime Control and Law Enforcement Act
P.L. 103-382, the Improving America's Schools Act of 1994
P.L. 103-66, the Family Preservation and Support Services Provisions
P.L. 103-3, the Family and Medical Leave Act
P.L. 103-82, the National and Community Service Trust Act
P.L. 102-321, the Alcohol, Drug Abuse, and Mental Health Administration
    Reorganization Act
P.L. 102-166, the Civil Rights Act
P.L. 101-381, the Ryan White Comprehensive AIDS Resources
    Emergency Act
42 U.S.C. 1210, the Americans with Disabilities Act
P.L. 100-259, the Civil Rights Restoration Act
P.L. 100-360, the Medicare Catastrophic Coverage Act
P.L. 96-272, the Adoption Assistance and Child Welfare Act
P.L. 100-435, the Hunger Prevention Act
P.L. 100-485, the Family Support Act
P.L. 100-77, the Stewart B. McKinney Homeless Assistance Act

FIGURE 5.2

Recent federal entitlement policies that directly impact the social work delivery system and its clients.

Source: Lester, Mutepa, Manetta, & Schneider (1998).

TABLE
5.1

RESOURCES AND SERVICES AVAILABLE TO SOCIAL WORK CLIENTS

Health	Education	Safety and Justice	Community Organization	Financial Resource Services	Legal Services	Housing
Information and Counseling	Information and Counseling	Fire Prevention, Control, and Protection	Information and Referral	Emergency Assistance	Bankruptcy Services	Information and Counseling
Emergency Services	Diagnostic Evaluation and Testing	Crime Prevention and Protection	Community Education and Information	Information and Counseling	Domestic Relations	Relocation Assistance
Diagnostic Evaluation and Testing	Regular Education Services	Law Enforcement/ Police Services	Charitable Foundations	TANF	Separation and Divorce	Homeless and Transient Shelters
Home Health Care	Special Educational Services	Civil Liberties Organizations	Fundraising Services	WIC	Child Support	Rehabilitation, Repair, Renovation, and Restoration Services
Inpatient Medical Care	Vocational Education	Probation and Parole Services	Human Relations	General Financial Assistance	Protective Orders	
Outpatient Medical Care	Advanced Education	Detention Facilities	Civil Rights	Food Stamps	Testate and Probate Assistance	Mortgage and Loan Assistance
Dental Care	Technical Education	Incarceration Services	Community Planning	Social Security Services	Legal Defense Services	Furniture, Supplies, and Tools
Alternative Health Care	Tutoring	Aftercare Services	Neighborhood Development	Supplemental Security Income	Pre- and Posttrial Services	Public Housing
Rehabilitative Services	Textbooks and School Supplies	Delinquency Prevention Services	Economic Development (small business, industry, tourism)	Unemployment Insurance	Advance Medical Directives	Rent Subsidies
Medication, Supplies, and Equipment	Equal Opportunity Services	Disaster Relief	Occupational and Professional Resources	Veterans' Services	Immigration Services	Retirement Housing, Centers, and Communities
Screening and Prevention	Homebound Education	Civil Defense	Government and Political Systems	Worker's Compensation	Employment Law	Urban Homestead
Advance Medical Directive	Adult Education	Weather Services	Service Planning	Disability, Retirement, and Death Benefits	Contracts Law	Building/Housing Code Enforcement
Health Reporting and Statistics	Continuing Education	Land, Water, and Air Rescue	Volunteer Services	Private Health Insurance	Criminal Law	Fair Housing and Land Use
				Public Health Insurance (Medicaid, Medicare)	Victim Services	

TABLE
5.1

SOCIAL WORK RESOURCES AND SERVICES (CONTINUED)

Employment	Mental Health Services	Recreation and Culture	Alternative Living	Environmental Issues	Transportation	Food and Clothing
Information and Counseling	Information and Counseling	Information and Counseling	Information and Counseling	Hygiene and Sanitation Services	Information and Counseling	Information and Counseling
Job Development and Testing	Emergency Services	Activity Groups	Emergency Shelter Care	Beautification and Preservation	Car Pool Services	Emergency Services
Institutional and On-the-Job Training	Personal and Family Counseling	Arts Appreciation	Foster Family Services	Traffic	Emergency Medical Transportation	Free or Subsidized Assistance
Sheltered Employment	Diagnostic and Evaluative Services	Residential and Day Services	Group Homes	Environmental Health Inspection	Escort Services	Affordability and Availability
Job Placement Services	Hospitalization	Library Services	Residential Care	Hazard and Pest Control Services	Errand Services for Homebound	TANF
Assisted Employment Services	Self-Help Groups	Lectures, Discussions, and Exhibitions	Residential Treatment Facilities	Pollution Regulation	Public Transit Services	WIC
Homebound Employment Services	Social and Recreational Programs	Discount Services	Transitional Services	Water Supply	Discount Rate Services	Charitable Services
Equal Opportunity Services	Companionship Services	Special Programs for Handicapped and Disabled Populations		Licensing and Regulation for Alternative Living Services	Special Transit Services for Elderly, Disabled, Children	Ecumenical Assistance
Affirmative Action and Minimum Wage	Crisis Intervention					
	Bereavement Counseling					

Abuse, Neglect, and Exploitation	Family Planning	Consumer Protection	Adoption Services
Information and Counseling	Counseling and Information	Information and Counseling	Information and Counseling
Educational Services	Abortion Services	Regulation and Business Practices	Preadoption Evaluation
Protective Shelter Services	Pregnancy Assistance	Weights and Measures	Placement Assistance
Investigative Services	Infertility and Sexual Dysfunction	Safety Standards	Pre- and Postadoption Guidance and Support
	Adoption and Foster Care Services	Buyer Protection Services	

Numerous rights, entitlements, resources, services, and benefits are outlined in Figures 5.1 through 5.3 and Table 5.1. Specific information about rights, entitlements, resources, services, and/or benefits can also be found using the websites outlined in Appendix A.

According to Barker (1995), a *client* is an "individual, group, family, or community that seeks or is provided with professional services" (NASW CD Rom). In conjunction with this definition, the authors define *client advocacy* as *one* individual, unit (family, group), or entity (community, organization), as provided under social work advocacy's practice parameters set forth in this chapter and in previous chapters. It is important to note that, within this framework, a population cannot be considered a client, for it is represented under cause, administrative, or legislative advocacy (see Chapters 6, 7, and 8). Further, under client advocacy's practice parameters, a "client" cannot have fluid boundaries; this means that members of families, groups, organizations, or communities cannot fluctuate or be interchangeable. Anything other than a unit or entity with fluid boundaries would be considered a population.

Client advocacy is used not only in direct service, but also in clinical practice. "Most advocacy begins with the individual" (Hunter, 1979, p. 16). As Claxton (1981) stated, "advocacy is an essential first step in starting a relationship" (p. 48). For example, clients are frequently denied rights, entitlements, resources, services, or benefits by agencies and communities, which often intensifies individual hardship or distress. When practitioners use advocacy skills in the early stages of professional relationships, they can help reduce clients' problems and equalize their psychosocial environment. Using advocacy can also help build a trusting therapeutic relationship. Following such relief, both parties can engage in and concentrate on appropriate treatment strategies (Claxton, 1981). Melton (1983) further stated that "advocacy essentially is the means by which the environment can be more conducive to the development of ego strength and to therapeutic change" (p. 97).

Client advocacy is not a simple action; rather, it is a complex process requiring significant knowledge and skill. To support this assertion, McGowan (1974) studied advocacy practice in the social work profession. Her results reported that: *first,* the decision to use advocacy was often influenced by "the objectives, the nature of the problem, the sanction for advocacy, the channel agent and target systems"; *second,* "the primary determinants of the action were the practitioner's resources and the receptivity of the target system"; and *third,* "the use of communication and mediation rather than power were emphasized in the range of resources and techniques used" (Northen, 1995, p. 295). Based on these results, it is important to understand that client advocacy cannot simply be practiced by anyone, at any time, or in any situation; rather, it must rely on a generally accepted framework or guidelines, which is necessary for professional legitimacy and efficacy.

Concrete Services are those resources and supports necessary to function and provide normative welfare standards to individuals and families, which include food, shelter, clothing, and transportation.

Day Services are congregate resources, benefits and supports provided to a broad range of populations, specifically children, the elderly, and the disabled, by and within the community system.

Elder Services are direct and indirect assistance, provisions, and benefits necessary to support and sustain the elderly with their unique and specialized needs.

Emergency Services are those benefits and resources immediately provided to individuals and families in a state of crisis. Such services are only authorized once per individual or family.

Family Preservation Services are those programs and direct services that work to sustain and maintain families intact.

Home Health Services refer to medical, nursing, and follow-up care as well as speech, physical, and occupational therapies for homebound individuals.

Homemaker Services consist of domestic resources and supports, specifically meal preparation, nursing care, transportation, and laundry/housecleaning assistance, to help individuals remain in their own home.

Human Services refer to those activities and programs necessary to promote individuals' well-being and growth, particularly those unable to provide for their own needs. Six basic human services are identified: (1) personal social services, (2) education, (3) health, (4) income, (5) housing, and (6) public safety and justice.

Information and Referral Services consist of organized systems that provide detailed information about services, networks, and agencies to facilitate comprehensive community access to various forms of human services.

Institutional Services consist of health care, income maintenance, education, housing, and employment as well as guidance, counseling, and the development of mutual- and self-help groups, family planning, and resources for the elderly and children.

Intangible Services include cognitive supportive services such as psychotherapy, relationship-building skills, reassurance, and knowledge.

Personal Care Services provide help with daily personal hygiene care such as bathing, dressing, and grooming to indigent homebound individuals.

Personal Social Services provide community relationship-building opportunities and skills necessary to enhance social enjoyment.

Protective Services consist of interventions on behalf of individuals and families in vulnerable populations at risk of injury, maltreatment, or abuse from others and unable to manage their safety needs.

Public Health Services provide for health promotion and illness prevention, to include diseases and disabilities, within micro and macro communities.

Public Social Services provide programs and services to individuals in need specifically through the public, private, and voluntary sectors.

School-Linked Services include the development, implementation and delivery of programs and supports within community agencies necessary to provide health and social services to families and children. These agencies are located in close proximity to school sites for family accessibility.

Social Services promote the health and well-being of individuals and families in society in order to help them become self-sufficient.

Veterans Services provide programs, supports, benefits, and resources to individuals who previously served in the military.

Victim Services provide programs, supports, and resources to survivors and witnesses of violent crimes.

Youth Services consist of organizations and programs designed to meet the developmental, educational, and recreational needs of adolescents and young adults.

FIGURE **5.3**

Various types of services that promote the welfare of others.

Source: NASW Encyclopedia of Social Work 19th Ed. (Revised) CD Rom Version; and Barker (1994) CD Rom Version

Although *all* social workers can practice client advocacy (e.g., academics, administrators, clinicians, community organizers, direct service practitioners, policy practitioners, researchers, supervisors, educators, and trainers), direct service practitioners and clinicians are its largest constituent providers (Gibelman & Schervish, 1997). Based on research conducted by Herbert and Mould (1992), however, many direct service practitioners do not think they advocate for their clients as much as they should. Specifically, "the social work roles used most frequently by the respondents were as agents of social control and social brokers, *whereas they thought they should be doing counseling and advocacy most frequently*" (Herbert & Mould, 1992, p. 120). This same study identified the following factors as contributing to a diminished advocacy role: (1) bureaucratic constraints; (2) heavy work demands; and (3) perceived lack of advocacy skills and knowledge (p. 116). To help alleviate these problems, this chapter will identify, outline, and discuss those knowledge and skill bases necessary to practice appropriate client advocacy.

Read through the vignette in Case 5.1 about Sarah Woods's advocacy efforts on behalf of her client Zacharia Jones (see Figure 5.4); this case will help as the reader explores advocacy's framework and practice principles in the next sections.

A Good Samaritan? Or a Good Advocate?

As the supervisor of a social services agency, I had minimal contact with agency clients. However, one day not long ago an adult male stopped by my office unannounced. His clothing was tattered and disheveled, his hair was unkempt, he was unshaven, and his personal hygiene was significantly neglected. He said he was hungry and needed emergency assistance until he could find a job and get back on his feet. I asked if he ever received emergency services before; he said he applied not long ago but his request was denied. Concerned about this man's situation, I offered him something to eat and drink, asked for his name, and went to the file room to pull his case.

Upon returning to my office, I glanced through the documents in the file. To ease his apparent discomfort, I asked him to tell me about his current situation. He was in great emotional distress and thus eager to talk about his personal hardships. From our conversation that day I learned the following information.

(Continued)

Zacharia Jones was a 31-year-old African American born in Birmingham, Alabama. When he was 15 years old, his father unexpectedly suffered a massive heart attack and died a few weeks later. As the oldest son, Zacharia dropped out of high school during the 10th grade to get a job, although he pursued his GED at age 17, and enlisted in the Army once he turned 18. Following his permanent military assignment, Zacharia's mother was diagnosed with terminal cancer. To support his family, Zacharia sent most of his salary home. Stationed across the country with limited family contact, Zacharia was deeply concerned about his mother. As a result, his job performance suffered. Further, within a few months his girlfriend Kendra announced she was pregnant; the two immediately married. In order to support this new family, Zacharia ceased sending money home. The psychological stress was too much for him to bear, and Zacharia began to drink alcohol on a daily basis, which exacerbated his depressed mood, poor work performance, and sporadic job attendance. After several disciplinary conferences with his Commanding Officer, Zacharia was discharged from the Army two years early with a General rather than an Honorable Discharge.

Not long after his first daughter was born, Zacharia's mother passed away. With few technical skills in hand, Zacharia found work as a laborer with a local construction company. Because Kendra wished to remain home with their daughter, she refused to look for employment. This required Zacharia to work more than 12 hours a day, 7 days a week to meet the family finances. Unfortunately, even this consistent work did not provide enough money for this family to move beyond their basic needs, and Kendra criticized him incessantly. Thus, Zacharia increased his alcohol intake to alleviate his psychic pain. After two stormy marital years, Kendra announced she was pregnant again. Once their second daughter was born, Kendra consistently spent more money than the family income allowed, which placed a further strain on their already fragile finances. From this point forward the family situation spiraled downward. As Zacharia increased his daily alcohol intake, he experienced blackouts. Within a short period of time he lost internal and external control. When Kendra would nag him, he would hit her. Eventually the slaps turned into beatings. After multiple incarcerations for spousal abuse, and with continuous and increasing alcohol use, Zacharia could no longer maintain consistent employment. One day he snapped as he beat his oldest daughter and threw her across the room during a blackout; both her arms were broken and she had multiple fractures throughout her body. Zacharia was charged with felony child abuse, found guilty, and sentenced to three years in prison.

5.1   (Continued)

During his imprisonment, Kendra filed for and obtained a divorce. At rock bottom, Zacharia sought out counseling and worked through his multiple issues. Feeling good about the future, Zacharia was ready to begin his new life once released from prison. However, the past followed him into the present as Zacharia could not find decent work due to his felony conviction. Moreover, previous debts forced him to file for bankruptcy, and he did not have enough money to pay child support arrears. These were the primary factors that led him to my office, as he was evicted from his apartment last month and unable to find shelter. Zacharia once again hit rock bottom in spite of his multiple efforts to rectify his past problems and mistakes.

Now that I learned the factors surrounding Mr. Jones's specific situation and needs, I asked him what type of emergency assistance he thought could best help him. Because of his immediate distress, he was unable to identify specific concrete resources. Thus, I told him about several community resources available and outlined their advantages and disadvantages. Of these choices, Mr. Jones selected a transitional homeless shelter that would allow him a lengthier stay, and would help him find employment and locate permanent housing. Once this decision was made, I called the various shelters to find space available, reserved program space, and transported Mr. Jones to the shelter. Finally, I spoke with the Residential Director to offer additional assistance if it was necessary.

On my way back to the office, I was concerned about the denial of Mr. Jones's previous request. Since I did not see paperwork reflecting the request in the case file, I decided to search the computer. In doing so, I discovered that Mr. Jones had, indeed, made a request approximately three weeks prior. However, there was a "no action taken" notation below this entry. Curious, I located the intake worker and questioned her about this disposition. During our conversation I learned about an informal agency policy that denied emergency services for applicants with child support arrears. This policy perpetuated Mr. Jones's poverty. When I brought this problem to my supervisor's attention, I was told that the agency's hands were tied because it lacked adequate financial resources to accommodate all emergency requests. This informal policy was necessary to contain its expenditures. Something about this situation did not feel right.

Knowing that I could not single-handedly change this policy, I decided to research other jurisdictions to determine if similar problems were experienced. During my queries I found that another county experienced similar problems. However, internal advocates successfully developed a program to

5.1 (Continued)

rectify the problems and were, at that time, putting the program into action. In that regard, I spent several hours with the program director to learn about their action plan, and what factors were necessary to develop and implement the program. With an abundance of information, I returned to my agency and asked several colleagues to join a committee to address this issue. Together we researched relevant statistics, located available funding in an existing entitlement policy, collaborated with external organizations to ensure community availability, and outlined a presentation for the Executive Committee. Within three weeks our group successfully researched, designed, developed, and set forth the proposed program. I recently learned that the Board of Supervisors approved the proposal; and the program will be implemented within the next six months. Better yet, Mr. Jones now receives many entitlements previously denied.

Representation

1. *Exclusivity*
2. *Mutuality*
3. *Use of Forum*

Skills

1. *Listening*
2. *Speaking*
3. *Writing*

Influence

1. *Identify Issues and Set Goals*
2. *Get the Facts*
3. *Plan Strategies and Tactics*
4. *Supply Leadership*
5. *Get to Know Decision Makers and Their Staff*
6. *Broaden Base of Support*
7. *Be Persistent*
8. *Evaluate Advocacy Effort*

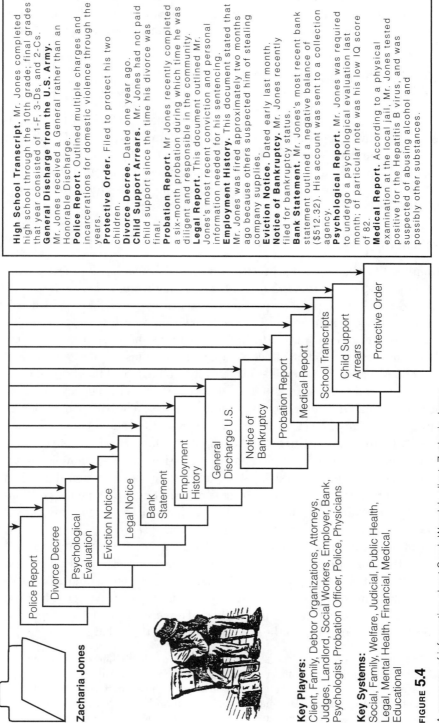

High School Transcript. Mr. Jones completed high school through the 10th grade; final grades that year consisted of 1-F, 3-Ds, and 2-Cs.

General Discharge from the U.S. Army. Mr. Jones received a General rather than an Honorable Discharge.

Police Report. Outlined multiple charges and incarcerations for domestic violence through the years.

Protective Order. Filed to protect his two children.

Divorce Decree. Dated one year ago.

Child Support Arrears. Mr. Jones had not paid child support since the time his divorce was final.

Probation Report. Mr. Jones recently completed a six-month probation during which time he was diligent and responsible in the community.

Legal Report. This document outlined Mr. Jones's most recent conviction and personal information needed for his sentencing.

Employment History. This document stated that Mr. Jones was fired approximately two months ago because others suspected him of stealing company supplies.

Eviction Notice. Dated early last month.

Notice of Bankruptcy. Mr. Jones recently filed for bankruptcy status.

Bank Statement. Mr. Jones's most recent bank statement outlined a negative balance of ($512.32). His account was sent to a collection agency.

Psychological Report. Mr. Jones was required to undergo a psychological evaluation last month; of particular note was his low IQ score of 82.

Medical Report. According to a physical examination at the local jail, Mr. Jones tested positive for the Hepatitis B virus, and was suspected of abusing alcohol and possibly other substances.

Zacharia Jones

Police Report

Divorce Decree

Psychological Evaluation

Eviction Notice

Legal Notice

Bank Statement

Employment History

General Discharge U.S.

Notice of Bankruptcy

Probation Report

Medical Report

School Transcripts

Child Support Arrears

Protective Order

Key Players:
Client, Family, Debtor Organizations, Attorneys, Judges, Landlord, Social Workers, Employer, Bank, Psychologist, Probation Officer, Police, Physicians

Key Systems:
Social, Family, Welfare, Judicial, Public Health, Legal, Mental Health, Financial, Medical, Educational

FIGURE 5.4

A summary of information about Sarah Woods's client, Zacharia Jones.

Whether she knew it or not, Sarah practiced good and effective client advocacy. Now let us look more closely at advocacy's framework and principles to see how Sarah used and applied these practice parameters in her advocacy efforts.

REPRESENTATION

As outlined and discussed in Chapter 3, representation is one of two fundamental objectives necessary for effective social work advocacy. Recall that exclusivity, mutuality, and the use of a forum are the required advocacy components of representation. In addition, social workers must demonstrate competence with their speaking and writing skills. The next sections will identify and discuss these components as they apply to this typology.

Exclusivity

As outlined in Chapter 3, exclusivity describes the *relationship* between the client and advocate as *focused on, centered on,* and *responsible to* the client. Under direct service practice parameters, social workers' first allegiance is always to clients. Friedman and Poertner (1995) support this assertion: "[T]he commitment of case managers to their clients must be unequivocal. Among other things, this means that effective case managers must not hesitate to advocate actions that make it possible for [a client] to be served in a normal environment, even if it is contrary to the desires of others in the agency" (p. 259). Sheafor, Horejsi, and Horejsi (1994) summarize the exclusivity perspective by stating that social workers' "willingness to assume the role of client advocate should arise from a desire to help [the] client, and never from a motive of dislike for another professional or agency or a desire for self-aggrandizement" (p. 405). Hardcastle et al. (1997b) stated that "for a social worker, starting an advocacy relationship is not too different from starting a therapeutic relationship. The client directs as much as possible. In turn, we try to demystify aspects of society about which we are knowledgeable" (pp. 357–358).

Under client advocacy, the most difficult barrier to exclusivity is determining the appropriate course of action while assessing the triangulated expectations of clients, agencies, and the larger society. Under our new advocacy model, how can practitioners rectify this discrepancy, particularly when those standards conflict with one another? The answer lies in the following excerpt, which is taken from the NASW *Code of Ethics* (1996):

> The primary mission of the social work profession is to enhance human well-being and help meet the basic human needs of all people, with particular attention to the needs and empowerment of people who are vulnerable, oppressed, and living in poverty. A historic and defining feature of social work is the profession's focus on individual well-being in the social context and the well-being of society.

Fundamental to social work is attention to the environmental forces that create, contribute to, and address problems in living. (p. 1)

In that regard, if an individual, agency, or entity contributes to, sustains, or condones client oppression, vulnerability, or poverty through word or action, practitioners are *obligated,* under the NASW *Code of Ethics,* to stand behind their clients, and not defer to an agency's or society's conflicting values and practices. In other words, social workers are simply unable to practice client advocacy if they cannot provide exclusivity to their clients. This does not mean they are not competent social workers; rather, it means they are not practicing appropriate social work advocacy.

For example, consider the opportunity for conflict by reviewing Table 5.1 and Figures 5.1 through 5.3. Then look closely at Figure 5.4. As you can see in this depiction, Mr. Jones is homeless. Which *rights* could apply in this situation? Certainly Mr. Jones would be eligible for any mandates under collective rights, and perhaps even legal rights contingent upon his circumstances. There should be no question that he would be free to enjoy his general rights. Human rights would preclude him from unlawful imprisonment, and he undoubtedly would qualify for welfare rights. On the other hand, what if Mr. Jones wanted to exercise his liberty rights? Under exclusivity, social workers must respect Mr. Jones's decision and help him work toward that goal.

In addition to rights, consider also the numerous *entitlement* policies and programs that could apply to Mr. Jones, identified in Figure 5.2. How would you determine which one takes priority over the others? Finally, Figure 5.3 outlines multiple *services, resources,* and *benefits* available to Mr. Jones in this situation. How would you distinguish which would best suit him in his homeless capacity? The reality is that, unless clients are incapable of making appropriate, necessary, and effective decisions about their short- and long-term welfare (as discussed in the next section), they are the *only* ones who can determine what is in their best interest. As professional practitioners, we are obligated to honor and respect those judgments and decisions, and help clients move toward their specific goals and objectives.

While the literature is clear that advocates have a responsibility to practice client exclusivity, social workers are frequently confronted with numerous barriers that hinder the process. To begin with, practitioners often have serious time constraints. According to Dane (1985), "the size of case loads and the emphasis on clinical intervention tends to pressure against the active maintenance of an advocacy role" (p. 509). Practitioners can also risk agency censure or lose professional status when providing advocacy with or for a client, particularly if the effort is controversial to the organization or community. Moreover, most agencies have policies with strict sanctions for violating internal practices and procedures. Frequently these policies can be detrimental to the client's welfare (Herbert & Mould, 1992; Nazario, 1984). "On the one hand, it is difficult to bite the hand that feeds you; on the other hand, it is simply irresponsible to ignore the impact of structural forces on the [client] while purporting to help" (Herbert & Mould, 1992, p. 126). Paradoxically, in such situations agencies can just as easily become the target of the advocacy effort. Herbert and Mould (1992) advise that "for frontline workers, advocacy must become a state of mind, an attitude of constant watchfulness to ensure the responsiveness of all systems to the clients they serve" (p. 128).

Critical Exclusivity Issue: Cultural Diversity

One of the most difficult challenges associated with client advocacy is providing exclusivity to those individuals different from us or from the norm. Consider the client who presents with a physical handicap in the fingers and hands and wants help learning to type; our first inclination is to openly discuss the cons of this request and redirect the client to other alternatives. Or suppose a lesbian couple asks for help with adopting a child; our value system may kick into high gear as we hope to avoid the encounter and the situation. Despite our deep-rooted biases and convictions, it is important to understand that social workers must demonstrate multicultural and diversity competency in order to practice appropriate exclusivity within the client advocacy context. Castillo (1997) defines culture as knowledge transferred from generation to generation, which includes "language, forms of art and expression, religion, social and political structures, economic systems, legal systems, norms of behavior, ideas about illness and healing, and so on" (p. 20).

So, just what types of individuals are different from us, and how do they differ? According to Flanagan and Flanagan (1999), four primary multicultural populations are prevalent in our society: (1) American Indians; (2) African Americans; (3) Hispanic Americans; and (4) Asian Americans. Each such culture has its own very unique set of value systems, traditions, and rituals relating to family roles and structures, relationship patterns, spirituality, language, symbols, acceptable and unacceptable behavior, and orientation toward those in authority. For example, where Hispanic cultures consider the male the dominant family member, African Americans typically consider the female as the head of the household. Other diversity issues center on gay and lesbian issues, religious issues, and individuals with physical, emotional, and intellectual disabilities.

Mutuality

Mutuality also describes the *relationship* between the client and social worker, although here it is *reciprocal, interdependent, equal,* and *joint,* and the worker and client *shares collaborative responsibility* with one another toward an identified, common goal. Flanagan and Flanagan (1999) state that "mutuality refers to a sharing process; it means that power, decision-making, goal selection, and learning are shared" (p. 152). This is not to say that the power relationship is equal, for there will always be a power differential between a professional and a client. Social workers should understand that they are obligated to advocate not only *for* clients, but *with* them as well. This process is empowering because it enhances those skills and techniques necessary for clients to identify and implement self-help practices when future needs arise. In fact, Friedman and Poertner (1995) reported that case managers *should ensure* that direct service interventions are modified to help clients and families acquire "the skills needed to advocate effectively for themselves" (p. 257).

To better understand this mutuality concept, take a look at Figure 5.5. According to Northen (1995), "[t]he client has the right to determine the action to be taken" (p. 295); Kirst-Ashman and Hull (1993) stated that advocacy "should never be carried out without the full knowledge and consent of the client" (p. 474). It is important to note that when mutuality is omitted from advocacy practice, practitioners are placed in dangerous positions because they represent clients without truly understanding what needs to be achieved (Compton & Galaway, 1994). Sheafor, Horejsi, and Horejsi (1994) further warn that: (1) social workers hoping to engage in client advocacy practice must ensure that clients both want and need professional advocacy assistance before such action(s) can take place. This should be accommodated through an explicit agreement; (2) clients must be fully apprised of the potential risks and benefits of advocacy outcomes; and (3) clients must be involved in every decision related to the advocacy effort (p. 404). It is also very important for social workers to evaluate their own motivation for their advocacy work. After all, advocates are human and are thus biased. Sometimes efforts to help those in need at this level can appear exploitive (Northen, 1995).

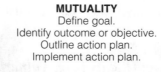

Advocate:
Uses professional skills, values, and services to help client meet goal intended to address unmet social need.

MUTUALITY
Define goal.
Identify outcome or objective.
Outline action plan.
Implement action plan.

→ **GOAL** ←

Client:
Works toward fulfilling unmet social need by openly discussing situation, and working collaboratively to define goal, identify outcome, and outline and implement action plan.

FIGURE **5.5**

An illustration of the concept of mutuality.

Why is it important for clients to remain involved during the advocacy process? Kirst-Ashman and Hull (1993) set forth the following reasons:

1. There is a greater chance for success when clients help plan the intervention and participate in its ongoing efforts.
2. When clients are involved in developing interventions, they are more likely to use and value their outcomes and resources.
3. There is a high probability that outcomes and resources are appropriate to the person and situation when clients have direct involvement in the process.
4. Clients experience efficacy when involved in actions that help meet their needs and reach their goals.
5. Direct involvement induces active participation, which is important for those clients who lack self-esteem and a support network. (p. 479)

Moreover, when clients are directly involved in the advocacy process, practitioners can evaluate not only their motivation, but their ability to participate in its activities. It should be noted, however, that the ultimate decision about when to advocate (or when not to) is determined by the social work practitioner. For example, when it is clear that the effort will fail, it is important to stop the endeavor before committing further manpower and financial resources (p. 480).

Recall that Chapter 2 identified six values associated with social work advocacy, specifically: (1) respecting the dignity and rights of the individual; (2) giving voice to the voiceless; (3) promoting self-determination; (4) providing compassion and relief from suffering; (5) using empowerment and strengths strategies as interventions; and (6) recognizing and promoting social justice. To reinforce these values, Claxton (1981) recommends that "advocacy by the social worker may also be necessary if the transactions between people do not enhance one's dignity, individuality, and self-determination, or if citizens and the collective society do not take mutual responsibility to realize these values" (p. 46).

Critical Mutuality Issue: Clients from Vulnerable Populations

As previously mentioned, some clients do not have the cognitive ability or emotional capacity to make appropriate, necessary, or effective decisions about what is in their best interest. Most of these clients fall within vulnerable populations (i.e., children, the elderly, persons with mental disabilities, individuals with serious mental illnesses, etc.). When advocating with, for, or on behalf of these clients, the mutuality concept must be revised to accommodate their multiple cognitive and emotional limitations. In many situations, the practitioner's first inclination is to utilize *parens patriae,* a legal doctrine that provides the state with guardianship responsibility for individuals unable to care for themselves (Barker, 1995; Melton, 1983). However, we know that the *parens patriae* ideology can be paternalistic and often promotes harmful attitudes and practices.

Advocacy for clients from vulnerable populations should not be taken lightly. When performed inappropriately, this type of advocacy can reinforce many of the concepts social work attempts to negate. As an unintended consequence, it communicates that clients are unable to resolve their own problems, which can reinforce negative self-esteem. In addition, long-term advocacy fosters dependency on the practitioner-advocate, which can activate transference and countertransference issues for both parties (Claxton, 1981; O'Connor & Ammen, 1997). In that regard, advocacy for clients from vulnerable populations should be time-limited to the specific problem at hand. Another negative outcome can develop when practitioners become so involved in their advocacy role that their treatment becomes ineffective. Also, social workers might develop a sense of power as well as a need for gratification after a successful advocacy effort. Finally, when clients develop a sense of gratitude following a successful advocacy outcome, it might be difficult for them to express negative feelings toward the practitioner, "thus hindering the (therapeutic) relationship" (Claxton, 1981, p. 48). Therefore, it is important that practitioners follow recognized and established practice parameters when advocating on behalf of clients from vulnerable populations, and remain attuned to their own needs and aspirations as well.

Two theoretical approaches are available to practitioners when advocating for clients from vulnerable populations. The first, family advocacy services, builds on those relationships with natural advocates; the other, the client support and representation (CSR) model, builds upon the needs approach using a strengths-based perspective. Gerhart (1990), however, cautioned that practitioners should first assess whether clients' inability to make decisions on their own behalf results from temporary impairments, or from impairments that reflect long-term psychological, neurological, or emotional limitations (p. 265). This assessment will determine the necessity and appropriateness for these types of advocacy approaches.

Family Advocacy Services   Family advocacy services combine both family-centered and strengths-based theoretical approaches. Specifically, the family advocacy services model was designed to build bridges between clients, families, and the larger community in order to support efforts to access necessary and appropriate services and resources. Although the four principles and seven practice implications listed in Figure 5.6 were previously outlined for children with emotional disabilities, we find them relevant to all vulnerable population client groups.

Cole (1995) summarized the family advocacy services ideology when he said "[t]he family unit . . . must be the primary object of therapeutic attention

and, individually or as a group, family members must become primary participants and, as soon as possible, leaders in the treatment process" (p. 193). It is
important to note that the families and support systems are frequently constant
and influential contributors to clients' biopsychosocial growth (Dane, 1985).

The Client Support and Representation (CSR) Model   When natural
advocates, that is, families and caregivers, are not available to clients from vulnerable populations, advocacy efforts should be structured around client
needs. *Needs* are defined as "any identifiable condition which limits a person
or individual, or a family member, in meeting his or her full potential" (Kettner
et al., 1990). Based on this approach, four specific need categories are outlined
below:

- *Normative need.* Needs measured by societal standards or norms.
- *Perceived need.* Needs that individuals deem necessary to rectify
  hardships or problems. Perceived needs fluctuate contingent upon
  individuals and/or their unique situations.

Family Advocacy Services

Principles	Practice Implications
1. If clients from vulnerable populations are best served in normal community environments, it is essential that family caregivers play an active role in decisions and treatment planning.	1. The key to achieving the client's treatment objectives and goals is the *relationship* between the caregiver and the service provider.
2. It is important for society and the larger community to accommodate the needs of those families that care for these clients.	2. Family systems should be used to identify and access family strengths, not family problems.
3. Caregivers are the best source of information as regards their own needs and the needs of clients.	3. Family caregivers are capable of identifying the support necessary to provide effective and efficient client care.
4. Family caregivers have strengths that can and should be acknowledged and utilized by communities and direct service practitioners.	4. Professionals should make sure that the physical and emotional needs of family caregivers are routinely assessed and provided in a timely manner.
	5. Family caregivers should *never* be denied information about clients or their disabilities. In fact, family caregivers should be provided with as much information as they need and want to effectuate the client's treatment plan.
	6. Family caregivers should be met and served in their own community, which should include meeting them at work or in the home, if and when required.
	7. Family and community strengths should be used to obtain the resources necessary to provide appropriate client care.

Source: Ronnau (1995).

FIGURE 5.6

Principles and practice implications of family advocacy services.

- *Expressed need.* Stated met or unmet needs.
- *Relative need.* Needs evaluated by existing service standards of one community against another community of equal size and proportion (pp. 48–50).

Initially designed for individuals with serious mental illness facing homelessness during the 1980s, the CSR model recognizes and uses the needs approach as well as a strengths-based perspective. Freddolino and Moxley (1992) stated that "the CSR model is based on a positive view of the client which precludes the use of deficit conceptions of social functioning. . . . [R]ather than emphasizing deficiencies that can undermine the self-worth of clients, the problems identified by clients are conceptualized as *normal needs* shared by many people within our society. The client is perceived as a person who, like the advocate, has specific wants, desires, and aspirations" (pp. 339–340).

The CSR model was designed to empower clients by providing them with self-help techniques and skills for present and future use. Advocates' goals are to help clients identify what they want and need, and to further work with them to accomplish those goals (Freddolino, Moxley, & Fleishman, 1989). The most frequently noted needs expressed by this population included "access to basic living resources, with strong needs expressed for income, shelter, and employment or job training" (Freddolino & Moxley, 1992, p. 338). The CSR model recognizes the advocate as a *catalyst* for the client; self-determination is considered the core value. Intervention in CSR builds on the following psychosocial rehabilitation processes: "(1) engagement; (2) assessment of advocacy needs; (3) setting objectives and identifying tasks; (4) maintaining relationships across space and time; (5) problem-solving and on-going needs assessment; (6) monitoring problem resolution; and (7) evaluation" (Moxley & Freddolino, 1990, pp. 342–344). Specific information related to these processes will be discussed later in this chapter in the section entitled "Influence."

Use of a Forum

As outlined in previous chapters, forums are necessary and mandatory for effective social work advocacy practice. You may recall that Chapter 3 identified a forum as a session or meeting where issues, concerns and viewpoints can be expressed with decision makers or influential persons. Advocacy forums have specific and identified rules, procedures, and expectations that ensure ongoing practitioner efficacy and accountability to client objectives and goals. Under client advocacy, several forums are available to practitioners and their clients.

Teams   Teams are one of the most effective and commonly used forums available to the practitioner-advocate. Teams consist of professional, paraprofessional, and/or voluntary members with specialized knowledge, training, and/or experience. Team members work collaboratively with one another to accomplish treatment and prevention objectives and goals. Teams also organize to ensure effective and appropriate client service implementation. The primary assumption of the team approach is that client needs are numerous and complex; as such, no one professional or discipline can effectively address and resolve all of them in a timely and effective manner. The team's responsibilities are to:

1. Provide initial and ongoing client assessments and/or diagnoses
2. Determine treatment modalities as well as the provision of resources and care
3. Review the quality and standards of client care and interventions
4. Determine and review service and agency coordination
5. Identify thematic or systemic problems that repetitively occur
6. Review case management plans and goals to determine appropriateness
7. Ensure that case management plans and goals are properly, efficiently, and effectively implemented
8. Develop and/or provide ongoing daily assistance for difficult or vulnerable clients, as well as their support systems
9. Open systemic channels of communication (Collins, 1989; Gerhart, 1990; Peterson & Urquiza, 1993; Sands, 1991; Stroul, 1995).

According to Gerhart (1990), "[s]ocial workers can become indispensible in providing information about a person's social resources, in paving the way for a hospitalized patient's return to the community, and in maintaining the patient in the community through the location and coordination of services. *Thus, the information provided by social workers significantly helps team members in shaping and directing treatment teams*" (p. 43). Of the multiple team approaches, those listed in the following text are the most prevalent.

Interdisciplinary or multidisciplinary teams. This type of forum has, in its membership, representatives from diverse professions and disciplines to include, among others, psychiatrists, psychologists, social workers, neurologists, nurses, recreational therapists, speech and language pathologists, occupational therapists, opthalmologists, oncologists, optometrists, pediatricians, pharmacologists, and housing specialists (Dane, 1985; Gerhart, 1990; Sands, 1991).

Intradisciplinary teams. This team has characteristics similar to the interdisciplinary team, although its members are within the *same* profession and discipline. Intradisciplinary team members have expertise in specialized problem areas (e.g., developmental disabilities, elderly, abuse and neglect, juvenile justice, etc.).

Case management teams. While this type of forum has characteristics similar to the interdisciplinary team, its primary objective is to develop ongoing relationships between the client and multiple professionals to ensure continuity of care. A case management team will include approximately three to six professionals from diverse professions; collaboratively, they provide around-the-clock client services and care (Gerhart, 1990).

Treatment teams. Gerhart (1990) describes the treatment team as those professionals "responsible for ongoing treatment and discharge planning" (p. 42). Treatment teams usually consist of individuals directly responsible for clients' ongoing, daily needs and care.

It is important to note that teams do not always function optimally. For example, practitioners will often find a diagnostic bias among members of the same profession or specialty. Many team members may also have skill deficits. Further, a client's behavior or functioning may be confused or misinterpreted by professionals, sometimes with devastating consequences. In addition, because assessments can be difficult to make without a full and accurate client history, some members tend to protect erroneous team decisions rather than take corrective action when these are eventually discovered (Dane, 1985). When these types of conflicts arise, Compton and Galaway (1994) suggest that practitioners employ the following strategies to help reduce tension between team members while continuing as a client advocate:

1. Be comfortable with the area of competency you bring to the team. Recognize that while all team members have competencies that differ, no single team member is omnipotent. As such, practitioners should have confidence and comfort in their ability to advocate for clients, particularly when the advocacy effort falls within their area of expertise and competence.
2. Understand advocacy's timing. Specifically, recognize the political environment and set priorities to help determine which issues to advocate for and which ones to defer.
3. Learn how to advocate. Advocacy requires a well-reasoned position, free of provocation or attack (pp. 507–508).

Legal, Judicial, and Administrative Proceedings   The second type of forum most frequently used by direct service practitioners is the legal, judicial, and administrative systems. Three specific processes are available to clients and practitioners within these systems: (1) adversarial (concerning disputes and arguments); (2) accusatorial (concerning burden of proof); and (3) fairness (concerning equity and equality). These types of proceedings involve:

1. *Child welfare.* Includes social workers' participation in abuse, neglect, and dependency hearings; foster care and adoption proceedings; domestic violence hearings; permanency planning hearings; and juvenile justice issues
2. *Criminal law.* Includes social workers' assistance during initial investigations, arrests, formal charges, initial court appearances, bail hearings, attorney retentions, preliminary hearings, pleas, pretrial motions, trials, sentencings, and appeals

3. *Custodial issues.* Includes social workers' participation in adoption hearings, entrustment proceedings, termination of parental rights hearings, child welfare hearings, paternity issues, surrogate parenting, and accessing confidential adoption and birth records

4. *Custody and child support.* Includes social workers' participation in the appointment of a guardian *ad litem,* as well as primary caretaker issues, parental morality, property distribution, parental sexual preference, race and religion, joint and interstate custodial issues, nonparental visitation and custodial rights, paternity issues, child support collection, and interstate support problems

5. *Disabled adults.* Includes social workers' participation in the limitations and consequences of incompetency, as well as guardianship authority, responsibility, and appointment; self-imposed guardianship; representatives for benefit receipts; agency agreements; powers of attorney, living wills, and trusts; case management; and protective services

6. *Domestic violence.* Includes social workers' participation in protection hearings and protective orders; battered women's syndrome, child abuse and neglect hearings, and elder abuse and neglect proceedings

7. *Health care.* Includes social workers' participation in clients' right to receive medical care, as well as informed consent of adults, adults' right to refuse life-saving treatment (competency versus incompetency), medical care of children, and legal issues related to human reproduction (such as birth control, sterilization, abortion, and new reproductive technologies)

8. *Immigration and naturalization.* Includes social workers' involvement in helping immigrants obtain visas, as well as communicating alien rights; participation in deportation hearings; asylum, refugee, and extradition issues; citizenship and naturalization issues; and criminal matters

9. *Institutionalization.* Includes social workers' participation in the voluntary and involuntary admission of individuals with mental illness, as well as the developmentally disabled; clients' right to refuse treatment; clients' right to humane treatment in the least restrictive environment; clients' right of restraint freedom and seclusion; institutional employment; clients' right to privacy and personal property; First Amendment rights and freedoms; transfers; nursing home residents' rights; and prisoners' rights

10. *Juvenile justice.* Includes social workers' participation in custodial hearings, detention hearings, adjudicatory hearings, and dispositional decisions

11. *Marital issues and disputes.* Includes social workers' participation in common law and homosexual marriage issues, invalid marriage issues, interstate recognition, property issues and agreements (prenuptial and antinuptial), divorce, and alimony
12. *Mental health commitments.* Includes social workers' participation in legal authority and commitment standards, commitment hearings, procedural safeguards, and commitment of minors
13. *Public primary and secondary education.* Includes social workers' participation in discrimination hearings (such as race, wealth and alienage, sex, and disability), truancy issues, and disciplinary matters (such as corporal punishment, expulsion from school, and grounds for punishment), as well as the education of handicapped children (Melton, Petrila, Poythress, & Slobogin, 1997; Saltzman & Proch, 1990; Weissbrodt, 1989).

Sancier (1984) noted that "sometimes families need help dropping a hopeless prosecution, or lawyers must be dissuaded from insisting on courtroom testimony from an already frightened victim of child sexual abuse; sometimes the obvious need for an interpreter has been overlooked" (p. 3).

It is important to understand that although individuals and families are not regulated, current culture has become more litigious with respect to family affairs. Because federal and state governments do not interfere with individual and family rights based on civil rights protections, unbiased, third-party mediators are often asked to make decisions on issues traditionally outlined as personal and private. "As the 'rules' for individual and family behavior and responsibility become less clear, people are turning to the courts for guidance" (Spakes, 1987, p. 31). It is important for social workers to understand that these forums can be used beyond the traditional role of protecting the rights of the disempowered; specifically, decisions made in these forums impact developing social policies. As such, the legal, judicial, and administrative systems are very important advocacy forums for client advocacy representation.

Direct Practice Supervision   In professional social work, supervision is a managerial tool used to provide guidance and support to direct service practitioners. The traditional supervisory model involves one hour of consultation between the practitioner and supervisor each week. In that forum, individual cases are discussed and reviewed; treatment and service plans are assessed and modified. In many circumstances, decisions made will directly impact clients and their families. For example, practitioners and supervisors will often brainstorm alternative resources and actions for clients; they can also conjointly activate available formal and informal community resources (Carrilio, 1998; Friedman & Poertner, 1995). As such, direct practice supervision is a very important client advocacy forum.

Social Support System   One of the most important, yet oft neglected, forums available to practitioners is the client's social support system, which is composed of natural supports and social networks. Natural supports are considered intact relationships developed through daily, routine interactions over long periods of time. Social networks, on the other hand, comprise individuals who share mutual support through unique relationships. Natural supports and social networks often consist of family, friends, coworkers, and neighbors; they can also include individuals accessible through repetitive interactions in community programs and support groups (Northen, 1995; Sands, 1991). Ronnau (1995) stated that "[i]n the long run . . . it is the informal resources . . . [that] will sustain us—friends, neighbors, grandparents, aunts, uncles, cousins, retired teachers, coaches, and church volunteers" (p. 299).

Within support systems, "significant others help [clients] mobilize their personal resources; provide the material means and skills that are essential to improve the situation; and provide emotional support for efforts to cope with the problems" (Northen, 1995, p. 297). Clients' support systems are very important under client advocacy because they can buffer ongoing stress, and perpetuate meaningful involvement in the external community (Doherty & Dougherty, 1997; Sands, 1991). It is important to note, however, that some social networks have a negative impact on individuals within the group. For example, many networks will reinforce or sustain deviant behavior, while others will require conformity to peer norms. Further, some social networks maintain inflexible boundaries and thus demand or exclude others from membership or participation (Northen, 1995).

When advocates meet with members of clients' support systems, not only are they working with groups, they are also meeting in a forum. As such, practitioners should focus on "mobilizing the network as a source of support for clients; maintaining an effective network or one of its parts or repair an ineffective network; managing tension or conflict among the parts; seeking to add a new cluster to an impoverished or incomplete network; and disengaging clients from maladaptive affiliations with members of a network" (Northen, 1995, p. 299).

Peer Supervision and Support   The practitioner's support system is equally important and effective for identifying client advocacy goals and objectives as is the case with the client's support system. For example, colleagues use informal supports to share insights with one another about treatment plans and community resources. Because support systems encourage mutual trust and respect, they also enhance client proactivity. Consequently, mutual peer support helps professionals "identify the needs of families, develop individualized service plans, maintain consistency and continuity for the families, and deal with changes and crises" for the clients they serve (Carrilio, 1998).

Mediation   Chandler (1985) defines mediation as a "resource for handling conflict between people by providing a neutral forum in which disputants are encouraged to find a mutually satisfactory resolution to their problems" (p. 346). In this forum, mediators are always neutral third parties; their responsibilities are to (1) listen to the disputing parties, (2) facilitate open and honest communication, (3) obtain factual information, and (4) resolve dispute through compromise or other alternatives. It is important to note that mediation is an alternative to systemic judicial proceedings. Mediations have effectively resolved numerous disputes, to include conflicts between landlords and tenants, consumers and merchants, and neighborhoods and communities (Chandler, 1985).

Miscellaneous Forums   Other advocacy forums that are not discussed in detail here, but are certainly important, include meetings with review boards, school boards, parent-teacher organizations, insurance companies, licensing boards, professional associations, referral sources, counseling services, and consumer advocate groups (Eriksen, 1997; Kirst-Ashman & Hull, 1993; Northen, 1995).

Communication

In Chapter 3, basic guidelines for communicating through effective speaking and writing offer client advocates a foundation from which they can develop their skills. The general principles and procedures for persuasive writing and speaking hold true for all advocates, regardless of orientation. Because client advocacy is traditionally based on one-to-one and small group relationships, the first part of this section will focus on developing listening skills. It is within the context of "listening" that practitioners obtain the material information necessary to accomplish advocacy efforts. Such information can be as simple as determining *what* the client needs or *when* the client needs it.

An example of an effective client advocacy effort that directly resulted from the use of listening skills is that of Jose Nazario, an 18-year veteran with New York City's Mobilization for Youth. Several years ago, Nazario was interviewing a Hispanic family for housing assistance; at that time he learned that the family's children were placed in long-term foster care. The mother expressed concern about the length of this placement, approximately 10 years. After hearing the family's concerns, Nazario explored this situation with the foster care service agency; he discovered that one of the children had been sexually abused by her foster father over many years. In addition, Nazario also learned that the foster mother made numerous complaints to the agency about this molestation. Litigation ensued, and a $225,000 award was "assessed against the agency 'for violating a foster child's right to be free from physical and sexual abuse by her foster father'" (Nazario, 1984, p. 6).

Listening   Listening is very important to effective client advocacy. Greenstone and Leviton (1993) identified several guidelines to help maximize listening skills and techniques in direct practice:

1. Listening is a necessary component for the accurate exchange of information. It thus allows practitioners to explore clients' feelings, perspectives, knowledge, life skills, life domains, experiences, and underlying motives. When social workers use good and effective listening skills, clients tend to relax. In addition, effective listening establishes and enhances trust between the practitioner and client, as well as other parties involved.
2. Listening is a very difficult skill to learn; it not only requires consistent practice and use, *it also requires responsiveness*. While listening, practitioners should not only *hear* the information verbally provided, they should also *observe* body language as they interact with clients.
3. *Hearing* verbal information involves (a) determining the content and context of the information provided, (b) identifying extra emphases placed on words or phrases, and (c) identifying unusual speech patterns or recurring themes during the conversation. Practitioners are cautioned to not let their minds wander, or attend to other tasks, while the client is speaking; it is counterproductive to the session and to the advocacy process.
4. Practitioners should recognize and interpret nonverbal cues by *observing* clients' body language. Nonverbal language includes sighing, wincing, yawning, frowning, rapid eye blinking, avoiding eye contact, looking around, acting bored, flipping through paperwork, tapping fingers or feet, and "watching the clock." Watching for and recognizing body language cues provides the practitioner with valuable information. For example:

- Closed fists or crossed arms and legs could indicate *defensiveness*.
- Open or spread hands, or leaning forward, could indicate *openness*.
- Hands clasped behind the head, "steepled" fingers, or feet placed on a desk or table could indicate *confidence.*
- Glancing sideways at the practitioner, avoiding eye contact, or pointing the body toward an exit could indicate *suspicion.*
- Sitting on the edge of a chair, tilting the head, maintaining eye contact, or leaning forward could indicate *cooperation* (Greenstone & Leviton, 1993).

Speaking   Knowing how to interview others is a very important skill for direct service practitioners and can be used in all forums, casual or structured. Understanding the guiding principles of an interview not only will help practitioners structure productive interviews, but will also help them understand the semantics when they are being interviewed themselves (e.g., while testifying at judicial proceedings or in legal depositions). Such guiding principles are outlined below:

1. Know and understand your goals in advance; state them clearly in the beginning.
2. Set a comfortable pace and climate for the interview.
3. Clarify your role and what you anticipate from the interviewee.
4. Set forth and clarify your expectations. Ask for the interviewee's expectations, and clarify any that are unclear.
5. Explore information or responses that directly address your goal.
6. Facilitate responses in subtle, nondirective ways.
7. Sort and refine information, when necessary and appropriate.
8. Support the interviewee's participation in the process as well as his or her responses.
9. Set future expectations. (Flanagan & Flanagan, 1999).

Highlight 5.1 provides several important operational components necessary in the interview process.

Writing   Maintaining appropriate documentation is crucial to client advocacy. Specifically, information recorded during professional endeavors will ultimately become part of the case file and the advocacy effort. Regis (1994) reported that the best way a social worker can be prepared for court is "to anticipate . . . that the case might come to court—*and to keep meticulous*

| 5.1 | *The Interview* |

Stages of an Interview
GREETING
- Identify yourself and clarify or confirm your role.
- Create a pleasant, relaxed environment.
  OPENING. The opening provides the interviewee with a clear understanding of what to expect.
- Explain the reason for the interview.
- Give the interviewee an approximation of how much time it will take.
- Give the interviewee some idea of what information you already have.
- Summarize what you hope to learn during the interview.

Influence (continued)

BODY. The interview develops through dialogue and questioning.
- Ask the interviewee to discuss what (s)he feels is important.
- Begin with broad, general questions and move to more specific questions.
- Avoid leading questions, double questions, and bombarding.
- Use closed questions to zero in on a topic.
  CLOSING
- When closing, tell the interviewee when (s)he may expect to hear from you again.
- Refer back to the matter discussed with a concluding statement.
- Recap plans or decisions made.

Guidelines for Interviews
1. Begin with broad questions and move to more specific questions.
2. Avoid leading questions and emotional remarks.
Tone of voice, wording and moral implications can communicate bias and hamper rapport.
3. Use CLOSED questions to zero in on a topic.
4. Use reinforcement to encourage continued talking.
"I see," "Uhha." Repetition of one or two words from respondent; nod head; lean forward.
5. Use silence to encourage talking.
6. Use transitional phrases to purposefully guide the interview.
Transitions can be derived from prior questions or statements or can introduce a new or related topic. "You mentioned that . . ." "Let's talk about that a little more."
7. Use feedback (descriptive rather than evaluative; sharing).
8. Listen to the interviewee's questions and respond accordingly.

NOTE: If you sense the interviewee's discomfort with a question, retreat and rephrase it. Do not underestimate how someone else might perceive a question that is actually harmless or factual.

Source: Adapted from *The Comprehensive Training Program for The CASA/GAL (1989)*, NY: The Edna McConnell Clark Foundation, with permission.

---

records of his or her involvement in the case" (p. 12). Fernandez (1980) advises that practitioners "keep a log of all telephone calls and letters to [decision makers], and be sure to record the date and time. After a meeting . . . write a *letter of understanding* of what occurred at the meeting" (p. 82).

It is important to note that documentation not only includes records of telephone calls and meetings, but also includes official and unofficial files, personal case notes, and video and audio interview tapes. Such documentation is extremely important for practitioners representing clients in advocacy forums. Saltzman and Proch (1990) state that practitioners "cannot always rely on . . . memory . . . without documentation, a good case may be greatly weakened or even destroyed. Moreover, a lack of documentation increases the probability that evidence will be inconsistent and therefore less credible" (p. 53). Other written documents needed in direct service practice include court reports, treatment and service plans, referrals, biopsychosocial assessments, psychological evaluations, case reviews, intake reports, and hospitalization summaries.

INFLUENCE

Influence is the second essential action of social work advocacy. In order to be effective, advocates must persuade those decision makers with the power, authority, and resources necessary to change client conditions. It should not be surprising to learn that many direct service practitioners believe they have very little power to influence change for their clients. Friedman and Poertner (1995), however, stated that "the power to influence people is essential. In some situations, the case manager's ability to *influence* the judge to allow the child to live at home is the only power he or she has" (emphasis added) (p. 265). While these authors make a very important and accurate point, the concept of influence should never be trivialized under client advocacy. Rather, influence should be considered a core concept.

According to Friesen and Briggs (1995), influence is identified as "the ability of one person to affect or alter the behavior of another" (p. 73). It is interesting to note that this definition also describes, in part, the therapeutic relationship and direct service practice. Influence relies on three sources of power: (1) personal characteristics, (2) opportunity, and (3) expertise (Friesen & Briggs, 1995). It is virtually impossible to effectively influence others without a combination of all three power sources. It should be noted that practitioners have these power sources immediately available within the professional relationship. As such, social workers *do* have the power to positively influence clients' lives. When this power is used timely and effectively, they *can* effectuate important and necessary changes in their clients' environments.

Consider the following examples of influential client advocacy practiced through the years:

- Clinical social workers shifting their focus from ongoing and routine treatment to helping clients and families develop advocacy skills; then mobilizing those skills to help shape the services offered to and from other organizations and agencies (Petr & Spano, 1990)

- Social work practitioners using their specialized knowledge and expertise to improve resource availability and continuity of care to enhance effective and appropriate service delivery (Lash, 1996)
- Social workers appealing systemic decisions that negatively impact the delivery of services, such as decisions imposed by managed care organizations or bureaucratic and hierarchical administrations
- Case managers initiating and participating in judicial proceedings to obtain restraining or protective orders for victims of domestic violence (Peled & Edleson, 1994)
- Clinicians writing formal outpatient treatment plans for judicial proceedings in order to help maintain nonoffender clients in the community in lieu of institutionalization (Ashford, Macht, & Mylym, 1987)
- Case managers and practitioners identifying and enrolling children from low-income families in the new State Children's Health Insurance Program, where health care premiums are either free or significantly reduced

The authors outline and discuss in the text that follows the eight principles discussed in Chapter 4, and further supplement them with information useful for client advocates. In addition, information regarding groups that have effectively used influence as part of their advocacy efforts can be found in most of the websites outlined in Appendix A.

Identify the Issues and Set Goals[2]

Practitioners need to take the time and energy necessary to effectively and efficiently identify the client's problem before they set advocacy goals. In that regard, the authors provide here methods used to identify problems, criteria necessary to select and prioritize problems, and insight relating to organizing problem orientations.

Problem Identification   As discussed in Chapter 4, identifying the client's problem is the very first step in social work advocacy. At the direct service level of intervention, the client's problem is *always* a source of physical, emotional, behavioral, social, and/or psychological pain, and is frequently an individual or family hardship (O'Connor & Ammen, 1997). Such problems include difficulty in one or more of the following life domains: (1) physical health; (2) education; (3) safety and justice; (4) finance; (5) legal; (6) housing/living status; (7) employment; (8) mental health; (9) recreation; (10) culture; (11) transportation; (12) family planning; and (13) abuse, neglect, and exploitation. Based on these

---

[2]For purposes of this chapter, the terms *issue* and *problem* are being used interchangeably.

extensive variables, an organized operational process should be used to identify and outline the specific problem parameters. Although sometimes this process occurs in progressive stages, more often it occurs simultaneously.

Understand the client's background and history. In many instances, the first thing practitioners must complete is a comprehensive assessment of the client's background and history. This task will involve various levels of interaction with clients, families, caregivers, as well as corollary community agencies and alternate service providers (Cole, 1995). At a minimum, the following client issues should be discussed at this stage:

1. Biological, psychological, social, behavioral, and emotional stressors
2. Existing and potential strengths and weaknesses
3. Internal and external outreach capacity, as well as available supports and resources
4. Need for a thorough psychological, medical, or psychiatric assessment
5. Risk of harm to self or others
6. Motivational level for change and/or treatment. (Hepworth & Larsen, 1993; Peterson & Urquiza, 1993; Sands, 1991)

Ask basic questions. Basic questions answer the *who, what, when, where, why,* and *how* of the presenting problem. The first question should always be "what is the problem?" As answers emerge, important characteristics and stressors should be extracted and prioritized. Information obtained should also be verified, clarified, and thoroughly documented. Schloss and Jayne (1994) outline several additional questions that can help build a working foundation; addressing them will also help eliminate a too narrow perspective of the problem:

1. Who is affected by the problem? Who benefits from the problem's continuation? Is someone's status or welfare sustained by its continuation?
2. When did the problem first start? Has it been continuous, or was it a single, isolated instance? Is it worse at certain times and better at others? What started or enhanced it? How or why did the client notice it? How did it impact the client?
3. What kinds of changes would help resolve the problem? How would you know when the problem was adequately addressed and resolved?
4. What has been done thus far to address the problem? What was the end result? Should that intervention be continued, or should another be implemented?
5. Are there laws and regulations relating to the problem at hand? Practitioners should refer to the NASW *Code of Ethics* for professional guidance.
6. Under what time frame should the problem be resolved? How long should the entire process take? (p. 235)

Throughout this analysis, it is important that practitioners clarify others' views in order to keep the process moving in the appropriate direction.

Identify key factors. With solid information and interpretation in hand, the next step is to identify the key factors that relate to the problem and the client. Key factors are identified, in part, by answers to these and other questions:

1. What themes, events, individuals, and/or systems are constant for the client? How do they affect the problem?
2. Do these factors have an identified role in the client's functional capacity?
3. Has the client established any primary or secondary relationships as a result of this problem? If so, what are their dynamics? Are these relationships functional or dysfunctional? Do they help or hurt the problem?
4. Are specific cognitive, experiential, or behavioral attributes consistent with the client and the problem?
5. How is this problem perceived by family members or significant others?
6. Do ethnic, cultural, and/or spiritual factors contribute positively or negatively to the client or the problem?
7. Are there any special circumstances associated with this problem? If so, should they be allowed to continue?

Identifying key factors helps practitioners build a framework around the problem, and provides the structure necessary to continue the advocacy process.

Identify the intended and unintended consequences. A consequence is a variable that occurs when the identified objective or goal is accomplished. For example, a client is accepted into a transitional homeless shelter; *therefore, he will receive food, clothing, and shelter while he remains in the program.* On the other hand, an unintended consequence is an unexpected corollary variable that also occurs when the intended objective or goal is accomplished. For example, although the client receives food, clothing, and a physical dwelling while he remains in the transitional shelter, *he has difficulty finding a job because, as a shelter resident, he is stereotyped as a deadbeat. This community attitude thus perpetuates his homeless situation.* It is important that practitioners anticipate any adverse intended or unintended consequences at this stage, if possible.

Clarify the theoretical perspective. Before setting the goal, practitioners should clarify the problem's theoretical perspective. Questions that help guide this process are: Is the problem chronic, or the result of a crisis? Did poor judgment or irresponsible behavior contribute to the problem, or did it result from inadequate skills and resources? Did the community or system fail to follow through with contracts made with or for the client? These answers help determine which theoretical perspective would be the most effective and appropriate for the client's presenting problem (i.e., crisis intervention, behavioral theory, cognitive theory, systems theory, etc.). Woods and Hollis (1990) noted that "[t]heories vary in many ways. They differ greatly, for instance, in the emphasis they put upon the client-worker relationship: its nature and its importance in treatment" (p. 486). For these and other reasons, it is important for practitioners to identify the operating theoretical perspective before engaging in the advocacy process.

Set the Goal(s)   As mentioned in Chapter 4, goals are intended outcomes designed to reduce or alleviate symptoms associated with presenting problems. At the client advocacy level of intervention, practitioners should identify four types of goals: (1) immediate or short-term, (2) intermediate, (3) long-term, and (4) outreach. With respect to a homeless client, an *immediate goal* would be locating appropriate shelter for that evening. An *intermediate goal* would be to help the client secure appropriate shelter until he or she finds employment and income. A *long-term goal* would be to help the client obtain the necessary skills and resources for ongoing self-sufficiency. An *outreach goal* would target the jurisdictional board of supervisors or a similar organized decision-making body to address the issue at the community or societal level.

Get the Facts

In this section, the authors outline information that client advocates need to know, and how to go about getting this information.

Sheafor, Horejsi, and Horejsi (1994) imparted the following wisdom: "[B]efore you engage in a confrontational tactic, be sure you understand the facts of the matter. Do not base your decisions on hearsay or on one-sided descriptions of the situation . . . get the facts before you decide how to proceed" (p. 405). In direct practice, facts are obtained throughout the professional relationship. However, fact finding should not only focus on clients and their problems, it should also concentrate on external factors that contribute to the problems. For example, entitlement program eligibility requirements often change contingent upon federal, state, and local policies; this type of information is very important to direct service practitioners. If a teenage mother presented with an undernourished child not long after losing her WIC eligibility, that information would be important to the practitioner and crucial to the advocacy process. According to Cole (1989), "[I]t is particularly important for a social worker . . . to be current on entitlement programs because patients' conditions or illnesses can be a determining factor in eligibility. A pregnant woman may be eligible for Medicaid for only a limited period of time, but that insurance coverage may be crucial to her or her family's financial situation during the months of pregnancy" (p. 83).

How do practitioners get the facts? Once again, they ask questions. Some questions practitioners should consider at this stage include:

- Who controls decision making?
- What is the formal power structure?
- What is the informal power structure?
- Who controls the budget or who sets priorities for use of money?
- How does the political system impact upon the system or agency?
- What are the channels for complaints or grievances?
- Who are actual or potential change agents within the system? Outside the system?
- What are the sources of resistance to change in the institutions? (Fernandez, 1980, pp. 83–84)

Plan Strategies and Tactics

According to Altman et al. (1994), a *strategy* provides a broad plan and approach for achieving advocacy goals, while *tactics* are the specific actions and events designed to carry out the strategy. Both strategies and tactics are integral to the client advocacy process. In addition to the strategies and tactics identified in Chapter 4, the following are necessary to enhance effective client advocacy practice.

Strategies   *Do No Harm.* The first and most important strategy under the client advocacy typology is to do no harm. As Spakes (1987) reported, "[T]here is growing evidence that, despite their best intentions, the efforts of social workers . . . are doing more harm than good" (p. 35). This is best demonstrated when practitioners favor the victim to the exclusion of all others; critical information, observations, and strengths related to the problems are thus overlooked. Consider, for a moment, children removed from biological homes based on abuse or neglect allegations. Practitioners' first instincts are to place these children in long-term foster care and ostracize the parents. From that point forward, parents' movements, behaviors, and attitudes are scrutinized, and negative assessments are recorded on official documentation. However, what about circumstances where abuse allegations are unfounded based on misinterpretations by unrelated third parties? There are also situations where multiple and cumulative psychosocial stressors, such as the loss of a job or the death of a loved one, are contributing factors to family dysfunction. The reality is that children placed in foster care are often lost in the system, with parents deprived of many legal rights. More often than not, children would benefit from remaining in the home with supportive community services such as day care or respite, thus rebuilding and enhancing family functioning (Nazario, 1984; Spakes, 1987). Herbert and Mould (1992) further advised practitioners to stray from strategies that publicly threaten their agency. Remember, today's solutions often turn into tomorrow's problems.

Develop a strong working knowledge base. Certainly you have heard the phrase "knowledge is power." Within client advocacy relationships, power and action are usually synonymous. What kind of knowledge is important at the client advocacy level? Weil, Zipper, and Dedmon (1995) outlined the following knowledge as crucial to the client advocacy process:

1. An understanding of case management's function and process, as well as its role within the family and with other service providers
2. Accurate and current information about relevant legislation, as well as state, local, and organizational policies
3. Current information about client confidentiality, particularly agency and professional policies and procedures
4. How to access networks of resources and services
5. The ability to assess and improve interprofessional and interorganizational relationships
6. Current information about family functioning, to include the interrelationship of stress between the family system and its individual family members
7. A comprehensive understanding of the therapeutic relationship (client assessment through termination)
8. An understanding about each aspect and level of mental health services, to include in-home and community-based interventions, residential care, day treatment, and hospitalization (pp. 227–228).

It is also important for practitioners to have comprehensive knowledge about the legal and judicial systems. Without this knowledge, advocates will undoubtedly fail to meet the criteria and expectations of critical legal mandates. For example, reports typically need to be filed prior to judicial and administrative hearings; such reports frequently determine client outcomes. Further, as mandated reporters, practitioners are expected to report abuse and neglect allegations to appropriate authorities. Once again, knowing the expectations and requirements of legal mandates will help social workers effectively advocate with and for clients (Sancier, 1984).

Collaborate. Collaboration is one of the most effective strategies under client advocacy. Collaboration is important because it builds the knowledge base and strength for successful advocacy efforts. According to Bailey and Koney (1996), "collaborative efforts are interactive structures that emphasize the creation of a partnership among parties in which joint participation ideally leads to the achievement of a common goal" (p. 605). Under client advocacy, collaborative efforts include resource sharing, providing or enhancing effective and efficient service delivery, and realigning power structures (Bailey & Koney, 1996). Dane (1985) further advised that collaborative efforts help maintain and sustain clients' natural support systems over the longer term.

Tactics *Obtain up-to-date and relevant information.* Fact finding extends beyond the analytical process described earlier in this chapter. It requires that practitioners look for answers from other sources. How do practitioners find information necessary to help them achieve their client advocacy effort? The most effective method is the interview (see Highlight 5.1), which can occur through face-to-face interactions, on the telephone, through secondhand interviews recorded on video or audio tapes, and through records and reports. Another method is to secure accurate and up-to-date information related to the problems, issues, organizations, systems, and procedures. Fact finding is important for two reasons: first, "advocates require an in-depth knowledge of the subject if they are to achieve consideration. Second, without such research, potential advocates may not become aware of unsatisfactory condi-tions that [clients] are experiencing" (Claxton, 1981, p. 52).

Provide hands-on training. Many clients lack the skills and resources nec-essary to function optimally. However, with the multiple limitations and bur-dens placed on professional practitioners, it is necessary to teach clients and their support systems advocacy skills and techniques. It is important to note that members of support systems will remain with clients longer than social work practitioners. Thus, hands-on training is more productive and effective in the long run. The long-term results and rewards are clear; the more training prac-titioners provide to clients and supportive members, the greater the likelihood of long-term success. Further, this support and training allows clients and sup-port systems to maintain shared control of their unique situations. Overall, this type of work has reinforced family members' reliance on one another "as a basis for the support and empowerment" (Dane, 1985, p. 506).

Initiate legal action. Practitioners should identify and mobilize legal action of concern or distress to clients. "Social workers . . . should not be passive col-laborators in the system, but should be active, aggressive advocates for their clients, even if this means confronting the system head-on. The way to con-front the system is through the system itself—through knowing and applying, and challenging and changing, the law" (Nazario, 1984, p. 5). It is important to note that changes made on behalf of oppressed, vulnerable, and indigent pop-ulations are frequently initiated to comply with established laws, not from a sense of humanitarianism. If practitioners truly want to help their clients, they need to be part of the system, particularly if it has a destructive capability. Nazario (1984) further notes that not only do practitioners have a moral obli-gation to initiate legal action on behalf of clients, "they are in a position to know what needs changing" (p. 5).

Provide expert testimony. Numerous opportunities exist for practitioners to be influential in the legal, judicial, and administrative processes. "In fact, lawyers are becoming aware that 'independent' social workers can be excellent resources and powerful expert witnesses if they are properly qualified" (Spakes, 1987, p. 36). Since social work practitioners typically obtain experience in public and private agencies and organizations, they understand how bureaucracies function. On the other hand, because these practitioners are no longer a part of those systems, they can usually accomplish more than agency representatives. This objective testimony can effectively counterbalance the testimony of agency workers. Sancier (1984) noted that "there are social workers who have demonstrated competence, made themselves indispensable to lawyers, and forged mutually respecting alliances that work to the benefit of clients" (p. 3). However, Hardcastle et al. (1997b) warn that any testimony can have a detrimental impact on clients; some of the multiple risks can include anger from family members and friends, retaliation, or a reduction of benefits (pp. 366–367).

Supply Leadership

You may recall that Chapter 4 identified leadership as change. Tropman (1997), however, stated that "[l]eadership involves taking new steps and thinking about new ideas and approaches" (p. 29). He further identified two aspects to leadership: (1) defining a future, and (2) creating conditions and attitudes that encourage others to contribute to the change effort. Nazario (1984) stated that "the role of social workers should not consist of simply following agency policies and procedures . . . social workers should be reaching out much, much more . . . we should be in the forefront" (p. 7).

Why is it important to integrate leadership into client advocacy? First, clients often present with the "symptoms of the mental and moral health of their communities" (Doherty & Dougherty, 1997). When clients engage in social work relationships, they are often burdened with numerous social anxieties such as community safety, job security, financial stress, and inaccessible health care. As practitioners, our job is to help clients relieve or resolve their multiple stressors. Even when successful at the micro level, practitioners often send clients back to unhealthy communities. How can advocacy efforts be successful without effective long-term change? Second, clients identify social workers as community leaders. To not offer appropriate and effective leadership is to encourage client dependency and passivity. Third, clients are not only consumers but producers of mental health. Consider, for example, community self-help groups such as Alcoholics Anonymous, Narcotics Anonymous, and Adult Children of Alcoholics. These groups are not run by professionals; rather, they are organized and managed *by* the community *for* the community. It should be noted that these groups are some of the most successful and effective recovery programs available. In other words, to not empower clients to promote change within their own communities is the equivalent of perpetuating unhealthy communities.

Recall the extract from the NASW *Code of Ethics* outlined earlier in this chapter that stated, in part, "[a] historic and defining feature of social work is the profession's focus on individual well-being in the social context *and the well-being of society.*" How can this goal be accommodated under client advocacy? First, make it part of your practice to ask clients to give back to their communities. Encourage them, for instance, to vote in local, state, and national elections or to participate in community and civic actions. Second, ask colleagues to do the same in their practice, and to become more involved in community service. Finally, get involved yourself! Join an advocacy group and take a stand on an important social issue.

Get to Know Decision Makers and Their Staff

As discussed throughout this chapter, direct service practitioners are in constant and direct contact with decision makers and staff in their endless client representation capacities—as members of interdisciplinary teams; through work with collaborative ventures; while working with lawyers, judges, administrators, legislators, and colleagues; and through work with families and other agencies. As such, advocates have endless opportunities to engage in this practice principle. Friedman and Poertner (1995) advise that "[t]he most significant impact a case manager can have . . . is developing a positive relationship as a supportive ally and as an advocate" (p. 264). It is important to note, however, that relationships are based on respect as well as an understanding that decision makers maintain certain roles with various functions as part of that process. This means that, in order to develop positive working relationships, advocates should get to know them as individuals, understand and respect their role in the system, recognize their individual strengths, and praise their good work. This suggests spending time with them to develop strong working relationships. Sheafor, Horejsi, and Horejsi (1994), however, warn that practitioners need to recognize and respect appropriate chains of command; in other words, do not request conferences with decision makers until after you have met with their staff (p. 405).

Broaden the Base of Support

Because the social work profession has made a commitment to serving underprivileged, disenfranchised, and oppressed populations, its practitioners must be willing to facilitate and change the quality and quantity of available service delivery and client care (Ruffolo & Miller, 1994). According to Nazario (1984), "social workers . . . should not be passive collaborators in the system, but should be active, aggressive advocates for their clients, even if it means confronting the system head-on" (p. 5). In addition to the general guidelines discussed in Chapter 4, advocates should actively participate in team meetings, join community and civic organizations, serve on local community services boards, and volunteer time and expertise to community projects and programs. Nazario (1984) noted that through his work with various community boards, he has successfully ensured that many clients otherwise underrepresented were adequately and appropriately served in their communities. Hardcastle et al. (1997b) suggest numerous other ways to bring people together—support groups, health fairs, recycling parties, community education, and day camps (p. 364). Hunter (1979) reported that a nutrition site committee developed after a social worker encouraged elderly citizens to use their jurisdiction's existing community services. Endless opportunities exist to use advocacy parameters while broadening your base of support.

Be Persistent

Persistence is more than an action or activity; it is an attitude that guides social workers in their day-to-day practice and activity. Persistence is not only a skill, it is also an inherent value. Herbert and Mould (1992) advised that "it is social work practitioners who must take primary responsibility for incorporating the advocacy role into their day-to-day practice" (p. 128). In many social service settings, advocates often feel they do not have the time and energy to push decision makers into action on an ongoing basis. It is important to understand that decision makers and their staff are just as busy as practitioners. Without the drive and force to support the advocacy effort, requests or demands for action will fall through the cracks. How can social workers be persistent? Team meetings provide opportunities to call advocacy partners into action. Telephone calls, requests for meetings, letters, petitions, and public hearings are always effective strategies. Herbert and Mould (1992) advised that short-term pain turns into long-term gain. Practitioners should realize that they need to ensure that services, rights, resources, entitlements, and benefits do not favor the system at the expense of the client.

Evaluate Your Advocacy Effort

Evaluating advocacy actions and efforts is not only an important practice principle, it is essential to client efficacy. In addition to the guidelines provided in Chapter 4, practitioners should evaluate client advocacy efforts with the client and their support systems multiple times throughout the process as well as once the outcome has been achieved. This can be done during meetings, after court hearings, and through ongoing communication. One evaluation process is to assess the client's outcome. For example, did the effort achieve its stated purpose and goals? Was the client's problem relieved or resolved? Evaluation also needs to address client satisfaction. It is important that advocates understand that client relationships and objectives may need to be restructured during the evaluation process. Evaluation also provides the foundation for work with other clients in the future. Regardless of orientation, advocacy actions cannot be completed without using evaluation as an applied and practiced principle.

SUMMARY

Client advocacy is a specialized practice area that requires specific skills and techniques; its purpose is to protect, enforce, and ensure clients' rights, entitlements, resources, services, and benefits. Client advocacy is specific to *one* individual, unit (family, group), or entity (organization, community). Under these dimensions, "client" boundaries cannot be fluid; rather, its membership must be fixed. According to scholars, client advocacy is practiced by more than 50% of direct service providers and clinical practitioners.

Under client advocacy, representation and influence remain fundamental objectives, as identified, described, and discussed within the general advocacy framework. However, numerous differences exist under client advocacy practice parameters. For example, under exclusivity, social work practitioners must have knowledge of and competency with multicultural and diversity issues. Mutuality presents numerous challenges, as advocates often represent clients from vulnerable populations such as children, the elderly, persons with mental disabilities, and individuals with serious mental illness, to name a few. Forums most often used under client advocacy are interdisciplinary, multidisciplinary, intradisciplinary, case management, and treatment teams; legal, judicial, and administrative proceedings; direct practice supervision; and social support systems. In addition to speaking and writing skills discussed in previous chapters, listening is of paramount importance for effective client advocacy.

There are also numerous differences with respect to influence that should not be ignored. While the nine practice principles remain intact and are necessary components to influence decision makers and other related parties, several specific nuances have changed. Three client advocacy strategies and four tactics are highlighted here:

> *Strategies:* (1) do no harm, (2) develop a strong working knowledge base, and (3) collaborate.
>
> *Tactics:* (1) obtain up-to-date and relevant information, (2) provide hands-on training, (3) initiate legal action, and (4) provide expert testimony.

DISCUSSION QUESTIONS

1. What are the requisite elements of client advocacy, and why are they important?
2. How is *client* defined under client advocacy practice parameters, and what characteristics distinguish it from *client* under cause, legislative, and administrative advocacy?

3. What is the primary mission of client advocacy, and where should its practice parameters stop?
4. Which social work principles and values are found under client advocacy?
5. *Exclusivity* describes the relationship between the client and advocate as "focused on, centered on, and responsible to the client." What are some of the characteristics and practice parameters specific to advocacy?
6. What are the short- and long-term benefits to the client associated with effective mutuality? What do clients gain? What do social work practitioners gain?
7. What theoretical approaches provide the foundation for advocacy with vulnerable populations? Outline several principles and practice implications for each.
8. Identify the various advocacy forums and discuss their differences as well as their importance to the client advocacy process.
9. Why are listening skills important to effective client advocacy?
10. Identify why influence is necessary to effective client advocacy, and discuss the nine steps necessary to accomplish this goal.

RECOMMENDED READINGS

Flanagan, R. S., & Flanagan, J. S. (1999). *Clinical interviewing.* New York: Wiley.

Freddolino, P. P., & Moxley, D. P. (1992). Refining an advocacy model for homeless people coping with psychiatric disabilities. *Community Mental Health Journal, 28*(4), 337–352.

Friesen, B. J., & Poertner, J. (1995). *From case management to service coordination for children with emotional, behavioral, or mental disorders: Building on family strengths.* Baltimore, MD: Paul H. Brookes.

Gerhart, U. C. (1990). *Caring for the chronic mentally ill.* Itasca, IL: F. E. Peacock.

Kirst-Ashman, K. K., & Hull, G. H., Jr. (1993). *Understanding generalist practice.* Chicago: Nelson-Hall.

Ronnau, J. (1995). Family advocacy services: A strengths model of case management. In B. J. Friesen & J. Poertner (Eds.), *From case management to service coordination for children with emotional, behavioral, or mental disorders: Building on family strengths.* Baltimore, MD: Paul H. Brookes.

Cause Advocacy

*I have never been able to turn down a good cause. I've come to see all injustices,
no matter how small or seemingly unrelated as linked.*

MAGGIE KUHN, FOUNDER OF THE GREY PANTHERS

OVERVIEW

Social work advocates regularly help individual clients or a family succeed in
obtaining services or righting an injustice. But, as Sunley (1970) stated so
accurately, "[social] workers struggle time after time to rectify wrongs suffered
by clients. Sometimes they succeed . . . but they are too often aware . . . that
ten or a hundred other people *in similar circumstances* continue to suffer for
lack of [effective] intervention" (p. 347). When human rights violations, injustice, or indignity transcend one person or family, social workers have the
opportunity to advocate for a remedy needed by several clients or even other
people unknown to them. This is often known as *cause advocacy,* that is,
addressing problems affecting a large group or class of persons with similar
concerns. In fact, some argue that *cause* advocacy is a logical extension of
client advocacy, that is, the individual's case serves as the basis for broader
action in changing policies or conditions for a larger group, be they abused or
neglected infants, single mothers with AIDS, homeless mentally ill persons, or
elderly persons with disabilities (Holmes, 1981).

Taylor (1987) speaks of this client-to-cause progression as a *dynamic* relationship between information and action. Social workers may notice similarities in the type of problems individual clients have, and, after repetition after
repetition, they determine to act to effect change in policies, laws, or practices
affecting specific groups or large numbers of persons with similar problems
(Hepworth et al., 1997).

Among the various terms describing cause advocacy are the following:
"class advocacy, systems advocacy, community advocacy, group advocacy, and
citizens advocacy" (Erickson et al., 1991; Fiedler & Antonak, 1991; Gerhart,
1990; Kirst-Ashman & Hull, 1993; McCullagh, 1988; Panitch, 1974; Schloss &
Jayne, 1994; Sheafor et al., 1994; Traczek, 1987; Williams, 1986). While each
of these terms has its own particular emphasis, the authors describe cause
advocacy as *promoting changes in policies and practices affecting all persons
in a certain group or class, for example, the disabled, welfare recipients, elderly immigrants, or battered women.* Cause advocacy may be required when
problems result from conditions beyond the client's ability to change or influence them as an individual. Cause advocacy also reflects social work's fundamental commitment to the person-in-environment perspective by attempting
to modify external conditions that are deleterious to a group of people
(Mickelson, 1995).

Cause advocates will seek changes in law and public policy, and they may even bring lawsuits in order to promote a needed change. Examples of changes in public policy effected by cause advocates are: early laws prohibiting child labor; P.L. 94-142, The Education for All Handicapped Children Act of 1975; P.L. 99-319, The Protection and Advocacy for Mentally Ill Individuals Act of 1986; The Americans with Disabilities Act of 1990; and the U.S. Supreme Court decision, *Saenz v. Roe*, in 1999, which disallowed California's ruling to limit new state residents to welfare benefits received in their previous state during their first year's residency in California (Yoo, 1999). Cause advocacy is undertaken for efficiency purposes, since appealing one issue at a time is too costly and cumbersome (Paul, 1977).

In the following text we present both of the fundamental advocacy skills, representation and influencing, in the context of cause advocacy. Using the authors' new definition, social work advocates can incorporate this specialized knowledge and skills into their professional careers and interventions.

Nursing Homes Benefit from Community Advocacy

A community group formed a council to monitor the care of residents of a private nursing facility, to support family members of residents, and to help staff. No patients or family members were on the council. These advocates simply believed in the importance of nursing home reform and acted out of their Christian ethic. Nurse aides called the council's hotline one spring to report a litany of health code violations. They had seen an RN beating a resident in a wheelchair, they were understaffed, and there was a shortage of linens, poor housekeeping practices, and inadequate nutrition.

After documenting these problems as well as they could, the council filed a complaint with the Department of Health Services (DOHS) alleging 37 separate violations. On the same day, they held a press conference in front of the nursing home, describing in detail the situation of the residents. The group gave leaflets to visitors to give to residents who could submit anonymous complaints to the council. Over the next four months, reports of poor care continued to trickle out, and the council submitted them all to DOHS, which still did not insist that the facility comply with the law. So, the council began to pressure the owners.

Members of the council met with the county district attorney to demand that he bring a lawsuit against the facility, and within a month, a $250,000 lawsuit related to violations of the Fair Business Practices Act was brought. Then a woman resident died due to neglect of her diabetic condition. The

(Continued)

council again held a press conference and a candlelight vigil to focus attention on the facility. At a meeting, a letter was written with a list of demands and sent by certified mail to the owners. When the owners refused to respond, the council sent 30 members in cars, surprising the owners with a house call. When they were ordered off the premises, they broke into small groups and leafleted the neighborhood, asking readers to call the owners.

When the owners continued to refuse to meet directly with the council, members picketed the two real estate offices where the owners worked, demanding that they bring the facility into compliance or get out of the health care business. One month after this demonstration, the council held a victory celebration announcing that the owners had decided to sell the nursing home to a nonprofit nursing home corporation. Follow up reports indicated that the quality of life for residents had improved substantially.

[Case based on Williams, C. (1986). Improving care in nursing homes using community advocacy. Social Scientific Medicine, 23(12), 1297–1303.]

REPRESENTATION

Cause advocates must be focused on representing the concerns of a class of clients. They can represent them through skills in writing and speaking. In addition, social workers strive to communicate exclusively on behalf of their cause and to work jointly with a group, empowering individuals to speak up themselves. There are many public and private forums where cause advocates can choose to present their positions. The text that follows presents specialized applications to social work practice that a cause advocate would promote.

Exclusivity

From the definition in Chapter 2, a cause advocate would *focus singularly on the best interests of the group of clients, and consider the group's needs as the sole priority; all activities and actions would be designed to address the concerns of the group first and foremost.* The council in the Case 6.1 vignette illustrates how the advocates focused singularly on the best interests of the nursing home residents. All of their plans, strategies, tactics, and energy were aimed at benefiting the residents. Below are several questions with particular relevance to the cause advocate.

Who is the "client" when a cause advocacy initiative develops in the community? Is the client the group of actually afflicted people or the well-intentioned advocacy person(s) or group? Can a neighborhood group or voluntary association truly represent the actual views of the nursing home residents in Case 6.1? Or are they only persons who are *trying* to speak on behalf of the group? Are not a particular advocacy group's views embedded in value stances about what *they* consider to be the "best interests" of a given population?

Unlike working exclusively with one person, cause advocates must attempt to synthesize a large, relatively divergent group of personal opinions, whether they come from the afflicted group or concerned others. Care must be taken to be sure that the advocate and/or the community represent what the clients' needs are (Ross, 1977b). Even if actual members of a disadvantaged group speak from personal experience about the issues, they only represent their own views, not those of every person in the selected group. Acting exclusively on behalf of a group or cause is complicated because it is so difficult to determine clearly the exact point of view of the entire group.

To whom does the cause advocate owe the greatest loyalty? Do cause advocates give primary loyalty to the "cause," to the community group backing the cause, or to the actual group whose common concerns the advocate is hoping to resolve? The current NASW *Code of Ethics* (1996) in section 1.01 notes that the social worker's *primary* responsibility is to promote the well-being of clients; and under section 6.01, social workers are to promote the general welfare of society, from local to global levels, and the development of people, their communities, and environments. Care must be taken not to disconnect the afflicted group and its circumstances from the more abstract "cause" that advocates may be pursuing. Causes sometimes take on a life of their own and participants become competitive about winning the battles, not the war. The well-being of the members of the group should not be submerged in fighting willy-nilly for the "cause."

What happens to the "individual" in the group or large-numbered cause advocacy efforts? As Paul (1977) stated, cause advocacy is issue-oriented, not individual-oriented. It focuses on a problem, not a person. It has as its goal a common need, not a unique need. It is initiated because of a similarity of problems and unmet needs. Cause advocacy is also undertaken for purposes of efficiency; it simply takes too much time to do some things "one person at a time." When decisions are considered that are based on the "general welfare" or "common good," it is possible that the cause advocate may lose sight of the individual person. Paul (1977) reminded the cause advocate that advocacy "must keep the common interest and the individual need in balance, remembering that, at its most profound meaning, the mission of advocacy is the rights of the individual" (pp. 28–29).

Can a cause advocate ever remain "impartial"? While professional social workers must always refrain from imposing their own values and interests over and above the self-determination of clients, cause advocates who assume an "impartial" or neutral attitude usually end up supporting the status quo (Mickelson, 1995). The authors agree with Mickelson (1995) that advocacy is attempting to bring about change, and advocates who are impartial cannot create public pressure on those with power. The NASW *Code of Ethics* (1996) clearly states that social workers must be concerned with the general welfare and participate in advocating change; advancing social, economic, political, and cultural values compatible with social justice; eliminating discrimination; and improving basic living conditions.

Mutuality

> *During our campaign, I also learned something about my own philosophy of advocacy. I believe that social work is most effective when it helps people solve their own problems, rather than solving them for them. I think the concept of empowerment should be the key to the field of social work. Empowering citizens is not as dramatic or glamorous or even as quick as "marching on Washington," but I believe it is more effective and long-lasting.*

JONATHAN

For "cause" advocates, *mutuality* incorporates other social work values such as self-determination and empowerment. Collaborating *with* a group or class of people such as the homeless mentally ill or battered women may be, in fact, more difficult than representing one individual because, whenever there are several people involved, there will be several different dimensions and proposals to consider. Decision making for the cause advocate would ideally take place with a majority of the afflicted group participating. Achieving consensus or even informed decision making remains a goal-to-be-achieved for most advocates.

Then there are some client groups who will never be able to speak or participate on their own behalf: infants who are abused, severely mentally ill persons, the developmentally disabled, and incompetent elderly persons. If such groups are the clients, who can legitimately represent them? Self-determination simply cannot be obtained here (Mickelson, 1995), and yet, someone must speak and act or grave dangers may overtake these vulnerable persons. In these cases, professional standards, moral codes, and/or religious values can be used as guidelines to determine what is in these clients' best interests. Most governments have already established agencies and policies for these populations, but as history has indicated, there may still be room to improve them when human dignity and respect for each person are not valued highly. Advocates who try to assist such groups usually attempt to decide about the well-being of the group of afflicted persons in a manner the latter would *likely* choose.

Basis for Mutuality   The premier social work principle of "begin where the client is" forms the basic rationale for the mutual relationship between the cause advocate and a class of vulnerable persons such as foster children, foreign refugees, AIDS victims, or nursing home residents (Riley, 1971). When there is a difference in perception about what is important or what issue should be pursued, advocates should go with the clients because the "person wearing the shoes knows best where the shoes pinch" (Riley, 1971, p. 379; Schloss & Jayne, 1994).

Another fundamental social work principle undergirding mutuality is the principle of self-determination. What does this group of clients want? What are their expressed needs? Even though cause advocates may suggest activity to improve certain conditions or to ensure persons' rights are honored, advocates are bound to respect the wishes of the group of clients (Hepworth et al., 1997). If a group of battered women do not wish to give testimony about arrest policies at a public legislative hearing, then advocates should not sacrifice client preferences for their own future-oriented desire to effect change (Holmes, 1981). Advocates should go no further in advocacy actions than the group wishes to go. (See the ethical discussion on pages 204–205.)

Mutuality also implies "partnering" in designing, implementing, and evaluating services. It is important to decide about advocacy actions based on the knowledge, expertise, and needs of the clients, and not only on those of the providers (Moxley & Freddolino, 1991). Support groups, clients, and professional social work advocates can pool their knowledge, skills, and experiences in order to advocate effectively. Ross (1977b) rejected inequality between advocates and clients and suggested that advocates adopt a willingness to be criticized, to listen to group concerns, and be humble in the exercise of judgment.

Another basis for cause advocacy is the goal of empowering people to participate in decision making. Mickelson (1995) notes that enhanced self-respect, confidence, knowledge, self-esteem, and skills are usually upgraded when empowerment is a basic principle used by advocates. Schloss and Jayne (1994) state that "the consumer remains the center of all decisions regarding his or her life" (p. 246). Kirst-Ashman and Hull (1993) give several reasons for promoting empowerment-based collaboration: (1) chances for success are higher if clients participate; (2) clients are more likely to use and value resources they had a hand in developing; (3) resources are more likely to be appropriate when clients have helped create them; (4) clients gain a sense of effectiveness; and (5) working with others provides a sense of participation and a support network.

Pitfalls   The following observations represent dimensions of mutuality to which cause advocates should be particularly sensitive:

    1. If cause advocates do not involve those who are disadvantaged, for example, nursing home residents, the homeless mentally ill, victims

of domestic violence, juvenile offenders, and so on, in the planning and decision making, then they can quickly be labeled and dismissed by authorities as *outside agitators* (Williams, 1986). Advocates can avoid this dilemma by seeking participation by representatives from the afflicted group.

2. Without the involvement of those affected by unjust policies or inadequate resources, cause advocates can easily become *paternalistic,* claiming to know the interests of clients more thoroughly than the clients themselves (Ross, 1977b). Richan (1973) urges that cause advocates refrain from taking over too much responsibility, and that they promote client action rather than stepping in for them. This author also suggests using the term *claimant* when referring to clients or classes of clients because it suggests "persons asserting just prerogatives, not [client] pleading for special acts of mercy" (p. 224).

3. There is a temptation to advocate for "services" to people in need, leading to a failure to empower groups of clients or "have-nots" in deciding their own destinies (Williams, 1986). O'Connell (1978) urged advocates to promote the "transfer of power so that the groups in need of service gain their own political and economic power to be able to represent themselves effectively" (p. 198). Commendable as developing services is, Kirst-Ashman and Hull (1993) urge advocates to help clients help themselves and never act as advocates for clients when they can advocate for themselves.

4. Cause advocacy may also involve risks, antagonisms, ill-will, or backlash that need to be considered carefully before implementing an action. Williams (1986) and Johnson (1995) point out that a new program for one group of clients may take away funds from another. Retaliation may be a threatening reality for members of a group such as tenants in public housing or residents in a nursing home. Evictions and transfers are very real problems. Persons may become very fearful, believing they have more to lose than gain if they participate in certain activities. Advocates should ascertain that no other means for alleviating the problem is available. The expected risks should be carefully explored, necessary resources need to be identified, facts should be verified, and clients must be made aware of the possible consequences. In any case, advocates should go no further in implementing actions than the clients wish to go.

Ethical Dilemma Gerhart (1990) raises a question often encountered by cause advocates: "Should representation be made on behalf of clients who have not given their consent to such representation?" (p. 277). Can a social work advocate take steps to improve clients' circumstances when they have not asked for or do not want that service or support (Johnson, 1995)? Do cause advocates respond to their own sense of unfairness or outrage or to the wishes of clients? At issue here is the fundamental question of client self-determination.

The homeless mentally ill offer a realistic example of this dilemma because many times they will resist any kind of confinement or regulated living situation. They wish to be left to live on the street, suffering from malnutrition, poor health, or even exposure to freezing to death in winter. Should they be forcibly transported to shelters? A mentally ill person who fails to take medications may decompensate and harm others and him- or herself. Should this individual be forced to take medications? Should housing violations such as rats, unsafe buildings, unsanitary facilities be reported when clients say they may be evicted if the authorities are told?

Kirst-Ashman and Hull (1993), among others, assume that advocacy should never be carried out without the full consent and knowledge of the client. But what about the clients who are incompetent and unable to grasp fully the situation endangering themselves? Gerhart (1990) suggests that there are no easy answers, but this type of ethical dilemma should be resolved on a case-by-case basis. The authors believe that advocates should assess the clients' competency to make decisions and honor it when feasible. The advocate can consider what the clients would have wanted if they were still competent. The advocate can assess the danger to clients or others. The advocate can try to balance the rights of the clients with the rights of others. The principle of "do no harm" is applicable here and offers guidance in decision making.

Use of a Forum

Cause advocates frequently use public hearings, budget sessions, councils, town hall meetings, local and state government hearings, the courts, as well as smaller forums such as staff meetings, supervisory sessions, internal agency committees, and task forces. Here they are able to raise awareness about issues (Shanker, 1983). In addition, they must know well the procedures used by participants in each forum. For cause advocates, there are three particular emphases to be aware of: (1) the basic rationale for agency hearings; (2) grievance procedures; and (3) litigation of issues in court.

Rationale for Agency Hearings   Why do agencies use forums, that is, administrative hearings or appeal procedures? Hagen (1986) pointed out that there are two general types of issues raised in hearings: questions about the level of benefits and questions about exclusion from a program. Cause advocates often find themselves dealing with decisions about benefits and exclusion. Is this scenario always negative? On the positive side, agencies recognize that program benefits or eligibility requirements may not automatically fit every client or client group, and professionals are allowed some discretion in their decision making involving the rules. A hearing may be viewed as an attempt by the agency to foster fairness, control for administrative discretions, and to ensure administrative justice (Hagen, 1986). Most agencies have outlined steps to appeal decisions so that if their system is working imperfectly, clients have the opportunity to ask for reconsideration (Sunley, 1970). While cause advocates may view a hearing as an adversarial event, the authors urge caution. Arguments and requests should be framed for presentation according to the notions of fairness and justice implicit in the hearing process. Using this assumption may lead to a quicker resolution than picking a fight.

When Grievance Procedures Are Absent   Where there are no appeal procedures, advocates should first urge agencies to establish effective grievance procedures regardless of the service or benefit provided. While more-established agencies may already have such procedures in place, newer service providers may not yet have developed a mechanism to deal with clients' complaints. Rather than resorting to lengthy legal litigation, advocates and agencies are recognizing that alternative forums such as grievance hearings, human rights committees, or other administrative mechanisms can secure speedy and efficient resolutions (Fiedler & Antonak, 1991; Moxley & Freddolino, 1991).

Courtroom Litigation   The use of litigation or legal action for procuring constitutional and statutory guarantees has become an integral part of advocacy on behalf of groups that have been denied access or rights (Levy, 1970). During the past two decades, according to Fiedler and Antonak (1991), many advocacy efforts on behalf of the mentally retarded have focused upon securing legal rights in a courtroom forum. Cause advocates may team up with lawyers to test policies in court regarding their constitutionality or dramatize the consequences so that legislators will change policies. Class-action litigation or test cases are major tools for access to justice, but they require resources and a lengthy period of time. As suggested above, it is advised to seek alternative forums for speedier resolution of issues affecting clients.

Public Arena   One forum of importance to cause advocates attempting to influence public opinion is access to and skilled use of the media. Important media and technology guidelines are presented in the following section.

Communication

In Chapter 3, the basic guidelines for effective speaking and writing provide cause advocates a solid foundation for communication. The general principles and procedures for persuasive writing and speaking hold equally true for all advocates, including cause advocates. In this section, the special focus will be on reaching out to the general public through *media* outlets such as television coverage, radio talk shows, and the print media. Cause advocates often do not appear to have good methods for reaching beyond a rather small core of "believers" and gaining wider audiences and persons unaffiliated with their cause (Mondros & Wilson, 1994). This section presents (1) purposes for using the media, (2) rules for successful media coverage, (3) methods of gaining access to the media, and (4) specific tips on dealing with the media.

Purposes for Using the Media   Bobo et al. (1996) and Shaw (1992) caution that getting media coverage, in and of itself, is not a demonstrable result. Advocates may say that media exposure will "obviously help the public understand the issues," or that the media will "usually support their position" on a human rights issue. However, many fail to evaluate the actual use of the media to achieve their goals, have no strategic plan that includes use of the media, and naively trust the media to cover events in such a way as to elicit broad public support (Shaw, 1992). Getting on television or newsprint coverage is not enough without prior planning and strategic thinking.

Altman et al. (1994), Bobo et al. (1996), and Mondros and Wilson (1994) believe that strategic media coverage can help win real improvements in people's lives. Among the purposes for employing the media in an advocacy campaign are:

1. Positive reports in the media can influence public opinion and accelerate attention to an issue, putting it on the public agenda.
2. The media can increase the knowledge of decision makers and the public about the issues.
3. Getting media coverage gives participants a sense of empowerment by seeing their pictures or remarks in the press or on television.

Cause advocates should seek media coverage that is integrated into the overall plan of an advocacy effort. Remember, media coverage is a means to an end, not an end in itself. Clarifying the purposes of a media strategy will usually assist advocates in achieving their goals more directly.

Rules for Successful Media Coverage   Following are a number of rules for using media coverage successfully (Altman et al., 1994; Shaw, 1996).

Use the media for results, not coverage. Cause advocates' strategy for using the media should include two dimensions: (1) illustration of a problem (cause), and (2) proposals for specific, implementable solutions. Media sources move quickly from a "hot" story to the next "hot" story. Immediate coverage evaporates, and the issue becomes lost to the public in a few days. If advocates have a proposed concrete solution at hand, they can often continue to get media exposure because there is a story line to follow and additional news items will be uncovered. Shaw (1996) provides a wonderful example of how lack of heat and hot water in homeless hotels coupled with his demand for new legislation by city supervisors enticed his city's media to follow the story over time, eventually resulting in a feature story, "a day in the life" of elderly homeless residents, that was picked up by the national media. Emergency legislation that went into effect in three days was passed due to the pressure from city, state, and national sources.

Choose a media spokesperson carefully. A savvy spokesperson is essential in communicating with the news media. The first key is to formulate the message you want to project before actually meeting with reporters or camera crews. To avoid damaging remarks or poorly thought-out comments, a spokesperson should prepare the basic message and not engage in long, rambling discussions with the media.

The second critical question becomes: Who should speak? A member of the affected constituency or a staff member of the organization? Generally, a spokesperson from the afflicted group should speak, since this principle is based on empowerment. During the course of the cause advocacy, leaders can identify one or two persons from the group who have good communication skills; these natural speakers can provide reporters with a "real person with real problems" interview, and a positive story usually results (Shaw, 1996). Staff persons who are comfortable with speaking in public, deeply committed to the cause, and available on short notice are good choices. It is best to choose only one or two persons so that the message is consistent and the media begin to identify a name and face and know whom they can contact.

Call on investigative reporters. While much of the "investigative" reporting done today features celebrities, private lives, and scandal, there are still producers and reporters who will explore issues of social change. Locally, advocates should become familiar with reporters with a record of investigative stories and establish relationships with them. Even though it is more challenging, advocates should not be reluctant to contact national programs such as *60 Minutes, Dateline,* or *20/20,* or the Center for Investigative Reporting. In every case, doing your homework, getting the facts, identifying key persons, and providing solid information is crucial. Obtaining such coverage offers a wonderful opportunity with a powerful impact on your cause and clients.

Be forever on the alert and watch out for traps. The media love controversy and will ask questions that may encourage you to criticize your opponents, take radical stands, make allegations, or stir up emotional issues. Be prepared for this tactic and stick to your main points. It is also not a good idea to "speak off the record" because your words may come back to haunt you. Even if reporters appear sympathetic to your cause and take copious notes and photos, there is no assurance the resulting story will support your efforts. Editors will have the final say on the "spin" of the story. Written pages or packets of information distributed to reporters often can help control the emphasis of your story.

Respond to unfair, biased, or slanted media stories selectively (Shaw, 1996). What do advocates do when the media publishes an attack on the constituent group or the immediate issue? How can one counter subtle "objective" reporting that is based on quotes, facts, and photos selected to cast the cause in a negative light? Experienced advocates analyze the situation with the following questions:

1. Has this piece caused real harm to your issue or constituency? If not, it is better not to respond because this one unfair story will soon be forgotten by the public.
2. Does the criticism come from credible sources, and if so, is the bias central or collateral to the story? If it is only an aside or a brief comment, not involving clear factual error and unlikely to cause harm, it is best to ignore this criticism because your comments may fail the "crybaby" test.
3. Is the reporting clearly focused on your issue and demonstrably inaccurate or derogatory? Such attacks demand a response because they affect people's perception of your issue.

Advocates responding to media stories can use letters to the editor; send letters signed by respected community leaders; ask for a separate column in the newspaper; complain to the TV/radio producers and ask for a correction; contact another news outlet that can show how its competitor missed critical facts; buy full-page newspaper ads, correcting the facts; hold a protest in front of the media's offices; or link up with an elected official who can demand an investigation into the accuracy of the story.

Use think-tanks to your advantage. Today think-tanks such as the Brookings Institute, American Enterprise Institute, The Cato Institute, The Center for Public Policy, and many others employ scholars and scientists full-time to research and develop positions on every imaginable topic including social issues. Their influence is linked to the coupling of objectivity and wide-ranging access to newspapers, electronic media outlets, talk shows, and print sources. An article by a think-tank can have great impact supporting or attacking your issue. When possible, advocates should attempt to use think-tank materials or to interest them in their cause.

Methods of Gaining Access to the Media   There is a variety of ways to obtain media coverage (Altman et al., 1994; Bobo et al., 1996); a brief summary of each method follows:

Stage a newsworthy event. Often cause advocates will plan an event especially for the media or will invite the media to an activity they are carrying out in the community. Because the media are looking for newsworthy stories, advocates can plan their events with the media in mind. Creative and imaginative tactics can be used as well as offering photo-ops. Hundreds of advocates, for example, for the Mattaponi Indians in Virginia planned a six-mile march from their reservation to an important river that was going to be dammed to create a reservoir, posing disastrous effects on the economy of the tribe. Packets of information with research, position papers, phone and fax numbers, and the organization's purpose should be available for distribution. Prepare your spokespersons to meet with the media representatives.

Hold a news conference. Experts advise advocates to use press conferences very seldomly unless their issue is very "hot." If you have a significant or dramatic finding that may be controversial or a good human interest story, you may do well to call a news conference. Hold it in the morning, notify editors or reporters several days in advance, prepare press packets of information, and be sure the logistics of the setting are adequate. Distribute the press kit, make a brief statement, and then answer questions.

Issue news releases. Reserve the use of press releases for news that is significant, novel, or truly newsworthy. If you send out releases frequently, reporters and editors will not be able to distinguish what is truly important and will begin to ignore all of your releases. It is also important to think of "hooks" that will attract attention and give a face to your story. There may be an anniversary (fifth annual walkathon), a prominent person (Rosa Parks, the mayor), human interest (child rescued from foster home), or a seasonal event that ties into your cause. Follow up your news release with a phone call.

Follow these technical and professional guidelines when issuing a news release:

- Use organizational letterhead.
- Double-space the text.
- Write "For Immediate Release" or "Release on such and such a date" centered at the top of the release.
- Put the name, phone and fax numbers, and e-mail address of your contact person in the top right-hand corner of the news release.
- Write a concise, clear, and informative headline.
- Write the opening paragraph to include all major information: who, what, where, and when.
- Write the most important news in the opening and first paragraphs, followed by less important information in following paragraphs. This allows editors to know quickly if the story is newsworthy and what to edit out if they want to reduce your release.
- Write no more than two pages. End the release with the symbol: XXXXXXXX

Feed stories to feature writers or individual reporters. Once you have established relationships with reporters who are sympathetic to or assigned to your area, for example, human services, human rights, or local government, you can suggest stories or angles that they might want to consider for an in-depth feature article or interview. Sometimes, you may want to give your contacts the first opportunity to run a story.

Appear on radio and television talk shows. All local radio and television talk shows and special programs are looking for newsworthy, interesting stories for their listeners and viewers. If you establish relationships with the producers, they may learn to call you for an opinion or comment on a human rights issue. Some stations allow people to make their own statements on the air, free of charge.

Write letters to the editors of newspapers. The editorial page is the most widely read page except for the front page. Do not flood the paper with letters, but when you write, make your point a strong one. This is also a way to get "free" coverage of your issue.

[Ron Dear's tips for writing a letter to the editor (Jansson, 1999):

- Start with your specific reason for writing.
- Be timely and do not let the news get stale.
- Be brief: 200–250 words. Do not ramble.
- Address only one issue or topic.
- Give reasons for your views and cite data and facts.
- If you have expertise on the topic, say that you do.
- If you have relevant personal experience, state it.
- Be constructive: what alternative/solution would you offer?.
- Use lively writing, humor, logic, but be civil.]

Meet with editorial boards or editors-in-chief. Small papers' editors usually write the daily/weekly editorials, and large papers have a group who share this responsibility. While many may be conservative, it is helpful to meet with them and explain your issue. Put the editors on your press release listing. Even if they do not agree with you, they may allow you to print an op-ed piece.

Specific Tips on Dealing with the Media   The following are some specific ways to deal with the media for best results (Altman et al., 1994; Bobo et al., 1996).

Develop relationships with reporters who cover the human services area. A professional relationship with the reporters is crucial. You can never assume that you will become "friends" with them, but you should strive for honest, respectful dealings. Try to connect with the reporters who cover your area. Develop a reputation for providing reporters with timely, accurate information, which, of course, makes their jobs easier. Be prompt in returning phone calls.

Develop a media list. As you begin planning your cause activities and strategies, assemble lists of all the news media addresses and contact persons. All daily newspapers in the state, region, or locality can be listed as well as weekly papers. Keep track of these sources, updating names and phone numbers, and develop computerized labels for mailing. Make e-mail address network groups part of your regular contacts.

Notify the media that there will be a "photo-op." As you plan your event, consider a photo setting that will attract the photographers and television reporters. Use symbols, images, and visuals that will illustrate your message.

Politicians particularly like to be photographed, and a photo-op can be used to entice them to come for an interview.

Mail or fax press (news) releases. The purpose of a news release is to get your event covered. Using the standard format, mail or fax your story to your media lists three to five days ahead of the event. The release need not contain all the information you want to disseminate, but it should be written to attract the attention of the reader and be judged as "newsworthy."

Recognize that luck plays a role. Your well-planned event will be scooped by the outbreak of violence in a local school despite your best orchestration and hard work. On a slow newsday, your group's action may be a feature on the 6:00 P.M. news. Luck is a part of dealing with the media.

Prepare yourself for the interview. Before an interview, frame your message that will put your issue in the best light. Usually a message should have only three to five main points and you refer to them throughout the interview. Develop these points well, and make them vivid and memorable. Return to these main issues whenever the questioner tries to lead you astray.

Identify the targeted audience for each of the media outlets. Research the audiences of radio and television stations to discover which group of people they are targeting and to find out how you can reach the people you want to affect. Find out which reporters are assigned to certain beats.

Find out the deadlines for media programs or newspapers. Newsprint and electronic media all have certain deadlines to meet before production or printing, and advocates should learn these times and dates before scheduling news conferences and events. Television reporters appreciate morning coverage so their film footage can be processed easily before the evening news. Certain days of the week, frequently Mondays, sometimes offer more successful coverage in the newspapers.

Volunteer to provide a local angle on a national story. If you know of national or high-profile stories, you can call a media contact and suggest how your effort is a local version of the wider issue.

Hand out Rolodex or business cards to media people. A card with your group's name and numbers will make it easy for the media person to contact you for more information or to interview you about related issues or stories.

Thank the media people who help you or produce stories about your cause. Sending a note to the reporters or producers who assisted in getting your story out demonstrates your appreciation and builds continuing relations with these persons. Write to their supervisors and praise their contributions.

INFLUENCE

The second fundamental skill in this book's definition of advocacy is *influencing.* That is, advocates attempt to persuade or sway decision makers who have authority or the resources to change conditions that may be causing problems for a class or group of people. The authors outlined eight principles of influencing in Chapter 4. The following text provides additional information on influencing that is particularly useful for cause advocates.

Identify the Issues and Set Goals

The most critical decision for advocates is not which strategies or tactics to devise, but whether or not to become active on an issue in the first place (Eriksen, 1997). Is the issue significant enough to motivate people to action? What is the "cause" all about? Can it become a priority? Defining the issue is linked to both motivation and action for cause advocates. The authors provide below (1) methods of identifying issues, (2) criteria by which to select or prioritize issues, and (3) several tips on bringing issues to the attention of the public and decision makers.

Identification of Issues   Discovering the main issue(s) to work on is a key task in cause advocacy. Who knows what the real issues are? What is the "cause" in a nutshell? How can advocates find reliable sources to determine which problems to work on? Three answers provided by Mondros and Wilson (1994) are discussed in the following paragraphs.

Issues are expressed directly by the people who are burdened. Grievances and complaints stated directly by the group of persons who suffer from a loss of rights, injurious conditions, or lack of services are one of the best ways to discover key issues. If people are affected deeply and painfully by a condition, they will more likely be motivated to take action and to see it through. Self-expressed issues intensify the urge to act, to empower people by giving them an active role, and to help focus people's participation on an issue of great import to them. Informal conversations, door-to-door knocking, meetings at churches, clubs, and centers, "gripe" tables, phone calls, and surveys are among other methods used to obtain information directly from people. Advocates must temper their own beliefs sometimes and listen carefully to the people burdened by issues that reflect their (not the advocate's) needs and wants.

While key issues are generated directly from the people affected by conditions, advocates can try to convince them of other, important related issues. Issues identified directly by people may have other dimensions that they have not yet discovered, and advocates may try to educate and convince people of other important issues that are present. Vacant housing may be a concern expressed by the people in the neighborhood, but improving the housing stock and obtaining low-rate home improvement loans are clearly related issues. Working on these issues can be a natural extension of the primary issue as long as the advocate educates people along the way and does not superimpose his or her own preferences and values.

Issues are born out of the necessity to take action. An issue often appears suddenly in the community. Economic, political, or social events may occur that heighten awareness over a concern, and advocates can mobilize people to respond. A developer's plan to convert low-income rental housing currently used by new immigrants into higher-paying units for homeowners may appear in the newspaper. An advocate can attempt to organize residents, housing advocates, churches, legal aid groups, agencies working with immigrants and refugees, and interested citizens into a task force to address this issue. Urgency to act propels the advocacy group to organize, or serious losses may result.

Criteria Used to Select or Prioritize Issues   Advocates must work not only to identify issues, but also to select the best issues to work on. Knowing clearly what standards or criteria express the group's values, beliefs, and interests will help the advocate focus the group's efforts. Four criteria provided by Mondros and Wilson (1994) are discussed below.

Relevancy of the issue to the group's members. A "good" issue is one that members see as beneficial to themselves, know from experience what is at stake, and are willing to support by working on it. Moxley and Freddolino (1991) note that issues usually touch basic needs such as income, housing, legal problems, and health care. People have to be more than "interested" in the issue. If the issue does not motivate people to engage actively in the change effort, the advocacy will almost certainly fail. The cause must be popular based on people's feelings, and their willingness to participate and take on leadership roles.

Ability to pursue an issue successfully. Advocates should be concerned not only with people's participation, but also with their experiencing some level of success through their actions. Can an action be planned and implemented that resolves the issue within a reasonable time span? Long and difficult struggles pose motivational problems for members, especially new ones who may not yet have the confidence to stick with an abstract idea. Experts suggest starting with an issue that is easy to resolve and tackle more complex ones later on. Constant victory is not possible, but small victories along the way provide morale-building experiences needed to continue the effort.

Feasibility of pursuing the issue with available resources. Organizations or advocacy groups have only so much time and money. Will a particular issue be the best use of these scarce resources? Does the group have the expertise it needs to pursue the issue? Would it be better to work in a coalition of other similar groups to conserve resources? The group must conclude that the issue is "worth it" before committing resources, personnel, money, and time.

Importance of the issue in the community. Sometimes, events in the community or timing allow advocates to link their issue to what is going on around them. The larger environment often provides clues to important political and economical forces, and advocates can optimize their activities favorably within the current climate. Sometimes advocates may have to alert members about trends, a piece of legislation, or economic news that threaten their efforts. A "hate crime" committed against a minority family can be linked to pending legislation in the state capitol.

Tips for Bringing Your Issues to the Public and Decision Makers
Below are brief tips for addressing issues and using them effectively to succeed.

Members must reach a "working agreement." Since every issue is viewed differently to some degree by each participant, people must eventually come together to discuss the issue(s) and clarify its meaning. Differences must be aired and compromises reached; total unanimity is not likely. People must reach a "working agreement" that allows them to accept limitations and differences to be part of the bargain. It is time-consuming to achieve this, and seemingly endless conversation may take place, but advocates must ensure that people can share their perceptions, reach compromise, and agree to go ahead (Mondros & Wilson, 1994).

Advocates must attend to both participation and efficiency. Balancing "getting the job done" and "letting everyone have their say" is also a role of the advocate. It requires political skills, good communication, openness, setting limits, and courage to overcome conflict. One way to accomplish this is to ask the group regularly if they are ready to move on. If they are, consensus will have been reached; if not, they will not allow the conversation to be ended until a satisfactory resolution is reached.

Advocates can appeal to the "common good." In the midst of conflict, advocates may be able to appeal to a greater "common good" among the members. It can be pointed out that, despite their differences, both sides will benefit in some way and their cooperative efforts are truly needed.

Make connections among the issues. Educating people about issues often entails showing them the linkages between issues. If people come to meetings and see that their issue is a part of a state or national struggle, it may motivate them to stick with it. Linking issues expresses a central concern for social change, a feeling that inspires many who look at the larger environment instead of the individual level alone. Reducing truancy among middle-schoolers is linked to educational achievement which is linked to employability which is linked to stable family life (Mondros & Wilson, 1994).

Reframe your opponents' statement of the issue. When opponents attack your stance, instead of counterattacking, use the same terms they used to respond to the criticism. You need to put your own "spin" on the issue (Altman et al., 1994). Here are a few examples of reframing an issue: (1) "Smoking is a personal choice" becomes "People smoke because they become addicted"; (2) "Immigrant families destroy housing property" becomes "The city does not build enough low-income housing units"; and (3) "School dropouts end up on the street" becomes "Families need to provide special attention to adolescents."

Stay cool and focused on the issues. Adversaries will attack you or members of your group personally. Avoid falling into the trap of "bait and react." These name-calling exchanges usually degenerate into personal animosity and often hurt your group's public image. Take the high ground and focus on the issue (Altman et al., 1994).

Make the issue local and relevant. Use local statistics, local impact statements, local people, local volunteers, local photo-ops, and local resources to support your cause. People readily identify with something they already know, and if it is "close to home," they may move to action or be supportive (Altman et al., 1994).

Use multiple methods to learn more about the issues. If you have the money, mail questionnaires or conduct telephone interviews to find out views. Hold meetings at conventions or conferences to speak with others. Analyze economic and social data. Visit places where people congregate. Speak with community and church leaders (Mondros & Wilson, 1994).

Get the Facts

Cause advocates should be prepared for penetrating or hostile questions as they attempt to persuade decision makers to change policies, programs, or procedures (Sunley, 1970). Fact finding has long been considered the primary instrument of human rights investigations and enforcement (Rosenthal & Rubenstein, 1993). So, if you are advocating on behalf of foster children, you must have detailed information about children, troubled families, social service policies and agencies, research findings on foster care, and how the system works or does not work on behalf of foster children. Advocates without good information will easily be outmaneuvered by officials or opponents (Mondros & Wilson, 1994). Such information can be carefully organized into a sound and tightly reasoned case and presented to decision makers with a potential impact (Sheafor et al., 1994). In this section, the authors outline: what cause advocates really need to know, especially the law; how to document your facts; and several tips on the use of facts in your advocacy efforts.

Cause Advocates Must Know the Laws   Experts agree readily that familiarity with pertinent laws is one of the most important knowledge areas for cause advocates (Ad Hoc Committee, 1969; Gerhart, 1990; Holmes, 1981; Kirst-Ashman & Hull, 1993; Panitch, 1974; Sunley, 1970). Although they are not expected to be as conversant as lawyers, social work advocates are expected to know state statutes, constitutional law, important cases, client bill-of-rights, and agency regulations pertinent to their issue. Entitlements to benefits for clients are particularly tied up with the law. Access to these laws is not formidable, and librarians will assist anyone who asks for help in locating specific laws in state or federal constitutions. Each agency has copies or references to appropriate laws pertaining to their jurisdiction.

Others Areas of Knowledge and Factual Information   *Data on the issue itself.* In addition to the laws governing the problem, advocates should collect as much information and research findings on the issue as possible. Areas to be explored are: the number of people affected by the problem, demographic information, the history of the issue, the public's perception of the issue, existing solutions, alternative programs, who profits from this problem, how much will a solution cost, and who wants to maintain the status quo (Mondros & Wilson, 1994).

Knowledge of culture, government, institutions, organizations, and service systems. Clients usually have contact with certain institutions such as social service departments, schools, courts, mental health facilities, and hospitals. It is important for advocates to learn about the structure, hierarchy, staff, clientele, informal systems, procedures, and concrete services available in specific institutions. Advocates can also learn about the orientation of the agency and its attitudes toward clients, willingness to change, and reaction to pressure tactics (Moxley & Freddolino, 1991; O'Connell, 1978; Sunley, 1970). Cross-cultural perspectives will also enhance the advocate's understanding of client issues and attitudes (Lequerica, 1993).

Familiarity with the political and policy processes. Advocates pursuing a cause issue may end up in the legislative arena. (There are many things to know here, and the reader is referred to Chapter 7 on legislative advocacy.) Suffice it to say that it is important to know the key politicians, power brokers, legislative aides, and influential community leaders. Equally important is to know the rules and calendars of the policy-making body such as the state legislature or city council in order to be able to participate effectively. Budget surpluses or deficits, pending legislation, potential trade-offs and compromises, and political "hot topics" are also important "facts" to know (Mondros & Wilson, 1994).

Individual and societal rights of client group. Kirst-Ashman and Hull (1993) list client rights as the first knowledge area for advocates. They state that "rights are those protections and guarantees to which people or society have a just claim and cannot, in American society, be denied without due process of law" (p. 474). Both individuals and society have rights that are guaranteed by state and federal constitutions. For example, freedom of speech, the right to assemble, and Miranda rights are guaranteed to every citizen. Entitlement programs are guaranteed to those individuals who meet specific criteria. Certain disabled children are entitled to funding or education that the state or nation has mandated for them. (See Chapter 5, pp. 154–156.)

Avenues of appeal. Complaints about services or denial of benefits can usually be addressed through the appeal procedures of an agency. Before pursuing other actions for redress, it is important for advocates and their clients to follow the established appeal process so that officials cannot claim that the clients did not follow proper procedures (Holmes, 1981; Kirst-Ashman & Hull, 1993; Sunley, 1970). It is crucial to identify what protections clients may have and to know what the specific steps are in following up a complaint.

Knowledge of the "target" of your advocacy. It may take some digging, but it is crucial to discover who is truly responsible or can be held accountable for the issue facing the group. Public relations personnel are often dispatched to deal with an advocacy group, but they do not possess any real authority. It is also useful to find out what an adversary's vulnerabilities might be (such as late tax payments or fines) and to discover those with whom they associate (e.g., through country clubs, boards, and political parties). This information can often be used in negotiation sessions (Mondros & Wilson, 1994).

Sources to Use or Develop for Documenting Facts   (Altman et al., 1994) Advocates should know that there are many sources of information available to them if they are willing to search them out. Public documents, census data, community studies, white papers, legislative studies, and consultant reports are some examples, and most of them are available at no cost. Although more costly, studies or other research activities can be initiated to find appropriate facts.

Local media. News articles in local, state, and national newspapers can keep one up-to-date on an issue and provide vivid examples of how people or groups are affected. Letters to the editor often reflect how people are feeling. Radio talk shows and televised commentary sessions are helpful. Websites and e-mail chat rooms are becoming more potent in sharing opinions.

Minutes of meetings. Use the minutes of meetings from any public agency that must allow all citizens access to them. Newsletters from many groups or organizations will also reveal what issues are on their agenda and why they consider them important. They may also provide tips on the group's future plans.

Study reports, annual reports, issue papers. By reviewing these documents, which most agencies and organizations publish, advocates can learn what priorities are in vogue, positive and negative changes that are underway, proposed actions that may affect your issue, and the basis for positions taken on an issue.

Existing surveys. United Way agencies, regional planning commissions, county governments, city halls, universities, and other civic associations frequently do surveys about problems or issues concerning their communities.

Archives. Libraries and most agencies have stored vast amounts of information in their archives. A review of court records, agency files, statistical information, policy records, and school inventories may each yield helpful information to your cause.

Community resource inventory. Identify all of the agencies or resources that may be working on an issue similar to yours. This allows the advocates to know what resources are available to them and may also lead them to others who can become allies, coalition partners, and supporters.

Community leader survey. Seek out community leaders or key influential persons and interview them, exploring their attitudes, listening to their recommendations, and learning from them about how to proceed most effectively. Often, these individuals will suggest others to interview.

Focus groups. Using eight to twelve persons from the community, advocates can meet with them for two hours and probe their attitudes and beliefs about an issue. New ideas for action may also emerge. Be sure to have focus groups from all segments of the community.

Community opinion survey. Although this type of survey requires time, money, and expertise in survey research, it will yield information directly from those who may be beneficiaries or decision makers who influence policy. Be aware that sample selection, question phrasing, and analysis require special skills.

Tips on Incorporating Facts into Your Advocacy Strategies

Develop fact sheets. In order to update newcomers to the group and to summarize the issue succinctly, advocates can design a "fact" sheet describing their complaint, the progress made to date, the important information, objective data and findings, goals of the group, names and telephone numbers of contact persons, and the opposition's record on the issue (Mondros & Wilson, 1994). (See pp. 259–262 on legislative advocacy for more information on developing a fact sheet.)

Adversaries use facts to appear objective. Brager (1968) reminds advocates that issues are settled almost always on grounds that are nonfactual, that is, political, personal, or economic, but common practice is to make it appear that the decision rests upon "objective facts." Decision making is a complex mixture of facts and personal/political quirks. Advocates should recognize that they may have to assist adversaries by face-saving gestures or harmless generalizations in order to succeed. Facts are still important to an advocacy strategy, but, like most things, they are not the entire explanation.

Cause *advocates need the facts that* client *advocates know so well.* The premise of this chapter is the belief that issues affecting many individual clients are actually shared by many others similarly affected by conditions, laws, or circumstances beyond their control. Mickelson (1995) says that cause advocates cannot bring about changes without important data from client advocates who actually view the effects of social policy or conditions on individual clients. A cooperative relationship between macro and micro practitioners is obviously very desirable to improve many clients' welfare.

Power for social work advocates comes from knowledge and expertise. Advocacy includes an understanding and willingness to use power, that is, the ability to make others behave the way you want them to. Although social workers may not have power based on wealth, political or genealogical connections, public support, or authority, they have the power that comes from knowledge and expertise (Sheafor et al., 1994). Getting the facts, doing your homework, researching the issues, developing alternative proposals, applying expertise to problem solving, and knowing community resources can offset the lack of power based on other criteria, and allow the social work advocate to demonstrate power that can be refuted only by others with greater expertise and knowledge.

Interpret the notion of "facts" widely, not narrowly. An advocate's aim is not simply to amass data and facts and present them to decision makers in multiple charts, graphs, and tables. In addition to the "objective" facts, advocates must also find out how people and leaders in the community feel about the issue (Altman et al., 1994). What ramifications are there for the businesses, nonprofit agencies, governmental agencies, community institutions, and important systems such as the courts, schools, health care, or neighborhoods? Advocates must interpret the context into which objective facts will be introduced before deciding which among all of the facts will prove most beneficial to the cause.

Facts do not always change opponents' views immediately, but may have a long-term effect. The accumulation of facts and technical information may not be enough to convince opponents or decision makers to accept your proposed changes. Other personal or political factors may be too powerful to overcome at the moment. Nevertheless, policy makers or community leaders may alter their opinions over time, and the next time the issue arises, they may vote more favorably in your direction (Jenkins-Smith & Sabatier, 1994). Learning often takes place slowly, so advocates should not be discouraged or dissuaded from always gathering facts and using them.

Plan Strategies and Tactics

A *strategy* provides the broad plan and approach for achieving your goals, and *tactics* are the specific actions and events designed to carry out the strategy (Altman et al., 1994). Cause advocates strive to convince community, governmental, or private systems/institutions to change their policies and practices on behalf of some group. They often point out how the institution's purposes are being undermined by its own policies; and advocates offer support in identifying alternatives that promote rather than inhibit the system's goals (Riley, 1971). Getting these alternative proposals accepted requires an overall "game plan" that guides the choice of actions and tactics. *Strategy* refers to *how* the advocacy group intends to accomplish its job.

Strategies   The authors believe that a deliberative process of strategic planning will reduce fuzzy thinking and sharpen crucial decisions about the use of time, money, and activities. Some experts have described strategy development in overly general terms, such as Johnson (1995) who states there are but two main strategies to planning cause advocacy activities: influencing the political process and organizing people. Kirst-Ashman and Hull (1993) offer more specific advice in setting strategy in three areas of concern: understand the nature of the problem itself; know the rights, strengths, and resources of the clients; and assess the opponents carefully. While Johnson and Kirst-Ashman's directives are useful, they do not provide advocates with step-by-step guidelines to ensure a process that addresses beginning, middle, and ending action steps to follow.

The authors recommend that social work strategy development be based, first and foremost, on an analysis of the opposition's values, vulnerabilities, strengths, and power; secondly, on the selection of one of three broad-based strategies, that is, collaborative, campaign, or contest, that correspond to the assessment of the opposition; and, thirdly, on the selection of tactics that complement and reinforce the strategy chosen. (See Chapter 4 under "Plan Strategies and Tactics.") Additional advice is offered below in order to ensure successful strategy development for cause advocacy efforts.

Some advocates use the same strategy and tactics over and over. Just because one strategy or tactic works successfully in changing a bureaucracy's practice does not automatically mean it will work well in influencing a key politician to support your group's goals. Some people think that demonstrations are always the best way to promote an issue, because they "love" demonstrations. Others think that "getting everyone together to talk about it" is the most effective way to plan regardless of circumstances. Advocates must remember that a strategy or tactic is a means to an end, not an end in itself. It is more important that an action be effective and have an impact than that the advocates be familiar or comfortable with it. Analyzing the opposition and the nature of the problem carefully is the critical first step because it becomes the basis for determining what strategy or tactic will work best in this instance (Altman et al., 1994; Bobo et al., 1996).

Advocates can also become stuck in their thinking about how change occurs and may become blinded to other explanations. Some advocates believe all change requires large numbers of people confronting those in power. Some believe that all individuals with power are highly resistant to change. Others believe that the government is the major arena for change. Still others believe that change only occurs at opportune moments. Each of these views has some truth in it, but advocates must not allow rigid thinking to predominate in setting strategies. Usually, no one belief explains every situation. Advocates are urged to be flexible in their beliefs and allow creativity and innovation to be a part of their strategizing (Mondros & Wilson, 1994).

Advocates must link strategies to goals. Mondros and Wilson (1994) recommend that advocates link their strategies to four sets of goals: (1) Long- and short-term *outcome* goals, which focus on what the group wants to achieve or change. If the group wants to change drug-testing laws for welfare recipients short-term, they may want to influence key legislators in the upcoming legislative session; and (2) Long- and short-term *process* goals, which focus on strengthening the group's capacity to build support and proceed toward their desired change. Recruiting more members long-term may require social, "fun" activities. Strategies should not be selected in a vacuum because they always relate to a time-related goal.

Choose the strategy of "least contest." The question of how much pressure to exert always arises. Should the strategy be highly confrontational or behind-the-scenes maneuvering? Kirst-Ashman and Hull (1993) recommend that nonconfrontational approaches should be used before confrontational ones. "If a hammer will do the job, why use a pile-driver?" They suggest that using a more forceful approach can be considered when: (1) nothing that you have tried has worked; (2) you are absolutely convinced that clients are being treated unfairly and with grave consequences; and (3) you think you have a good chance at succeeding by causing a confrontation (as opposed to wasting your energy).

Power is always a factor. When attempting to choose strategies to change behaviors, the element of power is always present. Who can influence someone else to act differently? Who can prevent something from happening? Advocates need to analyze the power sources by asking questions like these: How many people do we need to persuade? What is the basis of their power (elected or appointed officials)? Do they have a reputation for being tough? What have they done in the past when confronted with proposals? Do we know someone who knows them? What are they afraid of losing? (See Bobo et al., 1996.)

Be wary of co-optation. Berry (1981) warns of being co-opted by agencies when setting strategy. He suggests that bureaucracies take the path of least resistance and if your group lets itself be co-opted, they will quickly take advantage of it. You may be offered "privileged" access to information or you may be asked to collaborate on an ongoing basis. If your group wants to continue to represent the public interest effectively, you must consider the price of being dependent on agency or elected officials (Shaw, 1996). Your group may have to be willing to forsake good relations when an agency does something with which you disagree. Berry (1981) says you may have to burn a bridge and then rebuild it. Advocates must let officials know when they are right and when they are wrong (Shaw, 1996).

How to reach mutual decisions between advocate and members. The authors agree with Mondros and Wilson (1994) that strategic decisions should be reached *mutually* by advocates and members of the cause effort. Strategic and tactical decisions should rarely be made by the advocate alone or by a small, select group. Discussions needed to reach a decision are important in order to engage, empower, and educate members. People invest themselves more if they played a part in determining a decision. People can also express their fears and reservations about a strategy or tactic, and the advocate can point out the real risks, potential benefits, and the possibility of losing as well as winning. These conversations help people assess their chances for success realistically.

Tactics   Once a strategy is determined, then advocates and members must agree upon *tactics,* that is, the specific action or event that will allow participants to carry out the strategy. What tactic will influence the opposition to

How Do You Discharge an HIV-Infected Person?

The AIDS Long-Term Care Access Project (ALCAP) was founded in 1990 in Chicago to respond to the frustrations of hospital discharge planners who experienced great difficulty in placing persons with human immunodeficiency virus (PWHIV) infections in community or residential home care options. Seven Chicago hospitals serving the largest proportion of people with AIDS were usually unable to place them in nursing homes. The street wisdom in the social service community was that no nursing home would care for an HIV-infected person. And even if they could place them, they were fearful about the quality of care.

Earlier advocacy efforts in the late 1980s had been tried. In order to dispel the belief that infectious diseases precluded admissions, the state health director sent a letter to all nursing homes stating the expectation that homes would admit anyone requiring care. Legislation was passed that established a better reimbursement system. Social workers were asked to refer discrimination incidents to the U.S. Office of Civil Rights. Even with these initiatives, no admissions took place by January 1990.

A local AIDS service community group took up the cause. They organized a conference to bring together nursing home providers, state policy makers, and service agency professionals. The conference was cosponsored by more than 25 public and private agencies. Ideas generated at this conference became the foundation for ALCAP.

But, ALCAP was essentially a volunteer effort functioning informally through social work field students and a volunteer coordinator. Funding became an issue and project expenses needed to be identified. And who was going to offer funds? In the end, HIV-related and other health resources were convinced to help out, but the latter group needed plenty of education.

With some funding, ALCAP established an information line to help consumers and their advocates access long-term care services. A nursing home fact sheet was developed and distributed to callers. ALCAP members also began giving on-site technical assistance. They helped prepare staff for an HIV admission and conducted half-day seminars, in-service programs, and resident satisfaction surveys. Educational conferences prepared facility owners, managers, and staff to care for persons with AIDS. A newsletter was also distributed to all licensed nursing homes in the state.

After 18 months, a survey by ALCAP revealed that there were staff training and admission changes. Almost two-thirds of the facilities reported training for HIV/AIDS care, 85% within the past two years. Seventeen percent of the facilities reported they had received applications for an AIDS

Continued

admission and that of these, 36% indicated that they had actually accepted AIDS patients. ALCAP finally saw some progress toward integrating AIDS care into Chicago nursing homes.

[Case based on Marder, R., & Linsk, N. L. (1995). Addressing AIDS long-term care issues through education and advocacy. Health and Social Work, 20, 75–80.*]*

---

make the desired change? In Chapter 4, the authors recommend selection of one of three strategies—collaboration, campaign, or contest—based on an assessment of the opposition; tactics are then chosen to complement the strategy. Devising tactics is limited only by one's imagination and creativity. (The reader is urged to review pages 59 to 84 in Altman et al., 1994, *Public Health Advocacy,* for an extensive description of tactics.) Following is a listing of several tactics (without description) in each of the three categories of strategies (Altman et al., 1994; Bobo et al., 1996; Johnson, 1995; Mondros & Wilson, 1994; Panitch, 1974):

COLLABORATIVE TACTICS

Conduct studies, analyses, and surveys
Prepare fact sheets
Offer expert testimony
Create interagency committees
Initiate demonstration projects
Provide consultation
Document complaints
Give personal compliments and public support to officials
Develop proposals and alternatives

CAMPAIGN TACTICS

Sponsor community or public hearings
Request accountability sessions
Gather petitions
Take positions
Join a coalition
Conduct lobbying visits
Do letter-writing
Educate the public
Do electoral work, campaigning, and voter registration
Act as a watchdog or monitor

Communicate with the opposition's allies
Criticize unfavorable actions publicly
Seek enforcement of existing laws

CONTEST TACTICS

File a complaint
Plan demonstrations, marches, or actions
Organize protests and picketing
Conduct boycotts
Plan prayer vigils
Arrange a media exposé
Organize civil disobedience
Initiate legal action

Advocates must link tactics to resources. In developing tactics, cause advocates must be aware of available resources because no group possesses unlimited resources, and outcomes depend at least partly on current resources. The authors view tactics as pressure points for change of an opponent's behavior. Kirst-Ashman and Hull (1993) and Mondros and Wilson (1994) suggest several categories of tactical resources: (1) *People* are the best resource, especially if there are sizable numbers. Decision makers count heads. Celebrities, clergy, experts, key leaders, and volunteers can also be viewed as "people" resources in supporting your cause. (2) *Power and prestige* can be linked to your cause by obtaining the commitment of corporations, key leaders, local or national celebrities, organizations, and groups with reputations for integrity and effectiveness. (3) *Timing and sequencing* of an event can be effective. Be aware of calendars, holidays, special events, and religious holidays. Tactics can be escalated from initial, low-level confrontation to more aggressive, extended actions. (4) *Drama* can be used to illustrate your position through humorous or creative portrayals of a problem. A crowd of fifty persons all dressed as Abe Lincoln draws attention to discriminatory practices. (5) *News of a social, economic, or political nature* can be used to support your cause. Studies of current conditions, magazine articles, white papers, "inside tips," and newspaper accounts serve as resources to highlight an issue in the community. (6) *Money* enables a group to purchase material things or promotional time to gain attention and improve the presentation of a problem.

Learn how to motivate people to act and carry out tactics. Many people are hesitant or fearful to express and act upon their concerns. They are uncomfortable or unfamiliar with the tasks of implementing a strategy, and they may also fear retaliation from their actions. Mondros and Wilson (1994) suggest three techniques to sustain motivation:

1. *Reflection,* where members are helped to understand better the meaning and context of the issue. Advocates can clarify problems,

offer information, point out biases, and educate people about the issue and target. The advocate can also agitate and personalize the issue, get people worked up, focus their anger, and build emotion. People can visit the sites or scenes of their concern or meet with the opposition leaders to experience personally what conditions or personalities are like.

2. *Vision* means seeing oneself differently; advocates can help people build confidence in themselves, reminding them of their talents, past successes, skills, and capacities. Training sessions may be relevant here whereby people can reevaluate the situation and their roles in improving things.

3. *Reducing fear of taking risks* is also important. People do not want to be embarrassed, lose prestige and status, or become overly anxious about their futures. Many fears are "perceived" threats, and advocates can help expose people to the reality of an action. Make the action "fun" with social and informal gatherings, dinners, parties, celebrations, and singing.

Cause advocacy often leads to legal action or lawsuits. Sheafor et al. (1994) state that during the past 20 years, most of the reforms in mental health, mental retardation, disabilities, special education, and welfare grew out of lawsuits. (Review P.L. 94-142, The Education for All Handicapped Children Act of 1975; P.L. 99-319, The Protection and Advocacy for Mentally Ill Individuals Act of 1986; The Americans with Disabilities Act of 1990; and the U.S. Supreme Court decision, *Saenz v. Roe,* in 1999, which disallowed California's ruling to limit new state residents to welfare benefits received in their previous state during their first year's residency [Yoo, 1999].)

Cause advocacy by definition involves groups or classes of persons, and the courts often become the forum for interpreting laws and regulations. Agencies try to avoid lawsuits because they are expensive, time-consuming, and permit problems to be known to the public (Kirst-Ashman & Hull, 1993). Implementation of legal decisions also becomes a source of tension when an agency attempts to interpret the law very narrowly (Fabricant & Epstein, 1984). Advocates must remain vigilant in seeing that the spirit or intent of the law is retained.

Tactics may rely on "shock" to produce change. Jenkins-Smith and Sabatier (1994) argue that the only way that change of policy will occur is through some shock coming from outside (external to) the system, and then advocates can exploit this opportunity to their advantage. In Virginia, in 1998–99, mental health advocates pressured the governor to increase mental health funding and services soon after the U.S. Department of Justice served notice that it was investigating one of the state institutions for criminal neglect in the death of a mentally ill resident. The governor made mental health a priority and tried to take political credit for the reforms suggested by the advocates. Outside events or "shocks" in themselves do not necessarily lead to change, but they offer opportunities for advocates to reinterpret conditions to the public or decision makers.

Become an expert at providing information. Although providing information is usually classified as a collaborative tactic, it is useful to be perceived as the expert on a topic in any cause effort. Berry (1981) offers research findings that indicate that "high" information capability groups were much more likely to be consulted by decision makers than "low" capability groups. More than just transmitting the opinion or views of the group, advocates can increase their credibility by providing research-based information and scientific data. Advocates can also disseminate their information widely at hearings, through news releases, and through the media because the opposition most likely will not provide facts contrary to their position.

Assumptions about power. Kirst-Ashman and Hull (1993) offer five assumptions to consider when reflecting on the use of power in promoting their causes:

1. Those who hold power are generally reluctant to give up that power.
2. Those who hold power generally have greater access to resources than people with less power.
3. Resources in general, including power, are not distributed equally.
4. Conflict among people and between people and institutions is inevitable.
5. You must have power in order to change existing organizations and institutions.

Social work advocates can readily offer expert power, but should also be aware of the dynamics of power in any cause effort. Power is a reality, but not beyond influence.

Tips on tactics. Altman et al. (1994) offer several short tips for tactical planning:

- Distinguish between working hard and working smart!
- Have a backup plan in case your initial tactic fails!
- Be able to mobilize a network of influential persons on short notice!
- In the game of advocacy, being "right" does not guarantee winning.
- Remind the public and decision makers of your position frequently.
- Be scrupulously accurate in all written and spoken statements.

A Chicago Agency Expands Its Emphasis to Include "Taking up a Cause"

United Charities, a long-standing family agency in metropolitan Chicago, provided, as many agencies in the middle of the 20th century did, services primarily to individuals. Family-centered diagnosis and treatment were increasingly the primary methods used by the agency by the 1960s. But, by 1971, a policy shift took place on the board of directors. The agency was to continue to give primary emphasis to the provision of personalized services to individuals, families, and groups, but now was to also develop a public affairs program that would address conditions beyond the control of a client.

United Charities set up a social policy department that would focus on larger issues and their impact on individuals and families rather than on a case-by-case basis. Various "cause issues" were chosen by the agency in the next decade and a half.

One cause was "utilities advocacy." More and more clients complained of needing emergency assistance to keep the utilities hooked up. United Charities decided to assist in negotiating with the government and the utility to modify their regulations for low-income consumers.

Another cause was "housing initiatives." Agency staff expressed concern continually over the lack of affordable housing for their low-income clients. There were 80,000 persons on the waiting list for federally subsidized housing. There were more than 25,000 homeless in the city. State planning and responses to this issue were absent. United Charities played a role in creating a major housing coalition, educating legislators, and securing endorsements from key power players.

[Case based on Erickson, A. G., Moynihan, F. M., & Williams, B. L. (1991). A family practice model for the 1990s. The Journal of Contemporary Human Services, 72(5), 286–293.*]*

Supply Leadership

Cause advocates face many challenges as leaders because many times, they are the "paid" staff persons who use their skills to organize volunteers and develop other leaders. Bobo et al. (1996) believe that the professional organizer's role is to facilitate others to do things to build up the organization rather than the leaders doing it themselves. But, there are times when advocates must step up and provide direction and focus. As the authors point out below, cause advocates are required to balance several leadership traits and obtain special knowledge and skills in order to bring a cause to a successful conclusion.

Leadership Traits   Among the many traits associated with leadership, cause advocates often must demonstrate the following.

Commitment. Perhaps the first step in leading a cause effort is for the advocate to make a personal commitment to the issue and persons behind the issue. Without this level of energy, advocates may not be able to devote themselves sufficiently and exclusively to overcoming the barriers that afflict a group of people (Bobo et al., 1996; Sunley, 1970).

Self-discipline. Advocates who are organizing volunteers or groups of individuals cannot afford to act impulsively. It is important to analyze and think ahead coolly about the consequences of decisions made either by the advocate or the group. Building trust and cooperative relationships internally and externally with other agencies requires a reflective, three-steps-ahead kind of person (Sheafor et al., 1994).

Ahead of followers, but not too far. Leaders must seem to lead, states Cameron (1966) and Stewart et al. (1989), and they must be a little ahead, a little wiser, a little more informed than their followers. But if they are too far ahead, pushing too much too soon, confidence and trust may be lost and the leader will be without followers. Leaders without a sense of the desires of their members will fail to satisfy their members and will be out of a job (Eriksen, 1997).

Charisma. Most advocates do not have the awe-inspiring personalities of Martin Luther King, Jr., Mahatma Gandhi, or Eleanor Roosevelt, but they can be persons who can articulate what others feel, desire, or imagine but cannot put into words or action (Stewart et al., 1989). According to Altman et al. (1994), "leaders need to maintain the energy of the group, and motivate members by conveying a sense of hopefulness, optimism, and possibility for success" (p. 9). Bobo et al. (1996) state that leaders must have confidence and self-assurance while also being able to ask for help.

Pragmatism. Successful advocates also must bring a healthy skepticism, common sense, honesty, tact, efficiency, organizational expertise, fund-raising skills, recruitment skills, goal-setting skills, and a can-do attitude to the cause effort. Goals that are too idealistic or unattainable are replaced with more achievable ones that reflect the resources of the group and the political environment (Stewart, 1989).

Adaptable. Probably no one person can adapt to all of the pressures, events, conflicts, and dilemmas encountered in implementing a cause advocacy effort. Incidents occur and advocates must respond or appear to be controlled and helpless in the wake of events. Advocates who can adapt themselves to different audiences and crises without appearing to cave-in to pressures and demands may produce both short- and long-term successes. Reconciling differences diplomatically among group members and employing group members' unique talents toward the goal of the cause are often required. Leaders must seem to be in the forefront of necessary change without sacrificing values, norms, and beliefs of the members (Stewart, 1989).

Developing Leadership   Bobo et al. (1996) inform advocates in no uncertain terms: "[I]f you are not developing leaders, then you are not building the organization" (p. 93). Alinsky (1971) applied the term *leader* to all members other than paid staff in order to stress the importance of all participants and their contributions. A basic question is raised by Bobo et al. (1996): How do we get people to feel that they own this group, take responsibility, and work to keep it going? Advocates can spend a significant amount of time in the process of developing members into leaders (Mondros & Wilson, 1994).

A related question is: Who is a potential leader? One guideline is to recognize that leaders have a base of support and can bring people with them to meetings. These leaders will be people who speak the same language as the group members, share the same values, are trusted, can motivate others, and are in tune with the community (Bobo et al., 1996). Identify persons in the group who are charismatic, who can get people to work together. Although a few natural leaders exist, most organizations have to develop their own leaders. Advocates can start developing leaders by:

- Watching for signs of leadership in early meetings. Is the person politically astute, energetic, reliable, articulate, and loyal to the cause?
- Allowing persons to emerge or evolve as leaders from the membership.
- Discovering the self-interests of the potential leader. What return will he or she get from acting as a leader? respect? new skills? new allies? photo-ops? social activity? excitement? contacts?
- Having private conversations with potential leaders to uncover their interests.
- Carefully reviewing any position or task you may ask the person to do in order to allay fears or confusion.
- Not expecting one person to have all the leadership qualities you want.
- Analyzing the abilities of members and breaking the jobs down into manageable pieces, assigning a person to take responsibility for each piece.
- Providing praise and recognition for acts of leadership.

Understanding Group Dynamics   Cause advocacy is by definition based on groups: building groups, maintaining group consensus, resolving group conflicts, group decision making, group identity, strengthening group cohesion, and so on. Kirst-Ashman and Hull (1993) note that the successful advocate and leader understands the "group processes" of resistance to change, nonverbal communication, informal and formal structures, and decision making by groups. One certain area of knowledge and skill for the cause advocate is understanding the dynamics of groups. There is a vast literature on this topic; the authors recommend that readers spend considerable time studying it.

One important variable is group cohesion, which represents the bonds among members of a group who feel tied to one another, have a sense of solidarity, hold similar values, and believe strongly in a common goal or cause. Advocates can encourage and deepen the cohesion among the group by encouraging members to share in discussions and decision making. Time can be allotted not only for formal meetings, but also for informal socializing before and after meetings and events so that people can come to know each other better (Mondros & Wilson, 1994).

When discussions get too heated or bogged down, the advocate should know when to step in and suggest ways to reach a conclusion. Conflicts are a healthy outcome of group meetings, but disagreements and tensions, if left unattended, can weaken the group's ability to succeed. Compromise and resolving conflict will keep people working together. Sometimes meeting with individuals will help reduce the tensions.

Smart advocates will try to build a history of cohesive actions to establish the group's credibility, prestige, and power (Eriksen, 1997). The main point here is that advocates must be familiar with group dynamics and develop skills to enhance the inner workings of the group.

Students with Disabilities Have Complaints—MSW Students Organize

At Alvin Weller University in 1999, students with disabling conditions felt that they were not being listened to by the university Director of the Office of Students with Disabilities, and that accommodations guaranteed by the Americans with Disabilities Act (ADA) of 1990 were not readily provided. Rooms for meetings were not accessible for wheelchairs. Professors were not paying attention to university policy regarding students' requests for assistance with exams and lectures. Because some of their friends were among the frustrated, disabled students, a small group of MSW students decided they were going to advocate for a better response to and appropriate accommodations for their disabled peers. They had a cause!

First, the students debated how to raise the university's awareness of this issue. They drafted a petition calling for the administration to take three actions to improve delivery of services to students with disabilities. The three actions were: (1) conduct a thorough review of the university's compliance with ADA by hiring an outside expert consultant; (2) develop and implement

(Continued)

an ongoing monitoring system to evaluate services to students with disabilities; and (3) develop and implement special programs designed to educate and raise awareness of disability issues within the university.

Next, the students obtained 800 signatures from the university community for the petition. They believed that this step would get the issue into the larger community. They also organized a panel of credible experts to speak on disabilities at a Social Justice conference; this included the university Director of the Office of Students with Disabilities. Some of these same panelists were interviewed on video prior to the conference. During the panel presentation, the facts were presented as impartially as possible, and students believed that they had raised awareness a notch.

Another tactic was to obtain the official approval of the social work faculty and the dean of the school. At a faculty meeting, students distributed the petition, aired the video, and spoke to the faculty rather passionately about signing the petition. Here the students' plans nearly went awry. Due to selected editing of the video, the Director of the Office of Students with Disabilities appeared to be unfairly criticized, and faculty began asking pointed questions about the facts. One student advocate pleaded, "A lot of people have been affected, I mean, a lot!" The base of support from faculty began to fracture as some faculty began to defend the Director, and the students were losing ground quickly. Suddenly, the dean of the school spoke and refocused the conversation toward the petition, clarifying for faculty some of the circumstances, and personally asking them to support the students' efforts. Wisely, the students had already been working with the dean all along, and their initiative was saved by the dean's powerful recommendation.

With the faculty's approval, the students moved ahead with their petition to a higher level in the university administration where they began discussing the three actions that they believed would increase support for students with disabilities.

Get to Know Decision Makers and Their Staff

Effective cause advocates establish relationships with decision makers for the same reasons all advocates do: to influence the person(s) who have the power to give them what they want (Bobo et al., 1996). (See Chapter 4.) Particular advice directed toward cause advocates is centered around two questions: (1) Does a cause advocate target institutions or individual decision makers? and (2) How do decision makers react to proposals for change from advocates?

Does a cause advocate target institutions or individual decision makers? Alinksy (1971) and Bobo et al. (1996) believe that the "target" of an advocacy campaign is *always* a person. For them, the fundamental rule of organizing is expressed in the dictum, "Personalize the target!" Alinsky and others argue that it is impossible to develop hostility against inanimate structures like a bureaucracy or a corporation. Mondros and Wilson (1994) also suggest that targeting an individual person helps to structure decision making by "identifying who must be influenced, who must be held accountable, and whom the group is up against" (p. 145). Such personification allows advocates and their members to feel that winning is possible because a person(s) may have human responses to a complaint, such as fairness, guilt, loyalty, ambition, vanity, and "a soul" (Bobo et al., 1996). It is also easier to apply direct pressure on an individual such as the CEO of a corporation or an agency administrator whom advocates can confront in person or whose friends/associates can be petitioned (Mondros & Wilson, 1994).

Others believe that it is more effective to target institutions or "the system" (Rothman et al., 1977). They suggest that institutional targets are more visible and acceptable to advocates. Mondros and Wilson (1994) note that "if you get people focused on an individual person, then all of their anger and what they wanted to do is directed at that person as opposed to directed at [the system or] source of the problem" (p. 145). Taking on an individual also is more risky, since the person may resent personalized attacks and may not want to ever have anything to do with the advocacy group again. Wise advocates note that one never knows when you may need your current adversary as a future friend.

The authors agree with Mondros and Wilson (1994) that this dilemma is about the role of conflict in advocacy. Do advocates feel more comfortable confronting an individual or a faceless institution? Is it easier to "fight city hall" or the mayor? Perhaps it is natural to shy away from conflict altogether, but in the long run, issues requiring change will need to be addressed directly with decision makers. The authors believe it is individuals who need to be influenced or persuaded. Accepting conflict as normal is imperative. Preparing for it, providing accurate information, and fashioning feasible alternatives are the most effective responses.

How do decision makers react to proposals for change from advocates? Some suggest that decision makers simply resist any change in the status quo or that people with power usually do not want to give any of it up (Kirst-Ashman & Hull, 1993). Levy (1970) appeals to us to try to comprehend the great complexity of effecting change and influencing persons who make policy. He noted that several factors are typically involved in a decision maker's perspective about proposed changes: (1) psychological aspects of personally held values such as equality and ideological beliefs such as a limited role for governments; (2) if the decision maker is an elected decision maker, there is the desire to be reelected; (3) special personal interests such as deaf children because the decision maker has one; (4) pressures from politically powerful allies or constituents; (5) the state of the economy and the availability of funding; (6) allocation decisions subject to scrutiny by staff and the public; and (7) lack of authority by certain levels of decision makers to change programs. These seven dimensions will assuredly be found in varying degrees in reaction to any proposals for change. Advocates must take them into account.

Decision makers are influenced not only by cost-effectiveness statements, but also by the opinions of those who "count" in the eyes of the decision maker. This may or may not be in the "best interest" of the people or the cause, but often is very significant in determining the direction of a decision maker's opinion (Levy, 1970). Advocates do well to identify the persons or groups to whom decision makers listen.

Broaden the Base of Support

Cause advocates can be more successful when they find existing individuals, groups, or agencies who are concerned with the same issues and join forces with them (Altman et al., 1994; Sheafor et al., 1994). Some scholars (Jenkins-Smith & Sabatier, 1994) even suggest that there is enough evidence to argue that an advocacy coalition approach to change meets the requirements of a causal theory. Because cause advocates are usually seeking to influence social and political systems on behalf of a group(s) of people rather than a person-to-person change, a community, state, or regional coalition of persons or agencies is often employed (Shanker, 1983; Trazcek, 1987). The authors present in the following text seven additional directives particularly aimed at cause advocates seeking to broaden their base of support: enlist key, influential persons; seek multileveled coalitions; obtain support of senior administrators; remember that everything is political; do not do it all yourself; work on multiple issues at the same time; and use the Internet and World Wide Web.

Enlist key, influential persons. Wisdom says not to take on a cause all by yourself or even with your small group. The pressure required for changes in agency policy, state laws, and complex regulations demands powerful forces in order to succeed. Cause advocates should seek out individuals or groups that are already well established in the community and enlist them in support of their cause (Altman et al., 1994; Gerhart, 1990; Gormley, 1981). Their presence or testimony at a hearing, letters of support signed by them, or behind-the-scenes contacts frequently persuade decision makers to change their opinions or at least give credibility to the cause effort. By asking various leaders to identify who they perceive as "powerful," advocates can soon identify which persons or groups to seek out.

Seek multileveled coalitions. Becoming a part of a coalition that already has broader support is also an excellent idea. Often there are groups that have local, state, regional, and national organizations. The National Alliance for the

Mentally Ill (NAMI) is one such multileveled agency with local, state, and national chapters. Participating with such a coalition provides new access to funding, greater information resources, contacts, models and strategies to review, and a network of like-minded advocates (Schloss & Jayne, 1994). When attempting to offer alternatives, it is also a good idea to consider multi-leveled sources such as state dollars combined with federal dollars, incorpo-rating regional bodies in the planning, state and federal courts, federal agencies, and national organizations.

Obtain support of senior administrators. If agencies form a coalition in order to collaborate on solving a problem or proposing new alternatives, advo-cates should seek out approval for this effort not only from interested staff mem-bers of an agency, but also from the senior administrators. Experience shows that if the directors or executives of an agency do not solidly support or believe in the cause effort, they most probably will not allow their agency to participate sufficiently and effectively in the work that needs to be done (Pearl & Barr, 1976). Questions arise over staff time, commitment of resources, and decisions about strategies and tactics; senior administrators usually want to have a say in these decisions, and it is best to secure their participation beforehand.

Remember that everything is political. Many cause efforts must relate their immediate issue to the larger societal or community context (Williams, 1986). Negligent nursing home practices, for example, are a reflection of the larger long-term health care delivery system and growing demographics of an increasingly aging population. Nonheated rooms for homeless residents in low-cost hotels are a symbol of the community's disregard for homeless citi-zens and lack of enforcement of existing regulations and codes. In order to solve most issues, it is necessary to form a political base that will have some long-lasting, persistent presence, capable of exerting pressure on key decision makers who have the power to change things.

Be careful or you will be doing it all yourself. If advocates are not alert to promoting participation broadly in their planning, discussions, and decision making, members of the group may gradually fade away and leave the work to the advocate (Ross, 1977b). Initial enthusiasm among members must be main-tained as much as possible so that future actions will enjoy the support and energy of many participants. Cause advocates need to focus not only on the tasks that need to be done, but also on maintaining the motivation and inter-est of the members. This is a difficult balancing act, but reflects the normal dynamics of all group building.

Work on multiple issues at the same time. Some advocates believe that their efforts should focus solely on a single issue, or otherwise the members may be overwhelmed, loss of focus will occur, actions will be diluted, and scarce resources will be spent ineffectively. Everyone will be "spread too thin." Although these are dangers, it is also important to recognize how issues are interrelated. For instance, working with immigrants includes housing, employment, education, cultural acclimation, and communication. Mondros and Wilson (1994) state there are several advantages to working simultaneously on several issues:

1. People learn about the many forces affecting them when they work on multiple issues and see their effort not so much as problem solving, but as social change.
2. Issues naturally lead one to the other, and affected people usually need help in multiple areas.
3. Working on several issues at the same time may attract new funding sources and diverse people who will support the cause effort. Different people like to help on special areas, and if your effort is broad enough, it can include their interests.
4. Multiple issues provide relief from boredom with only a single issue, and if the group "loses" a battle on one issue, it may be winning on another one. Morale of the members is easier to maintain if there are little victories along the way. Success in some form is very essential to maintaining group morale and motivation.
5. Having more than one issue to consider readily leads to priority setting where the group can decide which issues are primary and which are secondary. This helps to focus the group and commit resources more efficiently.

Use the Internet and World Wide Web. In addition to using the Internet for fact finding, advocates can develop electronically linked groups of persons or coalitions. E-mails, discussion groups, and newsgroups can all provide a method of organizing individuals into a more coherent source of influence. Such online advocacy planning is advantageous because it shrinks distances and eliminates time as barriers to effective advocacy. Establishing e-mail linkages with small groups (or even large groups) promotes communication and decision making. There are usually low expenses associated with e-mail activities. Traditional methods of broadening one's base will be needed, but new experiments with electronic advocacy warrant support (McNutt & Boland, 1999).

Finally, Fiedler and Antonak (1991) remind the cause advocate that there are three basic reasons for broadening one's base of support: (1) to mobilize the maximum number of people concerned with an issue; (2) to view the issue from several different angles; and (3) to avoid the situation where similar agencies or groups make contradictory statements, failing to speak with one voice.

Be Persistent

Cause advocates must adhere to the notion of *persistence* in their advocacy because many, if not most, of their "causes" will not be resolved in a short time period. A cause is usually an issue firmly entrenched in the community or in an agency's operation, and it is not likely to be changed quickly because a few people think "changing it would be a good idea." Giving up early on achieving one's goals will always produce failure. The authors discussed in the following text provide additional pertinent advice to cause advocates.

Sheafor et al. (1994) and O'Connell (1978) remind the cause advocate that a major requirement of effective advocacy is stamina, sticking to a task, and seeing it through to the end. Altman et al. (1994) adds that "follow-through" is a particularly important element of persistence. If one's group has a reputation for not following through on commitments or agreements, it is very difficult to expect others to support the advocacy effort. In fact, opponents will simply wait until you give up or go away.

Discouragement is another issue affecting cause advocates and their partners (Gormley, 1981; Morgan, 1983). Some advocates "burn out" when their cause is not successful immediately. Initial setbacks or failure to achieve the ideal solution at once are frequently the source of low morale and dropout rates. Great care must be given to planning the advocacy effort so that small victories can be achieved along the way.

Cause advocates must also deal with another dimension of persistence, and that is trust (Brager, 1968; Ross, 1977b). Ongoing relationships depend upon trust, and a failure to "be there" in good times and in bad times will weaken the relationship of the advocate to the client group. Clients or client groups come to trust the advocate when they see him or her working with them over a long period of time and through periods of adversity.

Jenkins-Smith and Sabatier (1994) caution advocates about realistic time spans required for influencing change. A 10-year time span is considered very realistic for many issues because it is difficult to alter quickly the knowledge and beliefs of decision makers. While a decade may seem to be a pessimistic view, at the very least, it warns the advocate that persistence over several years may be in order to achieve the desired goal. A review of many major pieces of legislation at both the federal and state level reveals that it took many years to pass legislation on behalf of the mentally ill, handicapped children, the disabled, the aged, and so on. But with determination, advocates finally achieved benefits and resources for their cause and group.

Evaluate Your Advocacy Effort

How can cause advocates evaluate their effectiveness? How can they prove their efforts truly made a difference? Serious evaluation studies take a great deal of time and work, and change is hard to prove, especially long-term effects. Berkowitz (1982) stated that most community activities or social change programs are not evaluated at all. The reasons most commonly given for failing to conduct evaluations are:

1. Evaluation as a concept threatens the average worker, who may fear poor performance assessments or lack the knowledge of evaluation techniques. Berkowitz (1982) encourages advocates to realize that evaluations are simply "checking" on the results of what you do and making adjustments as needed. They also include evaluating how well something is done. These activities are daily experiences for all humans and should not be viewed as unusually difficult or strange.

2. Evaluations take time. Someone has to plan an evaluation, design instruments, collect data, tabulate, analyze findings, and disseminate the results. Advocates must determine how much time to allocate to evaluation rather than to service. If a program is evaluated well and leads to more resources or more effective outcomes, evaluation clearly justifies a proportionate investment of time and energy.

3. The results of an evaluation may be discouraging, threatening the advocate's position, implying a loss of credibility, bruising egos, and subjecting one's efforts to criticism. Berkowitz (1982) recommends that advocates learn to accept the truth about their efforts and have confidence that the results, if used to improve the program, will benefit everyone in the long run.

4. Evaluation requires technical skills and methods that the advocate may lack. In fact, there are some sophisticated methodological skills needed for valid research design and analysis. But, by using common sense, advocates can also generate data that, while imperfect, will provide useful information. Contracting with a technical researcher is another way of importing the expertise needed.

The reasons for undertaking evaluation of advocacy activities are:

1. Since advocates are usually interested in producing change, you cannot tell if change occurred without some type of evaluation. Detecting change implies measurement at point X and again at point Y. Did cause advocates' efforts have anything to do with the resultant change?

2. Success is a major factor in cause advocacy. If advocates and their members never succeed in changing conditions or influencing decision makers, membership usually drops off, morale is lowered, and the spirit of engagement dies down. Winning or seeming to win breeds confidence, raises spirits, attracts new members, generates publicity, improves chances for funding, and projects an image of power in the eyes of others (Mondros & Wilson, 1994). Consequently, evaluating the advocates' cause is important because it helps to define success.

The following text describes some ways in which cause advocates can assess or measure their successes. Mondros and Wilson (1994) propose four types of achievements or successes to which cause advocates aspire: achieving instrumental changes, developing leadership, developing organizational resources and capacities, and increasing the public's awareness of the cause effort and its issues.

Achieving Instrumental Changes   Securing the changes sought by the advocates is the focus of instrumental change. Was a desired change actually achieved? Did the state legislature pass the bill on preventing violence against women that the group was pursuing? Did the group persuade the agency to allocate 200 more section 8 housing certificates? Instrumental change is the primary type of change sought by most advocates: the attainment of benefits or improvement of conditions for a client group. Such demonstrable achievements keep current members motivated, inculcate a sense of pride and confidence in members, attract new members, let others know the group is a "winner," and invest power in the group in the eyes of the community.

Developing Leadership   Advocates frequently strive to teach members new leadership skills, to empower them to articulate their own vision of the world, and to make decisions competently. Indicators of success here are demonstrated by members assuming new responsibilities, by members taking on leadership tasks such as identifying issues and planning strategies, and by new members joining the group. Advocates who are sensitive to members' feelings about themselves and each other can encourage or challenge members with "easy" or "tough" campaigns, depending on the state of their leadership abilities. Helping individuals toward "small victories" will increase members' confidence in themselves and their abilities to make change.

Developing Organizational Resources and Capacities   Advocates also pursue strategies to strengthen the organization or group, helping it to grow, increasing its recognition, and finding funding. Indicators of success here include: numbers of new members, name recognition in the community, an increase in grants or dues, and even public attacks on the group by public officials who recognize the group as powerful. Successes should be widely publicized and used to raise money and enhance the reputation of the group.

Increasing the Public's Awareness   Public attitudes should change as a result of the groups' efforts. Indicators of success are positive media reports, editorials and letters to the editors, invitations to testify or speak at meetings, requests to join a coalition, and public opinion polls. Mondros and Wilson (1994) warn that instrumental change does not always follow attitudinal changes. Some propose that change actually comes before opinion shifts. Advocates are urged to proceed toward change on the assumption that public attitudes will eventually follow.

Steps in the Evaluation Process   Finally, the authors offer a summary of the necessary steps to follow in the evaluation process. Many texts are available with in-depth treatment of research and program evaluation techniques and methods; this section is not a substitute for them. However, the eight steps outlined here summarize the essential tasks required to evaluate one's cause advocacy efforts (see Berkowitz, 1982, pp. 155–167).

Step One. Make a commitment to evaluating your advocacy activities because it is very easy to let other activities supplant evaluation. Be willing to open yourself and your work to criticism, be honest, and be ready to transfer what is learned to your future efforts.

Step Two. Specify the purpose of your evaluation effort. Why are you doing the evaluation—to prove that things are going well, to produce results for funders, or to improve the operation of the organization? Ask yourself what you plan to do with the results after they have been analyzed.

Step Three. Identify the goals of your advocacy effort. Hopefully, you have already set goals; your task now is to see if your efforts have indeed produced the result you sought at first. Clarify goals early and often; evaluation of them will reveal the results you have or have not obtained. It is not ethical to conduct your advocacy activities and then proceed to formulate some goals.

Step Four. Select specific criteria by which the goals will be assessed. Evaluation must be based on preselected criteria. There are *outcome criteria* such as actual improvements in service, survival of the group, awareness by people of your efforts, support expressed by members and nonmembers, attendance, participation and responsibility sharing, requests for new services, spin-offs, income, and incidental effects. These can each be highly defined and used as criteria. There are also *process criteria* such as the personal feelings of accomplishment, learning, and satisfaction levels of the participants. *Input criteria* include time, people, contacts, and money as indicated by total numbers of hours, volunteers, dollars, and so on. *Cost-effectiveness criteria* include dollar cost per hour of service, time cost per hour of service, average client fee per unit of service, dollar cost per contact, and so on. Advocates should choose variables consistent with initial goals and by the ease of measurement.

Step Five. Set expected levels for each criterion you have selected. At first, advocates may not be able to "guess" the right numbers, for example, getting 100 or 200 new members, raising $5,000 or $10,000 with a raffle, training 50 or 150 volunteers, and so on. If experience shows that numbers are too high or too low, then future decisions will support an adjustment. When numerical values are tied to specific program objectives, they lend themselves readily to measurement.

Step Six. Take measurements on each criterion after the program has been operating. You must preplan when you will count or log items. Feedback forms or tallies must be designed. Measure before the program starts if at all possible. Keep records, establish baseline data, and use them to assist your other evaluative efforts.

Step Seven. Analyze the results, draw out the conclusions, and make recommendations. Usually, there will be numerical results, and advocates will need to interpret them in the context of the community or activity. Comparing them to other research findings is helpful.

Step Eight. Use the recommendations in practice. Many evaluations never get beyond the seventh step because organizers and advocates often pursue the line of least resistance. All the problems mentioned before may surface: deflated egos, hurt feelings, revision of plans, new energy required for different areas, starting over or nearly over, and so on. The best strategy is to build evaluation into the routine program operation, and then everyone will expect to use the results without much hesitation.

SUMMARY

Cause advocates address problems affecting a large group or class of persons with similar concerns. Some argue that *cause* advocacy is a logical extension of *client* advocacy, that is, an individual's case serves as the basis for broader action in changing policies or conditions for a larger group. Cause advocacy depends on the effective use of this book's two fundamental advocacy skills: representation and influencing. Whether fighting for a cause at local, state, or national levels, social workers can provide leadership in resolving problems that affect groups of people and meet their obligation to the NASW *Code of Ethics.*

DISCUSSION QUESTIONS

1. How are "cause" advocacy and "client" advocacy linked together?
2. Why do some experts say that cause advocacy is issue-oriented, not individual-oriented?
3. Why is it difficult sometimes to identify the "client" in cause advocacy?
4. Which social work principles and values are found in cause advocacy?
5. What steps can be taken to ensure that cause advocates do not become paternalistic or dominating?
6. Discuss how you would plan strategies to gain access to media coverage for your cause.
7. Why is it difficult to obtain consensus on the issue or problem for which you wish to advocate?
8. What should a cause advocate do when group members are afraid to use a tactic that requires them to demonstrate their position publicly?

9. Why is understanding group dynamics so important in leading a cause advocacy effort?
10. What advantages and disadvantages are there in evaluating the outcomes of an advocacy effort?

RECOMMENDED READINGS

Altman, D. G., Balcazar, F. E., Fawcett, S. B., Seekins, T., & Young, J. Q. (1994). *Public health advocacy: Creating community change to improve health.* Palo Alto, CA: Stanford Center for Research in Disease Prevention.

Berkowitz, W. R. (1982). *Community impact: Creating grassroots change in hard times.* Cambridge, MA: Shenkman Publishing.

Bobo, K., Kendall, J., & Max, S. (1996). *Organizing for social change.* Santa Ana, CA: Seven Locks Press.

Gerhart, U. C. (1990). Advocacy. In *Caring for the chronic mentally ill* (pp. 270–285). Itasca, IL: F.E. Peacock Press.

Mondros, J. B., & Wilson, S. M. (1994). *Organizing for power and empowerment.* New York: Columbia University Press.

Legislative Advocacy

> *Social workers should be aware of the impact of the political arena on practice and advocate for changes in policy and legislation to improve social conditions in order to meet human needs and promote social justice.*
>
> NASW *CODE OF ETHICS* SECTION 604(A) (1996)

OVERVIEW

Jansson (1999) implores social workers to recall that legislative advocates have significantly improved the well-being of millions of Americans. He highlights federal policies like Medicaid, food stamps, the Americans with Disabilities Act, and child care programs. At the state and local levels, advocates have influenced legislators to introduce and pass numerous proposals in the health and human services arena (Influencing State Policy, 1999). At the dawn of the 21st century, social workers have a new chance to influence social policy and legislation by paying close attention to the "new Federalism," which gives the states greater authority over benefits, rules, and priorities for clients (Schneider & Netting, 1999). Legislative advocates, who know how to address new problems and seek support and resources for disadvantaged persons, can raise public expectations about the rights and needs of all citizens.

The authors agree with Richan (1996) who appeals to social workers to remember that the drama of public policy has no final curtain call. Legislative advocacy is never over. Without the determined and constant involvement of social work advocates representing clients in legislative arenas, responsive and progressive policies may not be formulated and implemented. The NASW *Code of Ethics* reminds each social worker of the responsibility to advocate for legislation and policies that support social justice (section 604[a]).

In order to pursue its commitment to legislative advocacy today and in the future, the profession of social work must also recognize a past ambivalence. In the 1980s, Wolk (1981) noted that, despite some political activity such as letter-writing, discussion of issues, and financial contributions, social work professionals appeared to play a minimal role in shaping policies and decisions at the local, state, and national levels. In the 1990s, Figueira-McDonough (1993) continued this observation, noting that social work legislative advocacy in the United States is practiced only to a modest extent. Ezell (1993) has summarized recent literature on the political activity of social workers, noting some growth in political involvement of social workers since the Reagan years in office, but recognizing that nearly half of the solicited social workers could be identified as "politically inactive."

Why are social workers less than fully active in the legislative arena? We can summarize the known barriers to effective social work participation in legislative advocacy: limited knowledge of the legislative process; disdain of politics and deal making; impatience regarding the length of time required to make change; a preoccupation on clinical issues and professionalization criteria; and lack of content on legislative advocacy in professional educational curricula (Ezell, 1993; Mahaffey, 1972). This chapter cannot explore these barriers with the necessary depth and analysis. We propose that first social workers must acknowledge this gap in the profession; then leaders must create state and national structures to address and remedy this situation. Influencing State Policy, for example, is a national group committed to improving the effectiveness of social workers in state legislative arenas (see its website at www.statepolicy.org).

We present in this chapter both of the fundamental advocacy skills, that is, representation and influencing, in the context of legislative decision making. Social work advocates can incorporate this specialized knowledge and skills into their professional careers and interventions.

Convinced by a Constituent: A Mental Health Parity Bill in Virginia

Noran Sanford and John Salay of Virginia Commonwealth University, MSW students in 1999, personally lobbied committees in the Virginia House of Delegates to pass Senate Bill 430, a bill that would require insurance companies to cover serious mental illness on parity with physical illnesses. They worked with a state lobby group called the Mental Health Association of Virginia as part of a project for a MSW foundation policy/macro class.

Noran and John made personal appeals to each of the 14 members of the powerful House Corporations, Insurance, and Banking Committee (CIB) by using fact sheets, meeting with aides, answering questions, incorporating research findings into a cost-effectiveness argument, and using value-laden arguments when meeting with delegates.

They discovered that a key delegate on the committee represented John's voting district, and during the initial conversation, he opposed the bill. The delegate was very fiscally conservative. Noran and John made a presentation in order to persuade him to support the bill. They noted that the delegate paid close attention to what John was saying. Leaning heavily on the value of fiscal responsibility, John pointed out the "true" costs to many Virginians.

The bill passed the CIB committee with John's delegate casting the deciding affirmative vote. They then followed the bill through the remaining

(Continued)

journey to the full House and Senate where it passed by a comfortable margin. An estimated one million Virginians were affected by this bill, and more if you include family members. John and Noran stated that "two student-citizens, armed with facts and a polite demeanor, can make a difference," and "legislators are eager to have access to the facts surrounding an issue." John and Noran's advocacy was recognized as the most outstanding MSW student entry in the annual national contest, State Policy Plus Two. (For more information, visit the website www.statepolicy.org.)

REPRESENTATION

As Dluhy (1981) notes, "advocates frequently represent their clients in the political process" (p. 20). In fact, advocates have many different opportunities to communicate the concerns of their clients to legislators, committees, caucuses, at rallies, before the media, in policy briefs and proposals, letters, e-mail messages, news releases, testimony, and so on. When social work legislative advocates represent the ideas and concerns of a client to decision makers, they are also attempting to empower their clients to plead their own case and stand up for their own desires. In the American democratic tradition of government, all citizens have a constitutional right to assemble, to express their ideas to their elected representatives, and to "be heard." This far-reaching expression of representation and self-determination is at the heart of legislative advocacy.

Exclusivity

In Chapter 2, the authors described how the advocate should focus solely on the needs of the client, be client-centered and responsible to the client, and see the client's need as the sole priority. In legislative advocacy, this requirement remains the same, but it is subjected to unique pressures. Two areas particularly impinge on exclusivity: (1) the need for coalition building, and (2) the oft-necessity of negotiation and compromise in order to reach agreement on legislative proposals and bills.

Need for Coalition Building   Coalition building refers to one of the basic principles of this book, that of "broadening the base of support." It is nearly impossible for a single-minded group to be powerful enough to achieve its goals by itself. Operating "solo" usually fails due to lack of staffing, inadequate analytical resources, intense competition for media attention, limitations in perspectives, and inability to maintain attention to the issues over time. Many groups form a coalition with others who share common values and goals, and through the combination of resources, they hope to achieve a more unified and powerful status.

Beyond these benefits, threats may exist to the social work advocate's *exclusive* representation of a client or client group. Sometimes the original reason, that is, the client's specific need, for joining a coalition is lost or subverted in the process of developing or merging with the coalition's strategies. What may have been once a clear match of values and goals changes into a secondary or less significant item on the agenda. Advocates realize soon that their clients' concerns are no longer a primary or relatively exclusive issue for the coalition. Special funding, for example, sought for employment of the mentally retarded by a group may be swallowed up by a larger coalition initiative for funding community services for the chronically mentally ill.

Decisions about how much time and energy the advocate should exert on the coalition's agenda versus the priority of the client's concerns and rights need to be made. This may become difficult because cutting down on activities or leaving a coalition may signal a spirit of uncooperativeness or a perception by other members that the advocate is unwilling to support joint activities. Long-term relationships with a coalition must also be considered, and there may be partial solutions that allow the advocates to continue to support the coalition, but still focus largely on their clients. Although such assessments must be made, advocates must ultimately judge how well their clients' needs are being served.

Necessity of Negotiation and Compromise   In advancing a proposed piece of legislation in the decision-making processes, it is rare that amendments or changes are not introduced. In fact, some believe that only legislation that is amended stands a chance of passage due to the need to address the multiple concerns of legislators. In watching the course of a bill that reflects the needs of clients, advocates often see the original proposal diverted off course slightly, become watered-down, and sometimes, end up an empty shell of its original self.

Hence, the question becomes: *how much negotiation and compromise can social work advocates accept without sacrificing the exclusivity of their clients?* Advocates often face the reality that a bill may not pass successfully in any form at all. They must judge how much dilution of their client's needs is acceptable and when it is imperative to draw a line and indicate that too much compromise is harmful to the client. Prior to involvement in heated debates and discussions, it is recommended that advocates decide *in advance* just what the bottom limits of their positions are and identify the point beyond which they will not compromise. If the clients must give up some level of autonomy, benefits, or rights, then the advocates must be ready to represent their clients at a level that at least minimally protects their well-being and prevents harm.

Mutuality

Legislative advocacy is based firmly on mutual respect, empowerment, and joint decision making between social workers and their clients. The advocate must be careful not to take over too much responsibility for identifying needs and setting a legislative agenda, or in regard to the clients' right to help themselves. A paternalistic attitude of knowing "what's best for the client" must be avoided.

There are many opportunities for mutual collaboration during legislative advocacy. In selecting issues, both clients and advocates can work together in identifying specific concerns. Sometimes, the client can become the spokesperson for a bill and can provide testimony before committees or at public hearings. Lobbying efforts by clients are often among the most effective because their representatives are more likely to listen to a constituent's concern. Attendance and participation during planning or strategy sessions is also an opportunity to cooperate mutually about activities and problem solving. Efforts must be made to share updates on the status of bills and their progress through the legislative system. If changes in the legislation are going to be introduced, sharing this information with clients in a timely fashion indicates mutual respect.

In the legislative arena, pressure affecting the balance of mutual respect and decision making flows chiefly from the chaos of legislative decision making. Final, last-minute changes often occur that allow for minimum input from anyone not physically present during a discussion or verbal exchange. If advocates have been in communication consistently with the clients prior to and during the legislative session, then they will most likely be able to represent the mutual interests of clients accurately. Reports of such changes need to be given to the clients as soon as possible. If the changes are opposed by the client, then advocates must attempt to alter the previous decision(s).

Use of a Forum

I could comment at an ADOPT meeting this week because I attended Child Advocacy Day; I spoke up at a team meeting because I knew how to access the General Assembly through the Internet website. Participating in legislative advocacy makes me realize more than ever how it relates to social work and to me, a clinical practitioner.

STEPHANIE

Legislative advocates frequently represent their clients in forum-type settings such as public hearings, caucuses, testimony before committees, monitoring debates on the floor of a legislative chamber, budget hearings, and other meetings where concerns and issues are expressed before lawmakers. Advocacy in a forum setting includes the three following characteristics: (1) the forum is an opportunity to raise awareness; (2) forum members have the capacity to make decisions; and (3) the forum uses a specific set of procedures. Following are some specific ways that legislative advocates may affect these dimensions.

Opportunity to Raise Awareness   Many question the value of testifying in a forum and its effectiveness in influencing legislators, but few doubt that such public discussions boost the level of consciousness about an issue. A White House Conference on Poverty Among Children elevates the topic nationwide and sets the stage for further review and attention. A state commission on long-term care can highlight an increasingly difficult health care issue and may offer recommendations for legislators to evaluate. Nearly all organizations devoted to influencing legislation participate in forums, providing testimony at hearings and before committees (Schlozman & Tierney, 1986).

Capacity of Forum Members to Make Decisions   In the legislative arena, all of the elected officials are decision makers, authorized to make decisions about policy, budgets, and programs. There is usually a hierarchy among decision makers, and failure to know who influences what and whom is a recipe for disaster. Every committee has a chairperson and a vice-chairperson who hold particular sway over the agenda and procedures of their committee. Members who are appointed to a committee by legislative leaders each bring a particular background, party affiliation, values, interests, and skills with them. Social work advocates are wise to learn who these decision makers are along with their priorities. Ultimately, the passage or failure of a bill will rest with the legislators because they are officially and constitutionally elected to make decisions on the business of their district, state, or region.

Specific Procedures   Every legislature has a set of rules that it follows in order to conduct the enactment, amendment, or elimination of laws. These procedures are usually historically based and hide-bound in tradition, meaning that they rarely change. To be an effective advocate at the legislature means to know intimately the rules of governing, the daily running of committees and subcommittees, stages of the passage of a bill, deadlines, types of decisions made, and arcane rules of conduct. If, for example, an advocate did not know how to obtain sponsorship of a proposed bill, the initial process of enacting legislation would fail. If advocates were not aware of the "crossover" rules during the legislative session, they would not know how to influence effectively the legislators who will receive the other chamber's bills. Each state legislature publishes its rules and procedures and makes them available to anyone who asks.

The following paragraphs provide additional information for social work advocates to use in participating in legislative forums.

In general, social workers appear very unlikely to give testimony before legislative committees according to a study by Ezell (1993). In his study of political activities of social workers, *providing testimony* before local, state, or federal legislative committees was the *least frequent* political activity. Approximately 91% of the respondents did not give testimony versus 9% who did. Writing letters to legislators or public officials was the most frequent activity. Due to the nature of their jobs, macro social workers testified more frequently than micro workers.

Ezell (1993) does not suggest any inferences from these data, but it appears that, for whatever reasons, professional social workers do not often use legislative forums as a means to represent their clients. Among the reasons, we speculate, are: (1) continuing ambivalence among social workers about their role in politics; (2) discomfort with politics because it deals with power; (3) an unease with politics because it is a "dirty business"; (4) lack of training in representation during professional education; and (5) the belief that testimony is not very effective.

Studies have shown that testifying at forums is a widely used method of influencing legislators (Berry, 1977; Schlozman & Tierney, 1986). But Milbrath (1963) and Dear and Patti (1981) point out that open forums are not always recognized as an effective way to influence legislators. Changing opinions through testimony is questionable, since legislators often make up their minds early or use staff and colleagues as trusted sources of information. Personal contacts, letter-writing, monitoring legislation, and providing research results appear to work better. However, Eriksen (1997), Dear and Patti (1981), and Richan (1996) point out that testimony in a forum can provide the following effects:

- Forums offer a chance to publicize an issue for a relatively low cost because most of them are covered by the media.
- A forum draws public attention to a particular bill.
- Legislators often use a forum to mobilize public opinion.
- Forums provide a safety valve for strong emotions and allow vocal factions their "day in court."

Segal and Brzuzy (1998) point out that elected officials and legislators all live in the public eye. It is crucial for them to meet constituents and continue to demonstrate their commitment to them. One tactic a social work advocate might pursue is to organize a public forum about a pertinent topic or policy and invite the legislators to attend, especially if the meeting promises positive exposure. One must be sure to schedule it at a time that the legislator is available (not during a session); usually it is a good idea to ask the staff what the best time is. Extend a written invitation followed up by phone calls. Plan to invite the media to ensure the greatest impact. Be prepared for changes. Testimony by constituents, clients, or services providers should be planned in advance.

For more information and suggestions on how to give testimony before a legislative forum, see the following section under the heading "Speaking."

Communication

Representation includes communicating ideas and concerns on behalf of clients to those able to produce the desired change or improvement of conditions. As advocates, social workers are called upon frequently to speak and to write about the issues that affect their clients. Whether speaking or writing, advocates should never underestimate the importance of the message, the words, and the language used to refer to issues. Words often communicate fears or move emotions as well as provide information and facts. A poor choice of written or spoken words may make the advocate's job difficult. Words symbolize values; care and respect for the meaning of words are crucial in a legislative advocate's task of representing clients.

Speaking   The term *testimony* is most often used when referring to speaking publicly about a concern before a legislative forum, for example, hearings, committee and subcommittee meetings, and commissions. Three areas for the social work advocate to be aware of are: (1) the effectiveness of testimony, (2) rules for preparing and giving testimony, and (3) preparation of clients to give public testimony.

Effectiveness of testimony. Melton (1983) notes that while testifying is a "glamour" tactic, many legislators state that testimony is rarely as effective as personal contact. Sometimes a legislator who is wavering on an issue or needs more information can be persuaded by testimony (Dear & Patti, 1981), but most lobbyists and advocates feel compelled to give testimony to make certain that their views are put on the record. Some also say that testimony before state legislatures is more effective than that before Congress because state legislators, who often lack staff, are more likely to rely on testimony as sources of information (Melton, 1983). According to Richan (1996), to give or not give testimony is a moot question because he believes that forums and hearings are an integral part of the political process and there is little chance they will be eliminated. If not absolutely effective, testimony is still necessary.

Rules for preparing and delivering testimony. Most testimony is based on a written statement about two pages long, according to Kleinkauf (1981). (Jansson [1999] suggests submitting a document up to 20 pages long, but we believe that he recommends this length only when statements can be delivered several days in advance of the testimony.) Testimony should be organized as a summary of the arguments, data, research findings, and analysis of the proposed policy. It is best to limit the statement to three or four major points.

It should be clearly written, with no jargon, using factual data and citing sources. Case examples may also illustrate the impact of the policy. Sharwell (1978) advises the advocate to start and end the statement with the strongest points and leave the less crucial ones in the middle.

There are several reasons for submitting a prepared written statement to the committee before which one is testifying:

1. The statement will become part of the permanent record of the committee.
2. Such a document indicates a professional, serious approach to the issue.
3. Extended discussion of the issues beyond the time limits of the hearing may be possible; detailed information and data can be included.
4. The news media is likely to use already-prepared written materials.
5. The testifier is forced to be carefully organized and disciplined in choosing words, data, and strategies for expressing ideas.

The advocate should give a copy of the written statement to committee members before speaking. Usually, this means coming to the podium with copies in hand and giving them to the clerk for distribution to members behind the desks or tables.

Advocates should come early to the meeting room and listen to others giving testimony so that when their turn comes, they will be familiar with the line of questioning, the size of the room and audience, and location of the podium. Practicing your testimony in front of a mirror or fellow advocates beforehand will increase confidence and reduce nervousness.

Oral presentations must win the attention of the committee and keep members involved (Kaminski & Walmsley, 1995). Originality and creativity are essential. Advocates often use a symbol or a visual item to gain attention. Buttons with a message (Support Our Seniors!) or a small item such as a key (Unlock the waiting list!) or a stack of previous reports on crime among teens that have never been implemented are effective visual aids. Vivid case examples are also effective if they link the testimony to the bill or legislation under discussion.

Advocates should begin by introducing themselves, their organizational affiliation, past personal experience, and expertise in order to establish their credibility as a witness. They should then begin testimony by recognizing the chairperson and thanking him or her for allowing them to speak. A statement for or against a proposed bill or action is then made, followed by a summary of recommendations and an explanation of why advocates are interested in the bill, how they arrived at their conclusions, and who will benefit and who will be harmed. The problems should be briefly outlined, and preferred solutions or alternatives should be offered. Graphs, charts, or visual aids should be used if possible. Testimony is typically limited to five to ten minutes. At the end, recommendations are summarized, and the advocate should offer to answer any questions.

Look upon the questioning period as an opportunity to elaborate on the major points and recommendations of the testimony. The usual themes of this period are: feasibility, cost, benefit, and impact of the recommendations (Kaminski & Walmsley, 1995). Be sure to understand clearly the nature of the question or ask to have it restated or clarified. Be brief and concrete, using examples if possible. Many questioners will be friendly, but honest differences will arise. This is an essential part of the narrowing down process in policy making (Richan, 1996). Try to avoid a debate because the legislator usually wins on home turf. Stand your ground and inject your arguments or restate your position and acknowledge there is room for disagreement. If asked a question that you cannot answer, *never* fake or bluff it. Say that you will get this information right after the session.

Preparation of clients or celebrities as testifiers at legislative hearings. The testimony of clients or community residents can be even more effective than that of service providers or experts according to McInnis-Dittrich (1994). Personal experiences with their emotional tone often make very persuasive testimony. Such self-representation also empowers clients. Celebrities or "big names" draw significant public attention to an issue or proposal, and their testimony is almost always taken seriously. If Michael Jordan or Madonna decided to testify about transracial adoption policies, we can believe this issue would receive major attention.

The risk involved in a client or well-known person's testifying is that the person is entering an adversarial environment where hostile questions are as frequent as friendly ones. Inadequate preparation or a case of nerves may also cause problems. Advocates must be confident that clients and celebrities will speak clearly and with conviction. It is very important to coach and prepare them for what may happen during and after their testimony. An orientation session should be held beforehand, outlining expectations, warning of pitfalls, providing key arguments, alerting them to potential questions, telling them who the committee members are, and advising them not to express any reservations before the committee (Berger, 1977; Mahaffey, 1972). Role-playing is a suggested strategy for some clients who are nervous about testifying. With adequate preparation, these individuals can provide powerful testimony, far beyond what advocates could do themselves.

Writing   Writing skills are important resources used by social work advocates in legislative settings. Perhaps the most valued characteristic of written legislative documents is brevity—short and to the point. Because of the multitude of demands on legislators' time, succinct and clearly written papers and policy briefs are highly valued (Melton, 1983). The authors suggest particular attention should be given to: (1) letter-writing, (2) policy briefs, (3) bill drafting, and (4) several small but important tasks like news releases, thank-you notes, and letters to the editors.

Letter-writing. This activity is the "meat and potatoes of political action" according to Mattison and Storey (1992). These authors point out that "someone" in the legislator's office reads all of the incoming mail and files these letters; when an issue arises for legislative action, the weight and size of the folder often makes a difference. The debate between writing individualized letters versus form letters is ongoing, but the authors believe that both techniques are useful. Legislators are impressed with personally written letters from constituents or groups, and a high volume of "form" letters and postcards also receives positive attention.

When advocates write letters to decision makers about proposed legislation, they should keep in mind these basic guidelines:

- Keep the letter short and concise.
- Identify the name and bill number of the legislation about which you are writing.
- State your reasons for writing and state your position, citing facts, statistics, and personal experience.
- Do not assume the legislator knows as much as you do about the legislation.
- Be constructive. If you oppose the legislation, suggest alternatives.
- Remember you are writing to an elected official. Do not engage in name-calling or threaten the official if he or she disagrees with you.
- Remind the legislator (when possible) that you live in his or her district.
- Request a reply to your letter. Include your full name and address.

Researchers (Ericksen, 1997) agree that letter-writing is one of the top three methods used by advocacy groups to present the substantive and political merits of a position.

Policy briefs. These are one- or two-page documents that provide a detailed set of arguments on both sides of a question with supporting evidence (Richan, 1996; Segal & Brzuzy, 1998). A policy brief comprises an analysis of existing law, a clear statement of the problem, new proposals and points of view, rationale for changing existing policy, specific recommendations, and the likely objections to the new proposal (Jansson, 1999; Kaminski & Walmsley, 1995). Armed with this brief, advocates can confidently argue a case for a new proposal or effectively oppose existing laws.

Richan (1996) proposes that a policy brief is composed of a series of arguments based on the following four questions:

1. Is there a need for a change?
2. Will the proposed plan or proposal meet the need? How will it improve things?

3. Is the plan feasible? Cost or constitutional questions often arise here.
4. Would the proposed benefits of the plan outweigh any harmful or unintended consequences?

If advocates prepare policy briefs using these questions, it will take an equally effective counterproposal to stop it.

Richan (1996) suggests that advocates think of the brief as a resource paper rather than a document to circulate among policy makers, unless one wants to share it with friendly legislators. The policy brief should be built from the general to the specific, and background information should be brief and accurate. Once your case is put together as completely and thoroughly as possible, then attack your own case by raising objections and then rebutting them. The policy brief should help advocacy groups unify and present a consistent message to legislators, based on the same facts and arguments.

Bill drafting. Drafting bills and legislative proposals is another writing task critical to influencing the policy-making process. It requires both knowledge of the law and familiarity with existing regulations, policies, and programs related to the proposed legislation (Kirst-Ashman & Hull, 1993). Many social work advocates tend to retreat at this stage because they believe that only lawyers or specialists can draft such proposals (Herman & Callanan, 1978). This is an unfortunate conclusion, since anyone who is able to write in brief, concise, and understandable language can convert his or her ideas into a written bill.

Most legislative proposals are sent to an already-existing unit, sometimes called a "legislative service," where the draft bill will be reviewed by an attorney. Suggested refinements in language are made, the intention of the bill is clarified, and meticulous attention is paid to the composition of the bill. With assistance from staff, advocates can draft a bill that can be sponsored by legislators, who may also want to inject some of their own ideas into it. Many states now require or strongly urge legislative bills to be written in easily understandable English. Balancing coherent language with the need for precise wording is an ongoing tension, but one that is demanded by legislators and citizens alike.

Other important writing tasks. These include tasks such as writing thank-you letters, news releases, and letters to the editor. It is crucial to write *thank-you letters* to all—legislators, staff, and group members—who have helped your legislative efforts whether they were successful or not. Be a generous loser as well as a good winner (Eriksen, 1997). Friends were there when you "wanted" something, and it is appropriate to thank them when you "got" something. And, remember, there is always another legislative campaign down the road, and your group may need help again.

News releases are a writing task for advocates who are trying to get the news media to cover their legislative agenda, particularly in daily newspapers.

(Specific guidelines for writing a news release can be found in Chapter 6 on cause advocacy, p. 210.) Suffice it here to say that, unless the news release contains a story with a very newsworthy angle, it is unlikely to get published (Richan, 1996). Although advocates need to identify what they want to say and to whom, newspaper editors will decide if the message has relevancy to their readership. If a news release is going to citizens of a certain district, it is a good idea to send a copy of it to their senator or delegate to let them know you exist and are communicating with their constituents.

Letters to the editor are another writing assignment that legislative advocates can use. (Specific directions on writing a letter to the editor can be found in Chapter 6 on cause advocacy.) Richan (1996) suggests that letters to the editor can be used to influence policy making. Access to the papers and their readership is easy, so it is a good way to advocate for a bill. He suggests that letters are most effective when they "(1) are part of an organized effort involving several persons but (2) do not look that way" (p. 291). Group members commit themselves to responding to each other's letters and keep raising different dimensions of the bill or its impact over a given length of time, always citing the previous letter as a hook. Not only readers look at letter columns; editorial writers, columnists, and reporters also regularly scan them. Sometimes the paper will run an editorial based on a letter to the editor. Such a letter can play an effective role in influencing legislative issues.

INFLUENCE

Before taking on this advocacy project, I was cynical about my ability to impact legislative policy. I believed it took an army of people to get legislators to listen. This advocacy effort made me realize that one or two citizens—or social workers—can make a difference, especially if they use a strategy for influencing change.

DARLENE

Knowledge and skills in influencing others is as important as effective representation in legislative advocacy. The policy arena offers one of the most available opportunities for social work advocates to attempt to change or modify regulations or laws that adversely affect their clients. Each of the eight principles of influencing is presented below with a special emphasis on their application in the policy-making process.

Identify the Issues and Set Goals

Legislative advocates realize that their first challenge is to get an *issue*, that is, a matter of critical importance, on the agenda of enough legislators so that it will be considered seriously and endorsed for positive action. Since legislators are asked annually to reckon with hundreds of possible proposals, it is very important for advocates to identify issues that will gain and hold the attention of these decision makers. Likewise, once an issue has been agreed upon, advocates must set realistic *goals,* that is, a clear statement of their hopes, expectations, and desires. In the legislative arena, advocates often attempt to secure *reasonable* goals, not *absolute* ones, because there are many other competing issues and only finite resources. Such goals may be the result of compromising, but more often, they reflect the hard realities of trying to influence the legislative process.

The authors have identified the following specific questions for legislative advocates: (1) How can issues be classified in the legislative arena? (2) What is the best way to frame a legislative issue so it gets on the agenda? and (3) What can advocates do to set realistic legislative goals for their issues?

How can issues be classified in the legislative arena? Issues proposed as bills in the legislative process are seldom equal. Success in passage of a bill depends on many factors that may or may not be subject to the advocate's ability to influence. Dear and Patti (1981) suggest that there are certain issues that have a *low probability* of passage:

- High fiscal impact: the bill would require substantial allocation of money.
- Major social change: many people, agencies, and programs would be affected. Service delivery system may be altered greatly. Eligibility for services may be expanded significantly.
- Unpopular content: the bill refers to a topic or group contaminated by popular opinion as corrupt, worthless, or despicable. Unmarried teen mothers, the homeless, and welfare "queens" fall into this category.

There are also certain issues that have a *high probability* of passage:

- Low fiscal impact: implementation costs are low or absent.
- Minor or no social change: proposed changes are minimal corrections or small clarifications of regulations.
- Popular content: the public is favorable or sympathetic to the topic or group receiving the benefits of the bill. Education issues and child abuse proposals often fall into this category.

Advocates can use this analysis to determine an initial course of action tempered by a reasonable hope of success. However, the advocate's skill and credibility, the available resources, the patron(s), the size of the constituency, and the number of similar bills introduced will also affect decisions about formulating bills. There is no magical formula, but this analysis is an excellent starting place.

What is the best way to frame a legislative issue so it gets on the agenda? Advocates must find the written language that expresses the issue in such a way that legislators are motivated to act on their behalf. Advocates can learn what issues and problems are personally important to legislators and can demonstrate that their solution will help the legislator solve the problem. Asking for more money, more authority, or greater social work status will never inspire legislative action (Eriksen, 1997). There must be salable reasons for a legislator not only to act, but also to sell the proposal to other legislators.

The Advocacy Institute (1990) suggests that the issue should be framed to convey unity and values such as justice, fairness, equity, and truthfulness. It should address not just the narrow concerns of the advocacy group, but the widest possible group of potential supporters. In the United States, citizens and legislators resonate with surprising unanimity to core public values such as freedom, security, family, health, fairness, opportunity, and caring. They typically respond negatively to unfairness, government or corporate oppression, harm, deceit, greed, favoritism, and dependency. The authors suggest that the more these positive values are framed within an issue, the more likely it is to be supported, and that if the opposition can be linked to the negative values, the chances of additional support are enhanced.

Pearl and Barr (1976) recommended that an issue be as specific as possible. Morgan (1983) recommended that the change or issue be precisely defined. Building agreements results from persuasive packaging of information that clarifies the problem and demonstrates feasible and desirable solutions. The Advocacy Institute (1990) suggests that simplicity, clarity, and focus on a small number of themes are effective when framing an issue. Eriksen (1997) urges advocates to define issues in terms of consumer or client needs and cost reductions.

For example, a proposed bill in one state legislature was introduced to disallow the subpoenaing of therapists' notes for state criminal court cases. (It is already disallowed in state civil courts and in federal courts.) Rather than framing this bill as protecting the rights of the therapists, the advocates highlighted the need to protect consumers, to promote confidentiality, and to encourage free and complete access to mental health services without fear of unexpected consequences. The issue here is defined as preserving a citizen's right to service.

What can advocates do to set realistic legislative goals for their issues? In light of the resistance faced by legislative initiatives addressing social change and of the political pressures for competing resources, social work advocates must develop realistic goals for their efforts. Recalling that a goal is "knowing what one desires or hopes for," Dear and Patti (1981) offer no universal solution, but note that there are two alternatives: (1) reduce the scope and costs of a proposal to avoid rejection by the legislature, and (2) proceed with the initiative, even though chances are slim for passage, in the hope of achieving some small gain through compromise. The drawback to the first alternative is providing fewer resources to pressing social problems and the consequent delay in solving the issues. Drawbacks to the second alternative are greater chances for defeat and loss of credibility.

Richan (1996) proposes another distinction for advocates to use when setting goals: work either for incremental goals, or work for fundamental change goals. The former goals are aimed at making modest improvements in the legislative arena and moving steadily toward minor, but important changes that will affect clients. The latter is aimed at basic change and transformation of a program or service delivery system. For example, the current welfare system is constantly being tinkered with, reformed, and redesigned, while many argue that proposed initiatives do not go far enough. Which approach is best? There are arguments for pursing each or both of these goal-oriented activities; but whichever one chooses, it will affect the strategies and tactics advocates must plan.

Patti and Dear (1975) recommended that social workers actively promote their clients' interests in the legislative arena, but be cognizant that their efforts are only one element in an "array of interacting forces" and pressures that affect the legislative process. Social work advocates will never be able to anticipate or control all of the contingencies that arise in influencing decision makers, but they can become part of the process. These authors remind us that success can be measured, not in terms of absolute achievement of goals, but in how close advocates come to achieving them.

Richan (1996) also reminds advocates for the poor and champions of the vulnerable that their clientele are often the targets of simplistic solutions—cut off welfare, get a job, lock them up—and that too much energy may go into answering the critics rather than thinking through exactly what is desired. For example, if you don't approve of current health insurance coverages, then what do you suggest instead? Without alternative ideas and proposals, advocates will be unable to know what they really want and unable to communicate it to others.

Get the Facts

Facts are the fuel that drive the policy process (Morgan, 1983). Mattison and Storey (1992) suggest that there are two general types of facts that are useful in legislative advocacy efforts: (1) facts about the problem itself, and (2) facts about the people affected by the problem and the people possessing influence over solving it. Facts must be uncovered that demonstrate there is a problem, what the magnitude of the problem is, what will happen when there is a failure to take action, and how much solving the problem will cost in the annual legislative budget. Accurate knowledge of legislative processes is also crucial.

The authors have identified the following questions related to fact finding for legislative advocates: (1) What types of facts are useful in legislative advocacy? (2) Is the legislative process rational and data-based? (3) Where should legislative advocates look for facts, and how should they use them to promote their legislative agenda? and (4) What about technology and legislative advocacy? Each question is answered in the text that follows.

What types of facts are useful in legislative advocacy? In marshaling relevant facts to support legislative advocacy initiatives, it is important for advocates to obtain or know facts about the following: (1) the problem and the people to be affected by legislation, (2) the legislative process, (3) fiscal information, (4) the law, and (5) the political environment.

The most crucial "fact" is to demonstrate as accurately and clearly as possible the real needs of clients. The problem must be assessed, documented, analyzed, and researched carefully, addressing the history and dimensions of the problem, impact on clientele, human costs, and effects on communities and society. Factual evidence is preferred to anecdotal, but both are useful. In legislative arenas, it is important to compare the needs of clients with others and show why these clients are worse off and in more need of a proposed policy (Dluhy, 1981).

Mahaffey (1972) urged social worker advocates to realize that in order to influence the political process, they must first understand it. It is important to know the actual processes and procedures about "how a bill becomes a law" in any city council, state legislature, or Congress. Likewise, it is good to know the structure and composition of the chambers where decisions are made. It is crucial to know, for example, that most state legislatures, while part-time, operate on a year-round basis even though they may meet officially for only a few months in legislative session. Legislative committees meet throughout the year to study issues. Knowing this "fact" is essential to being an effective advocate.

Costs of new legislative initiatives are important facts to develop and support (Johnson, 1995). A fiscal analysis includes start-up and first-year costs and ongoing expenditures (Haynes & Mickelson, 1997). In practice, the merits of a bill do not always predominate, but as Kirst-Ashman and Hull (1993) point out, bills that ultimately require spending less money are more likely to pass.

Advocates must know what the existing laws and regulations related to their issue are so that they can indicate what this new bill will add or take away. A careful reading of laws and regulations often reveals options or loopholes previously unnoticed (Ericksen, 1997).

Advocates need to know the facts about the political environment as well as the problem or processes. How receptive are legislators to a bill? Which legislator would be sympathetic? Here the advocates should complete in-depth profiles of legislators including voting records, interests, prejudices, those with a family member with a similar disorder as that which your group is advocating for, and their political vulnerability.

Is the legislative process rational and data-based? Many advocates assume that the unadorned facts will convince legislators to support their bills, and often become disillusioned when they fail to be persuasive. Such an advocate might say, "How could anyone not see the importance of this bill and the enormous benefits it gives to the mentally ill? The 'facts' are right there if only they would look at them!" Patti and Dear (1975) reminded us that it is essential to recognize that legislative decision making is rarely an entirely rational process. Legislators face a myriad of forces that impinge on their decision making, altering priorities and allowing complex motives to enter into the rational process. Political self-interest, the views of their constituents, personal values, life experiences, precedents, and the need to balance not just one value, but many values are among the reasons that a clear, compelling logic and the obvious facts do not always win out.

However, the importance of rational, logical argument and solid facts should not be minimized, even though there are limits. Social work advocates should grasp the topic and be able to assemble, use, and present facts whenever called upon. Alone, the facts may not be adequate, but without them, the advocate will have very little to say. A final note by Melton (1983): successful advocates combine rationality and commitment. Facts presented without a sense of personal commitment to the bill or issue are usually not as convincing.

Where should legislative advocates look for facts, and how should they use them to promote their legislative agenda? It is usually very expensive and time-intensive to design a credible statistical study, gather the data, and analyze it in order to produce reliable, primary data. Sometimes, to get crucial statistics, a group will have to conduct its own study. However, there is a nearly infinite source of information available to anyone who is willing to spend time looking for it. Richan (1996) reminds us that such information is easily accessible and much of it is free for the asking in libraries, on websites, and in government agencies and legislative bodies. Commissioned studies, surveys, polls, funded research, clearinghouses, and state and community associations often produce findings useful to advocates. In Appendix A, the authors have listed some of the common websites and several of the legislative document sources that are readily available.

When it comes to using the facts effectively, the following ideas are suggested:

1. Use the information and data gathered in the research to start an awareness and educational campaign for the legislators, the general public, and professional groups. Speeches, videos, overhead transparencies, and posters can be developed.

2. Facts should be presented in a crisp, one-page handout. This handout should feature the facts, pinpoint the needed change, promote the bill, and be attractively designed and pleasing to the eye (Morgan, 1983). It is a good resource to put in the hands of a legislator.

3. Kaminski and Walmsley (1995) note that advocates usually collect more information than they can use in the typical one- or two-page fact handout. They suggest that the additional information be made into appendices and attached to other documents or handed out at hearings or inquiries.

4. Smith (1979) noted that in a study of legislators, 47% gave the following reason for listening to advocacy groups: *provision of information.* It seems only logical that advocates should furnish their own data, facts, studies, analyses, and statistics to legislators on a regular basis.

5. If you do use statistical data in handouts or presentations, Richan (1996) advises the advocate to: (1) Be clear about what is being measured, particularly the difference between frequency (total number) and rate (the ratio between actual cases and possible cases); (2) Give the time period, for example, from January 1, 1999, through December 31, 2002; and (3) Identify the geographical area clearly, for example, state, county, city, region, or nation.

What about technology and legislative advocacy? Timely and accessible information is crucial to advocates' fact finding and strategies. With the Internet, speedy access to information creates new opportunities for advocates to influence legislators and the policy-making process (Bryer & Magrath, 1999). In Figure 7.1, the Virginia legislature's web page, readers can see clearly how much information is available to them with the click of a mouse on the computer screen. Advocates can readily follow legislation and bills on a daily basis. They can search for other laws, regulations, studies, and court decisions. By entering the number of a particular bill, they can learn about the current or final status of the bill. Social work advocates must also begin to explore the use of e-mail, websites, discussion groups, and e-petitions to contact legislators and to rally support for their positions. McNutt and Boland (1999) state that information technology is revolutionizing the practice of political advocacy in the United States. Although "electronic advocacy" or "online advocacy" is still developing, these techniques represent a direction in which effective advocates will most likely go. Considerable research needs to be done to assess the effectiveness of such advocacy, but there is little doubt about the growing awareness and use of high-tech tools for the future.

Legislative Information System
2000 Session

Bill Tracking:	*convened January 12, 2000*
Bills and Resolutions:	*status of individual bills and related information*
General Assembly Members:	*member sponsored legislation*
Standing Committees:	*legislation referred to committee*
Meetings:	*House and Senate committee meeting schedule*
State Budget:	*budget bills, committees and summaries*
Daily Floor Calendars:	*legislative agendas*
Minutes:	*record of floor sessions*
Statistics:	*session statistics*
Comprehensive Index:	*subject index of bills, resolutions and documents*
Lobbyist-in-a-Box:	*VIPNet's subscription based bill tracking service*

Searchable Databases:

Bills and Resolutions:	*session legislation*
Code of Virginia:	*statutory law*
Virginia Administrative Code:	*state agency rules*
Rules of the Supreme Court:	*court rules*
List of Legislative Studies:	*House and Senate documents*

Past sessions: 1994 - 1995 - 1996 - 1997 - 1998 - 1999

Check out the *Virginia Legislative Information System* subscription service for additional information.
If you need help using the system take a look at *LIS hints.*

FIGURE **7.1**

The Virginia legislature's web page.

Lobbying for the "Hate Crimes Bill"

One of my interests in advocating for social change is the issue of gay rights. I attended the Virginians for Justice Lobbying Day on February 2 and learned that this group was particularly excited about the "hate crimes bill," Senate Bill (SB) 159, that provided protections and penalties for crimes based on hate, discrimination, and bias. There was a general consensus that this bill had a very good chance of being passed this year.

I was paired up with an experienced lobbyist and spent the day visiting various senators and their staff. I was surprised at how easy it was to gain access to most of the senators. Even the senators who were opposed to SB159 were polite and listened to our opinions of the merits of the bill. The patron of the bill, Senator Patsy Ticer, was also very helpful about advising us as to the senators who were undecided on the bill.

On the next day, I attended the Courts of Justice subcommittee #1 meeting because SB159 was on the agenda. Senator Ticer introduced the bill and informed the committee that there were a few people available to testify on behalf of the bill. After the testimony, there were a few remarks from the committee members, but there seemed to be a lot of tension surrounding this bill. One of the senators moved to have the bill "passed by indefinitely," but the ensuing vote was tied, sending it to full committee on the next day by default. Senator Ticer seemed to be very discouraged and said she wanted more support for the bill. She asked me if I were a heterosexual who was willing to testify for the bill in the committee session the next day. I said I would be honored to do so.

I consulted the lobbyist for Virginians for Justice about my testimony, and he gave me a few tips, asking to see a copy of it before I testified. I also consulted my literature on how to testify and worked through most of the evening, developing a five-minute speech. This was more difficult than I thought it would be. I had much I wanted to say, but if I said too much, it might do more harm than good.

Because my speech was to be short, it was my intention to try to catch the attention of the senators in the committee. I realized that a "run-of-the-mill" speech would be totally ignored. I wanted to convey the message that this bill was not just about gays and lesbians wanting something for themselves, but that it was a matter of civil rights and giving all of our citizens protection from hate just for being different. I included a piece of personal information about my grandmother who was a Cherokee Indian; she always warned me not to let anyone know that I was an American Indian because of discrimination and hatred.

(Continued)

I arrived early the next day and met with the lobbyist who made some small changes in my testimony. I was nervous about testifying once I sat down in the formal and rather large committee chamber. To make matters worse, the meeting started about two and a half hours late. The lobbyist decided to have me speak first with the intention of surprising the opposition with a "heterosexual" going first on behalf of this bill.

Before our bill, the senators took up another bill dealing with individuals spying in public restrooms. One of the senators cleverly managed to use the word homosexual *in this discussion, and I think this set the tone for the opposition. He covertly conveyed the message that homosexuals were deviant and a possible threat to society.*

While giving my testimony, I noted that I had the full attention of the entire committee when I talked about my ethnic background. Opponents of the bill were leaning forward when I explained I was not fully Caucasian. I think their minds were made up, but it was somehow consoling to me that they were listening. The bill was voted to be "passed by indefinitely" by a vote of 9 to 5. I felt very disappointed and was surprised how the defeat of the bill affected me physically. I felt as if I had been hit in the stomach.

Surprisingly, the lobbyist and other members of Virginians for Justice left the room in high spirits. They viewed the process as a victory, as the bill advanced further this year than it ever had in the past. They were having an impromptu meeting with Senator Ticer and talking strategies for next year. This scene reminded me of the work and time frame that goes along with changing or making policy.

Marcus L. Stiglets

Plan Strategies and Tactics

Effective advocates plan their strategies first, before taking action (Eriksen, 1997; Schlozman & Tierney, 1986). Usually, a small group assembles and takes a broad and long view of the proposed legislative initiative, sets priorities, develops flexible goals, decides which battles are worth fighting for, and then settles down to the task of determining how they will achieve what they hope for. A decision about an overall plan or a broad blueprint (*strategy*) must be made, followed by selection of the day-to-day, nitty-gritty actions (*tactics*) that are designed to carry out the strategy (see Chapter 4). Organization of these efforts and the distribution of assigned tasks to individual advocates are required before and during a legislative session.

The reader must recall that choosing a strategy is based on assumptions about human behavior and why persons actually modify or change their opinions. Selection of a strategy usually depends on first learning what the opponents are like, for example, hostile, indifferent, or favorable, and then developing an approach that has the best chance of persuading them to agree with the advocate's position. We examine legislative strategies and tactics below under collaborative, campaign, and contest categories.

Collaborative Strategies and Tactics   When a legislator is perceived to share many of the basic values of the advocate, has cooperated previously on similar issues, seems to be uninformed, or may simply need more information, a collaborative strategy is usually appropriate. There is little if any conflict between the advocate and the legislator, with open communication flowing easily between the two. The advocate must remember to provide an adequate rationale and political cover for the legislator in seeking his or her support of the proposed bill. A collaborative strategy can be carried out by using the following tactics.

Meet with legislator and staff. Personal meetings with legislator and staff are common practice for advocacy groups (Rickards, 1992). These meetings should be well planned and viewed as a means to presenting information to the legislator or staff member. Advocates should identify themselves as constituents whenever possible and politely present a position on an issue with accompanying personal or client anecdotes. The meeting should be brief, concise, friendly, and informative. Leave a fact sheet and business card, and send a thank-you note. If one arranges for a photographer or local newspaper for the visit, it may increase the chances of actually meeting the legislator. Politicians are eager to be photographed.

Provide information. Legislators are faced with hundreds, even thousands of complicated bills and only gain a substantial understanding of a few of them. They are forced to rely on staff, colleagues, and advocates for information. Lack of information is often an obstacle that can be overcome by providing facts and researching issues for legislators. Smith (1979) noted that the most important factor determining a group's influence was the capacity of the group to provide lawmakers with technical and political information. This information should be timely and available when it is needed; it should be balanced and credible, aimed at solving problems, not propagandistic and narrow; and it should provide the basis for alternative proposals and feasible options (Patti & Dear, 1975).

Provide fiscal impact data. Perhaps the most significant information advocates can provide to decision makers is cost-related. Legislators will want to know how much a new or modified policy will cost, pure and simple. Careful fiscal analysis by the advocates is required, covering start-up costs, first-year costs, and ongoing costs such as staff, overhead, and special equipment. In-kind contributions should be calculated accurately. Human costs can also be calculated, including what it would cost if the proposed bill were not passed or how much human suffering would continue (Haynes & Mickelson, 1997).

Use a supportive legislator to introduce a bill. It is important to obtain as many sponsors of proposed legislation as possible because it will increase the likelihood of passage. Knowledge of the interests, values, and voting records of legislators will help advocates determine whom to ask to introduce a bill and lead the fight during the legislative session. In addition to sympathetic legisla-tors, advocates should also try to enlist bipartisan support, leaders of the majority party, and key powerful legislators who are respected among their colleagues (Kirst-Ashman & Hull, 1993).

Draft legislation jointly. The most hazardous segment of the policy process is often the most overlooked. Drafting a bill means choosing the language and inserting the dimensions of the solution that translate the advocate's preferences into tangible and verbal form (Jansson, 1999). This is a very important task, and advocates should attempt to participate fully in finalizing the wording of the proposed legislation. Collaborating with legis-lators represents an opportunity to introduce options and services that may go by unnoticed.

Conduct a legislative workshop. Bringing together various groups, legisla-tors, experts, community leaders, clients, and constituents can provide advo-cates with a device to heighten awareness, educate participants, and decide on future actions. Advocates may want to organize a workshop around their high-est priority issue and devote time to discussing and analyzing it in order to learn what proposal or option would be likely to pass. Supporters of a bill can also be identified based on their participation in the workshop.

Campaign Strategies and Tactics   When a legislator is perceived to be neutral, indifferent, or apathetic about a proposed initiative, advocates will choose a campaign strategy. These legislators share fewer values, have dif-ferent attitudes, and have little invested in the outcome of the legislation. Their relationship with the advocates may be cool or distant, and perhaps this encounter is the first time they have worked side by side. The legisla-tor may have a "show me" attitude, compelling the advocate to use persua-sive skills effectively. Some conflict and tension probably exist. At one time or another, the advocate and legislator may have been on opposite sides of another piece of legislation. A campaign strategy can be carried out by using the following tactics.

Lobby legislators one-on-one. Smith (1979) cited studies pointing to the importance of interaction between legislators and advocates, indicating that greater frequency of contact between them led to more change in the legisla-tors' opinions. Richan (1996) and Melton (1983) state that the most direct way of influencing a legislator is by talking with him or her in person. Mahaffey (1972) suggests the following characteristics for lobbyists: friendly, articulate, outgoing, flexible, persuasive, able to work independently, patient, good listener, and good strategizer. Segal and Brzuzy (1998) state that the key to effective lobbying is to stay focused on the issue of concern. Lobbying can also be thought of as an *exchange* where the advocate wants action on a bill and the legislator wants to be reelected (Richan, 1996). If advocates have a power base behind them, policy makers will pay more attention to their requests.

Educate the public. It is not at all surprising that citizens are often unaware of complex policy and political issues, since even lobbyists find it difficult to keep up on proposed bills or amendments. Bills often do not appear to be of interest to the average person (Kirst-Ashman & Hull, 1993) because the proposals are directed at unpopular audiences or small groups. Advocates must try to demonstrate to people how their own interests are tied to the well-being of often marginal groups. Informed persons usually participate more in the democratic process (Hoechstetter, 1996).

Use the media. To keep an issue alive and gain public support, publicity is a necessity. Elected officials pay attention to media coverage and respond to the views of the general public (Morgan, 1983). Advocates gain power by having access to the media (Amidei, 1982; Segal & Brzuzy, 1998). Dorn et al. (1998) recommend developing a media plan integrated with the lobbying effort. The aim is to raise the visibility of an issue and help shape the terms of the debate. Among the media methods are: press releases to local, daily, and weekly newspapers and TV/radio news programs; letters to the editor; fliers, handouts, and newsletters; interviews on radio and TV; posters; online news message boards; news conferences; feature stories with a human interest focus; op-ed commentary; talk shows on radio or TV; key newspaper columnists; periodical journals and magazines; and paid advertisements. (See Chapter 5, the section on communication, for additional information on use of the media.)

Organize letter-writing campaigns and phone calls. A 1977 study by Berry found that nearly half of responding lobbyists perceived letter-writing campaigns as effective. Segal and Brzuzy (1998) stated that congressional staff listed spontaneous constituent mail as important. The most effective letters are clear, personal, handwritten, and not mass-produced (Segal & Brzuzy, 1998). The letter should be no longer than one page, positive and courteous, explicit about the issue, offer one's own point of view, factual, and provide alternatives. Request a written response, and include your name and address. The same guidelines apply to making a telephone call or leaving an e-mail message.

Use power people. Affiliation with persons within the "establishment" or power structures of a state or community can increase the leverage that advocates can apply. These individuals usually know legislators and the legislative process, and their opinions are typically respected. They may be more comfortable with behind-the-scenes advocacy, but they can also prove very effective in public appearances. Business groups and political action committees tend to exert significant influence over policy making (Segal & Brzuzy, 1998).

Refer to precedents. Decision makers often are willing to support a policy if it has been tried before (Eriksen, 1997). Even if the policy failed, there may be justification for trying it again. Initiating a brand-new, never-been-tried-before idea is something that makes many legislators nervous. Hence, advocates should strive to illustrate how the policy has worked elsewhere, what the cost savings have been, what outcomes and impact there were, and how it will assist a given client group now.

Take the high moral ground. In order to overcome apathy or indifference among legislators, advocates can often take the high moral ground. It places the decision makers in a moral context that is usually hard to reject or dismiss (Kaminski & Walmsley, 1995). Legislators will need to declare themselves on an issue of justice, poverty, or fairness in order not to appear too detached from citizens' lives and problems.

Monitor the legislative process carefully. In order to keep track of the progress of a bill and to prevent obstacles from developing, advocates frequently use individuals to monitor a piece of legislation on a regular basis at meetings, hearings, and so on. These persons must be patient, often wait long hours, and keep records of voting patterns. A monitor will also be able to alert others to crises, get help in responding to word changes or amendments, note absent committee members, provide information, or call the media. Even though monitors usually do not speak publicly, their mere presence in the committee room often reinforces a legislator's previously stated position (Van Gheluwe & Barber, 1986).

Contest Strategies and Tactics   When a legislator is perceived to be hostile, unwilling to listen, nonsupportive of a bill, and shares few, if any values in common with the advocate, it is usually time to employ a contest strategy. There may be open conflict between the advocate and legislator. Distrust is high and so is disagreement about the importance or outcomes of the legislation. Here, advocates might be lucky enough to change behaviors, but not beliefs or values.

The question of degree of conflict is important to consider in legislative matters because advocates must weigh carefully whether to burn bridges and heighten conflict to intense levels. In years to come, today's opponents may be tomorrow's allies. There will be more issues in the future, and alienation of legislators is a risk that should be measured very prudently. Differences should remain professional, not personal, and at no time do the authors recommend behavior that is contrary to the NASW *Code of Ethics*.

Schlozman and Tierney (1986) found that legislative advocacy groups ranked protests and demonstrations as the lowest means of influence. Patti and Dear (1975) advise advocates to realize that, under most circumstances, heavy-handed, coercive, and confrontational tactics are usually counterproductive. Sometimes a demonstration will mobilize the opposing side and result in a public argument leading nowhere. At other times, a visible protest action will harden the opposition, resulting in even greater resistance to the proposed change. Advocates must try not to tarnish the public image of the legislator unnecessarily because making a legislator look bad is risky, undermining his or her image with constituents back home. Using threats is also risk-filled because they usually create antagonisms and remove future access to the legislator involved.

When does one decide to hold a protest or demonstration? (It is assumed that advocates have already tried a conventional collaborative or campaign style effort as described above and made little or no progress.) Jansson (1999) and Melton (1983) suggest that a protest tactic can be used when: (1) a group does not have access to decision makers; (2) an issue or bill has not reached a significant level of public consciousness; (3) considerable conflict is necessary to secure enactment of a controversial bill; or (4) legislators continue to ignore an important issue. In these circumstances, in order to advance a proposed bill or issue, advocates need to organize carefully their actions in order to maximize effect and minimize loss of goodwill or alienation from supporters.

Legislative advocates who lead demonstrations must cope with these tensions simultaneously:

- Nurturing and sustaining their own organization
- Choosing tactics that maximize exposure to the media
- Influencing legislators capable of approving a bill
- Influencing others with greater resources and influence to team up with them (Lipsky, 1968)

Although there are risks involved for legislative advocates in organizing demonstrations and protests, there are times when the issue at stake is too important to gloss over and direct action is called for. A protest can also motivate members, attract new members, increase solidarity, and gain credibility for a group (Eriksen, 1997). Long-term success nearly always includes other policy strategies in addition to protest activities. Legislative advocacy calls for courageous action tempered by seasoned judgment.

Supply Leadership

Jansson (1999) points out that legislative advocates need an organized group to advance legislative proposals. Without leadership, efforts to influence legislation will probably go in different directions, voices will give conflicting messages, and ultimately the group's efforts will be impaired. Typically, legislative advocates need to supply leadership by: (1) identifying key tasks such

Adopting Kids: Not by Homosexuals

Sarah E. Morris, a student at Ball State University, Muncie, Indiana, influenced legislation in the state of Indiana that would have banned homosexuals from adopting children or becoming foster parents.

She organized students on campus and gathered 300 signatures on a petition that was mailed to the governor, state patrons of the bill, and local representatives. Ms. Morris created a series of packets to distribute for people to sign and mail to the state legislature. She and other students flooded the legislators on key committees with over 5,000 hand-delivered letters, obtained critical media coverage, and collaborated with other statewide organizations. One attempt at amending the bill offered language that would ban "unmarried" people from adopting. The bill quickly failed in the full Senate.

Three thousand homosexual families would have been affected by the bill. Ms. Morris stated that "one motivated person can create change" and that it is important to "know whom you are trying to influence and frame your argument in a way that compels them to agree with you."

---

as lobbying, testifying, research, letter-writing, liaisoning to committees, developing policy briefs, and organizing demonstrations; (2) assigning these tasks to specific persons; and (3) monitoring the completion of these tasks during the legislative process. Generally, the big secret behind effective leadership is breaking large projects down into manageable pieces and then identifying people to take responsibility for each piece (Bobo et al., 1996).

The authors also believe it is important to be aware of these related questions: (1) Has the profession of social work provided effective leadership in legislative and policy matters in the past? (2) What are key leadership tasks in the day-to-day activity of a legislative advocate? and (3) What personal qualities characterize leaders in legislative advocacy?

Has the profession of social work provided effective leadership in legislative and policy matters in the past? Meinert argues persuasively that social workers are basically reactors rather than shapers of the basic directions of social legislation (Pardeck & Meinert, 1994). He observes that social workers are less involved in the formulation and legislation of policy and more likely to be found implementing and evaluating it in organizational settings. Meinert also notes that social workers have always had philosophical and value positions that support legislative initiatives, and that historical figures such as Jane Addams, Harry Hopkins, and Wilbur Cohen were effective leaders in policy. But, with a few exceptions like Michael Sherraden, recent leaders have not

been very successful in bringing major policy initiatives to fruition, particularly at the state and national levels.

Why has social work leadership been ineffective in this arena? Meinert
offers three explanations. First, the National Association of Social Workers
(NASW) acts assertively about those policies that are mainly self-serving for its
membership. Licensure and third-party payments have been consistent objectives over the past 20 years with less energy and resources devoted to policy
initiatives benefiting clients such as welfare reform. In fact, NASW closed
down its Center for Social Policy in 1995. Second, for decades, social work
leadership has been aligned exclusively with the Democratic Party and its
intellectual and ideological sentiments. It has been rare to find instances when
social work examined policy proposals objectively and rationally, free from the
unquestioned acceptance of the Democratic Party's principles. Other legislative proposals are often rejected on the basis of their ideological origin and not
on their merits. Many times, this affiliation has removed the profession from
participating in national or state debates. Third, with its emphasis on clinical
issues, social work often identifies concerns related to individual problems,
and it fails to suggest policies, structures, and programs to address them. This
approach reduces the profession to a residual or remedial role, ignoring the
creation of policies to improve the environment in which persons can achieve
greater levels of functioning and well-being (Pardeck & Meinert, 1994).
Current and future leadership of NASW will need to move the membership
away from these three tendencies if the profession is to become truly effective
in formulating policies that carry benefit for clients needing economic, social,
or just redress for their concerns.

*What are key leadership tasks in the day-to-day activity of a legislative
advocate?* Leadership can be most effective when advocates:

- Provide accurate information to legislators. A majority of legislators do
  not trust one single source of information (Denny et al., 1989;
  Herman & Callanan, 1978; Melton, 1983), and reliable information
  from an advocacy group will usually increase its credibility over time.
- Know the entire legislative process from A to Z. Expert knowledge of
  the procedures and rules often prevents harmful omissions and
  promotes strategic interventions. It is crucial to know the "route" of
  the bill.
- Develop and follow a calendar-based plan of action that encompasses
  the many important dates and deadlines of the legislative process such
  as hearings, committee votes, budget meetings, and so on.
- Identify key legislative leaders who are important to the outcome of
  the proposed bill and match them with a constituent or member who
  can interact or express concerns. A good leader also knows their staff
  members and secretaries.

- Monitor the opposition and anticipate their arguments so that they can be publicly answered. Find out what they are thinking and doing.
- Search for allies to join in a coalition or endorse the group's position or bill.
- Keep members and constituents informed about a bill's status and ask for needed action at the appropriate time. Leaders may coach or educate individuals to complete a certain task like testifying or lobbying.
- Develop materials and identify expert resource persons who can be used to persuade legislators. Policy briefs, fact sheets, and suggested action plans can be distributed as needed.

What personal qualities characterize leaders in legislative advocacy? There are, of course, many qualities that intermingle in an effective leader's personality. While no one formula or recipe works in all cases, Smith (1979) noted that legislators value leaders with stable personal qualities such as wisdom, respect, reliability, and sound judgment. In fact, this author suggests that reputation is an important resource in itself, particularly the most crucial characteristic of inspiring confidence and trust. Pawlak and Flynn (1990) also noted that "active" leaders are essential in the legislative arena. Some leaders establish political ties and purposefully position themselves to be asked to serve on task forces or committees. Others simply make it their business to get involved in the community, meet legislators or commissioners, and volunteer to contribute their time, knowledge, and energy to committees or activities. Amidei (1982) urges leaders to speak up in public when elected officials are present and ask questions about their positions on issues. She also notes that "doing nothing," for example, not challenging misinformation in the newspapers, television, and other media, is more damaging than most think.

Get to Know Decision Makers and Their Staff

Legislative advocates, who crave to influence legislators and their staff members, go to great lengths and exert much energy to do so. But there are limits in time and stamina, and advocates must carefully choose which legislators they seek to know more intimately. Why is knowing a legislator so important? Simply put, knowing the legislators and their staff members is part of a crucial recipe for achieving a successful legislative agenda (Amidei, 1991; Dear & Patti, 1981; Denny et al., 1989; Haynes & Mickelson, 1997; Herman & Callanan, 1978; Kleinkauf, 1986; Melton, 1983; Patti & Dear, 1975; Pearl & Barr, 1976; Richan, 1996; Smith, 1979).

The authors have also identified these four related questions: (1) Which legislators should advocates get to know? (2) Why bother to get to know

Students Organize to Advocate at the Legislature in North Carolina

At East Carolina University, many social work graduate students choose direct practice over indirect practice, frequently failing to see the connection between policy and direct practice. Two professors, Powell and Causby (1994), concluded that students as well as practitioners often lacked knowledge and skills about influencing the political arena, and too easily accepted the focus on changing individuals rather than on altering the system itself or combining both strategies.

To help students recognize their capabilities as advocates, the professors recalled an incident when an influential state legislator responded to a student question about how the students could become a part of the process. "To make a difference, you need to go to the state capitol, press the flesh of the lawmakers, sit down with them in their offices, and briefly, but forcefully advocate for your beliefs." The legislator offered to assist anyone who came to Raleigh.

The professors decided to have students prepare child/family advocacy positions that would be likely to appear before the North Carolina legislature and, as a class, spend time actually advocating their positions. Before the beginning of the legislative session in early spring, the students began identifying elected representatives in their own communities, leaders in the fields of mental health and social services, and other advocates such as John Niblock, the president of the North Carolina Child Advocacy Institute. They also researched existing statutes and identified amendments, revisions, and deletions that were being proposed. They tried to calculate the anticipated costs of implementing new proposals. Professors ran classroom exercises in lobbying, negotiating, and testifying. Students were required to write position papers or policy briefs. Practical details were discussed, such as proper attire, making eye contact when speaking, using the correct title, and time and location of hearings.

Soon, students and professors experienced mounting anxiety because "Legislative Day" was just around the corner. Would their "homemade" handouts be out of place amidst the slick materials of the professional lobbyists? Would the students be considered "do-gooders" by the lawmakers? As they traveled to Raleigh on April 17, they were excited, but prepared for failure.

One student was selected by her peers to testify on their behalf before a Senate legislative committee considering a family preservation statute. The professors walked the halls of the legislative building, seeing and hearing students actively engaging legislators and their aides in their offices. Students

(Continued)

were cornering lobbyists about a proposed cut in funding for women's shelters. A social worker elected to the Senate gave a stirring presentation to the students and commended them for their efforts. As they rode home that evening, one student said, "We, as social workers, made ourselves visible today."

Debriefing the experience later, students acknowledged being apprehensive and "scared." They said they were afraid of the "unknown." Some students thought this assignment would be a waste of time, a way to fill class time. They were very skeptical about the process. The professors held out the offer that students might also begin to see this assignment as a chance to make a difference or a "real" opportunity.

Afterwards, many students stated that they felt empowered because of the skills they learned, their new knowledge of the process, and the pride they took in walking the halls of the capitol with their social work colleagues. All of the students noted that this experiential exercise in legislative advocacy had helped them bridge the gap between practice and policy.

---

legislative staff? (3) How do advocates actually get to know legislators? and (4) What motivates legislators in general?

Which legislators should advocates get to know? Richan (1996) points out that advocates need to know whom to court and to whom to direct their arguments. Some research has identified factors related to effectiveness as legislators (Dear & Patti, 1981; Denny et al., 1989; Kleinkauf, 1988; Patti & Dear, 1975; Smith, 1979), and among influential legislators (whom advocates would want to know) are those who:

- Serve as committee chairpersons
- Sit on key committees dealing with human services
- Have a reputation for substantive expertise and in-depth knowledge on a topic
- Possess exceptional knowledge of procedures, rules, traditions, personalities, and formal and informal processes of the legislature
- Are assured reelection, because they are freed from political considerations and can be influenced by the merits of a case
- Have a moderate image, causing other legislators to believe that the bill is not an irresponsible departure from existing legislation
- Represent the advocate's (or other group members') home voting district, thus allowing greater access to the legislator and leverage as a constituent

- Are part of the party leadership or majority party such as majority leader, minority leader, whip, or caucus officers
- Are actually willing to exercise their influence actively in support of a bill
- May have a large constituency of the targeted group such as low-income housing tenants, welfare recipients, or unemployed in their district
- Have sponsored prior legislation and have a voting record supporting similar legislation desired by advocates
- Serve on the boards of agencies that provide services to the targeted group or have family members who serve
- Contact the advocacy group for information or support, indicating a predisposition toward the advocate's goals
- Have a fairly positive outlook on the advocate's concerns and issues
- Know that their constituents strongly support a proposed bill
- Operate effectively in bipartisan relationships

Why bother to get to know legislative staff? It is common wisdom that the way to influence a legislator's vote is to have an inside track to his or her legislative aides. Kleinkauf (1988) reminds the reader that the staff member's first job is to protect and advance his or her boss's interest and power. But it is also clear that staff exert a critical force on the policy process (Herman & Callanan, 1978; Mattison & Storey, 1992; Melton, 1983; Patti & Dear, 1975; Richan, 1996). Experts point out several reasons why knowing the staff member is so useful to an advocate. Staff members usually:

- Are more accessible than the legislator
- Assist in defining the issues and drafting legislative proposals and reports
- Generate and filter the flow of information used as the basis for a decision
- Possess more technical, sophisticated, or expert knowledge than the legislator
- Can give more time and attention to advocates
- Do not think immediately about the voter/constituent dynamic like their boss
- Attend hearings and monitor various committees
- Serve as the liaison between the legislator and constituents and lobbyists
- Initiate policy ideas and use information given to them
- Arrange for testimony by advocates and plan contacts with legislators
- Negotiate differences and compromises on a bill's language

Only an amateur advocate would say that they were irritated because they "only talked to an aide." Richan (1996) makes a useful distinction between ultimate and intermediate targets of influence. The aide is usually the intermediary through which advocates can reach the legislator.

How do advocates actually get to know legislators? The last impression advocates want to give to a legislator is that they come around only when they need something. In order to get to know legislators in more depth, advocates should try to:

- Visit personally with the legislator. Make an appointment. Be friendly, courteous, and as brief as possible. Bring along no more than three companions. Have a specific request to ask for, and leave a one-page handout or letter conveying your concerns so that they will go on the record. Thank them for their time in a follow-up letter. Personal contacts are one of the most effective means for influencing legislation.
- Identify what committees, subcommittees, commissions, or other offices your legislators serve on. It may be surprising to discover how powerful they are. Attend some sessions.
- Study the political leanings, interests, and voting record of the legislator. Determine the religion, ethnic group, family history, background, and profession to which the legislator belongs. Perhaps the legislator has a family member with a particular illness or disability. Knowing facts, attitudes, and values will prepare you for discussions and later meetings.
- Use friend-to-friend contacts in order to meet a legislator or official. In most groups, there is usually someone who has a friend who knows "the senior senator" from upstate.
- Invite the legislator to meet with clients or service providers by hosting a meeting at an agency or civic center. It will give him or her a chance to encounter persons with real needs and give you an opportunity to serve as the legislator's guide and source of information.
- Attend hearings or committee meetings where the legislator is present or presiding and introduce yourself before or after the session. Congratulate him or her on running a smooth exchange of ideas.
- Ask legislators to speak at a special forum or before a group of constituents. Usually there is the opportunity for the legislator to speak and to answer questions. Both the advocates and legislator learn more about each other.
- Give an award to a legislator or key staff member for efforts on behalf of the advocacy group. If there is a dinner, you may want to ask the legislator to be the main speaker. A dinner occasion or reception also provides one-on-one opportunities for people to chat with the legislator.
- Work closely with those who know their way around the legislature and who have considerable experience and knowledge of people and procedures.

What motivates legislators in general? How does a legislator decide to cast his or her vote? Mattison and Storey (1992) reduce legislators' motivation down to a simple and countable formula: votes and money. While there is much truth in this statement, the issue is more complex. Below are other factors identified by U.S. Representative Lee Hamilton, D-Indiana (*Congressional Record*), that serve as a rank order of motivators for most legislators:

1. *Constituents.* On issues where the constituency expresses a strong preference, a legislator is almost certain to favor them in a vote.
2. *Colleagues.* Other legislators are important sources of information; they often are well-informed on an issue, can frame their advice to another legislator's needs, and are available at the time of the vote.
3. *Lobbies.* Interest groups and associations are available to offer factual and essential information as well as innovative ideas to a legislator.
4. *The executive.* A governor or president of the United States has great influence on the legislative process due to excellent sources of information, ability to initiate legislation, ease of appealing to the people, and capacity to set a legislative agenda.
5. *Party leadership.* Although the party leadership has some effect on a legislator's vote, it is really the leaders in the legislative body, such as the Speaker or majority and minority leaders, who have more influence.
6. *Media.* Legislators usually consider how their votes will play in the news media. The media is also good at setting an agenda by drawing attention to it.
7. *Staff.* Most legislators rely on their staff to assist them in evaluating legislative proposals due to pressure-filled schedules and lack of technical knowledge.

Although legislators seek information and help from many sources when they prepare to vote on complex and controversial issues, they realize that they alone will be held accountable for their votes.

Broaden the Base of Support

Roberts-DeGennaro (1986b) noted that "more than any single organization, a *coalition* of organizations can effectively alter policy" (p. 308). Success in "fighting back" in periods of austerity often depends on the effective use of coalitions to shape public opinions and influence the political process. Coalitions are almost a tradition in the legislative arena (Bistline, 1981). Joint efforts are so common that the groups lobbying on their own without allies are the exception to the rule. Ninety percent of organizations in Schlozman and Tierney's (1986) research sample reported that they belong to a coalition.

In Washington, the nation's capital, and in most state capitals, there are scores of coalitions representing the interests of groups with particular emphases such as disabilities, mental health, aging, child abuse, domestic violence, juveniles, health care, nursing homes, and so on. Coalitions interested in mental health, for example, include the Mental Health Group, Consortium for Child Mental Health Services, National Prevention Coalition, National Mental Health Leadership Forum, Ad Hoc Coalition on National Alcohol and Drug Abuse, Consortium for Citizens with Disabilities, and Consortium of Family Organizations, all of which work to influence legislators.

Eriksen (1997) presents several reasons why coalition building in the legislative arena is growing: (1) the increasing complexity of government; (2) the need for clout in defining the policy debate and influencing policy outcomes; (3) the increasing numbers of interest groups and the resultant decrease in each group's clout; (4) the government's need for predigested policies; and (5) legislators' need to build majorities without being criticized for favoring special interests.

The authors have identified three questions as foci on coalitions: (1) What are the principal benefits of coalitions in the legislative setting? (2) What are the different types of legislative coalitions? (3) What special advice exists on building and maintaining effective coalitions?

What are the principal benefits of coalitions in the legislative setting? Bills that have wide sponsorship and support are more likely to become law (Kirst-Ashman & Hull, 1993). By maximizing the number of organizations in a coalition involved with a legislative initiative, chances of success are higher. Coalitions create a very useful outcome called *clout* (Wittenberg & Wittenberg, 1989), which is particularly helpful when a bill is initially proposed (Herman & Callanan, 1978).

Legislators often demand testimony from coalitions about an issue in order to identify issues and test the depth of support for certain dimensions. Effective coalitions have an opportunity to introduce provisions and key wording of bills (Rickards, 1992). Defining the terms during a debate on policy often results in gaining some control over the policy outcomes (Eriksen, 1997).

Coordinated activities and consistent statements from a coalition avoid the pitfalls of disjointed or contradictory statements coming before legislators. A unified front assures legislators that the issues at hand are agreed upon by the major players. In addition, the workload and division of labor is shared among several groups. With many requests for general information and a need for sophisticated analyses of pending legislation, no one person or group can likely accomplish these tasks alone (Jansson, 1999; Ross, 1992). Contacting legislators and their staff alone constitutes an enormous task that can be eased by dividing up the labor and time requirements.

What are the different types of legislative coalitions? Bistline (1981) and Rickards (1992) suggest there are two types of coalitions: (1) temporary, ad hoc, or single-issue coalitions; and (2) ongoing, formal, more permanent coalitions. The former is usually created to focus on a single piece of legislation or one issue that may be emotionally charged, and it usually disbands once its

goals are achieved. A coalition on removing lead from old paint in one particular public housing project would be a temporary coalition.

The latter, more permanent type of coalition serves broader goals and usually has a staff, stated goals, and specific responsibilities. It is concerned with
the ongoing influencing of legislative activities such as drafting amendments,
committee processes, floor actions, and analyzing key provisions. A formal
coalition concerned with children's mental health services might be comprised
of organizations like the National Association of Social Workers, the American
Psychological Association, the National Council of Community Mental Health
Centers, and the National Association of State Mental Health Program
Directors. Each of these groups would contribute resources to the coalition in
pursuit of its mission and goals.

What special advice exists on building and maintaining coalitions?
Eriksen (1997) suggests creating coalitions of nontraditional allies. A business
lobby can be linked with child advocacy groups. Be careful not to "write off"
another group or political party as "too conservative" or unsympathetic to a
bill. Dear and Patti (1981) also suggest that bipartisan sponsorship is a method
to influence a broader range of legislators. This advice recognizes the importance of compromise, negotiation, outreach, and creative effort needed to
improve the chance of a bill's passage.

Very large, politically active organizations with well-known reputations,
plenty of resources, and perceived clout can be targeted for membership in a
coalition. Many times they join, not to gain information, but to provide it. Such an
organization may not participate actively or may merely lend its name, but most
coalitions welcome their presence (Eriksen, 1997). The American Association of
Retired Persons (AARP) with over 35 million members is a good example here.

Coalitions must be formed early, well before the legislative session begins.
If one waits until the formal session has begun or is about to begin, it is usually too late to influence legislators and provide ideas or wording to a bill.

Some client groups have no natural constituency upon which they can
count for support, for example, homeless children, battered spouses, and
abused infants. It is more difficult to build a coalition around these groups.
Often, advocates can look for nontraditional groups to form a coalition. In the
case of homeless children, school teachers and administrators, teacher unions,
PTAs, and home builders might be interested in the welfare of these clients.

Be Persistent

Mahaffey (1972) noted that social workers often become impatient about the
prolonged time involved in creating legislative change, and some lack the persistence to deal with the compromises, negotiations, and uncertainties of the
political process. Complicating matters even more is the recognition that
"many of the problems we seek to alleviate legislatively . . . have been with us

for centuries and will take years to eradicate" (Mattison & Storey, 1992, p. 145). Proposing new legislation beneficial to disadvantaged persons usually requires an allocation of funding and a winning political rationale before policy makers adopt and sign it into law. There are often many serious roadblocks along the path toward the passage of such a bill (Yep, 1992). Finally, while being "politically active" sounds glamorous, individuals with little experience in the legislative process are surprised by many of the mundane tasks (telephone calls, waiting for appointments, stuffing envelopes, and so on), intangible rewards, and small payoffs that come with being "active" in the process.

DeLeon et al. (1982) have stated that legislative success takes time, energy, and above all else, perseverance. The authors believe that social workers will increase their effectiveness as legislative advocates by keeping in mind the following important dimensions of persistence: time frames, incremental change, vigilance, and how to handle defeat.

Time Frame   If advocates are pursuing a change in policy, especially a major one, they can count on spending several years on it (Richan, 1996). Jenkins-Smith and Sabatier (1994) suggest that using a decade as a time perspective is realistic. Because the legislative process is slow and exasperating, it is very important for social workers to have sober, down-to-earth expectations about the length of time it takes to achieve legislative goals. Patti and Dear (1975) reminded us that "depending on the nature of the bill and its opposition, the bill may have to be reintroduced and advocated in several consecutive sessions extending over several years" (p. 110). Medicare, a popular federal legislative victory, was introduced in consecutive legislative sessions from 1957 to 1965.

A legislative bill is rarely enacted the first time it is introduced. In most state legislatures, at the end of every two years, pending bills automatically die and have to be reintroduced for the next session. Patti and Dear (1975) pointed out that only a very small fraction of bills introduced into an annual legislative session is ever enacted. These authors further indicated that if the bill introduces a new or controversial concept or requires substantial funding, the probability for initial failure is even greater.

This perspective is indeed daunting for social work advocates because it requires long-term commitment and steady, unswerving motivation. However, this lengthy process also provides positive opportunities. By persisting in promoting a particular bill, social workers can meet several subgoals: (1) educate many people, including legislators, who need to become familiar with the bill; (2) identify points of resistance and disagreement to the bill that can be addressed in future proposals; (3) determine areas of compromise; (4) obtain press coverage to educate the public; and (5) cultivate the commitment of sponsors, coalitions, and new allies (Patti & Dear, 1975).

Legislative Processes Are Incremental   In modern societies, while radical change is unlikely to happen, incremental modifications often occur (Pearl

& Barr, 1976). The legislative processes of negotiation, compromise, give-and-take, and trade-offs require slow, often tedious attention and time. Parts of a bill may pass one year, and other elements of it must wait until a future date. Competing interests, current events, financial priorities, and political issues frequently, if not always, intrude on the passage of a bill. Typically, changes or amendments to bills should be encouraged because these bills usually get through the legislature with greater frequency than those without amendments (Kirst-Ashman & Hull, 1993). Social workers can learn to accept that change usually happens in small ways, and with an eye on overall goals, they can work persistently toward aspects of their goals within an incremental framework and not be discouraged by failing to get everything they wanted in one huge victory. Patti and Dear (1975) pointed out that compromise will be necessary, and advocates will have to settle for less than they desire. Morgan (1983) suggested that advocates always keep a temporary fallback position in mind. Of course, advocates should not bargain away issues that are primary to a client or involve basic values.

Vigilance   Decisions that impact thousands of persons are made frequently in split seconds in the legislative arena. Politicians are subject to influence from multiple sources, and their decision making can best be described as unpredictable and complex. Social work advocates must be able to spot a crisis and react quickly (Berger, 1977). In order to do this, advocates must check, double-check, and triple-check the status of the bill(s) they are promoting. They must never believe that their bill has been "sewn up." It is important to keep legislators and their staff reminded about the bill and to be available to provide information if requested. Eriksen (1997) uses the old saying, "It's not over 'til it's over," to remind advocates that bills and policies are continually being made, influenced, remade, and unmade.

Richan (1996) urges social work advocates to be vigilant and never give up in trying to get an appointment with a key legislator. He suggests going to a meeting where the legislator is scheduled to appear and try to provide testimony; after the meeting, try to shake hands and reiterate your position on the bill. Cornering a legislator requires creativity and vigilance, but it will eventually provide advocates with the opportunity to promote their bill.

After a bill passes through the legislature, social worker advocates must monitor it vigilantly on its way to the governor or president's desk and beyond. After a bill is signed, it will go to an agency where regulations will be drafted, offering another chance to influence the outcome of the bill. A rule of thumb: *whenever a policy moves from one arena to another, for example, from the legislative to the executive branch or from the state to the local level, monitoring is necessary.*

A government agency that opposes a bill becoming new legislation may try to blunt its impact by ignoring the details, framing the outcomes in negative terms, or dragging their feet in implementing it. Vigilance helps ensure that the intent of the legislation is retained all the way through implementation.

Defeat   Jansson (1999) reminds us that no single person or group is going to succeed continuously in the complicated playing field of policy making and legislation. Defeat of proposed bills is inevitable, and a watered-down version of a proposal is often all that can be salvaged. Advocating for powerless and vulnerable groups that lack political clout and money almost guarantees more defeats than victories.

Both Richan (1996) and Jansson (1999) believe that, in order to avoid the pessimism and self-recrimination that occurs in the wake of failed legislation, social work advocates must have a vision or perspective that is based on realistic expectations and standards. This vision is usually based on a belief in the ultimate success of one's cause, on a moral purpose that provides an ideal toward which one can aspire, and a determination that something can be done somehow. Richan (1996) calls this perspective a "mindset" and urges advocates to prepare to invest the time and effort over the long haul, become expert in their areas, and be on the alert for ways to promote an agenda that supports their bills.

Evaluate Your Advocacy Effort

The authors suggest three important dimensions in evaluating legislative advocacy: (1) evaluating a legislative advocacy campaign itself, (2) assessing the cost-effectiveness of legislation before and after passage, and (3) policy assessment after implementation.

Evaluating the Campaign   This first dimension focuses on measuring how effective certain activities are in promoting a successful legislative advocacy effort. Eriksen (1997) points out that findings vary widely on the effectiveness of strategies used to influence legislative processes. She states that some interest groups are seen as truly determining policy and others as having very little impact. Some groups are perceived as a powerful part of the political system and others as weaker than previously supposed. Some members of Congress complain that interest groups have become too powerful and intimidating (Schlozman & Tierney, 1986). Why? What actually helps lead to passage of legislative initiatives?

Researchers have had a very difficult job in actually determining what advocacy strategies are effective. Indeed, academic studies of interest groups have demonstrated few conclusive links between an advocacy campaign and actual patterns of influence. This does not mean that such patterns do not exist, but rather, it is very difficult to prove them (Loomis & Cigler, 1986). Certain factors or tactics may *increase the likelihood of success,* and advocates are advised to pay particular attention to them (Eriksen, 1997):

FACTORS LINKED TO SUCCESSFUL CAMPAIGNS
TO INFLUENCE LEGISLATION

- Link the issue to a constituency known to the legislator.
- Raise money and mobilize volunteers.
- Intensify the support of legislators who already support the issue.
- When a major issue is controversial and affects many people, increase the number of tactics used (and vice versa).
- Pay attention to details in the legislation to ensure the desired outcome.
- Use a moderate voice in discussing the issues.
- Work together with other organizations and have a unified agenda to present to legislators.
- Focus your demand as narrowly or technically as possible.
- Address less visible and nonconflictual issues.
- Try to block issues rather than promulgate new ones.
- Target the House of Representatives over the Senate (at U.S. congressional level).
- If advocates have contacts within the legislature who are concerned about the same issue, find a way to involve them.
- Develop as many resources as possible, although money is not *the* determining resource.
- Emphasize the merits of the legislation and why it should be enacted.
- The amount of time given to a campaign does not necessarily affect its success.
- Newcomers are encouraged to take the advice of the seasoned regulars.
- Lobbying is not a last-minute activity; it is the result of an accumulation of actions over time.

Heinz (1993) cautions that we cannot accurately predict legislative and policy outcomes. Hence, the success or failure of advocacy groups on key issues is also uncertain. Social work advocates can increase their chances for success by using as much scientific knowledge as possible and then hope that other uncontrollable factors will favor them.

Cost-Effectiveness of Legislation   This second dimension reflects legislators' interest in the cost-benefit of a policy. What will this policy actually accomplish for a reasonable cost? As Jansson (1999) states: "Assessment requires us to ask how, if at all, the world is different because a specific policy exists, and what, if any, difference it would make if we removed or modified the policy" (p. 390). How successful have community mental health centers been in preventing and treating mental illness and at what cost? Have child day-care policies proven effective in assisting single mothers to stay out of poverty? This type of questioning is at the heart of most policy-making decisions, and legislators often pose such questions to advocates, agencies, and bill sponsors.

One important time when this line of questioning takes place is in discussion *before* the passage of a policy. Legislators try to determine whether or not to proceed with a proposed policy by getting a clearer idea of the proposed policy before they cast a vote (Lyday, 1972). Few politicians will support legislation that appears likely to fail (Jansson, 1999). *Caution:* Advocates may make very extravagant claims that will result "if only the legislation they support is enacted" (Feldman, 1978). The virtues of the policy are magnified, the defects are overlooked, and supporters are labeled "good guys" and opponents are labeled "bad guys." This "oversell" may flow from the need to "get this bill passed," and not on the basis of well-researched data and pertinent findings. Retaining one's credibility is more important than passing a particular bill.

Policy Assessment   Another important evaluative stage in the life of a policy is after an existing policy has been implemented, and someone wants to know if it is flawed or meritorious (Jansson, 1999). Was the policy effective in actually doing what it was intended to do? Were people helped or harmed? Did it discriminate against some? Were there unintended consequences? Was a client's life or well-being improved or not?

Below are listed several well-established principles of policy assessment:

1. If an evaluation of a policy is desired at a future date, for example, in three years, then it is important to structure assessment procedures ahead of time, usually from the very beginning (Lyday, 1972). If care is not taken to collect certain data early on, then these data will not be available at the time one wants to perform an evaluation. While lacking the excitement of initiating a new program, establishing a method of gathering information about the ongoing outcomes and operation of the program is a very vital task.

2. Berk et al. (1985) noted that many quantitative evaluations of policies reflect relatively modest gains, a mixture often between no gains or modest changes in either a positive or negative direction. Consequently, these studies rarely provide definite and once-and-for-all answers to the merits of a policy or program. Evaluators may try to use their data less to prove than to argue for the merits of a policy. Findings may "suggest" continued support or modifications of a program and can be used in debate about the issues.

3. Political considerations often influence the interpretation of research findings (Jansson, 1999). Conservative politicians may debate whether the magnitude of a change in clients' behavior warrants future funding: "Shouldn't we expect more change than 15%?" They may also question the length of time the group was studied as being insufficient: "How can you tell in 15 months whether the new behavior will persist?" They can also question the weighting of the

criteria used by the evaluator: "Are increases in costs adequate relative to the improvement we expect on test scores?"

4. Policy evaluators try to eliminate rival explanations that critics can use to cast doubt on their findings (Jansson, 1999). Although beyond the scope of this book, it is important for evaluators to use specific design, sampling, and statistical procedures, as well as appropriate instruments, to decrease the chance that other explanations can account for the data and findings. This careful planning increases the confidence that one can place in a study's findings.

5. Evaluators are increasingly using a mixture of quantitative and qualitative research methods to give a more dynamic picture of the outcomes or processes of a policy (Jansson, 1999). Qualitative studies often give more attention to the context of a program in order to explain its success or failure.

6. Useful research should result in modifying programs. A feedback loop to the legislators or agency personnel is intended to convey the merits and weaknesses of a policy and suggest alternative ways to improve the existing policy. Advocates may also disseminate the findings of evaluative research to other groups or the public.

SUMMARY

Legislative advocates have significantly improved the well-being of millions of Americans through federal policies like Medicaid, food stamps, the Americans with Disabilities Act, and child care programs. At the state and local levels, advocates have helped pass numerous proposals in the health and human services arena. At the dawn of the 21st century, social workers have a new chance to influence social policy and legislation by paying close attention to the "new Federalism," which gives the states greater authority over benefits, rules, and priorities for clients. Legislative advocates who can *represent clients and influence decision makers effectively* can raise public expectations about the rights and needs of all citizens. Legislative advocacy is never over. The NASW *Code of Ethics* reminds each social worker of the responsibility to advocate for legislation and policies that support social justice (section 604[a]).

DISCUSSION QUESTIONS

1. How do social work advocates attempt to influence legislative proposals?
2. How is the legislative forum different from other public speaking settings?

3. What can advocates do to improve the chances that their issue will be embraced by a key legislator?
4. Why should legislative advocates devote time to evaluating how effective a policy is?
5. How can advocates remain persistent and vigilant in their quest to promote legislation?
6. What are the pros and cons of joining a coalition to support an important piece of legislation?
7. What is the first step in planning a strategy to influence a piece of legislation?
8. How many issues can be dealt with effectively by an advocacy group in the annual state legislative session?
9. Can you suggest ways in which social workers in the future can provide leadership for policy making?
10. What will happen to human services issues in the future if social workers do not participate actively in the policy processes?

RECOMMENDED READINGS

Amidei, N. (1992). *So you want to make a difference: Advocacy is the key.* Washington, DC: OMB Watch.

Dear, R. B., & Patti, R. J. (1981). Legislative advocacy: Seven effective tactics. *Social Work, 26,* 289–296.

Eriksen, K. (1997). *Making an impact: A handbook on counselor advocacy.* Washington, DC: Taylor & Francis Group.

Jansson, B. S. (1999). *Becoming an effective policy advocate: From policy practice to social justice.* Pacific Grove, CA: Brooks/Cole.

Pardeck, J. T., & Meinert, R. (1994). Do social workers have a major impact on social policy? Yes or no? In J. H. Karger, & J. Midgley, *Controversial issues in social policy* (pp. 93–106). Boston: Allyn & Bacon.

Richan, W. C. (1996). *Lobbying for social change.* New York: Haworth Press.

The good social worker doesn't go on helping people out of a ditch. Pretty soon, she begins to find out what ought to be done to get rid of the ditch.

MARY RICHMOND

OVERVIEW

Many agree with Richan (1980) when he states that it seems like a "contradiction to speak of *administration* and *advocacy* in the same breath" (p. 72). Why this puzzlement? First, Ezell (1991) points to stereotypes affixed to some administrators: highly conservative and cautious, maintaining the status quo, resistant to change, making rules and regulations that keep one from helping people, demanding endless paperwork and reports, looking down on creativity and innovation, afraid of controversy due to board of directors' reactions, fearful of offending funding sources. In this context, advocacy on behalf of clients is often thought of as targeted *at* administrators rather than being engaged in *by* them (Richan, 1980).

Secondly, the "culture" within some public and private social agencies frowns on potentially adversarial activities, thus inhibiting agency workers' ability to advocate openly for clients (Kirst-Ashman & Hull, 1993). Employees are discouraged from perceiving advocacy as a legitimate role in their job descriptions and performance (Herbert & Mould, 1992). Without administrative sanction, these social workers feel caught between following approved agency guidelines for practice and their professional ethos of pleading aggressively on behalf of a client. Fear of dismissal, reduced chances for advancement, large caseloads, and lack of advocacy skills all contribute to a negative influence.

Finally, advocacy that involves "promoting change from within" is also filled with uncertainty, lack of knowledge and skills, and fear of risk. Individual employees may want to change policies, programs, or procedures of their own agencies. This is called "internal advocacy." Unless the agency permits review and discussion of problems in a way that is perceived as nonpunitive, staff often do not engage in pushing for change of internal administrative policies or procedures.

In this chapter, we discuss two types of administrative advocates: (1) agency administrators who do engage themselves or their agencies actively in advocacy, and (2) administratively appointed "internal advocates" who are responsible for increasing the effectiveness of client services or addressing agency practices or procedures that are deleterious to clients (Patti, 1974). As the reader will see, there are many opportunities for administrators of agencies to advocate successfully for clients, causes, and legislation. In fact, administrators are often in key positions to lead advocacy efforts. Likewise, there are internal advocates who can effect great change within an agency. These positions are called different names:

ombudsman, client representative, and/or unit advocate. Their job descriptions include addressing agency policies or procedures that may be harmful to clients, investigating internal complaints by clients or families, evaluating events or incidents that affect clients and staff, and calling attention to violations of client rights.

We present in this chapter both of the fundamental advocacy skills, that is, representation and influencing, in the context of administrative advocacy. Using the authors' new definition, social work advocates can incorporate this specialized knowledge and skills into their professional careers and interventions.

REPRESENTATION

In the current context of cost-cutting pressures on administrators in nonprofit and public agencies, "speaking up" on behalf of clients requires great balance between focusing on present needs and ensuring future agency capability to meet its mission (Perlmutter & Adams, 1994). Administrators, agency employees, and internal advocates all experience the call to compromise in the struggle to address client demands while simultaneously facing inadequate resources and administrative constraints (Patti, 1980). Richan (1983) warns that "staying aloof" from representing client rights' issues is dangerous, because eventually, the agency will be at the mercy of others.

Exclusivity

Exclusivity describes the social work advocate as "focused uniquely, singularly, and solely on clients and their needs." While representing clients *exclusively*, there are particular issues for administrators and internal advocates. Among them are: (1) the ethical directive to represent clients exclusively *within* an agency, (2) the stress of working at odds in one's agency, (3) co-optation by bureaucracies, and (4) three steps that internal advocates can take to justify their activities to agency executives.

For administrators and internal advocates, Patti (1974) and Mailick and Ashley (1981) state that the source of legitimacy for advocacy is in their ethical obligation to the primacy of the client. (See 1996 NASW *Code of Ethics*, section 1.01.) Patti (1974) stated earlier that "where this obligation conflicts with loyalty to the employing organization's policies and procedures, the professional practitioner is committed to give precedence to client interests" (pp. 542–543). Taebel (1972) suggests that administrators view the traditional bureaucracy differently even to the point that an "agency would devote itself, even at the risk of self-destruction, totally to the client" (p. 38). Administrators and internal advocates need to be constantly alert to policies and procedures that favor the interests of the "system" at the expense of the well-being of clients (Herbert & Mould, 1992).

The stresses in exclusive representation of clients by internal advocates and administrators are real. How do they advocate against a policy or condition fostered by their own agencies, seemingly biting the hand that feeds them? How do administrators support advocacy efforts by their employees with the day-to-day contact with clients? How do they handle a serious deviation from agency policy or traditional practice? There are, of course, no easy answers to these questions. Administrators must attempt to see the contributions that employees are trying to make and open up channels of redress and communication as much as possible. Employees must try to bring their challenges to the appropriate forums. Herbert and Mould (1992) remind administrators that "organizations whose programs and policies are not informed constantly by the experiences of the front-line workers will inevitably become part of the problem rather than part of the solution" (p. 127).

There may also be the temptation for advocates to resolve some of the tension around the exclusive representation of clients by "co-opting" for a solution that may not include a strong focus on their clients. As Berry (1981) states, a bureaucracy will take advantage if a person(s) lets him- or herself be co-opted. There may be times when good relations must be secondary, when going public is required, and when bridges must be burned. These are complex decisions, but primacy of the client and other ethical directives offer guidance to the advocate in these situations.

There are three steps suggested by Patti (1974) that can be taken by administrative advocates to justify to supervisors, executives, or boards those actions taken exclusively on behalf of clients. Overall, the advocacy actions can be framed as contributing to the mission of the agency:

1. Advocates can demonstrate that they have special insight and skill into the problem and they can lead the agency to an effective solution. This competence must be supported by visible evidence such as a well-documented plan or a superior understanding of the issues.
2. Advocates can argue that their advocacy activities are congruent with the agency's stated mission. If respecting client rights and honoring entitlements are part of the agency mission, then advocates can show how the agency can fulfill its goals by advocating on behalf of the clients.
3. Typically, distortions and inadequate information cause poor understanding of issues and problems. By filtering new information into the agency, advocates can provide decision makers with needed feedback. Internal advocates can supplement the channels of communication in an agency.

These arguments may not be accepted by upper-level administrators or board members, but they raise the level of discussion to debates over values rather than funds or territory.

Mutuality

Mutuality reflects one of social work's most cherished values, that is, client self-determination. Administrative advocates continuously evaluate decisions in light of how an action reflects the actual will of a client or how much emphasis is placed on acting together with clients and/or empowering them to take action on their own behalf. This working relationship is one of collaboration and respect, not paternalism. For administrative advocates, there are special considerations of mutuality as illustrated in: (1) current trends, (2) the structure of agency decision making, and (3) personal orientation of administrators toward mutuality.

Current trends point to program administrators being asked to listen more closely to what clients have to say (Ingelhart & Becerra, 1995; Stockdill, 1992). Clients in the mental health, mental retardation, and child welfare fields are seeking greater interaction with policy makers and service institutions. They are being represented by associations such as National Alliance of the Mentally Ill, Children's Defense Fund, and Federation of Families for Children's Mental Health. Administrative advocates can view these associations as indispensable allies in clarifying priorities and seeking resources.

Taylor (1991) places particular emphasis on the structure of decision making used by an agency in advocating for clients. If an agency decides to make advocacy a priority, the board and administrators must design a structured system that allows for the involvement of people experiencing the problem or condition wherever possible. In the model of Lancaster City and County noted by Taylor (1991), there is a built-in opportunity for clients to participate in the definition of the problem and for staff to obtain direct information. Herr (1983) asserts that "the disabled can best speak about their needs, conditions, and concerns as they experience them throughout their own lives" (p. 214). This structure reflects a commitment to mutuality by the agency.

Richan (1983) exhorts administrators to develop a conscious "mutual" orientation toward clients and their problems. He believes that administrative advocates must regard the client as one who has the right and the capacity to participate maximally in directing his or her own affairs insofar as this does not abrogate the rights of others. Riley (1971) reinforces this perspective by noting that mutual-oriented administrators see their own organizations as planning *with* people rather than just *for* them.

Use of a Forum

Administrative advocates often appear at specific forums where clients' concerns can be addressed such as fair hearings and appeals, legislative meetings, judicial reviews, and staff planning groups. Effective representation of clients in these forums often depends on negotiating skills and mutual client-advocate representation. Successful administrative advocacy also depends on agency structures that can be designed to enhance the practice of advocacy. The following text presents several issues facing administrative advocates in forum settings.

Fair hearings are legally mandated grievance mechanisms for clients who are dissatisfied with an agency's decision about program termination and/or level of benefits. Theoretically, fair hearings are designed to foster fairness and to control for agency discretion in policy decisions. In practice, however, there are serious limitations: (1) agencies often fail to notify the client of their right to a file a grievance; (2) clients must risk confronting those who determine their benefits; (3) questions arise about client ability to function as an equal adversary in the complex regulatory system, using complex documents and cross-examination; and (4) clients with limited access to legal representation may try self-representation at great risk (Hagen, 1986).

Administrative advocates may be involved in these grievance procedures either in assisting the client to challenge a particular decision, or in representing the agency in adjudicating claims from clients. In both instances, the advocate should be aware of the following:

1. Clients have a right to be notified adequately of an adverse decision.
2. Clients have a right to be informed of the right to appeal an agency decision.
3. Hearings are adversarial in nature, but through an open, impartial presentation of views, an accurate and fair decision or resolution can be made.
4. Clients who self-represent usually are poor at cross-examination and challenging questionable agency rules and regulations.
5. The hearing must be respectful at all times of the client and allow for adequate preparation of the client's appeal, access to agency documents and manuals, and sufficient time to hear the facts and application of the policy to the client's challenge.

In public agencies, where decisions about clients' interests must fall within the boundaries of enabling legislation, agency discretion can also be challenged constitutionally by a *court judicial review*. This forum is an advanced procedure for public accountability of the administrative process, and it tests whether the agency has (a) exceeded its constitutional or statutory authority, (b) properly interpreted the applicable law, (c) conducted a fair hearing, and (d) not acted capriciously and unreasonably (Albert, 1983). Administrators may be called to defend agency actions or procedures in this forum, and internal advocates may use it to compel compliance with the intent of legislation.

Staff groups or committees are often used to assist in making decisions in many social service agencies, and their meetings fit the definition of *forum* as used in this book. Such groups may be mandated to resolve conflict over programs or policies or to design innovative responses to problems. Upper level administrators often initiate such groups at the lower levels of large, complex agencies as well as in smaller, informally functioning agencies. Effective representation before such groups, according to Villone (1983), however, may be difficult due to resistance to change by other agency staff. Strategic attention to agency/staff concerns must be given a high priority in attempts to use this forum as an advocacy tool.

According to Riddle and King (1977), *negotiation* is the most used advocacy skill within an administrative forum. Negotiation usually refers to discussing, conferring, and bargaining with another in order to reach an agreement. Administrative advocates typically will confer with others about alternatives or different proposals to meet the needs of clients. The advocate will start with the party most directly connected to the client in order to resolve an issue. If problem solving fails at this level, the client and advocate move to the next level of authority and so on until a satisfactory solution is found. There will be instances when the negotiation process becomes more confrontive and harder demands are laid down. Compromise may ease problem solving, but risks to clients' rights must be carefully weighed.

Hagen (1986) and Riddle and King (1977) encourage the social work advocate to actually accompany clients to hearings or other forums in order to support them in requesting the change needed from those responsible for the policy or program. This admonition reflects the "mutuality" that this book requires of advocates. Often, the advocate can interpret to professional staff what the client is proposing. If the client agrees, the advocate can actually represent the client during a hearing. It is not necessary to be an attorney to function effectively in most hearings.

If administrators want to promote advocacy in their organizations, they will have to design specific forums to accomplish this ambitious task. In Taylor's (1991) opinion, advocacy cannot be successful on an ad hoc basis: "Advocacy will not be pursued within an agency when no one is responsible for it" (p. 141). Model advocacy is discussed in greater depth in Taylor's (1991) article, but its chief characteristics are: (1) initial resistance to the idea of advocacy is normal and may come from board members, staff, or even the executive; (2) working to educate all staff and deal with objections constructively is crucial; (3) advocacy's cost-efficiency can often convince funding sources; (4) the advocacy structure must be accountable and involve input from every level of the agency; (5) study and action are linked; and (6) agency advocacy must include community professionals and clients experiencing the problems.

Communication

Speaking and Writing "Aiding the commissioner throughout was a superb command of language and what seemed at the time to be an uncanny ability to read his audience" (Richan, 1980, pp. 80–81). Effective advocates in administrative arenas usually possess excellent representational skills in speaking and writing. They have the ability to assess the audience accurately and anticipate the impact of information upon it. Careless words and rhetoric often result in misunderstandings that administrative advocates prefer to avoid. This section discusses several issues related to speaking and writing that may affect advocates as they represent clients within an administrative context.

Richan (1980) notes that administrators have more control over information in an organization and what gets communicated to whom than any other person. They generally have high access to sources of information and usually decide what pieces of it should be relayed to board members, staff, and clients. Likewise, a major task of the administrator is paying attention to the flow of information inside and outside of the agency. From this key positioning, administrative advocates can be prepared to use data to mobilize support, neutralize opposition, and raise relevant issues with appropriate audiences. In every speech and with every written memo or report, an administrator is able to influence the direction of policy making and program development.

Another word used in describing administrative advocates is *interpreter.* Both Richan (1980) and Riddle and King (1977) suggest that a crucial role for an advocate is to interpret the needs or demands of a client to other audiences. This representation most likely will take place in forums such as interdisciplinary team meetings, staff planning conferences, weekly treatment team meetings, hearings, or supervisory sessions. Through an interpretation, the advocate may highlight or downplay key aspects of a client's situation. Helping clients verbalize or write about their needs reflects the mutual relationship that is so important in social work advocacy. Haynes and Mickelson (1997) suggest that testimony by both the advocate and the client is extremely dynamic and offers dramatic opportunities to influence decision makers.

For internal advocates who speak up on behalf of clients/residents, Riddle and King (1977) strongly urge advocates to follow through to a successful closure of the issue if they wish to maintain credibility with staff and the clients/residents. In this sense, words are not enough; actions must also back up the words so that all participants can observe that the advocate is trustworthy and reliable. Addressing the negative impact of agency procedures on client self-determination in a residential program must ultimately produce changed procedures.

A key dilemma facing internal advocates and employees who want to change things from within is knowing that, by speaking out, they may either bear the disapproval of their peers and suffer isolation to some degree, or undergo ethical dissonance and loss of professional identity by failing to adhere to their *Code of Ethics* (Mailick & Ashley, 1981). The fear of losing the respect of colleagues and thus being excluded or ignored by the other staff is a real phenomenon. Developing the political acumen to assess which battles to fight and which issues to select is important for the advocate, who must never compromise the rights and privileges of his or her clients.

Albert (1983) reminds administrators and supervisory personnel that they are in the best position to understand a regulation's impact on services and clients. He urges these advocates to use the "comment" period, available during most hearings on new or amended rules and regulations, to point out, verbally or in written statements, what the impact of the regulations will be on clients. According to the author, a carefully drafted written statement or an intelligently structured verbal presentation at such hearings can be quite influential.

Simons (1988) points out that administrators are constantly attempting to persuade others to contribute time, money, energy, resources, or service required for effective service delivery. He believes that persuasion often involves producing changes through the provision of new information so that the target thinks, feels, or acts differently. In summary, here are some factors that an effective administrator would be conscious of when writing or speaking in order to persuade:

> *Emphasize advantages or rewards.* Show the individual how the change will satisfy their needs and desires. People need sufficient reasons to modify their behaviors.
>
> *Be comprehensible.* Use language that is readily understood and avoid jargon.
>
> *Show compatibility of values.* People will accept an idea if it is perceived as consistent with their current beliefs, values, and ways of doing things. Compatibility usually reduces risks.
>
> *Cite proven results.* When people can see the positive results of an action, they are more likely to adopt it. Pilot projects are very useful here.
>
> *Allow for trialability.* People are reluctant to commit themselves to an action that does not allow for a later change of mind. Find a way to let the idea be tried on a piecemeal basis.
>
> *Link the message to influential others.* People tend to adopt the same attitude toward an idea if that idea is held by someone whom they like or respect, and vice versa. Link the idea to someone who is liked by the target audience.
>
> *Avoid high-pressure tactics.* When people feel pressured to select a particular course of action either through the promise of rewards

or the threat of punishment, they usually look for alternatives to the position being advocated. It is better to offer a two-sided argument: first, acknowledge the merits of the other side and the limits of one's own position, and second, assure the audience that you appreciate their point of view.

Minimize threats to security, status, or esteem. People are not only rational, embracing an idea on its merits and accepting it thoughtfully; they are also emotional and have fears, perceiving threats to their status. The message must reduce defensiveness and discuss fears objectively.

Administrators can also provide leadership in the use of electronic and online resources to promote advocacy within and outside of the agency. Encouraging board members and staff to review websites and information sources available on the Internet is a good first step (see Appendix A, Internet and World Wide Web Advocacy Resources).

INFLUENCE

Like representation, knowledge and skills in influencing others is of utmost importance in administrative advocacy. Agency executives, supervisors, internal advocates, and staff members are in key positions to persuade others to alter policies or procedures that adversely affect clients. Each of the eight principles is presented here with an emphasis on unique advocacy dimensions found in administrative arenas.

Identify the Issues and Set Goals

We know that an "issue" is a matter of critical importance, a problem that may affect a significant number of people, or a substantive matter in dispute. Administrators and internal advocates face important "issues" daily, resolving them as effectively and efficiently as they can. Patti (1980) noted that issues related to program or service changes and issues related to procedures affecting workflow account for 40% of advocacy efforts by workers within an agency. Sosin and Caulum (1983) also point out that administrative level advocacy is concerned with convincing decision makers to alter agency regulations. Furthermore, Taylor (1991) demonstrates that the mission and goals of an agency set the parameters within which the board, administrators, and employees provide advocacy for clients or causes. The following paragraphs outline several of the typical issues that administrative advocates are likely to encounter.

Advocates may presume that organizations generally operate to minimize change and to preserve current procedural arrangements (Inglehart & Becerra, 1995; Kirst-Ashman & Hull, 1993; Terrell, 1967). Many agencies seem to change only when they are put under duress or when conditions have reached a point that they can no longer be ignored. Board members and administrators often prefer consensus-seeking processes and avoid "disruptive" advocates who want to resolve issues or problems differently. Attempts to change are often met initially with resistance because they upset the status quo.

The attitude of some human services organizations is hostile or negative toward its clients (Hepworth et al., 1997; Kirst-Ashman & Hull, 1993). These agencies may deny clients services, subvert rules, act secretively, keep clients ignorant of their rights, hide how workers and supervisors are actually performing, humiliate clients, fail to provide adequately for privacy and confidentiality, allow staff to make judgmental remarks about clients, fail to be on time for appointments, or use demeaning procedures. These internal organizational dynamics usually spill over into how clients are treated.

In many organizations, social work practice is dictated not by professional considerations, but by managerial practices such as daily work procedures, work norms, budget allocations, fiscal constraints, and the "comfort" that the agency has developed over the years (Jaffe, 1978). Jaffe suggests that the influence of management on practice and decision making has become a syndrome that actually rationalizes poor or low-quality services. This habitual manner of judging agency priorities results in decisions that are even defended by professional social workers.

Helping organizations are frequently faced with the issue of how to increase accessibility to services by clients (Hepworth et al., 1997). Advocates may identify areas where improvements can be made such as (1) scheduling during hours when clients are more available or on the weekend, (2) adjusting procedures to avoid long waiting lines, (3) locating agency centers in proximity to client neighborhoods, and (4) arranging for home visits or transportation. Vosburgh and Hyman (1973) also point out that agencies should not only make services accessible, but also ensure their delivery.

Within agencies, some clients may be denied resources or services for inequitable reasons that advocates attempt to counter. Among these reasons are (1) institutional racism; (2) discrimination based on age, ethnicity, gender, or income; (3) arbitrary decisions by staff; (4) lack of knowledge of resources available in the community; (5) client failure to assert rights; (6) failure of authorities to develop resources mandated by law; and (7) dysfunctional policies and procedures (Hepworth et al., 1997).

Internal advocates often attempt to improve the communication pattern between administrators and staff workers (Patti, 1980). Greater input by staff in decision making is a central issue in most agencies. This arena is typically viewed as the domain of administration, and resistance can be very intense. Because workers are affected by decisions about workflow, scheduling, agency procedures, and so on, they wish to have greater impact on how the decisions are made.

Many workers and advocates face the issue of inadequate resources, poor facilities, staffing shortages, lack of supplies, insufficient clerical assistance, and small discretionary funds. This issue, in Patti's (1980) opinion, is a difficult one to resolve because administrators resist efforts by others to enter their domain of budgeting and allocation of funds. Funding is what allows the administrator to direct and control the agency; suggested changes will usually be dealt with cautiously, if at all.

After an issue has been identified by the agency as a priority, advocates often experience difficulties in goal-setting. Taylor (1991) points out that successful advocacy agencies were more likely to have an established, structured goal-setting procedure and to have maintained consistent goals over the past five years. If there is no annual or semiannual goal-setting process in an agency, advocates often encounter great difficulty in addressing issues effectively.

Get the Facts

> *The meeting went well. After substantive, productive, and calm discussion of the issues raised by my proposal, the committee voted unanimously to adopt it for consideration. My effort was not without flaws. I could have spent more time in the fact-gathering phase. I could have formed an advisory group. But, I still learned a great deal about how to gather, process, and synthesize information. Even more importantly, I learned that one person can truly make a difference, providing she or he is willing to do the work.*
>
> BELINDA

"Miller knew his facts and could summon them up when challenged by reporters, hecklers, and antagonistic legislators" (Richan, 1980). Pawlak and Flynn (1990) tell executives to "know your stuff. Your credibility comes from being accurate, not exaggerated" (p. 310). Administrators have access to more facts and information than anyone else in the agency (Roberts, 1983) and, as advocates, can use them to benefit clients. Following are some specific dimensions of facts or fact finding as they pertain to administrative advocacy.

Patti (1980) urges administrators to pay attention to opinions of employees in lower administrative levels. Since these individuals know firsthand the needs of clients (*facts*) and also how the agency's services impact clients (*facts*), administrators and board members should view employees as a primary source of factual insight into agency activities. Ideas, criticisms, and recommendations derived from those delivering services should be sought by administrators and supervisory personnel and incorporated into the decision-making process.

In hiring practices, administrators are encouraged to find individuals with substantive skills in policy research (Berry, 1981). Such employees do not need to be well-published, doctoral-level persons, but rather individuals who know how to read the literature in the field, know whom to call for specialized information, and can collect data from primary and secondary sources. Although not the only skills needed in an agency setting, these fact-finding skills will contribute to the agency's capacity to develop and use facts and data consistently in its proposals and presentations.

Olley and Ogloff (1995) and Hagen (1986) all recommend that social work advocates be factually informed about their clients' rights and the procedures that must be followed to secure entitlements or benefits. Hagen (1986) notes that administrative appeals can be challenged by the facts and the application of those facts to the standards set by policy in the agency. Studies have suggested that many clients, especially inpatients, do not remember having their rights explained to them or receiving a copy of them. Even if they were informed, many do not demonstrate an adequate understanding of their rights. It behooves administrators and internal advocates to know the facts about clients' rights and agency procedures.

Albert (1983) recommends four fact-finding questions for administrative advocates to ask when attempting to interpret regulations on behalf of clients:

- Is there a statute in existence that gives the agency authority to pass regulations on the general subject matter before you?
- Is there a statute that is the authority for the particular regulation before you?
- Is the agency's interpretation of its own regulation consistent with the statute upon which it is based?
- Is the advocate's interpretation of the regulation consistent with the statute upon which it is based?

Internal advocates are in a unique position to access the facts about a client's request. Typically, an internal advocate has complete access to all facilities, patients, and file records (Olley & Ogloff, 1995). Advocates who represent residents in facilities are usually involved in fact finding related to quality-of-life issues, privileges, privacy, confidentiality, quality-of-care issues, treatment alternatives, choice of caregivers, second opinions, legal issues such as informed consent, compulsory treatment, and access to legal services. In particular, these authors recommend that advocates be very knowledgeable about the strengths and weaknesses of psychiatric treatments in mental health facilities. Understanding the treatment debates and appropriate policy and treatment alternatives is very crucial.

Plan Strategies and Tactics

In order to be successful, administrative advocates must plan and develop strategies and tactics that will permit them to achieve their goals either internally in the agency or externally in the community. Chapter 4 provides a working model from which administrative advocates can develop their own collaborative, campaign, and contest strategies and tactics according to the circumstances. The authors provide below additional insights that can be used to advocate for change, as outlined by Johnson (1995); Olley and Ogloff (1995); Pawlak and Flynn (1990); Richan (1980); and Rothman, Erlich, and Teresa (1977):

1. Promote innovations in agencies by initiating new ideas, programs, or services with a small-scale demonstration or with a small pilot group. If it proves successful, then it can be adopted on a larger scale.

2. Modify the goals of the agency by seeking new input from clients, community groups, advisory boards, or staff members. Rather than attempt to abolish the present goals, the administrator can introduce a process that will reexamine the mission and goals by including board and staff as participants.

3. It is important that administrators have the support of their boards. Pawlak and Flynn (1990) recommend that administrators not surprise board members by getting "out in front of the board" without first informing them of advocacy activities.

4. Clarify the role performance of staff members by regular evaluations. Staff development opportunities also can be provided to encourage staff to learn content and skills in new areas such as advocacy.

5. Proposing new ideas when the leadership of an agency or its board changes is an effective strategy. At that point, there is more willingness to examine the direction, mission, and programs of an agency and a greater chance of introducing longer-lasting modifications (Johnson, 1995).

6. Administrative advocates should make their advocacy proposals as nonadversarial as possible. This approach usually reduces fear and threats to individual staff. The use of informal techniques such as small group discussions, casual conversations, and making ample information available will also assist in alleviating concerns (Olley & Ogloff, 1995).

7. Richan (1980) reminds administrators that they have three important factors on their side as they consider advocacy initiatives: (a) the *formal authority to act,* which makes others less likely to challenge them and is a generally accepted norm; (b) *control over resources,* which makes allocating tangible things like money, materials, equipment, and personnel very useful in advocating on behalf of a client or cause; and (c) *control over information,* since the administrator usually has more access than anyone else to sources of information and channels of communication.

The authors advise advocates to use only those tactics that directly support a collaborative, campaign, or contest strategy and to follow the principle of parsimony, that is, use the most modest or least confrontational tactic that will accomplish the job. The reader will recall that tactics are day-to-day, short-term, nitty-gritty steps or actions designed to increase the probability that a proposed change will be adopted. The following paragraphs discuss some tactics and provide a brief description of each.

Allow your agency to become a mentoring or sponsoring organization. Briggs and Koroloff (1995) note that emerging groups or associations often need the support of established agencies to assist them in their developmental phase. As a mentoring agency, you may provide direct services, offer information, provide bookkeeping or check-writing, or serve as a fiscal liaison between a funding source and the fledgling organization.

Give information to advocacy groups. Administrative advocates usually have access to relevant knowledge, research studies, data, trends, documents, and ideas that may be beyond the capacity of a smaller, less well-funded local action group. Such groups actually depend on administrators for program information and studies (Stockdill, 1992; Terrell, 1967). Sharing this knowledge or developing fact sheets with advocates outside the agency may provide them with information that allows them to function more effectively in bringing about change.

Establish agency programs to address needed changes. Administrators can cooperate with agency advocacy groups, residents, schools, welfare agencies, health systems, and other human service organizations to seek funding and cooperatively design an effective program to address an issue(s). Unmet needs in a community can be addressed by creating the needed services and forming programs or projects to carry out the effort (Riley, 1971).

As an agency, take a position on an issue. Sunley (1970) suggests that throwing the weight of the agency behind an issue is often very effective. Through its contacts with the press, legislators, public officials, and other agencies, the agency can publicize an unmet need or injustice. Board members may be influential citizens with clout in the community. Taking a formal position is also likely to convey to staff and clients that the agency is committed to them and to issues affecting them. Pearl and Barr (1976) also suggest that an agency give an endorsement to specific causes or events if it is sought and given approval by board members.

Participate in demonstration projects. Even though demonstration projects are long-term in nature, an agency can focus on an unmet need such as poverty or mental illness among the homeless and demonstrate leadership in addressing a difficult problem (Sunley, 1970). If there is success on a small scale, then the results may be transferable to institutions or larger systems. Demonstration projects also yield information about the need for assistance and the impact on certain populations. Funding sources usually require such data before providing funding on a large scale.

Organize a workshop. Fox (1989), Pearl and Barr (1976), and Sunley (1970) all suggest that organizations can use workshops or conferences as a very effective advocacy tool. A workshop promotes three things: (1) it brings together a variety of constituents to consider a particular social problem; (2) it heightens public awareness of a condition or problem; and (3) it becomes a starting point for action for those who wish to pursue further steps. By presenting the facts on a condition in the community, participants often influence officials at agencies to change. Such workshops will also bring to the surface potential adversaries or issues that may block future actions.

Select a diverse mix of board members. In order to enhance an agency's credibility with the community, decision makers, funding sources, and citizen groups, Pearl and Barr (1976) recommend that administrators compose their boards with individuals from a variety of professions, agencies, government levels, laypersons, and activists. Although recruitment may be labor-intensive, it usually pays off in increased responsiveness to community issues and access to power and influential decision makers.

In coalitions, provide team-building training to improve effectiveness. Doss and Idleman (1994) studied the needs of community-based groups seeking to bring innovations to problem-solving situations. Team-building was listed as the greatest need. Other factors were the coordination of assessment efforts, regular meetings, clarification of the roles of all participants, and developing collaborative relationships among the members.

Hire a government relations staff person or lobbyist. Fox (1989) and Rickards (1992) recommend that agencies or groups that want to be heard on their issues hire someone who has experience in working as a lobbyist and who is knowledgeable about the issues. Despite the best intentions, administrators and their staff may not have the time to devote to contacting the decision makers or organizing volunteer members to make phone calls or write letters. By hiring an experienced person with skills in persuading decision makers, the agency or coalition of agencies stands a better chance of advancing its agenda and issues.

Send agency newsletters to relevant decision makers. Haynes and Mickelson (1997) recommend that advocates in agency settings routinely disseminate their agency's newsletters or other documents to state legislators, government officials, other agencies, and civic groups. The payoff is increased visibility and public awareness of the agency's agenda. In the future, the agency administrator and other decision makers may have already broadened their perspectives about each other and can more easily find common ground.

Be aware of relevant state statutes, client rights, and various professional standards. Internal advocates as well as administrators can often advance their client's cause by ensuring that appropriate and current state laws and regulations are applied fairly and regularly. Basic and fundamental rights such as the right to treatment, use of phones, privacy, access, benefits, and confidentiality are often abridged or encroached upon. Through expert knowledge of the existing policies and legislation, administrative advocates can effectively remedy conditions faced by clients.

Design internal advocacy programs to be proactive as well as reactive.
Advocates often wait for clients or patients to instruct them about what to do
or to identify an issue that is bothering them. The advocate then reacts to this
instruction by taking steps to remedy it. Olley and Ogloff (1995) suggest that
advocates should also work in a more preventative sense by educating clients
and their families about certain rights, privileges, benefits, and opportunities.
Some clients are unable to give direction due to mental illness or incompe-
tence, and some children may not be protected adequately. The advocate who
is proactive here can assist the client and other staff to understand the issues
and prevent a loss or abuse of rights.

Supply Leadership

> *My efforts may have laid the groundwork for the acceptance of a future pro-*
> *posal. Despite our inability to secure funds for the divorce mediation service, we*
> *learned that anything of value is rarely obtained with ease or for nothing.*
>
> MELISSA

Riley (1971) relates the story of an administrator who practices advocacy, but
states that "I can understand why people resist advocacy. Everything about it
makes me nervous. I like my job. I want everyone to like me. Politicians scare
me and reporters do too. I never know what my board members will think"
(p. 380). In a recent survey of Family Service Agency executives, Perlmutter
and Adams (1994) note that social work administrators may be limiting themselves to managerial roles rather than acting as institutional leaders or advocates. These authors fear that executives are focusing heavily on financial and
survival concerns while devoting little attention to positioning their agencies
for the future. Younger executives in their survey disclosed little hope for
advocating for services at the state and local levels, and expressed little interest in forging alliances with other nonprofits.

On the other hand, Ezell (1991) found in a study of social work administrators that macro (versus micro) practitioners more routinely saw advocacy as
a part of their jobs and were more likely to belong to organizations that take
public stands on issues. In a 1986 study by Reisch, effective advocacy organizations (as opposed to ineffective ones) were led by social work administrators.
Ezell (1991) notes that it is too narrow to perceive administrators as largely
responsible for constraining change; his research leads to the conclusion that
much change is actually initiated from above.

In sum, such divergent views provide little solace and clarity to those who
wish to lead their agencies and staff toward an advocacy stance. But, agreement
is clear about the role of leadership and its significance in advancing organizational and political agendas on behalf of clients. The following text outlines several key dimensions of leadership affecting administrative advocates today.

Factors that Contribute to Effective Administrative Advocacy   From the literature (Ezell, 1991; Kirst-Ashman & Hull, 1993; Mailick & Ashley, 1981; Richan, 1980; Roberts, 1983; Sunley, 1970; Villone, 1983) come several factors that contribute toward administrative advocates leading their agencies and staff effectively toward successful advocacy outcomes:

1. Administrators have the legitimate authority vested in their role by the board or officials who hire them. By virtue of this authority, leaders can initiate activities, promote discussions, set agendas, or facilitate change on many issues. Employees often believe that administrators have a "right" to influence them.

2. Most administrators have the power to obtain resources such as funding, grants, buildings and space, and material that would support a new program or shift emphasis within existing ones.

3. Within many agencies, administrators have access to more sources of information than anyone else. Controlling this information through its distribution, availability, and use gives the leaders additional leverage to lead.

4. Successful leaders frequently view staff not just as employees, but as members who are essential to the life of the agency, integrating them into the organization's formal and informal decision-making structures.

5. Administrative advocates often have access to sources of power that assist them in leading their agencies. "Reward" power is the ability to give positive reinforcements such as praise, salary, raises, recognition, and promotions to staff. "Coercive" power also exists whereby administrators can impose negative reinforcements on staff such as loss of position or title, demotions, replacement, poor evaluations, and reassignment.

6. Administrators provide leadership by modeling the behavior they hope for in their staff or board. Staff can judge by agency budget allocations whether or not the administrator truly believes in advocacy issues and projects. Leaders must also demonstrate a willingness to risk themselves for what they believe.

7. Effective leaders must keep their proposals feasible so that decision makers see that what is proposed can be carried out in practice. Great ideas that are impractical or resistant to implementation result in disastrous consequences.

8. Capable administrators should be well prepared and educated not only in technical aspects of their work, but also more broadly in macroeconomics, demography, policy analysis, and legislative and legal research.

One leadership model for successful administrative advocates includes the following capacities: (1) attention to mediating conflicts internal to the agency;

(2) policy development including innovation and translation of agency policy into program design; (3) managerial skills involving coordination and integration of the agency operation through fiscal, personnel, and information management; and (4) attention to the quality and responsiveness of services being delivered to clients.

Barriers to Administrative Advocacy   Barriers also exist that prevent or discourage administrative advocates from taking action (Ezell, 1991; Jaffe, 1978; Patti, 1974; Perlmutter & Adams, 1994; Richan, 1983). These are discussed in the following paragraphs.

Fear of dismissal. When advocates engage in dissent or disagreement with agency policies or have conflict with the board and administration, there is the possibility of job loss. Whether this threat is employed to neutralize advocacy efforts or not, it does confront the advocate with loss of income, negative job references, inconvenience, geographic mobility, and potential loss of professional identification.

Opportunities for job advancement. Employees who seek greater recognition, money, and status usually try to advance their careers through the administrative hierarchy. The potential costs associated with internal or external advocacy rise dramatically when issues of security, status, and upward mobility are considered. Approval by the board or superiors becomes a significant issue and may well modify advocates' behaviors.

Fiscal and operational concerns. Agency executives today are facing survival issues usually related to fiscal and operational concerns. Focus on managerial issues of reduced funding, defensive strategies, staff tensions, excessive workloads, complex client problems, and competition is so intense that the capacity for leadership is often undermined. Workers become conditioned to norms dictated by management considerations, not professional ones. Administrators become preoccupied with managing rather than leading. Leadership functions of strategic planning, defining and refining the agency mission, designing innovative services, serving new clientele, and formulating new policies are lost or diminished in an era of cost-cutting. Richan (1983) warns that the path to collective suicide is remaining aloof from the political and policy arenas. Others will make the important decisions affecting both clients and social work professionals.

Hatch Act and Internal Revenue Code 501(c)(3). Administrative advocates working for the federal government agencies and nonprofit agencies often believe themselves limited in the type and amount of advocacy and lobbying that they can undertake. (State and local governments also have some version of the Hatch Act policy in effect.) Violations of these statutes, which prevent employees from participating in partisan political activities, it is feared, may lead to job loss or loss of tax-exempt status. Pawlak and Flynn (1990) and Thompson (1994) note that it is understandable that fear and uncertainty exist, since these laws are very complex, they are interpreted differentially in judicial and administrative settings, and there are legislative amendments offering exemptions, inclusions, exceptions, contradictory opinion, and subjective listings of what is considered permissible (Haynes & Mickelson, 1997; Pawlak & Flynn, 1990, p. 311; Smucker, 1999; Thompson, 1994). (See Appendix B for a summary of the Hatch Act and for additional suggestions on determining how to decide to practice advocacy in an agency and Appendix C for a summary of the IRS 501(c)(3) and (4) regulations.)

Get to Know Decision Makers and Their Staff

It is clear from Chapter 4 that knowing personally those who are in a position to decide policies is crucial to an advocate's ability to influence or change decisions affecting a client. Administrative advocates initially seem to have ready access to decision makers because they may actually be one of the decision makers (administrator or executive director), an agency employee who works in the same building with decision makers, or an internal advocate hired by decision makers to represent the needs of clients. While it is true that these individuals are well positioned to influence decision makers, there are special principles for administrative advocates in "getting to know the decision makers." Among them are: (1) include advocacy within the agency structure; (2) recall that organizational decision making is not rational; (3) remember that internal advocates have advantages over external advocates—sometimes; and (4) make a list of decision makers every administrator should know.

Advocacy Within the Agency Structure   Administrative advocates are urged to encourage the development of plans and structures that include advocacy activities as part of the ongoing operation of the agency. Many agencies do not have an agencywide structure dedicated to advocacy (Sunley, 1970), and isolated efforts by the board or administrators such as letter-writing or passing resolutions have little effect. Staff and the agency itself see themselves as too small and inactive to accomplish more than long-distance connections to decision makers in the state or community. By using a planful approach through education and pilot projects, administrators can establish rapport over time with board members, encouraging them to become vital participants, rather than passive spectators, in influencing conditions affecting clients (Riley, 1971).

A structural model of advocacy outlined by Taylor (1987) is recommended as a place to start. (See Figure 8.1.) Following the model from the top and clockwise, an adminstrator begins with the purpose or mission of the agency, for example, to provide high-quality in-home health and personal services, and the agency goals and objectives, for example, to serve low-income frail elders in a given community and to achieve a unit cost at the lowest level possible.

From these benchmarks, the administrator analyzes how these parameters can be further developed from an advocacy perspective. Is there a great gap in services? Is accessibility a problem for some? Is there adequate funding?

With answers to these questions in mind, the administrator can then formulate agency advocacy goals and objectives in the form of a program. The administrator, board, and staff may want to increase the number of frail elders served in a 12-month period. They may want to do outreach to identify citizens eligible for in-home health benefits. They may want to advocate for greater funding to recruit and retain certified nursing assistants. Once the issues and goals are set, the administrator can lead staff and board in planning strategies and tactics that they can pursue. It requires organizing people, developing step-by-step actions, analyzing the opposition, and securing the necessary resources.

Using the plan of action developed, a program can be carried out and implemented over time. Not everything will go as planned, and adjustments will need to be made. The adminstrator should provide leadership, encouragement,

THE PROCESS OF ADVOCACY

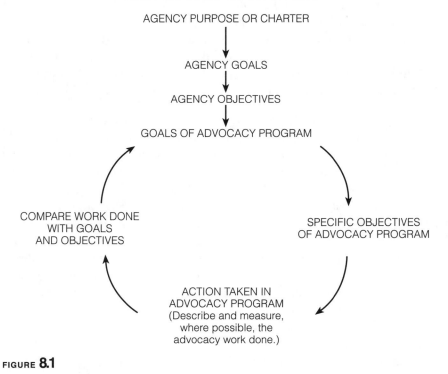

FIGURE **8.1**

A structural model of advocacy.

Source: Taylor, E.D. (1987). *From issue to action: An advocacy program model* (p. 125). Lancaster, PA: Family Service

and demonstrate the persistence required to carry out the advocacy activities. Afterward, the achievements of the advocacy effort should be evaluated and compared with the original goals and objectives. How many frail elderly were served? At what actual cost? What were unintended consequences? This is the cycle of advocacy behind Figure 8.1.

Decision Making Is Not Rational Sonnichsen (1989) reminds administrative advocates that organizational decision making seldom takes place in a rational, sequential fashion and often precipitates conflict and confusion. Many factors contribute to the irrationality of decision making in agencies: past history and reputation of the agency, key events, funding sources, members of the boards and their preferences, inner dynamics of staff, levels of trust between management and staff, communication channels, external forces in the community and society, and other factors too numerous to mention here. At the very least, advocates must try to understand the key decision makers and their staff who are in the middle of this dynamic process.

Advantages of Internal Advocates Internal advocates can be very effective in carrying out their role of representing the needs of those who cannot speak out or who do not have natural advocates within a service delivery system. These advocates are on the scene constantly and can inspect the machinery of the bureaucracy in order to see if client priorities are being met (Riddle & King, 1977). In-house advocates also can actually accompany a client with his or her requests to the decision makers and help clarify or negotiate the changes needed. Sitting in on treatment team meetings or meetings regarding the clients also allows the in-house advocate to ensure the clients' rights and needs are considered appropriately. If adequate solutions are not found at staff or supervisory levels, internal advocates may use their clout to go to the director's office for further review.

It is important to have good relations with the staff, and this often makes the internal advocate more effective than an external one (Olley & Ogloff, 1995). By working alongside staff in a facility or service system, internal advocates can overcome the usual apprehension, mistrust, and reservations. There are times that an external advocate may be able to exert more influence over a circumstance, but it is usually at a crisis point by that time.

Decision Makers Whom Administrators Should Know Administrators of agencies are urged in particular to get to know decision makers in certain sectors (Berry, 1981; Pawlak & Flynn 1990; Pearl & Barr, 1976). First, they should become involved in the local community and get to know county commissioners, members of city council, state representatives from the region, and civic, business, and religious leaders. "If you don't know anyone, you aren't going anywhere" (Pawlak & Flynn, 1990, p. 310). Second, they should develop a network of contacts within the government, particularly at the local and state levels. Sending copies of correspondence, reports, research studies, agency initiatives, newsletters, and other materials to these contacts will familiarize officials with your agency's initiatives. Finally, Pawlak and Flynn (1990) recommend establishing close contact with lower-level staff in government and other agencies in addition to the standard interactions with politicians and appointed officials. Much of one's influence can develop behind closed doors between the administrator and staff members.

Broaden the Base of Support

Internal advocates are encouraged to build support for their proposals for change in much the same way as external advocates do. However, in addition to building external support through coalitions, there is also a special emphasis open for most administrators and internal advocates: a focus on collaboration with others *within* the agency. The following text provides several key findings that will help administrative advocates become effective in expanding support for their proposals for change.

Herr (1983) urges advocates to build a confederation of advocacy organizations that could lead to a statewide structure. He envisions a durable coalition that would overcome the many barriers of coalition building such as duplication of efforts, limited resources and funds, multiple voices, and disorganized planning. Such collaborative efforts could strive to reach consensus on priority issues and identify uncovered geographic regions. Herr also notes that such cooperation and cohesion is still an isolated phenomenon.

Stockdill (1992), Pawlak and Flynn (1990), and Berry (1981) agree that administrators can accomplish more of their advocacy goals if they engage external allies to support them. These authors recommend that administrators: (1) listen closely to what consumers and families have to say, (2) recognize that associations are essential allies of the administrator in clarifying priorities and seeking resources, (3) note that providers need to be won over so they do not block efforts at change, and (4) look for client family members who are themselves trained professionals to help with planning policy development. Outside support will help agency officials reach their goals, and the agency's power position should be grounded on attentive groups with an enduring tie to the issues. Pearl and Barr (1976) also recommend that a successful community coalition uses *established* agencies to demonstrate its credibility and uses their collective influence to pursue change.

Internal advocates must learn to deal with anyone in a facility who has responsibility for a client(s). Staff members who are allied with a client are particularly important allies, and the advocate can obtain information from them about the client and his or her needs. The advocate must also maintain positive relationships with supervisors, treatment teams, upper- and lower-level staff, day and night shifts, and so on. By building support among all of these persons, the advocate will gain the credibility needed when it is time to advocate for a needed change.

Social workers who are members of interdisciplinary teams must walk a fine line between maintaining collaborative relationships with other professionals on the team and maintaining sufficient distance from the ever-present group norms that may conflict with social work values. Workers can build coalitions with others on the team with similar value orientations (Mailick & Ashley, 1981). Remaining an effective team member and preserving one's autonomy is the dilemma faced frequently by the advocate.

Johnson (1995) recommends that administrators foster broad participation by all levels of staff in the functioning of the agency. Including staff in various decision-making processes is encouraged because they see the issues or problems from a different vantage point, and if they are listened to, they will most likely support the new change. However, Taylor (1991) cautions that the process of advocacy is not an ad hoc enterprise, and that it demands consistent application and structures within the agency if it is to endure.

Be Persistent

In this section, the authors demonstrate how persistence is related to several facts about agencies, individuals in organizations, administrative processes, and changing large systems. Administrators and internal advocates can thus understand better the environment in which administrative advocacy takes place and strive to be persistent in their efforts.

Scotch and Lane (1972) remind us that organizations are not necessarily barriers to advocacy, but are mechanisms for achieving change *over time*. They state further that organizational support is a prerequisite for meaningful client advocacy. Without the financial resources, expert personnel, professional interaction, agency reputation, board members, and community sanction associated with an organization, most advocates could not sustain their efforts to improve conditions for their clients.

Typically, although not inevitably, organizations drift toward greater conservatism over time, shifting from their original ideals into greater emphasis on survival (Allen et al., 1995). Called "goal displacement," this drifting may occur slowly or rapidly depending on: (1) the rate of growth of the agency, (2) the intensity of the demands to secure resources, (3) attainment of legitimacy, and (4) the need for accountability to funding sources. Persistent and watchful attention to the agency mission is required by administrators, board members, and employees in order to avoid becoming "successful" (with the emphasis on survival) at the long-term price of weakening the agency mission.

The practice of meaningful internal advocacy can be a lonely effort, testing one's persistence. Riddle and King (1977) note that rewards and successes may be slow in coming. Building relationships with staff, persuading others in a context of mutuality, and establishing trust and confidence all require long-term efforts.

Social workers should consider how daily incorporation of advocacy into their work routines, despite heavy client demand and large caseloads, can be viewed as "short-term pain for long-term gain." Advocacy benefiting one client may well lead to improvements for others in similar situations, thus producing effects far beyond the precipitating cause. If social workers are persistent in monitoring the responsiveness of all systems serving clients, then advocacy can become an enduring mind-set and attitude leading to successful problem solving (Herbert & Mould, 1992).

Advocacy that is legitimized for all staff or vested in a particular person within an institution or agency can set the stage for many changes *over a period of time* (Riddle & King, 1977). By feeling the constant presence of an advocate, other staff ideally become more secure in advocating for the needs and rights of clients. The advocate will be called upon to double-check quasi-legal situations and to answer requests about rights of the client versus rights of the family or institution. Clients or residents are given hope because some rules actually change. They may also begin to self-advocate, following the pattern of advocates and staff who demonstrate advocacy in their job performance over time and through solving problems regularly.

Taylor (1991) is persuasive when she states that "advocacy will not be successful on an *ad hoc* basis" (p. 141). Reisch (1990) found that effective advocacy agencies were those that were likely to have maintained consistent goals over the past five years. These two authors urge advocates to understand that persistence, linked with other activities such as goal-setting, is vital to successful advocacy outcomes.

Recent data from a study by Perlmutter and Adams (1994) reveal less interest on the part of voluntary social agency administrators in advocacy skills than in computers and marketing to help keep agencies afloat. Younger respondents stated that they devote little energy to advocating for services within the local and state government sectors. These trends run counter to the research that suggests that the collective lobbying by nonprofit agencies contributed to the increases in social program expenditures in the 1960s and 1970s. Without strategies for persistent advocacy, we will experience less support from government sources and a worsening of the plight of clients.

Evaluate Your Advocacy Effort

Evaluation activities are designed to assess the effectiveness of service providers and to improve the quality of service to clients. In addition to the evaluation components in Chapter 4, there are several dimensions of evaluation that administrators and internal advocates can keep in mind that will assist them in their efforts to practice social work advocacy within an organizational context.

Herr (1983) notes that an evaluation plan is essential to the integrity of an agency's advocacy mission. But, while evaluation provides useful information to decision makers, it also creates fear and resistance. It is human nature to resent criticism and resist change, and although few persons accept criticism gracefully, fewer still learn and grow from critical information associated with programs in which they are involved (Sonnichsen, 1989). This phenomenon applies equally to administrators, program managers, and staff, all of whom may feel threatened by or become defensive about evaluative findings.

Administrative advocates do well to become students of organizational behavior and assess the influence exerted by the agency culture, traditions, and dominant decision-making processes. In order to be effective, advocates need to understand the organizational power structure, identify the major stakeholders, and acknowledge the political nature of decision making. Sonnichsen (1989) suggests the same goals for evaluators of agency programs.

Implementation of agency or legislative regulations is an important function carried out by administrators and agency employees, and it is frequently monitored by in-house advocates. Because of politics or pressure, new regulations or laws frequently are subject to not-so-subtle deviation from their original intent. Administrative advocates, by monitoring the course of implementation of policies, can develop evaluative data that can be used to ensure that the intended client need is met or service is provided (Albert, 1983).

Stockdill (1992) suggests that increased attention be given to using client family members in monitoring and evaluating mental health programs. Since the family members become familiar with nearly all aspects of the service system, they can provide invaluable insights into the quality of services provided to clients. Such collaboration between administrators, staff, and families also reinforces the "mutual" nature of social work advocacy as defined by the authors.

Administrative advocates may succeed more often if they advocate for changes based on an evaluation of organizational policy processes (Sonnichsen, 1988, 1989). The goal here is to assist in improving program effectiveness and in ensuring that program realities are represented in decision-making forums. For this to occur, a philosophy that values evaluation is required in the agency or among the top executives. Internal evaluation must be seen as a positive force that permits the agency to review core issues and traditional practices/rituals and to develop alternative approaches to improving service delivery rather than maintaining the status quo. In-house advocates should be given a highly visible spot in the agency with reporting responsibility to the upper levels of management as well as the opportunity to participate in policy-making decisions on an ongoing basis.

Internal Advocate Goes to the Boss

Michael Sidone, a long-term patient in Argent County Hospital, a mental health institution, is injured over the weekend by another patient and suffered a bruised face and strained back muscle. Eva Sidone, his wife, is not notified of the injuries by the treatment team. When she arrives on Monday to visit, Eva finds him in a distressed physical state. She asks the staff what happened and they tell her: "If he would stay out of other patients' rooms, he would not get into trouble." Eva reports her frustrating conversation with the staff to the internal (or patient) advocate at the hospital, Ms. Ardith Mimosas.

In her investigation, Ms. Mimosas uncovers violations of existing hospital procedure that calls for family members to receive notification by the hospital if there is any change in the patient's condition. She documents the status of the current policy in a written report and sends it to the chief hospital administrator. She then meets with the administrator to discuss the issue further. The chief administrator decides to emphasize this policy in subsequent memos and meetings, and staff in-service training is expanded to include recognizing the emotional needs of family members.

Source: Woodside and Legg (1990)

Blackfeet Tribal Officer Sues the Bureau of Indian Affairs

As head of a special trustee's advisory board and chairwoman of the Intertribal Monitoring Association on Trust Funds, Ms. Elouise Cobell filed a law suit in 1996 against the federal agency, the Bureau of Indian Affairs (BIA) for depriving about 300,000 Indians billions of dollars that had accumulated in trust accounts created to compensate them for use of their land and to pass along royalties from the sale of natural resources. PricewaterhouseCoopers could not find documentation to support $10 billion of transactions.

As Treasurer of the Blackfeet Nation earlier, she questioned BIA officials about their recordkeeping and they said, "Oh, you don't know how to read the reports." Such treatment left Ms. Cobell mad. When the issue of the trust accounts seemed to go on the backburner, she and other plantiffs sued. Some

Continued

relatives and friends were angry with her. But her persistance brought the issue to a head. Said one observer, "Elouise moves with a quiet power that blew it out the water." Ms. Cobell says she would be as guilty of neglect as the government if she hadn't acted on her knowledge of the BIA's action. "As your eyes open, you would feel criminal if you didn't," she says.

Source: Fawcett (1999)

SUMMARY

In this chapter, we discussed two types of administrative advocates: (1) agency administrators who do engage themselves or their agencies in advocacy, and (2) administratively appointed "internal advocates" who are responsible for increasing the effectiveness of client services or addressing agency practices or procedures that are harmful to clients. Administrators often find themselves in key positions to lead advocacy efforts. They can establish structures for advocacy practice in their agencies and work with ongoing coalitions in the community. Internal advocates can effect great change within an agency as ombudsmen, client representatives, and/or unit advocates. Frequently they address agency policies or procedures that are harmful to clients, investigate internal complaints by clients or families, evaluate events or incidents that affect clients and staff, and call attention to violations of client rights. By developing knowledge and skills in representation and influencing, administrative advocates advance their clients' interests in effective and significant ways.

DISCUSSION QUESTIONS

1. What is your personal experience with "administrators as advocates"? Can they really serve as advocates?
2. What are some of the reasons why agencies resist making advocacy a "normal" part of their mission?
3. Is internal advocacy as important as external advocacy? Why or why not?
4. Why is it so important for advocates to know the factual circumstances of a client's right(s) to entitlement benefits?

5. In what ways can administrative advocates improve their ability to persuade others to change policies or programs?
6. What can in-house advocates do to overcome the fear and suspicion other staff members may have toward them?
7. How does an agency actually advance the goals of an advocate?
8. What is the best method(s) to learn how to negotiate and to probe for solutions?
9. If agency administrators have the greatest access to information, why do they often appear reluctant to share it widely?
10. How does an employee decide the amount of job risk he or she is willing to take about an issue in the agency that affects clients negatively?

RECOMMENDED READINGS

Ezell, M. (1991). Administrators as advocates. *Administration in Social Work, 15,* 1–18.

Perlmutter, F. D., & Adams, C. T. (1994). Family service executives in a hostile environment. *The Journal of Contemporary Human Services, 75,* 439–446.

Reisch, M. (1990). Organizational structure and client advocacy: Lessons from the 1980s. *Social Work, 35,* 73–74.

Richan, W. C. (1980). The administrator as advocate. In F. D. Perlmutter & S. Slavin (Eds.), *Leadership in social administration* (pp. 72–85). Philadelphia: Temple University Press.

Simons, R. L. (1988). Generic social work skills in social administration: The example of persuasion. *Administration in Social Work, 11,* 241–254.

Taylor, E. D. (1991). The role of structure in effective agency advocacy. *Social Work with Groups, 14,* 141–151.

part four

CONCLUSION

CHAPTER 9
ADVOCACY TRENDS AND
PRACTICE IMPLICATIONS

ADVOCACY TRENDS AND PRACTICE IMPLICATIONS

There is no rule that says that once we have acted on behalf of a specific client
we must let the matter die there. We have a responsibility not to.

RICHAN (1973)

OVERVIEW

By now you have read about social work advocacy's history, studied the various
definitions analyzed and applied through the years, absorbed and assimilated a
new definition, and learned about its general framework and specific practice
parameters. You have also read several chapters applying the general advocacy
framework to the following social work orientations and practice areas—client,
cause, legislation, and administration. The authors hope that they have stimu-
lated your interest. You may now be wondering how social work advocacy will
be practiced in the new millennium and, more importantly, what issues will predominate. This final chapter will address these and other related issues.

9.1

Based on numerous child abuse crises, the Massachusetts NASW chapter and a
dozen college deans raised $10,000 to research and report on the ineffectiveness,
high cost, and inhumane treatment of its child welfare system. According to the
NASW News (July 1999), "Our Children and Families: A Social Work Statement
Addressing Child Abuse and Neglect," released in March 1999, documented high
caseloads, a "small percentage of licensed social workers in the system and an inadequate number of effective prevention programs" (p. 8). This report also outlined a
proposed model of reform and reorganization using prevention, early intervention,
and protection as the foundation. Since the document's release, legislators, the interim social services commissioner, and the media have taken a great deal of interest in
Massachusetts's child welfare system, and have requested meetings with the project's
organizers to discuss the findings and proposal.

WHOM DO ADVOCATES REPRESENT?

Over the past 125 years, advocacy's client base has, in many respects,
remained the same; in other respects it has significantly changed. During social
work's earliest years, those individuals directly impacted by advocacy practice
were under the auspices of mental health, corrections, and indigent legislation.
In later decades, advocacy's client base shifted to immigrants and oppressed
groups such as women, children, and minorities. During the 1930s, advocacy's
client base changed focus as it supported individuals suffering from extreme

financial hardship during the Great Depression. Numerous safety net entitlements were thus proposed, enacted, and implemented in subsequent years.

Although these historic client populations have remained constant throughout social work's history, numerous biopsychosocial stressors have changed the dynamics of our constituent populations. For instance, at the beginning of the 20th century, nuclear and extended families were the norm. With the shift toward women's professional emancipation in the 1920s, divorce was commonplace and single-parent families were accepted. Contemporarily, step, blended, adoptive, biracial, and homosexual families have joined the ranks of nuclear and extended family structures and relationships. "Female-headed households—single mothers with children—are the fastest growing type of family" in our society (Day, 1989, p. 11). Numerous advocacy efforts have addressed and continue to address issues for individuals and groups within these populations. We anticipate that the future will hold new challenges as families continue to diversify, particularly as infertility interventions such as surrogacy, *in vitro* fertilization, third-party sperm/egg availability, and scientific technology continue to advance and be accepted by mainstream society. In conjunction with these accepted medical practices, children abandoned by or terminated from biological parents will be difficult to place in future years. These children will become clients based on their continued vulnerability.

Advocacy has also helped indigent, vulnerable, and displaced populations for more than a century. Historically, those most frequently represented were immigrants, women, and children. Where immigrants were predominantly from European backgrounds, those currently represented are primarily of Central American, South American, and Asian descent. Social workers continue to advocate with, for, and on behalf of individuals within all these populations, although their constituent groups have been expanded to include other minorities such as individuals with physical, emotional, and mental disabilities; the frail and isolated elderly; refugees; homosexuals; and war veterans, among others. As our world becomes more complex through time, many of these populations will undoubtedly integrate into mainstream society, and others needing advocacy attention and efforts will emerge.

Because social work is often perceived as paternalistic in nature, there has been a move toward "consumerism" over the past decade. In essence, clients represented by social work practitioners are now identified as purchasers of services. Since consumers are better educated and more sophisticated than they were throughout history, many feel they command the right to hold providers accountable for quality of care and service delivery. As such, consumers are often involved in every phase of planning, delivery, and service evaluation. Under this model, personal autonomy and consumer choice are ensured, which includes the ability to choose and change providers, as well as the ability to establish advance directives. "In the social service arena, concern for consumer choice has led to . . . increased choices about the institutions from which they can seek and receive human services" (Stern & Gibelman, 1990, p. 16).

In order to help guide this process, the National Mental Health Association outlined numerous consumer rights, which include, among others: (1) choice, (2) grievance procedures, (3) emergency care, (4) ombudsman services, (5) information, (6) treatment decisions, (7) services, (8) appeals, (9) confidentiality, (10) access to records, (11) access to advocates, and (12) reasonable convenience, among others (Gabriele, 1997; Pritchard, 1997). Based on these and other variables, advocacy's client base will continue to shift and change throughout and beyond the 21st century, which will thus make advocacy practices more accountable to its clientele.

9.2

Following the wrongful death of a 16-year-old boy who died of asphyxiation while being restrained at an inpatient psychiatric hospital in North Carolina, a recent University of Pennsylvania MSW graduate was asked by his dean to participate in a research project designed to uncover "the way psychiatric facilities conduct business" (O'Neill, 1999, p. 4). Terrance Johnson agreed to work with CBS's *60 Minutes* on this project. Rigged with a hidden camera and videotape recorder, Johnson was hired by Charter Pines Hospital in Charlottesville, North Carolina, as a mental health technician. During his period of employment, Johnson found and recorded numerous shocking incidents to include: (1) the facility used undertrained and undereducated employees to facilitate mental health groups, restrain children, and complete mental health assessments on patients; (2) professionals wrote session notes about patients not seen; and (3) counselors were encouraged to emphasize patients' negative characteristics in order to obtain insurance reimbursement. Following this research and exposure, the University of Pennsylvania's School of Social Work developed a seminar using this material to highlight using the media as an agent of social change.

WHICH ISSUES TYPIFY ADVOCACY?

Social workers have historically and traditionally advocated for social justice issues as well as basic human rights. During the turn of the 20th century, prevalent social justice issues centered on minimum social standards that included: (1) living wages; (2) reasonable working hours and conditions; (3) available and appropriate education; (4) sufficient and adequate food, clothing, and shelter; (5) recreational opportunities; (6) individual safety and security; (7) health care and medical intervention; (8) accessible transportation; and (9) freedom from government corruption (Tucker, 1913). Moving through the next few decades, financial stability and family security were often highlighted as prominent social issues. As organizations emerged to address deficits related to these issues, individual and institutional discrimination emerged, to include the traditional *isms* (i.e., racism, sexism, and ageism, among others). These issues continue to highlight a large part of our advocacy work.

In conjunction with social justice issues, practitioners also advocate for basic human rights. According to the Universal Declaration of Human Rights:

> [A]ll human beings are born free and equal in dignity and rights. They include "positive rights" such as the right to life, liberty, and security of person; to recognition as a person before the law with equal protection; to a nationality; to freedom of thought, conscience, and religion and "negative rights" such as protection from slavery or servitude, arbitrary arrest, detention, or exile. They also include the economic, social, and cultural rights indispensable for dignity and development; the right to work, including equal pay for equal work; and the right to a standard of living adequate for health and well-being, including food, clothing, housing, medical care, and necessary social services. (Witkin, 1998, p. 197)

These rights expand upon constitutionally mandated laws enacted to accord immigrants equal opportunities in our society. Unfortunately, not all individuals and organizations are committed to ensuring equal rights to all constituents and related populations.

Social justice and human rights continue to be integral to social work advocacy practice. Consider, for example, the following federal authorizing legislation proposed and enacted during the last decade of the 20th century:

- P.L. 105-89, the Adoption and Safe Families Act of 1997
- P.L. 105-33, the State Children's Health Insurance Program
- P.L. 104-204, the Mental Health Parity Act of 1996
- P.L. 104-91, the Health Insurance Reform Act
- P.L. 103-66, the Family Preservation and Support Services Provisions
- P.L. 103-3, the Family and Medical Leave Act
- P.L. 102-321, the Alcohol, Drug Abuse, and Mental Health Administration Reorganization Act
- P.L. 102-166, the Civil Rights Act
- P.L. 101-381, the Ryan White Comprehensive AIDS Resources Emergency Act
- 42 U.S.C. 1210, the Americans with Disabilities Act
- P.L. 100-259, the Civil Rights Restoration Act
- P.L. 100-360, the Medicare Catastrophic Coverage Act
- P.L. 96-272, the Adoption Assistance and Child Welfare Act
- P.L. 100-435, the Hunger Prevention Act
- P.L. 100-485, the Family Support Act
- P.L. 100-77, the Stewart B. McKinney Homeless Assistance Act

On one level, social workers advocate for the development, enactment, and implementation of these and other policies; on another level, social workers advocate within micro and mezzo communities to ensure these entitlements not only are available, but also are accessible to clients. Efforts devoted to these issues constitute a large part of social work advocacy.

Fair and equitable employment has also been a prominent focus for advo-cacy practitioners. The turn of the 20th century presented several employment challenges as the workforce shifted from agriculture to manufacturing. At that time, immigrants, women, and children were often exploited by factory owners, employers, and other decision makers. The turn of the 21st century has pre-sented similar challenges as the workforce has shifted from manufacturing to information processing and service delivery. With computers and advanced technology replacing the skilled and unskilled labor force, more and more indi-viduals have been forced into low-paying, low-satisfaction tertiary service posi-tions such as food service, housekeeping and cleaning, retail and sales, customer service, and so on. These types of positions rarely pay much beyond the mini-mum wage, hardly livable wages in our advanced and automated society. Further, the availability of advanced technology has promoted an employer-friendly workforce. According to Hoechstetter (1996), "corporate downsizing has added to the problem. So far in the 1990s, about one in every 20 workers has lost their jobs . . . only about 35 percent of displaced workers are finding jobs at pay equal to or higher than the jobs they lost" (p. 88).

During and following the 1930s, numerous safety nets were implemented to ensure economic protection for vulnerable populations. Many entitlement programs that we take for granted—including Medicaid, Medicare, Old Age Disability, Social Security, unemployment insurance, and so on—were insti-tuted during that era. However, during the 1990s the federal government began to demonstrate its retreat from this commitment. Block grants became the political norm in an effort to transfer program implementation and fund-ing responsibilities to state and local grants.

Recall that Chapter 1 discussed the increasing political shift from direct, hands-on involvement to privatization over the last two decades. This

---

9.3

Throughout 1998, social workers observed the profession's centennial by identi-fying with and acting on early social work traditions. Among them were NASW's Pennsylvania and North Dakota chapters. The "Poor People's Summit," held at the Temple University School of Social Administration on October 9–11, 1998, high-lighted social workers supporting indigent people in the community, particularly working welfare recipients. Specifically, social workers from these two chapters pub-licized and facilitated this event; those who attended the Summit were asked "to either give financial assistance to groups that want to attend or to give their time by volunteering at the event" (*NASW News*, October 1998, p. 4). Support included help with child care, accommodations, fundraising, and developing presentations for the event. As part of the Summit, recent SUNY/Rockport social work graduates "organ-ized a rally, press coverage and a dinner for Kensington Welfare Rights Union mem-bers who toured the nation during the summer to publicize their stance that U.S. welfare reform violates principles of the United Nations' 1948 Universal Declaration of Human Rights" (*NASW News*, October 1998, p. 4).

"new federalism" was designed to decentralize the federal government's role for social welfare entitlement programs while simultaneously reducing and balancing the national deficit. Thus, power and authority are being transferred back to the states. It is important to note that these programs are crucial to the survival of vulnerable, displaced, and at-risk populations. Within broad federal guidelines, states have the flexibility to design, structure, and implement entitlement programs around their specific constituents or economies. In order to advocate effectively for social work clients, practitioners need to understand the numerous hidden political agendas built into block grant ideologies and methodologies:

1. While block grants emphasize reducing and balancing the federal budget, they concurrently target reduced discretionary funding for domestic programs.
2. While the federal government has transferred power and authority back to the states, it has also reduced future economic growth through block grant capitation. Thus, during economic hardships or recessions, states will need to increase jurisdictional taxes, restrict program eligibility, or reduce individual and group benefits in order to maintain these devolved entitlement programs. (Bailey & Koney, 1996)

Grant funding currently supports most contemporary social welfare programs. This devolution will have a detrimental snowball effect for vulnerable and displaced populations; its long-term impact will not be realized for several decades. In addition to budget controls, other detrimental variables include restrictions on entitlement allocations, selective tax reductions, and means-tested benefits for individuals and families identified as socially responsible. Federal protections, fair hearings, grievance procedures, and equitable benefit and equal access measures will be minimized among the states (Weil, 1996). As part of this devolution, social workers should expect to see continued social service privatization efforts that include offers of purchaser of service (POS) agreements and other enticements meant to attract agencies and practitioners into service provision (Edwards, Cooke, & Reid, 1996). "Unless consumers, social workers, and other local leaders provide input into these processes, there remains a substantial risk that decentralization and competition will inevitably perpetuate a quantity-over-quality approach to service delivery or cause the states to engage in a 'race to the bottom'—a race to cut welfare benefits faster than their neighbors, thereby endangering the well-being of the most marginal members of society" (Bailey & Koney, 1996, p. 604).

Exactly how does new federalism impact social work clients? To begin with, the quality and quantity of service delivery has significantly declined. Crucial staff positions have been eliminated, and specialized services are often restricted. Preventive interventions are either minimized or nonexistent, and crisis intervention has become standard practice. Public service organizations

---

9.4

During late 1997 and early 1998, as welfare reform legislation was being discussed and drafted, several NASW chapters actively advocated against the punitive policies under consideration. Several chapters, including New York and Colorado, testified before legislators about the egregious provisions proposed. In addition, Mississippi chapter members, social work students, and faculty distributed approximately 5,000 brochures about "What Clients Should Know About MS's Welfare Reform Plan" throughout the state. These brochures, left at social service agencies, grocery stores, county health departments, and Head Start offices, "outlined benefits, requirements for receiving them and situations that would bring sanctions and loss of benefits" (*NASW News,* January 1998, p. 13). Chapter members also collected stories about welfare reform effects on clients that they planned to share with legislators and policy makers. The New Mexico chapter's advocacy focused on the effect welfare reform would have on the state's 22 federally recognized Indian tribes (*NASW News,* January 1998, p. 13).

---

are now required to monitor contracted services, which deflects manpower and resources to document accountability rather than service provision. Policy decisions are often delayed, which creates individual and community frustration. As competition for federal aid intensifies, states with minimal federal assistance will need to raise taxes or reduce services. These combined factors have increased personal hardship for vulnerable and displaced populations. According to Weil (1996), "with all of these trends, the nonprofit and government sectors, in which most social workers practice, will face great challenges in dealing with local social problems and needs" (p. 39).

How do we address the problems associated with these restrictive policies? First, practitioners need to get more involved in federal, state, and municipal policy development using legislative, administrative, and cause advocacy practice parameters. It is important to note that legal, judicial, and administrative forums are frequently used to impact policy change. As discussed in Chapter 5, the courts are increasingly asked to make decisions on issues such as procreation, inheritance, marriage, divorce, child support, adoption, termination of parental rights, and the rights of unwed fathers and grandparents. According to Spakes (1987), "the issues are becoming more complex as judges balance the competing interests of spouses, children, state governments, and other concerned parties (including communities, agencies, natural parents, foster parents, surrogate parents, grandparents, and adoptive parents)" (p. 31). Decisions made in these proceedings directly impact social policy legislation. As such, this corollary trend provides numerous opportunities for advocates to impact social policy development in routinely accessible forums.

Social service agencies need to further develop interorganizational collaborations that involve clients in grassroots efforts to ensure unified success:

> In a political and social climate where individual input often is overshadowed by larger, more organized groups, the community-based collaborative structure allows individuals and local organizations to work together, thereby increasing their collective power and resources to effect change. Ensuring the active participation of consumers, residents, or neighborhoods in these collaboratives makes them community based. (Bailey & Koney, 1996, p. 605)

As discussed throughout this book, social work practitioners have the knowledge, skill, and values necessary to initiate and lead these collaborative, community-based initiatives. This is an area that needs increased social work and advocacy focus. Finally, social workers must provide more aggressive and effective client advocacy strategies to ensure that clients receive the services and benefits they are entitled to under law.

Health and mental health care are other advocacy issues prevalent throughout social work history. During the turn of the 20th century, the focus was on institutionalizing those individuals considered dangerous to society. However, following deinstitutionalism efforts during the 1980s, advocacy's primary focus has been to provide a continuity of quality health and mental health care to consumers in the least restrictive environment, that is, within communities and families. Issues pertinent to health and mental health fall within the domain of managed care.

Recall that Medicaid managed care was a by-product of social policy and entitlement devolution designed to contain costs, facilitate high-quality health care services, and increase access to Medicaid. These policies and practices have since transformed our fee-for-services health care delivery system into the country's most popular health care vendor (Poole, 1996). Managed care consists of numerous strategies to ensure that the health care system provides fiscal responsibility and acceptable quality services; it "is now the primary model under which health and mental health services are delivered in the for-profit, nonprofit, and public sectors" (Poole, 1996, p. 393).

Managed care has become standard practice across the nation because it reduces or eliminates those health care services deemed ineffective or unnecessary. Underlying principles include (1) controlling utilization costs to reduce budgets, (2) providing financial incentives to those health care providers that limit client services, (3) managing treatment plan case reviews through preestablished criteria, and (4) using primary care physicians as gatekeepers for health and mental health care (Berkman, 1996). Based on the swift immersion into the behavioral health care system, practitioners must quickly adapt to and understand managed care's regulatory requirements, legal mandates, technical service provisions, and reimbursement protocols (Gibelman, 1999; Poole, 1996). Among the litany of new services and terminology, social workers should understand the similarities and differences between preferred provider organizations, exclusive provider organizations, health maintenance organization plans, managed indemnity plans, and point-of-service plans, as well as a host of new terminology including capitation financing, service bundling, and cost-efficiency (Berkman, 1996; Poole, 1996).

Gibelman (1999) reported that "mental health is the fastest growing area of social work practice. [As such,] managed care has the potential of limiting the role of social workers, as well as the quality and quantity of services available to the clients" (p. 305). Exactly how does managed care impact clients and social work practitioners? First, it limits confidentiality, freedom of choice, self-determination, quality of care, service availability and accessibility, informed consent, research protocols, client rights, and participation in treatment decisions. Managed care also restricts professional autonomy, blurs professional roles, and enhances job insecurity (Poole, 1996).

9.5

In February 1999, Stephen Gorin, the Executive Director of NASW's New Hampshire chapter, delivered a message to President Clinton about the need for a federal patients' bill of rights. Citing the fact that (1) families are often denied access to specialists because physicians are given incentives to limit their number of referrals, and (2) consumers are frequently denied the right to appeal health care decisions, Gorin urged that President Clinton "hold out for legislation that will provide real protection and ensure the accountability of managed care organizations to consumers" (Slavin, 1999, p. 4).

Social work practitioners should understand that managed care's success or failure will be measured by individual and collective responses to these and other changes. For example, if practitioners respond as victims, managed care will become more destructive than constructive. Those practitioners capable of measuring outcomes rather than caseloads or methodologies will have a better chance of survival than those who do not. In addition, Poole (1996) noted:

> [P]olitics will be a major factor as well. Professionals who demonstrate political savvy will survive at a greater rate than their counterparts. It is critical, therefore, that we become promoters of change—not bystanders—in this environment. We must move out of our offices into the political space that extends beyond our professional systems. Forming alliances and coalitions, staffing key committees and task forces, writing action proposals, and taking part in policy making—these and other tactical measures can win social work a place at the negotiating table of managed care. (p. 358)

Confidentiality and Access to Records

Reamer (1998) noted that practitioners are "attracted to the profession primarily because of social work's abiding concern about values germane to human rights, welfare rights, equality, discrimination, and oppression" (pp. 489–490). Based on these factors, it is not surprising that confidentiality is a core social work practice value. Confidentiality has been a consistent tenet of social work practice, and it is an ethical requirement mandated by the NASW revised *Code of Ethics*. "Confidentiality has been seen as crucial in developing a trusting relationship with the client . . . and a necessary fiduciary responsibility to clients" (Rock & Congress, 1999, p. 254). According to legal mandates and accepted practice parameters, client confidentiality can only be breached when there is imminent risk of danger to self or others; even these practice parameters have multiple restrictions to confidentiality disclosure. Despite the multiple legal obligations and ethical responsibilities practitioners have to clients, the combination of managed care and advanced technology has magnified confidentiality issues in mental health practice settings.

According to Rock and Congress (1999):

> [M]anaged care companies eavesdrop on treatment when they need to know why a person is seeking treatment, the type of treatment provided, as well as the content of treatment. It is standard practice in contractual agreements between managed care organizations and providers to have a "boiler plate" clause requiring that the managed care organization have access to all records and details of treatment. (pp. 256–257)

These practice parameters, in conjunction with the rapid transmission of shared information, pose an increased threat to client confidentiality. Computerized databases, facsimile transmissions, voicemail reports, and Internet accessibility are used by managed care organizations to facilitate easier access to mental health records. The National Mental Health Association advises that "records should be disclosed only as needed for the provision of services. Even then, disclosure should be made only with the consumers' consent and after an explanation of the purpose and scope of the disclosure. These disclosures should be noted in the consumers' treatment records" (p. 29).

9.6

On October 21, 1998, seven social workers were among 25 individuals who presented testimony to New York City and state elected officials, as well as staff at the Office of Public Advocate, at a public hearing "on the status of mental health care" and the adverse effect for-profit health care has on patients; the hearing was held at the Hunter College School of Social Work. This advocacy event, moderated by the president of NASW's New York chapter, addressed at-risk issues prevalent in the for-profit health care sector, to include confidentiality preservation and the person-in-environment. Social workers also distributed "critical incident reports" previously used "to gather information about consumers' adverse experiences with managed care" (*NASW News*, January 1999, p. 6).

WHERE DO SOCIAL WORKERS ADVOCATE?

As discussed in previous chapters, advocacy is practiced in clinical, direct service, administrative, legislative, and judicial settings. However, more recently advocacy has been moved within the arena of advanced technology. The specific advanced technology we speak of includes interactive communication and instantaneous information accessibility and retrieval. What started out as tools to increase effectiveness and efficiency for the military and corporate sector has since turned into vital necessities for small business and personal use. These tools include facsimile machines, digitally operated voicemail systems, pagers, cellular phones, and multiple-party telephone conferencing. But the most important tools demanded by the market are computers, which include both personal and laptop as well as network and mainframe accessibility. Corresponding tools include various software programs designed to enhance the quality of business and personal life. Continued demand for these products provided the impetus for increasingly sophisticated technology and software, which opened the door to cyberspace and the information highway, better known as the Internet or World Wide Web.

The Internet "is a vast global network that enables computers of all kinds to share services and correspond directly, as if they were part of one giant machine. It has the capacity of changing many of the ways in which people interact and communicate" (Myrick & Sabella, 1995, p. 38, as quoted in Giffords, 1998, p. 243). Examples of interactive communication available on the Internet include e-mail, mailing lists and listservs, the World Wide Web and gopher search engines, bulletin boards, conferences, chats, and interrelay chats.

The Internet offers wonderful opportunities that will impact positive social change. Specifically, grassroots organizations and coalitions can network and exchange information in order to (1) obtain funding information and opportunities, (2) obtain information and relevant research, (3) problem-solve with others, and (4) learn about firsthand experiences relating to important issues and problems. While the Internet offers many unique and fascinating services to assist practitioners with their advocacy work, it also presents numerous challenges. First, practitioners will need continuous education and hands-on training to stay current with advanced technology. In addition, the social work profession needs to provide opportunities and strategies to help diminish the digital divide, or the gap between individuals with access to computers (and thus information) and those without access (Weil, 1996).

Numerous alternate trends have also emerged to help practitioners and clients engage in various levels of advocacy. For example, beginning as early as the 1970s, practitioners have used telephone conferencing to facilitate self-advocacy for disabled and home-bound clients (Weiner, 1998). More recently, technology-based telephone and computer groups have become the norm for these and other populations. Schopler, Abell, and Galinsky (1998) identified the following client groups (in addition to the two mentioned above) that have been successful with this form of advocacy: (1) cancer and HIV/AIDS patients; (2) sexual abuse survivors; (3) elderly clients; and (4) emotionally and chronically ill clients (p. 255). Cellular telephones provide instantaneous communication, which is crucial for those practice areas reflecting abuse and neglect.

9.7

In response to the South Carolina court system using its child abuse statutes to incarcerate drug-addicted pregnant women based on potential harm to the fetus, and the South Carolina Supreme Court's decision to uphold the legitimacy of the statute for these same purposes, the NASW "signed on to an *amicus curiae* brief in support of a women who was jailed under South Carolina's child abuse and neglect law for using cocaine during her pregnancy" (*NASW News*, April 1999, p. 4). Notwithstanding the constitutionality and confidentiality factors associated with this case, the NASW and its South Carolina chapter emphasized a treatment focus rather than punishment. According to the NASW, punishment threatens the best interests of the child by destabilizing the family unit. Thus, the child's and society's interests would be better served by treating rather than punishing the client.

How Do We Ensure Appropriate and Effective Advocacy?

We ensure appropriate and effective advocacy by working to increase and improve community integrity. This is done by building and improving community collaboration. We also promote and enhance multicultural diversity and organizing. We work for the best interest of vulnerable populations. This is best accomplished by promoting and enhancing a family-centered approach to legislation and intervention. These two approaches are outlined in more detail below.

Promote Cultural Competence

Cultural competence is another trend necessary for effective advocacy practice. Weaver (1999) stated that "cultural competence is a recognition of the profession's ethnocentric foundation" (p. 217); it mandates that practitioners not only represent community and cultural diversity, but that they be well trained and experienced in providing culturally competent services. According to Altman et al. (1994), professional awareness of cultural competency is becoming more and more important:

Our society is no longer a melting pot where ethnic minorities are assimilated into the dominant white culture. We are a salad bowl of many ethnic communities that are holding onto their identities and cultural values. As we embrace this diversity, our health promotion focus will be increasingly multi-cultural, making our advocacy efforts more relevant to the growing variety of our communities (p. 14).

Cultural diversity also means working with "communities of color, women, gay men and lesbians, and socioeconomically disadvantaged groups" (Uehara et al., 1996, p. 613). When practitioners embrace multiculturalism, they commit themselves to ending oppression and exploitation represented through classism, racism, sexism, xenophobia, and homophobia.

According to the National Mental Health Association, practitioners should work to ensure that cultural competence is reflected at every practice level. As part of this effort, members of diverse cultural groups and populations should be included on advisory committees as well as other policy-making groups. This should include the following:

1. Emphasis on the importance of adapting services to meet consumers' unique needs based on their cultural differences
2. Providers who are culturally competent, which includes understanding: (a) culturally based traditions, particularly attitudes about healing systems; (b) specialized assessment and treatment techniques for ethnically diverse groups; (c) dynamics of monocultural, bicultural, interfaith, and biracial families; and (d) appropriate linguistic skills or the availability of linguistic support services
3. Membership on all policy-making bodies that reflects the population's diversity
4. A quality assurance plan that includes regular monitoring and improvement based on indicators that evaluate services to minority and other culturally diverse groups
5. Training on cultural competence for providers and at all levels of governance (Gabriele, 1997; Pritchard, 1997)

9.8

Russell Redner, a Native American social worker, has been an advocate of Indian causes for more than 25 years and continues to advocate on behalf of Native Americans and Native American causes every day in his capacity as Director of Pyramid Lake (Nevada) Social Services. In addition to helping minimize strained relationships between Native Americans and Hispanic communities using effective leadership skills, Redner has been working with "the Paiute tribal council to put into operation a six- to eight-bed therapeutic group home for children who must now be placed in out-of-state homes, some as far away as Oregon" (*NASW News*, November 1998, p. 12). As part of this proposed residential treatment program, Redner emphasized using traditional Native American methods of healing, and teaching clients Native American history using the tribe's native language.

When assessing and advocating cultural competency, two questions should be asked. The first addresses questions of sensitivity. For example, how representative of the community is your group? Is it culturally sensitive? How culturally specific will your advocacy efforts be? Will you use language, metaphors, and expressions that the community of interest understands and feels comfortable with? Questions of responsiveness should also be identified. For example, do your group's issues address needs of minority communities, or only needs perceived by the majority society? Are your advocacy efforts responsive to the interests of diverse communities? (Altman et al., 1994).

Promote Family-Centered Services

Recall that Chapter 5 discussed family advocacy services, a model designed to build bridges between clients, families, and the larger community. These efforts provide the support necessary to access appropriate services and resources. It is important to note that this model was built from the family-centered services model. Its key principles and underlying approaches include the following:

PRINCIPLES
1. Respect for and acceptance of diversity across families
2. Respect for family autonomy, independence, and decision making in choosing the level and nature of intervention
3. Family/professional collaboration and partnership
4. Professionals must reexamine traditional roles and practices. Practices must promote mutual respect and partnerships
5. Services should be flexible, accessible, and responsive to family needs
6. Services should be provided in as normal a fashion and environment as possible, to promote integration of the child and family in the community

APPROACHES
1. Understand the client is one member of a family system
2. Caregivers as partners—collaboration in setting goals and priorities
3. Identify opportunities for communicative and social growth within family routines
4. Provide information and emotional support
5. Respect and support family decisions
6. Understand and respect cultural differences and family values
7. Help caregivers develop advocacy skills (Prizant, 1999)

If advocacy efforts are to be successful, both multicultural compentency and family-centered service must be in the forefront of practitioners' working knowledge base.

The Role of Social Work Education

Several authors suggest that in light of the never-ending changes in policies and services that negatively impact constituent clients, schools of social work are not doing a good job of preparing practitioners for effective and appropriate advocacy practice (Epstein, 1992; Herbert & Mould, 1992; Nazario, 1984; Ruffolo & Miller, 1994; Spakes, 1987). Criticisms range from deficiencies in the judicial development of social and family policies, to lack of adequate training in the developing legal and institutional systems. In addition, social workers are often disengaged from working with vulnerable and indigent populations; they are also ill prepared to represent clients in the multiple destructive systems and forums. According to Weil (1996):

> Social workers need skills to stay ahead of rapid information development and social change. Continuing education strategies will become more important, and schools of social work will need to integrate new methods of learning. They must prepare for this revolution by teaching practice methods that help clients cope with accelerating social change and that help people understand local, national, and global changes so they can find sustainable niches in the growing global economy. Social workers need skills to help break down the social alienation of poor and middle-class groups. (p. 37)

Spakes (1987) advised that "judges and lawyers are constantly seeking reliable information and sound research which will assist them in making their cases and in guiding and informing their decisions" (p. 36). In addition, decision makers continue to recognize the importance of social science research in these forums, and the inadequacy of training in its interpretation and use.

Ruffolo and Miller (1994) recommend using social work field education to supplement classroom education. Using this practice area, students will receive appropriate practice with diverse consumer populations, particularly populations with special needs. These authors further advise using the advocacy/empowerment model of organizing, which involves four primary components: (1) outreach, (2) partnership, (3) direction planning, and (4) change. It is important to note that the following steps must be undertaken by the lead organization and the field office:

1. Involve the frontline community agency in discussion about the role of social work in the agency and the potential contributions of social work in the agency's development.
2. Ask questions to expand the agency's perspective on the role of social work students.
3. Validate the agency's expertise in addressing the consumer groups that it serves.
4. Discuss various options of developing viable student field placements at the agency (e.g., provide MSW supervision via the university faculty, develop MSW group supervision models, or use direct-line non-MSW staff to work in conjunction with an MSW off-site supervisor).
5. Discuss resources and supports that each participant can bring to the process. (Ruffolo & Miller, 1994, p. 311)

TRENDS TOWARD EMPOWERMENT

Self-Advocacy

In conjunction with consumerism, self-help groups continue to grow in size and popularity. Sommer (1990) identified self-advocacy as a movement where "individuals who share a common need or problem join together to create groups to deal with that need or problem" (p. 205). Existing self-help groups are organized to address and cope with shared physical or social problems like alcohol and substance abuse, single parenting, death and bereavement, and overeating (Stern & Gibelman, 1990). Levy identified the following criteria for defining self-help groups:

1. Help and support for members in dealing with their problems
2. An origin and sanction for existence resting with the group members rather than with external agencies
3. The organization relying on its own members' efforts and skills as the primary resources
4. Members who share a common core of life experiences and problems
5. Control of the organization residing with lay members (Sommer, 1990, pp. 205–206)

As noted in previous chapters, self-help groups are some of the most effective programs available to consumers. Self-help groups are growing in numbers throughout the country, particularly as their efficacy continues to increase. This type of advocacy should be embraced by social work practitioners in every area of advocacy.

This chapter is not designed to provide an all-inclusive discussion of effective and commonly practiced contemporary advocacy techniques and approaches. Rather, it is meant to highlight selected areas felt to be of interest and needing increased focus and attention. For a fuller discussion of commonly practiced advocacy techniques and approaches, please refer to the previous chapters of this book.

SUMMARY

As discussed throughout this chapter, advocates' client bases have both remained the same and changed in numerous respects. In addition to understanding who has historically been represented, it is important that practitioners look at today's issues to determine who tomorrow's clients will be. Several issues have been prevalent within advocacy's history, many of which apply by today's and tomorrow's standards. Social justice and human rights have been, and will continue to be, central to all advocacy efforts. Employment issues continue to present a challenge as our society shifts from manufacturing to information processing and service delivery. Federal entitlement programs will need continued focus as governments attempt to shift the responsibility to states and local jurisdictions. Managed health and mental health care, implemented to control costs and medical service delivery, will need continued focus as we enter the 21st century.

Social work practitioners should not only advocate in those forums described throughout this book, but should become increasingly involved with computer technology and the information highway. In addition, social workers should understand and have a strong working knowledge of multicultural competency issues as well as family-centered services, as they will lead many of our advocacy endeavors over the next decade or more. Finally, schools of social work should integrate advocacy practice into their curricula, as well as field work experiences.

DISCUSSION QUESTIONS

1. Discuss the differences and similarities associated with historic and contemporary advocacy representation.
2. Discuss the differences and similarities between historic and contemporary advocacy issues.
3. What did you find most surprising in this chapter? Why?
4. Select two examples of community or individual advocacy efforts presented in this chapter and discuss characteristics you found most important.
5. Discuss the elements of cultural competency and identify techniques and methods of incorporating this approach into an advocacy effort.
6. Discuss the elements of a family-centered approach and identify techniques and methods of incorporating this approach into an advocacy effort.

RECOMMENDED READINGS

Ewalt, P. L., Freeman, E. M., Kirk, S. A., & Poole, D. L. (Eds.). (1997). *Social policy: Reform, research and practice.* Washington, DC: NASW Press.

Gabriele, R. J. (Ed.). *Healthcare reform: A consumer, family and advocate perspective.* Alexandria, VA: National Mental Health Association.

Weil, M. O. (1996). Community building: Building community practice. *Social Work, 41*(5), 481–499.

Witkin, S. L. (1998). Human rights and social work. *Social Work, 43*(3), 197–201.

Internet and World Wide Web Advocacy Resources

AGING

Administration on Aging	www.aoa.dhhs.gov
Alzheimer's Association	www.alz.org
American Association of Retired Persons	www.aarp.org
Eldercare Web	www.elderweb.com
Gerontological Society of America	www.geron.org
National Aging Information Center	www.ageinfo.com
Senior.Com	www.senior.com
SeniorNet	www.seniornet.com

AIDS

AIDS Education Global Information System .	www.aegis.com
Children with AIDS Project	www.aidskids.org
HIV Insite	hivinsite.ucsf.edu

CHILDREN AND YOUTH

American Academy of Child and Adolescent Psychiatry	www.aacap.org
Annie E. Casey Foundation	www.aecf.org
Child Quest International	www.childquest.org
Children Now	www.childrennow.org
Children's Advocacy Institute's Clearinghouse on Children	www.acusd.edu/childrensissues
Children's Defense Fund	www.childrensdefense.org
Child Welfare League of America	www.cwla.org
Coalition for America's Children	www.usakids.org
Connect for Kids	www.connectforkids.org

National Center for Missing
and Exploited Children . . . .   www.missingkids.org
National Clearinghouse on Child Abuse
and Neglect . . . .   www.calib.com/nccanch
National Stand for Children . . . .   www.stand.org

COMMUNITY DEVELOPMENT AND WELFARE

Academy for Educational Development . . . . .   www.aed.org
Alliance for National Renewal . . . .   www.ncl.org
American Enterprise Institute for Public
Policy Research . . . .   www.aei.org
Chronicle of Philanthropy . . . .   www.philanthropy.com
National Association of Community
Action Agencies . . . .   www.nacaa.org
Neighbor Works . . . .   www.nw.org
United Way . . . .   www.unitedway.org
U.S. Social Services Administration . . . .   www.ssa.gov

CULTURAL DIVERSITY

Center for Equal Opportunity . . . .   www.ceousa.org
Chicano Latino Net . . . .   latino.sscnet.ucla.edu
Indians and Native Americans Program . . . . .   www.wdsc.org/dinap
LatinoLink Home Page . . . .   www.latinolink.com/index.html
National Advancement for the Association
of Colored Persons . . . .   www.naacp.org
National Black Child Development Institute . .   www.nbcdi.org
National Indian Child Welfare Association . . .   www.nicwa.org
National MultiCultural Institute . . . .   www.nmci.org
Native American Resources . . . .   www.pitt.edu/~lmitten/
                                                                             indians.html
NativeWeb . . . .   www.nativeweb.org

DISABILITIES

American Association on Mental Retardation . .   www.aamr.org
American Foundation for the Blind . . . .   www.afb.org
Disabled American Veterans . . . .   www.dav.org/contents
March of Dimes Birth Defects . . . .   www.modimes.org
National Alliance for the Mentally Ill . . . .   www.nami.org
The Arc Homepage . . . .   www.thearc.org
U.S. Department of Veterans Affairs . . . .   www.va.gov
U.S. Equal Employment Opportunity
Commission . . . .   www.eeoc.gov

DISASTER RELIEF

American Red Cross	www.redcross.org
Emergency Preparedness Information Center	TheEpicenter.com
Federal Emergency Management Agency	www.fema.gov
International Federation of the Red Cross	www.ifrc.org
International Committee of the Red Cross	www.icrc.org

FAMILIES

Alliance for Children and Families	www.alliance1.org
Children, Youth and Families Consortium	www.cyfc.umn.edu
Families and Work Institute	www.familiesandworkinst.org
Families USA	www.familiesusa.org
Family Resource Coalition	www.frca.org
Focus on the Family	www.fotf.org
Foster Parents Home Page	www.fostercare.org/FPHP
Kaiser Family Foundation	www.kff.org
National Association of Family-Based Services	www.nafbs.org
National Association for Family Child Care	www.nafcc.org
Planned Parenthood	www.plannedparenthood.org
Zero to Three: Center for Infants, Toddlers and Families	www.zerotothree.org

GAY/LESBIAN ISSUES

The Human Rights Campaign	www.hrc.org
Lesbian Mothers' Support Society	www.lesbian.org/lesbian-moms
National Black Lesbian and Gay Leadership Forums	www.nblglf.org
National Gay and Lesbian Task Force	www.ngltf.org
National Journal of Sexual Orientation Law	sunsite.unc.edu/gaylaw
National Latino Gay and Lesbian Organization	www.llego.org

GENDER ISSUES

Institute of Women's Policy	www.iwpr.org
National Fathers' Network	www.fathersnetwork.org
National Organization for Women	www.now.org

HEALTH AND HEALTH CARE

Agency for Health Care Policy and Research	www.ahcpr.gov
American Public Health Association	www.apha.org
Center for Disease Control and Prevention	www.cdc.gov

Food and Drug Administration	www.fda.gov
Health Care Financing Administration	www.hcfa.gov
Health Care Resource and Services Administration	www.hrsa.dhhs.gov
Healthfinder	www.healthfinder.gov
Health Gate	www.healthgate.com
MedConnect	www.medconnect.com
National Academy for State Health Policy	www.nashp.org
World Health Organization	www.who.org

HOMELESSNESS AND HOUSING ISSUES

Habitat for Humanity International	www.habitat.org
National Coalition for the Homeless	nch.ari.net
National Housing Institute	www.nhi.org
U.S. Department of Housing and Urban Development	www.hud.gov

MENTAL HEALTH

Bazelon Center for Mental Health Law	www.bazelon.org
The Center for Mental Health Services	www.mentalhealth.org
National Association of State Mental Health Programs Directors' Research Institute, Inc.	www.nasmhpd.org/nri
National Institute of Mental Health	www.nimh.nih.gov
National Mental Health Association	www.nmha.org

POVERTY AND HUNGER ISSUES

American Public Welfare Association	www.apwa.org
Food for the Hungry	www.fh.org
Institute of Research on Poverty	www.ssc.wisc.edu/irp
U.S. Department of Agriculture	www.usda.gov
Welfare and Families (Idea Central)	epn.org/idea/welfare.html

PROFESSIONAL AND ETHICAL ISSUES

American Counseling Association	www.counseling.org
American Medical Association	www.ama-assn.org
American Psychiatric Association	www.psych.org
American Psychiatric Nurses Association	www.apna.org
American Psychoanalytic Association	www.apsa.org
American Psychological Association	www.apa.org
The Association of Black Psychologists	www.abpsi.org
National Association of Social Workers	www.naswdc.org

PUBLIC POLICY AND SOCIAL JUSTICE ISSUES

Alliance for Justice	www.essential.org/afj
American Civil Liberties Union	www.aclu.org
American Public Human Services Association	www.aphsa.org
Amnesty International	www.amnesty.org
Center on Budget and Policy Priorities	www.cbpp.org
Center for Law and Social Policy	www.clasp.org
Civic Practices Network	www.cpn.org
Electronic Policy Network	www.epn.org
Equal Opportunity Publications	www.eop.com
HandsNet	www.handsnet.org
IGC Internet	www.igc.org
Influencing State Policy	www.statepolicy.org
Peace Corps	www.peacecorps.gov
Policy.Com	www.policy.com
Public Welfare Foundation	www.publicwelfare.org
Search Institute	www.search-institute.org
Welfare Information Network	www.welfareinfo.org

SUBSTANCE ABUSE

Alcoholics Anonymous	www.alcoholics-anonymous.org
Creative Partnerships for Prevention	www.CPPrev.org
Drug Abuse Resistance Education	www.dare-america.com
Join Together	www.jointogether.org
National Clearinghouse for Alcohol and Drug Information	www.health.org
Parents Resource Institute for Drug Education	www.prideusa.org
Substance Abuse and Mental Health Services Administration	www.samhsa.gov

VIOLENCE

National Network of Violence Prevention Practitioners	www.edc.org/HHD/NNVPP/
Partnership Against Violence Network	www.pavnet.org
The Sexual Assault Information Page	www.cs.utk.edu/~bartley/saInfoPage.html

The Hatch Act: Lobby Guidelines

The Hatch Act was passed by the U.S. Congress in 1939 and amended in 1993. The original act prohibited civil servants from serving as delegates to political conventions, engaging in partisan political activity, and having anything to do with political contributions. The 1993 amendment allows most federal and D.C. employees to engage in many types of political activity; however, the amendment does not extend this provision to state and local employees. The justification for the Hatch Act is that public employees should not be put in a position where they could be intimidated by elected officials. They also should not be put in a position where public funds could be used to further their political ambitions.

The United States Office of Special Counsel (OSC) promotes compliance by government employees in regard to the Hatch Act. The office provides two essential services: enforcement of the Hatch Act and rendering of advisory opinions by persons seeking advice about political activity under the act. You may request such advice by phone, fax, mail, or e-mail. Contact:

Hatch Act Unit
U.S. Office of Special Counsel
1730 M Street, NW, Suite 300
Washington, DC 20036-4505

Tel: 800-85-HATCH
   202-653-7143
Fax: 202-653-5161
E-mail: hatchact@osc.gov
URL: http://www.osc.gov

Federal Guidelines*

Federal Hatch Act DO'S

Federal employees may:

- Be candidates for public office in nonpartisan elections
- Register and vote as they choose
- Assist in voter registration drives

---

*For further information: These guidelines provide general guidelines about the interpretation of the Hatch Act. For specific information, federal employees should contact the Office of Special Counsel. Employees of state and local governments should consult with the attorney general of their respective states to render a ruling about any specific activity. Employee handbooks are a starting point for information on political activity. States may have conflict of interest laws that also apply.

- Express opinions about candidates and issues
- Contribute money to political organizations
- Attend political fund-raising functions
- Attend and be active at political rallies and meetings
- Join and be an active member of a political party or club
- Sign nominating petitions
- Campaign for or against referendum questions, constitutional amendments, municipal ordinances
- Campaign for or against candidates in partisan elections
- Make campaign speeches for candidates in partisan elections
- Distribute campaign literature in partisan elections
- Hold office in political clubs or parties

Federal Hatch Act DON'TS

Federal employees *may not*:

- Use official authority or influence to interfere with an election
- Solicit or discourage political activity of anyone with business before their agency
- Solicit or receive political contributions (may be done in certain limited situations by federal labor or other employee organizations)
- Be candidates for public office in partisan elections
- Engage in political activity while:
  - On duty
  - In a government office
  - Wearing an official uniform
  - Using a government vehicle
- Wear partisan political buttons while on duty

Reference: 5 U.S.C. chapter 73, subchapter III, as amended; 5 C.F.R. part 734; Pub. L. 103-359, § 501(k) (1994); website: www.osc.gov

State and Local Government Employees*

The Office of Special Counsel issues guidance that covers certain state and local government employees. Covered employees under the act are persons principally employed by state or local executive agencies in connection with programs financed in whole or in part by federal loans or grants. The act does not apply to the political activity of persons employed by educational or research institutions or agencies supported in whole or part by (a) states or their political subdivisions, or (b) religious, philanthropic, or cultural organizations.

It should be noted that some statutes make Hatch Act provisions applicable to other categories of individuals, for example, persons employed by private, nonprofit organizations that plan, develop, and coordinate Head Start and certain other types of federal assistance.

---

*For further information: These guidelines provide general guidelines about the interpretation of the Hatch Act. For specific information, federal employees should contact the Office of Special Counsel. Employees of state and local governments should consult with the attorney general of their respective states to render a ruling about any specific activity. Employee handbooks are a starting point for information on political activity. States may have conflict of interest laws that also apply.

State and Local Hatch Act DO'S

Covered state and local employees *may*:

- Run for public office in nonpartisan elections
- Campaign for and hold office in political clubs and organizations
- Actively campaign for candidates for public office in partisan and nonpartisan elections
- Contribute money to political organizations and attend political fund-raising functions

State and Local Hatch Act DON'TS

Covered state and local employees *may not*:

- Be candidates for public office in a partisan election
- Use official authority or influence to interfere with or affect the results of an election or nomination
- Directly or indirectly coerce contributions from subordinates in support of a political party or candidate

Reference: 5 U.S.C. § 1212(f), and chapter 15; website: www.osc.gov

ADDITIONAL READING

Bridges, M. (1993). Release the gags: The Hatch Act and current legislative reform—another voice for reform. *Capital University Law Review, 22,* 237.

Domanski, M. D. (1998). Prototypes of social work political participation: An empirical model. *Social Work, 43*(2), 156.

Salcido, R., & Seck, E. (1992). Political participation among social work chapters. *Social Work, 37*(6), 563.

Thompson, J. (1994). Social workers and politics: Beyond the Hatch Act. *Social Work, 39*(4), 457.

Wolk, J. L. (1996). Political activity in social work: A theoretical model of motivation. *International Social Work, 39*(4), 443.

Source: www.osc.gov

Lobbying by 501(c)(3) and (4) Agencies: Guidelines

C

Charitable organizations are one of the most effective vehicles for making use of citizen participation in shaping public policy. The federal government, including Congress and the Internal Revenue Service, supports lobbying by charities. Congress sent that unambiguous message when it enacted the liberal provisions under the 1976 lobby law. The same message came from the Internal Revenue Service in regulations issued in 1990, which support both the spirit and intent of the 1976 legislation.

The 1976 law is clear regarding what constitutes lobbying by charities. Following are key points about that legislation. They apply only to charities that have "elected" to come under the 1976 law. *[Those that have not elected remain subject to the ambiguous "insubstantial" test, which leaves uncertain which activities of charities related to legislation constitute lobbying and how much lobbying is permitted.]*

- The most important feature of the law is that it provides ample leeway for charities to lobby, and it protects those that elect the advantages of the 1976 rules from the uncertainties they would be subject to if they remain under the "insubstantial" test.
- Generally, organizations that elect the 1976 lobby law may spend 20% of the first $500,000 of their annual expenditures on lobbying ($100,000), 15% of the next $500,000, and so on, up to $1 million dollars a year! Equally important, there are eight critically important legislation-related activities which charities may conduct that are not considered lobbying by the IRS. (See section entitled "Exclusions from Lobbying" that follows.)
- Understanding what constitutes lobbying under the 1976 law is not difficult. In general, you are lobbying when you state your position on specific legislation to legislators or other government employees who participate in the formulation of legislation, or urge your members to do so (*direct lobbying*). In addition, you are lobbying when you state your position on legislation to the general public and ask the general public to contact legislators or other government employees who participate in the formulation of legislation (*grassroots lobbying*).
- The Internal Revenue Service encourages groups to elect to come under the 1976 law. The IRS has found groups that have elected are more often in compliance with the law than those that have not. Also, it is easy to elect. Just have your governing body vote to come under the provisions of the 1976 law and file the one page IRS Form 5768 with the IRS.

Exclusions from Lobbying

The main elements of the 1976 law are the provisions declaring that many expenditures that have some relationship to public policy and legislative issues are not treated as lobbying and so are permitted without limit. For example:

1. **Contacts with executive branch employees or legislators in support of or opposition to proposed regulations are not considered lobbying.** So, if your charity is trying to get a regulation changed, it may contact both members of the Executive Branch as well as legislators to urge support for your position on the regulation and the action is not considered lobbying.
2. **Lobbying by volunteers is considered a lobbying expenditure only to the extent that the charity incurs expenses associated with the volunteers' lobbying.** For example, volunteers working for a charity could organize a huge rally of volunteers at the state capitol to lobby on an issue and only the expenses related to the rally paid by the charity would count as a lobbying expenditure.
3. **A charity's communications to its members on legislation—even if it takes a position on the legislation—is not lobbying so long as the charity doesn't directly encourage its members or others to lobby.** For example, a group could send out a public affairs bulletin to its members, take a position on legislation in the bulletin, and it would not count as lobbying if the charity didn't ask its members to take action on the measure.
4. **A charity's response to written requests from a legislative body (not just a single legislator) for technical advice on pending legislation is not considered lobbying.** So, if requested in writing, a group could provide testimony on legislation, take a position in the testimony on that legislation, and it would not be considered lobbying.
5. **So-called self-defense activity—that is, lobbying legislators (but not the general public) on matters that may affect the organization's own existence, powers, tax exempt status, and similar matters would not be lobbying.** For example, lobbying in opposition to proposals in Congress to curtail charity lobbying, or lobbying in support of a charitable tax deduction of nonitemizers, would not be a lobbying expenditure. It would become lobbying only if you asked for support from the general public. [Lobbying for programs in the organization's field (e.g., health, welfare, environment, education, etc.), however, is not self-defense lobbying. For example, an organization that is fighting to cure cancer could not consider working for increased appropriations for cancer research to be self-defense lobbying.]
6. **Making available the results of "nonpartisan analysis, study or research" on a legislative issue that presents a sufficiently full and fair exposition of the pertinent facts to enable the audience to form an independent opinion, would not be considered lobbying.** The regulations make clear that such research and analysis need not be "neutral" or "objective" to fall within this "nonpartisan" exclusion. The exclusion is available to research and analysis that take direct positions on the merits of legislation, as long as the organization presents facts fully and fairly, makes the material generally available, and does not include a direct call to the reader to contact legislators. This exception is particularly important because many nonprofits that engage in public policy do conduct significant amounts of nonpartisan analysis, study and research on legislation.

7. **A charity's discussion of broad social, economic and similar policy issues whose resolution would require legislation—even if specific legislation on the matter is pending—is not considered lobbying so long as the discussion does not address the merits of specific legislation.** For example, a session at a charity's annual meeting regarding the importance of enacting child welfare legislation, would not be lobbying so long as the organization is not addressing merits of specific child welfare legislation pending in the legislature. Representatives of the organizations could even talk directly to legislators on the broad issue of child welfare, so long as there is no reference to specific legislation on that issue.

8. **It's not grassroots lobbying if a charity urges the public, through the media or other means, to vote for or against a ballot initiative or referendum.** It's direct lobbying, not grassroots, because the public in this situation becomes the legislature. Lobbying the public through the media is therefore considered a direct lobbying expenditure, not a grassroots expenditure. This is an advantage because charities are permitted to spend more on direct lobbying than on grassroots lobbying.

From the foregoing, it is very clear that there are many activities related to legislation that do not count toward lobbying expenditure limits.

Source: Charity Lobbying in the Public Interest
2040 S. Street, NW
Washington, DC 20009
Tel: 202-387-5048
E-mail: charity.lobbying@indepsec.org

References

Addams, J. A. (1892). Address on "How would you uplift the masses?" In *[Report of] The Sunset Club, Chicago, Forty-second meeting, held at the Grand Pacific, Thursday Eve., February 4, 1892*, pp. 10–12.

Addams, J. (1895). The settlement as a factor in the labor movement. In L. M. Pacey (Ed.), *Readings in the development of settlement work* (1950). New York: Association Press.

Addams, J. A. (1910). Why women should vote. In C. Lasch (Ed.), *The social thought of Jane Addams*. Indianapolis: Bobbs-Merrill.

Addams, J. A. (1912). My experiences as a progressive delegate. In C. Lasch (Ed.), *The social thought of Jane Addams*. Indianapolis: Bobbs-Merrill.

Addams, J. A. (1914). The larger aspects of the women's movement. In C. Lasch (Ed.), *The social thought of Jane Addams*. Indianapolis: Bobbs-Merrill.

Addams, J. A. (1915, October 22). Letter to Julia Grace Wales. State Historical Society of Wisconsin; Julia Grace Wales Papers.

Ad Hoc Committee on Advocacy (NASW) (1969). The social worker as advocate: Champion of social victims. *Social Work, 14*(2), 16–22.

Advocacy Institute. (1990). *The elements of a successful public interest advocacy campaign*. Washington, DC: Author.

Albert, R. (1983). Social work advocacy in the regulatory process. *Social Casework, 64*, 473–479.

Allen, S. M., Mor, V., Fleishman, J. A., & Piette, J. D. (1995). The organizational transformation of advocacy: Growth and development of AIDS community-based organizations. *The Journal of Applied Behavioral Sciences, 17*, 463–477.

Allen-Meares, P. (1996). The new federal role in education and family services: Goal setting without responsibility. *Social Work, 41*, 553–540.

Alinsky, S. (1971). *Rules for radicals*. New York: Vintage Press.

Alonso, H. H. (1996). Nobel Peace laureates, Jane Addams and Emily Greene Balch: Two women of the Women's International League for Peace and Freedom. *Journal of Women's History, 7*(2), 6–26.

Altman, D. G., Balcazar, F. E., Fawcett, S. B., Seekins, T., & Young, T. Q. (1994). *Public health advocacy: Creating community change to improve health*. Palo Alto, CA: Stanford Center for Research in Disease Prevention.

Altmeyer, A. J. (1955). The dynamics of social work. In *The Social Welfare Forum, 1955: Official proceedings, 82d annual forum, National Conference of Social Work, San Francisco, California*, May 29–June 3, 1955. New York: Columbia University Press.

Ambrosino, S. (1979). Integrating counseling, family life education, and family advocacy. *Social Casework, 60,* 579–585.

Amidei, N. (1982). How to be an advocate in bad times. *Public Welfare, 40,* 37–42.

Amidei, N. (1991). *Policy advocacy as social work practice.* (Unpublished paper).

Amidei, N. (1992). *So you want to make a difference: Advocacy is the key.* Washington, DC: OMB Watch.

Ashford, J. B., Macht, M. W., & Mylym, M. (1987, May–June). Advocacy by social workers in the public defender's office. *Social Work,* 199–203.

Association of Retarded Citizens (ARC). (1991). *Protection and advocacy* (position statement). Arlington, TX: Author.

Bailey, D., & Koney, K. M. (1996). Interorganizational community-based collaboratives: A strategic response to shape the social work agenda. *Social Work, 41*(6), 602–611.

Bailey, D., & Koney, K. M. (1996). Interorganizational community-based collaboratives: A strategic response to shape the social work agenda. In P. L. Ewalt, E. M. Freeman, S. A. Kirk, & D. L. Poole (Eds.), *Social policy: Reform, research and practice* (1997). Washington, DC: NASW Press.

Barker, R.L. (1995). *The social work dictionary* (3d ed.). Washington, DC: NASW Press.

Barnhart, C. L., & Barnhart, R. K. (1991). *World book dictionary.* Chicago: World Book.

Barrows, I. C. (Eds.). (1896). Preface. In *Proceedings of the National Conference of Charities and Corrections at the Twenty-Third Annual Session held in Grand Rapids, Mich. June 4–10, 1896.* Boston: George H. Ellis.

Beecher, N. B. (1983, Winter). Perspectives: Human service advocacy in the 1980s. *New England Journal of Human Services,* 53–54.

Benjamin, P. L. (1945). Techniques of social action: Securing social legislation. In *Proceedings of the National Conference of Social Work: Selected papers, seventy-second annual meeting, 1945.* New York: Columbia University Press.

Bennett, E. M. (Ed.). (1987). *Social intervention: Theory and practice.* Lewiston, NY: Edwin Mellen Press.

Bentley, K. J., & Walsh, J. (1996). *The social worker & psychotropic medication: Toward effective collaboration with mental health clients, families, and providers.* Pacific Grove, CA: Brooks/Cole.

Berger, E. M. (1977). The compleat advocate. *Policy Sciences, 8*(1), 69–78.

Berk, R., et al. (1985). Social policy experimentation: A position paper. *Evaluation Review, 9,* 387–431.

Berkman, B. (1996). The emerging health care world: Implications for social work practice and education. In P. L. Ewalt, E. M. Freeman, S. A. Kirk, & D. L. Poole (Eds.), *Social policy: Reform, research, and practice* (1997). Washington, DC: NASW Press.

Berkowitz, W. R. (1982). *Community impact: Creating grassroots change in hard times.* Cambridge, MA: Shenkman Publishing.

Berry, J. (1977). *Lobbying for the people.* Princeton, NJ: Princeton University Press.

Berry, J. M. (1981). Beyond citizen participation: Effective advocacy before administrative agencies. *The Journal of Applied Behavioral Sciences, 17,* 463–477.

Bersani, H., Jr. (1996). Leadership in developmental disabilities: Where we've been, where we are, and where we're going. In G. Dybwad & H. Bersani, Jr. (Eds.), *New voices: Self-advocacy by people with disabilities* (pp. 265–269). Cambridge, MA: Brookline Books.

Bevis, C. L. (1989). Community advocacy: The Tampa experience. In R. M. Friedman, A. J. Duchnowski, & E. L. Henderson (Eds.), *Advocacy on behalf of children with serious emotional problems* (pp. 57–67). Springfield, IL: Charles C. Thomas.

Bicha, K. D. (1986). Emily Greene Balch. In W. I. Trattner (Ed.), *Biographical dictionary of social welfare in America.* New York: Greenwood Press.

Bistline, S. M. (1981). Coalitions have grown up: They are broader, more sophisticated. *Association Management, 52–56.*

Blackburn, C. W. (1954). The citizen's responsibility for social action. In *The Social Welfare Forum, 1954: Official proceedings, 81ˢᵗ annual forum, National Conference of Social Work, Atlantic City, New Jersey, May 9–14, 1954.* New York: Columbia University Press.

Blackmar, F. W. (1900). Politics in charitable and correctional affairs: Report of the standing committee. In *Proceedings of the National Conference of Charities and Corrections at the Twenty-seventh annual session held in the City of Topeka, Kan., May 18–24, 1900.* Boston: George H. Ellis.

Blakely, T. J. (1991). *Advocacy in the social work curriculum.* (Unpublished paper).

Blankenship, J. (1966). *Public speaking: A rhetorical perspective.* Englewood Cliffs, NJ: Prentice-Hall.

Bobo, K., Kendall, J., & Max, S. (1996). *Organizing for social change. A manual for activists in the 90s* (2d ed.). Santa Ana, CA: Seven Locks Press.

Bouterse, A. D. (1948). Marshaling public support for social legislation. In *Proceedings of the National Conference of Social Work: Selected papers, Seventy-fifth anniversary meeting, Atlantic City, New Jersey, April 17–23, 1948.* New York: Columbia University Press.

Brager, G. A. (1967, January). Institutional change: Perimeters of the possible. *Social Work, 59–69.*

Brager, G. A. (1968). Advocacy and political behavior. *Social Work, 13*(2), 5–15.

Brager, G. A. (1969). Advocacy and political behavior. In National Association of Social Workers, *Changing services for changing clients.* New York: Columbia University Press.

Brager, G. A., & Holloway, S. (1978). *Changing human service organizations: Politics and practice.* New York: Free Press.

Bremner, R. H. (1967). *From the depths: The discovery of poverty in the United States.* New York: New York University Press.

Briar, S. (1967). The social worker's responsibility for the civil rights of clients. *New Perspectives, 1,* 90.

Briar, S. (1968). The casework predicament. *Social Work, 1,* 5–11.

Briar, S. (1977). In summary. *Social Work, 22,* 415–416, 444.

Bridgman, G. (1992). Does advocacy work? *Community Mental Health in New Zealand, 7*(1), 23–38.

Brieland, D. (1995). Social work practice: History and evolution. In *The encyclopedia of social work* (19th ed.). Washington, DC: National Association of Social Workers.

Brieland, D. (1997). Social work practice: History and evolution. In *Encyclopedia of social work* (19th ed. rev.). Washington, DC: NASW Press. CD Rom.

Briggs, H. E., & Koroloff, N. M. (1995). Enhancing family advocacy networks: An analysis of the roles of sponsoring organizations. *Community Mental Health Journal, 31,* 327–333.

Brown, P. (1981). The mental patients' rights movement and mental health institutional change. *International Journal of Health Services, 11*(4), 523–540.

Browning, P., Thorin, E., & Rhoades, C. (1984). A national profile of self-help/self-advocacy groups of people with mental retardation. *Mental Retardation, 22*(5), 226–230.

Bruno, F. J. (1948). *Trends in social work as reflected in the proceedings of the National Conference of Social Work: 1874–1946.* New York: Columbia University Press.

Bryer, D., & Magrath, J. (1999). New dimensions of global advocacy. *Nonprofit and Voluntary Sector Quarterly, 28* (4th Supp.), 168–177.

Bull, D. (1989). The social worker's advocacy role: A British quest for a Canadian perspective. *Canadian Social Work Review, 6,* 49–68.

Butler, A. W. (1906). Statistics: Report of the committee. In *Proceedings of the National Conference of Charities and Corrections of the Thirty-third annual session held in the City of Philadelphia, Penna., May 9–16, 1906.* Fort Wayne, IN: Fort Wayne Printing Co.

Cameron, W. B. (1966). *Modern social movements.* New York: Random House.

Campbell, J. F. (1978). Does school social work make a difference? *Social Work in Education, 1*(1), 4–18.

Carlton, T. O., & Jung, M. (1972). Adjustment or change: Attitudes among social workers. *Social Work, 17,* 64–71.

Carrilio, T. E. (1998). *California safe and healthy families model program: A family support home visiting model, Executive summary.* San Diego, CA: California State Department of Social Services.

Carroll, N. K. (1977). Three dimensional model of social work practice. *Social Work, 22,* 428–432.

Castillo, R. J. (1997). *Culture and mental illness: A client-centered approach.* Pacific Grove, CA: Brooks/Cole.

Chambers, C. A. (1963). *Seedtime of reform: American social service and social action, 1918–1933.* Minneapolis, MN: University of Minnesota Press.

Chandler, S. M. (1985). Mediation: Conjoint problem solving. *Social Work, (4),* 346–349.

Checkoway, B. (1995). Six strategies of community change. *Community Development Journal, 30*(1), 2–20.

Chin, R., & Benne, K. D. (1976). General strategies for effecting changes in human systems. In W. Bennis, K. D. Benne, R. Chin, & K. E. Corey, *The planning of change* (3d ed., pp. 22–45). New York: Holt, Rinehart.

Chronology, 1884–1894. (1968). In Encyclopaedia Britannica, Inc., *The annals of America: Vol. 11. 1884–1894. Agrarianism and urbanization.* Chicago: William Benton.

Chronology, 1895–1904. (1968). In Encyclopaedia Britannica, Inc., *The annals of America: Vol. 12. 1895–1904. Populism, imperialism, and reform.* Chicago: William Benton.

Chronology, 1905–1915. (1968). In Encyclopaedia Britannica, Inc., *The annals of America: Vol. 13. 1905–1915.* Chicago: William Benton.

Chronology, 1916–1928. (1968). In Encyclopaedia Britannica, Inc., *The annals of America: Vol. 14. 1905–1928. World war and prosperity.* Chicago: William Benton.

Clague, E. (1946). Social work in the new economic scene. In *Proceedings of the National Conference of Social Work: Selected papers, Seventy-third annual meeting, Buffalo, New York, May 19–23, 1946.* New York: Columbia University Press.

Claxton, L. M. (1981). Advocacy: an application to children. *Social Work in Education, 3*(4), 43–54.

Cohen, J. (1971). Advocacy and the children's crisis: An invited commentary. *American Journal of Orthopsychiatry, 41,* 807–808.

Cohen, W. J. (1954). Factors influencing the content of federal public welfare legislation. In *The Social Welfare Forum, 1954: Official proceedings, 81st annual forum, National Conference of Social Work, Atlantic City, New Jersey, May 9–14, 1954.* New York: Columbia University Press.

Cole, R. F. (1995). Case management to assure quality care in multiagency systems: Building standards of practice into a computerized clinical record. In B. J. Friesen & J. Poertner (Eds.), *From case management to service coordination for children with emotional, behavioral, or mental disorders: Building on family strengths.* Baltimore: Paul H. Brookes.

Collins, J. (1989). The advocate's role. In M. L. Henk (Ed.), *Social work in primary care.* Newbury Park, CA: Sage.

Compton, B. R., & Galaway, B. (1994). *Social work processes.* Pacific Grove, CA: Brooks/Cole.

Connaway, R. S. (1975). Teamwork and social worker advocacy: Conflicts and possibilities. *Community Mental Health Journal, 11*(4), 381–388.

Costin, L. B. (1983). *Two sisters for social justice: A biography of Grace and Edith Abbott.* Chicago: University of Illinois Press.

Coulton, C. J. (1996). Poverty, work, and community: A research agenda for an era of diminishing federal responsibility. *Social Work, 41*(9), 509–519.

Craigen, J. E. (1972). The case for activism in social work. In *The Social Welfare Forum 1972: Official proceedings, 99th annual forum, National Conference on Social Welfare, Chicago, IL, May 28–June 2, 1972.* New York: Columbia University Press.

Dane, E. (1985). Professional and lay advocacy in the education of handicapped children. *Social Work, 30*(6), 505–510.

Danstedt, R. T. (1958). An assessment of social action. In *The Social Welfare Forum, 1958: Official proceedings, 85th annual forum, National Conference on Social Welfare, Chicago, Illinois, May 11–16, 1958.* New York: Columbia University Press.

Danziger, S. H., & Weinberg, D. H. (1994). The historical record: Trends in family income, inequality, and poverty. In S. H. Danziger, G. D. Sandefur, & D. H. Weinberg (Eds.), *Confronting poverty: Prescriptions for change.* Cambridge, MA: Harvard University Press.

Davidson, W. S., II, & Rapp, C. A. (1976). Child advocacy in the justice system. *Social Work, 21*(3), 225–232.

Davis, K. E. (1993, March/April). The need for social workers to advocate. *Virginia NASW Newsletter, 4.*

Day, P. J. (1989). *A new history of social welfare.* Englewood Cliffs, NJ: Prentice-Hall.

Dean, W. R. (1977). Back to activism. *Social Work, 22,* 369–373.

Dear, R. B., & Patti, R. J. (1981). Legislative advocacy: Seven effective tactics. *Social Work, 26,* 289–296.

Degen, M. L. (1972). *The history of the Woman's Peace Party.* New York: Garland.

DeLeon, P. H., O'Keefe, A. M., Vandenbos, G. R., & Kraut, A. G. (1982). How to influence public policy. *American Psychologist, 37,* 476–485.

De Long, J. B. (1991). Depression. In E. Foner & J. A. Garraty (Eds.), *The reader's companion to American history* (pp. 279–283). Boston: Houghton Mifflin.

Demone, H. W., & Gibelman, M. (1984). Reagonomics: Its impact on the voluntary not-for-profit sector. *Social Work, 29*(5), 421–427.

Denny, E., Pokela, J., Jackson, J. R., & Matava, M. A. (1989). Influencing child welfare policy: Assessing the opinion of legislators. *Child Welfare, 68,* 275–287.

Devine, E. T. (1906). The dominant note of the modern philanthropy. In *Proceedings of the National Conference of Charities and Corrections at the Thirty-third annual session held in the City of Philadelphia, Penna., May 9–16, 1906.* Fort Wayne, IN: Fort Wayne Printing Co.

Devine, E. T. (1910a). The conservation of human life. In E. T. Devine, *The spirit of social work* (1976). New York: Arno Press.

Devine, E. T. (1910b). The attitude of society towards the criminal. In E. T. Devine, *The spirit of social work* (1976). New York: Arno Press.

Devine, E. T. (1911a). The tenement home in modern cities. In E. T. Devine, *The spirit of social work* (1976). New York: Arno Press.

Devine, E. T. (1911b). The substantial value of woman's vote. In E. T. Devine, *The spirit of social work* (1976). New York: Arno Press.

Devine, E. T. (1911c). The correction and prevention of crime. In E. T. Devine, *The spirit of social work* (1976). New York: Arno Press.

Devine, E. T. (1912, September 2). Letter from E. T. Devine to E. G. Balch. Swarthmore College Peace Collection, Jane Addams Papers, Series 1. From University of Illinois at Chicago: The University Library, Jane Addams Memorial Collection.

Devine, E. T. (1915, September 2). Letter to Jane Addams. Swarthmore College Peace Collection, Series 1.

Devine, E. T. (1939). *When social work was young.* New York: MacMillan.

Dluhy, M. J. (1981). *Changing the system: Political advocacy for disadvantaged groups.* Beverly Hills, CA: Sage.

Doherty, W. J., & Dougherty, P. (1997, May). *Working upstream: Therapy as public work.* Family Therapy Network Symposium. Washington, DC: The Resource Link.

Dorn, S., Teitelbaum, M., & Cortez, C. (1998). *Advocate's tool kit.* Washington, DC: Children's Defense Fund.

Doss, C. B., & Idleman, L. S. (1994). The county child abuse protocol system in Georgia: An interagency cooperation approach to a complex issue. *Child Welfare, LXXIII,* 675–688.

Drucker, P. F. (1967). *The effective executive.* New York: Harper & Row.

Dubler, N. N. (1992). Individual advocacy as a governing principle. *Journal of Case Management, 1,* 82–86.

DuBois, B., & Miley, K. K. (1996). *Social work: An empowering profession* (2d ed.). Boston: Allyn & Bacon.

Dumont, M. (1970, May/June). The changing face of professionalism. *Social Policy, 1,* 26–31.

Dunham, A. (1948). What is the job of the community organization worker? In *Proceedings of the National Conference of Social Work: Selected papers, Seventy-fifth anniversary meeting, Atlantic City, New Jersey, April 17–23, 1948.* New York: Columbia University Press.

Edwards, R. L., Cooke, P. W., & Reid, P. N. (1996). Social work management in an era of diminishing federal responsibility. *Social Work, 41*(5), 468–479.

Ehrenreich, J. H. (1985). The altruistic imagination: A history of social work and social policy in the United States. Ithaca, NY: Cornell University Press.

Epstein, I. (1968). Social workers and social action: Attitudes toward social action strategies. *Social Work, 13*(2), 101–108.

Epstein, W. M. (1992). Professionalization of social work: The American experience. *The Social Science Journal, 29*(2), 153–166.

Erickson, A. G., Moynihan, F. M., & Williams, B. L. (1991). A family practice model for the 1990s. *The Journal of Contemporary Human Services, 72*(5), 286–293.

Eriksen, K. (1997). *Making an impact: A handbook on counselor advocacy.* Washington, DC: Accelerated Development, a member of the Taylor & Francis Group.

Everett, J. R. (1982). *Religion in economics: A study of John Bates Clark, Richard T. Ely, and Simon N. Patten.* Philadelphia: Porcupine Press.

Ewing, D. W. (1974). *Writing for results.* New York: Wiley.

Ezell, M. (1991). Administrators as advocates. *Administration in Social Work, 15,* 1–18.

Ezell, M. (1993). The political activity of social workers: A post-Reagan update. *Journal of Sociology and Social Welfare, 20,* 81–97.

Ezell, M. (1994). Advocacy practice of social workers. *Families in Society: The Journal of Contemporary Human Services, 75*(1), 36–46.

Fabricant, M., & Epstein, I. (1984). Legal and welfare rights advocacy: Complementary approaches in organizing on behalf of the homeless. *Urban and Social Change Review, 17*(1), 15–19.

Family Word Finder. (1975). Pleasantville, NY: The Reader's Digest Association.

Fandetti, D. V., & Goldmeier, J. (1988). Social workers as culture mediators in health care settings. *Health and Social Work, 13*(3), 171–179.

Faulkner, C. E. (1900). Twentieth century alignments for the promotion of social order. In *Proceedings of the National Conference of Charities and Corrections at the Twenty-seventh annual session held in the city of Topeka, Kan., May 18–24, 1900.* Boston: George H. Ellis.

Favero, P. (1987). Professional values about community decisions: The advocacy question. *Journal of the Community Development Society, 18*(2), 54–68.

Fawcett, A. (1999). Indian woman, after years of struggle, brings suit to trial charging U.S. mishandled funds. *Wall Street Journal,* July 9, A16.

Feldman, S. (1978). Promises, promises or community mental health services and training: Ships that pass in the night. *Community Mental Health Journal, 14,* 83–91.

Ferguson, V. S. (1950). Fifty years of social work. In *The Social Welfare Forum, 1950: Official proceedings, 77th annual meeting, National Conference of Social Work, Atlantic City, New Jersey, April 23–28, 1950.* New York: Columbia University Press.

Fernandez, H. C. (1980). *The child advocacy handbook.* New York: The Pilgrim Press.

Fiedler, C. R., & Antonak, R. F. (1991). Advocacy. In J. L. Matson & J. A. Mulick (Eds.), *Pergamon general psychology series: Vol. 121. Handbook of mental retardation* (2d ed., pp. 23–32). New York: Pergamon Press.

Figueiria-McDonough, J. (1993). Policy practice: The neglected side of social work intervention. *Social Work, 38,* 179–188.

Fisher, J. (1935, April). Rank and file challenge: The first national convention of rank and file groups in social work. *Social Work Today, 5*–8.

Fisher, R. (1984). *Let the people decide: Neighborhood organizing in America.* Boston: Twayne.

Flanagan, R. S., & Flanagan, J. S. (1999). *Clinical interviewing.* New York: Wiley.

Flexner, A. (1915). Is social work a profession? In *Proceedings of the National Conference of Charities and Corrections at the Forty-second annual session held in Baltimore, MD, May 12–19, 1915.* Chicago: Hildmann Printing Co.

Flynn, L. M. (1989). The family phenomenon: The story of the National Alliance for the Mentally Ill. In R. M. Friedman, A. J. Duchnowski, & E. L. Henderson (Eds.), *Advocacy on behalf of children with serious emotional problems* (pp. 134–147). Springfield, IL: Charles C. Thomas.

Folks, H. (1911). The rate of progress. In *Proceedings of the National Conference of Charities and Corrections at the Thirty-eighth annual session held in Boston, MA, June 7–14, 1911.* Fort Wayne, IN: The Fort Wayne Printing Company.

Folwell, I. W. (1901). Legislation concerning charities special field of national legislation: Report of the committee on legislation. In *Proceedings of the National Conference on Charities and Corrections at the Twenty-eighth annual session held in Washington, D.C., May 9–15, 1901.* Boston: George H. Ellis.

Fox, D. M. (1967). *The discovery of abundance: Simon N. Patten and the transformation of social theory.* Published for the American Historical Association. Ithaca, NY: Cornell University Press.

Fox, P. (1989). From senility to Alzheimer's disease: The rise of the Alzheimer's disease movement. *Milbank Quarterly, 67,* 58–102.

Freddolino, P. P. (1990). Mental health rights protection and advocacy. *Research in Community and Mental Health, 6,* 379–407.

Freddolino, P. P., & Moxley, D. P. (1992). Refining an advocacy model for homeless people coping with psychiatric disabilities. *Community Mental Health Journal, 28*(4), 337–352.

Freddolino, P. P., Moxley, D. P., & Fleishman, J. A. (1989). An advocacy model for people with long-term psychiatric disabilities. *Hospital and Community Psychiatry, 40*(11), 1169–1174.

Freire, P. (1990). A critical understanding of social work (M. Moch, Trans.). *Journal of Progressive Human Services, 1,* 3–9.

Friedman, C. R., & Poertner, J. (1995). Creating and maintaining support and structure for case managers: Issues in case management supervision. In B. J. Friesen & J. Poertner (Eds.), *From case management to service coordination for children with emotional, behavioral, or mental disorders: Building on family strengths.* Baltimore: Paul H. Brookes.

Friedman, R. M., Duchnowski, A. J., & Henderson, E. L. (Eds.). (1989). *Advocacy on behalf of children with serious emotional problems.* Springfield, IL: Charles C. Thomas.

Friesen, B. J., & Briggs, H. E. (1995). The organization and structure of service coordination mechanisms. In B. J. Friesen & J. Poertner, *From case management to service coordination for children with emotional, behavioral, or mental disorders: Building on family strengths.* Baltimore: Paul H. Brookes.

Friesen, B. J., & Poertner, J. (1995). *From case management to service coordination for children with emotional, behavioral, or mental disorders: Building on family strengths.* Baltimore: Paul H. Brookes.

Frost, M. E. (1983, Winter). Perspectives: Human service advocacy in the 1980s. *New England Journal of Human Services,* 50–51.

Frost, M. E., Higgins, T., & Beecher, N. B. (1983). Perspectives: Human services advocacy in the 1980s. *The New England Journal of Human Services, 3*(1), 50–54.

Funk & Wagnalls Encyclopedia (1994). In *Infopedia: The ultimate multi-media reference tool.* © 1995 Future Vision Multimedia, Inc., a subsidiary of Future Holding, Inc. and its licensors. CD Rom.

Gabriele, R. J. (1997, October). Key contracting issues for consumers, families and advocates. In R. J. Gabriele (Ed.), *Healthcare reform: A consumer, family and advocate perspective* (pp. 31–35). Alexandria, VA: National Mental Health Association.

Gerhart, U. C. (1990). *Caring for the chronic mentally ill.* Itasca, IL: F. E. Peacock.

Gibelman, M. (1999). The search for identity: Defining social work—past, present, future. *Social Work, 44*(4), 298–310.

Gibelman, M., & Schervish, P. (1997). *Who we are: A second look.* Washington, DC: NASW Press.

Giffords, E. D. (1998). Social work on the Internet: An introduction. *Social Work, 43*(3), 243–253.

Gil, E. (1996). *Treating abused adolescents.* New York: Guilford.

Gilbert, N., & Specht, H. (1976). Advocacy and professional ethics. *Social Work, 21*(4), 288–293.

Gormley, W. T. (1981). Public advocacy in public utility commission proceedings. *The Journal of Applied Behavioral Science, 17*(4), 446–462.

Greenstone, J. L., & Leviton, S. C. (1993). *Elements of crisis intervention.* Pacific Grove, CA: Brooks/Cole.

Grosser, C. F. (1965). Community development programs serving the urban poor. *Social Work, 7,* 15–21.

Gutierrez, L., Alvarez, A. R., Nemon, H., & Lewis, E. A. (1996). Multicultural community organizing: A strategy for change. *Social Work, 41*(9), 501–508.

Hagen, J. L. (1986). Welfare fair hearings and client advocacy: A role for social workers. *Journal of Sociology and Social Welfare, 13,* 348–365.

Hallman, D. (1987). The Nestle boycott: The success of a citizens' coalition in social intervention. In E. M. Bennett (Ed.), *Studies in health and human services: Vol. 11. Social intervention: Theory and practice.* Lewiston, NY: Edward Mellon Press.

Halter, A. P. (1996). State welfare reform for employable general assistance recipients: The facts behind the assumptions. *Social Work, 41*(1), 106–110.

Hardcastle, D. A., Wenocur, S., & Powers, P. R. (1997b). Using the advocacy spectrum. In *Community practice: Theories and skills for social workers.* New York: Oxford University Press.

Harrington, M. (1962). *The other America: Poverty in the United States.* New York: Macmillan.

Hathway, M. (1944). Social action and professional education. In *Proceedings of the National Conference of Social Work: Selected papers, Seventy-first anniversary meeting, Cleveland, Ohio, May 21–27, 1944.* New York: Columbia University Press.

Haynes, K. S., & Mickelson, J. S. (1991). *Affecting change: Social workers in the political arena* (2d ed.). New York: Longman.

Haynes, K. S., & Mickelson, J. S. (1997). Influence through organizing others. In *Affecting change: Social workers in the political arena* (3d ed.). New York: Longman.

Heinz, J. P., Lauman, E. O., Nelson, R. L., & Salisbury, R. H. (1993). *The hollow core: Private interests in national policy making.* Cambridge, MA: Harvard University Press.

Henderson, C. R. (1899). President's address: The relation of philanthropy to social order and progress. In I. C. Barrows (Ed.), *Proceedings of the National Conference of Charities and Corrections at the Twenty-sixth annual session held in the City of Cincinnati, Ohio, May 17–23, 1899.* Boston: George H. Ellis.

Henderson, L. J. (1978). Administrative advocacy and black urban administrators. *Annals of the American Academy of Political Science, 439,* 68–79.

Henk, M. L. (Ed.). (1989). *Sage sourcebooks for the human services: Vol 8. Social work in primary care.* Newbury Park, CA: Sage.

Hepworth, D. H., & Larsen, J. A. (1993). *Direct social work practice: Theory and skills* (4th ed.). Pacific Grove, CA: Brooks/Cole.

Hepworth, D. H., Rooney, R. H., & Larsen, J. A. (1997). *Direct social work practice: Theory and skills* (5th ed.). Pacific Grove, CA: Brooks/Cole.

Herbert, M. D., & Mould, J. W. (1992). The advocacy role in public child welfare. *Child Welfare, 71*(2), 114–130.

Herman, M. H., & Callanan, B. V. (1978). Child welfare workers and the state legislative process. *Child Welfare, 57,* 13–25.

Herr, S. S. (1983). *Rights and advocacy for retarded people.* Lexington, MA: Lexington Books.

Higgins, P. S. (1978). Evaluation and case study of a school-based delinquency prevention program: The Minnesota youth advocate program. *Evaluation Quarterly, 2*(2), 215–234.

Higgins, T. (1983, Winter). Perspectives: Human service advocacy in the 1980s. *New England Journal of Human Services, 52.*

Hoechstetter, S. (1996). Taking new directions to improve public policy. *Social Work, 41*(7), 343–346.

Hoey, J. M. (1944). Social work concepts and methods in the postwar world. In *Proceedings of the National Conference of Social Work: Selected papers, Seventy-first anniversary meeting, Cleveland, Ohio, May 21–27, 1944.* New York: Columbia University Press.

Hollis, F. (1964). *Casework: A psychosocial therapy.* New York: Random House.

Holmes, K. A. (1981). Services for victims of rape: A dualistic practice model. *Social Casework, 62*(1), 30–39.

Horn, E. V. (1991). Advocacy for the traumatic brain injury professional. *Special Report #1*. Richmond, VA: Virginia Commonwealth University Rehabilitation Research and Training Center on Severe Traumatic Brain Injury.

Howard, D. S. (1952). Changing roles of public and private social welfare agencies. In *The Social Welfare Forum, 1952: Official proceedings, 79th annual meeting, National Conference of Social Work, Chicago, Illinois, May 25–30, 1952*. New York: Columbia University Press.

Hoyt, C. (1893). History of immigration. In I. C. Barrows (Ed.), *Proceedings of the National Conference of Charities and Corrections at the Twentieth annual session held in Chicago, Illinois, June 8–11, 1983*. Boston: George H. Ellis.

Hunter, J. B. (1979). Advocacy in action for the elderly. *Practice Digest, 1*(4), 15–17.

Hyman, D. (1983). A preventive approach to bureaucracy: The dialectical organization as a model for citizen's advocacy and ombudsmen. *Journal of Voluntary Action Research, 12*(4), 65–80.

Influencing State Policy. (1999). State policy differences. *Influence, 3*(2), 12.

Ingelhart, A. P., & Becerra, R. M. (1995). Service delivery to diverse communities: Agency-focused obstacles and pathways. In *Social services and the ethnic community* (pp. 205–239). Boston: Allyn & Bacon.

Jacobs, L. A. (1993). *Rights and deprivation*. Oxford: Clarendon Press.

Jaffe, E. D. (1978). On problems of loyalty: Who owns social work? *International Social Work, 21*, 38–42.

Jansson, B. S. (1994). *Social policy: From theory to policy practice*. Pacific Grove, CA: Brooks/Cole.

Jansson, B. S. (1999). *Becoming an effective policy advocate: From policy practice to social justice*. Pacific Grove, CA: Brooks/Cole.

Jansson, B. S., & Smith, S. (1996). Articulating a "new nationalism" in American social policy. *Social Work, 41*(9), 441–451.

Jenkins-Smith, H. C., & Sabatier, P. A. (1994). Evaluating the advocacy coalition framework. *Journal of Public Policy, 14*(2), 175–203.

Johnson, A. (1923). *Adventures in social welfare: Being reminiscences of things, thoughts and folks during forty years of social work*. Fort Wayne, IN: Fort Wayne Printing Company.

Johnson, L. C. (1995). *Social work practice: A generalist approach*. Boston: Allyn & Bacon.

Kahn, S. (1991). *Organizing: A guide for grassroot leaders* (Rev. ed.). Washington, DC: NASW Press.

Kahn, S. (1995). Community organization. In *Social Work Encyclopedia* (19th ed., pp. 569–576). Washington, DC: NASW Press.

Kaiser, C. A. (1952). Social group work practice and social responsibility. In *The Social Welfare Forum, 1952: Official proceedings, 79th annual meeting, National Conference of Social Work, Chicago, Illinois, May 25–30, 1952*. New York: Columbia University Press.

Kalas, J. W. (1987). *The grant system*. Albany, NY: State University of New York Press.

Kamerman, S. B. (1996). The new politics of child and family policies. *Social Work, 41*(9), 453–465.

Kaminski, L., & Walmsley, C. (1995). The advocacy brief: A guide for social workers. *The Social Worker, 63*, 53–58.

Katz, M. B. (1996). *In the shadow of the poorhouse: A social history of welfare in America* (10th anniversary ed.; Rev. and updated). New York: HarperCollins.

Kaufman, M. S. (1912, August 20). Letter to Jane Addams. Swarthmore College Peace Collection, Series 1.

Kellogg, P. U. (1938). As we find ourselves. *Survey, 74*(5).

Kennedy, D. M. (1991). World War I. In E. Foner & J. A. Garraty (Eds.), *The reader's companion to American history.* Boston: Houghton Mifflin.

Kettner, P. M., Moroney, R. M., & Martin, L. L. (1990). *Designing and managing programs: An effectiveness-based approach.* Newbury Park, CA: Sage.

Khinduka, S. K., & Coughlin, B. J. (1975). A conceptualization of social action. *Social Service Review, 49,* 1–14.

Kim, R. Y., Garfinkel, I., & Meyer, D. R. (1996). Is the whole greater than the sum of the parts? Interaction effects of three non-income-tested transfers for families with children. *Social Work Research, 20*(4), 274–275.

Kingsley, J. D. (1954). The citizen's responsibility for social action. In *The Social Welfare Forum, 1954: Official proceedings, 81st annual forum, National Conference of Social Work, Atlantic City, New Jersey, May 9–14, 1954.* New York: Columbia University Press.

Kirst-Ashman, K. K., & Hull, G. H., Jr. (1993). *Understanding generalist practice.* Chicago: Nelson-Hall.

Klein, A. R., & Cnaan, R. A. (1995, April). Practice with high-risk clients. *The Journal of Contemporary Human Services,* 203–212.

Kleinkauf, C. (1981). A guide to giving legislative testimony. *Social Work, 26,* 297–303.

Kleinkauf, C. (1988). Social work lobbies for social welfare: An Alaskan example. *Social Work, 33*(1), 56–57.

Kotler, P. (1972). The five Cs: Cause, change agency, change target, channel, and change strategy. In Zaltman, P. Kotler, & Kaufman, *Creating social change* (pp. 172–185). New York: Holt, Rinehart.

Kubler-Ross, E. (1969). *On death and dying.* New York: Macmillan.

Kurzman, P. A. (1974). *Harry Hopkins and the New Deal.* Fair Lawn, NJ: R. E. Burdick.

Kutchins, H., & Kutchins, S. (1978). Advocacy and social work. In G. Weber & G. McCall (Eds.), *Social scientists as advocates: Views from the applied disciplines.* Beverly Hills, CA: Sage.

Kutchins, H., & Kutchins, S. (1987). Advocacy and the adversary system. *Journal of Sociology and Social Welfare, 14*(3), 119–133.

Lane, R. P. (1946). An agency initiates social action. In *Proceedings of the National Conference of Social Work: Selected papers, Seventy-third annual meeting, Buffalo, New York, May 19–23, 1946.* New York: Columbia University Press.

Larcom, G. C., Jr. (1953). Democracy versus bureaucracy—The citizen's role. In *The Social Welfare Forum, 1953: Official proceedings, 80th annual meeting, National Conference of Social Work, Cleveland, Ohio, May 31–June 5, 1953.* New York: Columbia University Press.

Lardie, J. J. (1989). Advocacy strategies: An overview. In R. M. Friedman, A. J. Duchnowski, & E. L. Henderson (Eds.), *Advocacy on behalf of children with serious emotional problems* (pp. 45–53). Springfield, IL: Charles C. Thomas.

Lasch, C. (1965). *The social thought of Jane Addams.* Indianapolis, IN: Bobbs-Merrill.

Lash, M. (1996). Family-centered case management: Preparing parents to become service coordinators for children with ABI. In G. H. S. Singer, A. Glang, & J. M. Williams, *Children with acquired brain injury: Educating and supporting families.* Baltimore: Paul H. Brookes.

Lawrence, C. (1899). Necessity of uniform settlement laws. Delivered during the Report of Immigration and Interstate Migration Committee. In I. C. Barrows (Ed.), *Proceedings of the National Conference of Charities and Corrections at the Twenty-*

sixth annual session held in the City of Cincinnati, Ohio, May 17–23, 1899. Boston: George H. Ellis.

Leader, G. (1957). Social work in the political arena. In *The Social Welfare Forum, 1957: Official proceedings, 84th annual forum, National Conference on Social Welfare, Philadelphia, Pennsylvania, May 19–24, 1957.* New York: Columbia University Press.

Lee, Porter R. (1935). The social worker and social action. In P. R. Lee (Ed.), *Social work as cause and function and other papers.* New York: Columbia University Press.

Leighninger, L. (1987). *Social work: Search for identity.* New York: Greenwood Press.

Lenroot, K. F. (1935). Social work and the social order. In *Proceedings of the National Conference of Social Work [formerly the National Conference of Charities and Corrections] at the Sixty-second annual session held in Montreal, Canada, June 9–15, 1935.* Chicago: University of Chicago Press.

Lequerica, M. (1993). Stress in immigrant families with handicapped children: A child advocacy approach. *American Journal of Orthopsychiatry, 63*(4), 545–552.

Lester, L., Mutepa, R., Manetta, A. A., & Schneider, R. L. (1998, August 1). *Entitlement policies and programs: Internet access for social work professionals and students in the Commonwealth of Virginia.* Richmond, VA: Virginia Commonwealth University.

Levy, C. (1974). Advocacy and the injustice of justice. *Social Service Review, 48*(1), 29–50.

Levy, C. S. (1970). The social worker as agent of policy change. *Social Casework, 50,* 102–108.

Lewis, C. T. (1898). Minutes and discussions: The spoils system. In I. C. Barrows (Ed.), *Proceedings of the National Conference of Charities and Corrections at the Twenty-fifth annual session held in the city of New York, May 18–25, 1898.* Boston: George H. Ellis.

Lieberman, F. (1982). *Clinical social workers as psychotherapists.* New York: Gardner Press.

Linderholm, N. W. (1945). The social worker's responsibility for the reputation of the profession. In *Proceedings of the National Conference of Social Work: Selected papers, Seventy-second annual meeting, 1945.* New York: Columbia University Press.

Lipsky, M. (1968). Protest as a political resource. *American Political Science Review, 62,* 1144–1158.

Litzelfelner, P., & Petr, C. G. (1997). Case advocacy in child welfare. *Social Work, 42,* 392–402.

Loomis, B. A., & Cigler, A. J. (1986). Introduction: The changing nature of interest group politics. In A. J. Cigler & B. A. Loomis (Eds.), *Interest group politics* (pp. 1–26). Washington, DC: Congressional Quarterly Press.

Lourie, N. V. (1975). The many faces of advocacy. In I. N. Berlin (Ed.), *Advocacy for child mental illness.* New York: Brunner/Mazel.

Lurie, A. (1982). The social work advocacy role in discharge planning. *Social Work in Health Care, 8*(2), 75–85.

Lurie, H. (1935, July). Jane Addams. *Social Work Today,* 17–18.

Lyday, J. M. (1972). An advocate's process outline for policy analysis. *Urban Affairs Quarterly, 7,* 385–402.

Mack, J. W. (1912). Social progress. In *Proceedings of the National Conference of Charities and Corrections at the Thirty-ninth annual session held in Cleveland, OH, June 12–19, 1912.* Fort Wayne, IN: Fort Wayne Printing Company.

Mahaffey, M. (1972). Lobbying and social work. *Social Work, 17,* 3–11.

Mailick, M. D., & Ashley, A. A. (1981). Politics of interprofessional collaboration: Challenge to advocacy. *Social Casework, 62,* 131–137.

Martinez-Brawley, E. (1995). Community. In *Social Work Encyclopedia* (19th ed., pp. 545–548). Washington, DC: NASW Press.

Maslen, S. (1944). Methods of action on housing legislation. In *Proceedings of the National Conference of Social Work: Selected papers, Seventy-first anniversary meeting, Cleveland, Ohio, May 21–27, 1944.* New York: Columbia University Press.

Maslow, A. (1954). *Motivation and personality.* New York: Harper & Row.

Matson, J. L., & Mulick, J. A. (Eds.). (1991). *Handbook of mental retardation* (2d ed., Pergamon general psychology series, Vol. 121.). New York: Pergamon Press.

Mattison, G., & Storey, S. (1992). *Women in citizen advocacy.* Jefferson, NC: McFarland.

Mayo, L. W. (1944). The future for social work. In *Proceedings of the National Conference of Social Work: Selected papers, Seventy-first anniversary meeting, Cleveland, Ohio, May 21–27, 1944.* New York: Columbia University Press.

Mayo, L. W. (1948). Basic issues in social work. In *Proceedings of the National Conference of Social Work: Selected papers, Seventy-fifth anniversary meeting, Atlantic City, New Jersey, April 17–23, 1948.* New York: Columbia University Press.

Mayster, V., Waitzkin, H., Hubbell, F. A., & Rucker, L. (1993). Local advocacy for the medically indigent: Strategies and accomplishments in one county. *Journal of Health Care for the Poor and Underserved, 4*(3), 254–267.

McCormick, M. J. (1970). Social advocacy: A new dimension in social work. *Social Casework, 51*(1), 3–11.

McCullagh, J. G. (1981). Legislative advocacy for special needs children: A case example. *Arete, 6,* 23–33.

McCullagh, J. G. (1988). Challenging the proposed deregulation of P.L. 94-142: A case study of citizen advocacy. *Journal of Sociology and Social Welfare, 15*(3), 65–81.

McDougall, A. W. (1906). Publicity in charitable work in smaller cities. In *Proceedings of the National Conference of Charities and Corrections at the Thirty-fifth annual session held in the city of Richmond, VA, May 6th to 13th, 1908.* Fort Wayne, IN: Fort Wayne Printing Co.

McGowan, B. G. (1974). *Case advocacy: A study of the interventive process in child advocacy.* Doctoral dissertation, Columbia University, New York, NY.

McGowan, B. G. (1978). The case advocacy function in child welfare practice. *Child Welfare, 57*(5), 275–284.

McGowan, B. G. (1987). Advocacy. In A. Minahan (Ed.-in-Chief), *Encyclopedia of social work* (18th ed., Vol. 1). Silver Spring, MD: National Association of Social Workers.

McInnis-Dittrich, K. (1994). *Integrating social welfare policy and social work practice.* Pacific Grove, CA: Brooks/Cole.

McNutt, J. G., & Boland, K. M. (1999). Electronic advocacy by nonprofit organizations in social welfare policy. *Nonprofit and Voluntary Sector Quarterly, 28,* 432–451.

Melton, G. B. (1983). *Child advocacy: Psychological issues and interventions.* New York: Plenum Press.

Melton, G. B., Petrila, J., Poythress, N. G., & Slobogin, C. (1997). *Psychological evaluations for the courts: A handbook for mental health professionals and lawyers* (2d ed.). New York: Guilford.

Mencken, H. L. (1937). *The American language: An inquiry into the development of English in the United States* (4th ed.). New York: Alfred A. Knopf.

Mencken, H. L. (1966). *The American language: An inquiry into the development of English in the United States* (Supp. I). New York: Alfred A. Knopf.

Merriam Webster. (1994). In *Infopedia: The ultimate multi-media reference tool.* © 1995 Future Vision Multimedia, Inc., a subsidiary of Future Holding, Inc. and its licensors. CD Rom.

Meyer, A. E. (1956). Has the structure of social work become outmoded? In *The Social Welfare Forum, 1956: Official proceedings, 83rd annual forum, National Conference of Social Work, St. Louis, Missouri, May 20–25, 1956.* New York: Columbia University Press.

Mickelson, J. S. (1995). Advocacy. In *Encyclopedia of social work* (19th ed., pp. 95–100). Washington, DC: NASW Press.

Milbrath, L. (1963). *Washington lobbyists.* Chicago: Rand McNally.

Miller, H. (1968). Value dilemmas in social casework. *Social Work, 13,* 27–44.

Miller, S. M., Rein, M., & Levitt, P. (1990). Community action in the United States. *Community Development Journal, 25,* 356–368.

Mills, F. B. (1996). The ideology of welfare reform: Deconstructing stigma. *Social Work, 41*(7), 391–395.

Mondros, J. B., & Wilson, S. M. (1990). Staying alive: Career selection and sustenance of community organizers. *Administration in Social Work, 14,* 95–109.

Mondros, J. B., & Wilson, S. M. (1994). *Organizing for power and empowerment.* New York: Columbia University Press.

Morgan, G. G. (1983). Practical techniques for change. *Journal of Children in Contemporary Society, 15*(4), 91–102.

Moxley, D. P., & Freddolino, P. P. (1990). A model of advocacy for promoting client self-determination in psychosocial rehabilitation. *Psychosocial Rehabilitation Journal, 14*(2), 69–82.

Moxley, D. P., & Freddolino, P. P. (1991). Needs of homeless people coping with psychiatric problems: Findings from an innovative advocacy project. *Health and Social Work, 16*(1), 19–26.

Moxley, D. P., & Freddolino, P. P. (1994). Client-driven advocacy and psychiatric disability: A model for social work practice. *Journal of Sociology and Social Welfare, 21*(2), 91–108.

NASW News. (1998, January). Welfare: Chapters keep the pressure on. *NASW News, 43*(1).

NASW News. (1998, October). Helping the working poor scale summit. *NASW News, 43*(9).

NASW News. (1998, November). Protector of kids and a culture: A Native American social worker finds his niche. *NASW News, 43*(10).

NASW News. (1999, January). For-profit health care ills voiced. *NASW News, 44*(1).

NASW News. (1999, April). Drugs-and-pregnancy challenge revisited. *NASW News, 44*(4).

NASW News. (1999, July). Model child welfare system is devised. *NASW News, 44*(7).

National Association of Social Workers. (1996). *Code of Ethics.* Washington, DC: Author.

National Association of Social Workers, Ad Hoc Committee on Advocacy (1969). The social worker as advocate: Champion of social victims. *Social Work, 14*(2), 16–22.

Nazario, J. (1984). Confronting the system: How social workers can challenge—and change—the laws. *Practice Digest, 7*(2), 4–9.

Nees, R. (1936, January). Five letters from the field: Civil liberties in Michigan. *Social Work Today,* 19–20.

Neilsen, G. A., & Young, F. J. (1994). HIV/AIDS, advocacy, and antidiscrimination legislation—The Australian response. *International Journal of STD & AIDS, 5,* 13–17.

Netting, F. E., Kettner, P. M., & McMurtry, S. L. (1998). *Social Work Macro Practice* (2d ed.). New York: Longman.

Northen, H. (1995). *Clinical social work: Knowledge and skills.* New York: Columbia University Press.

Northwod, L. K., & Parker, M. (1984). The relative effectiveness of legislative campaigning in a school of social work. *Journal of Sociology and Social Welfare, 11,* 684–713.

Nulman, E. (1983). Family therapy and advocacy: Directions for the future. *Social Work, 28,* 19–22.

O'Brien, D., Richard, B., & Wein, F. (1989). *Influencing social policy: A reconsideration of the role of advocacy by social workers.* Paper presented at the Fourth National Conference on Social Welfare, Toronto, Ontario.

O'Connell, B. (1978). From service to advocacy to empowerment. *Social Casework, 59*(4), 195–202.

O'Connor, K. J., & Ammen, S. (1997). *Play therapy treatment planning and interventions: The ecosystemic model and workbook.* San Diego: Academic Press.

Olley, M. C., & Ogloff, J. R. P. (1995). Patients' rights advocacy: Implications for program design and implementation. *Journal of Mental Health Administration, 22*(4), 368–376.

O'Neill, J. V. (1999, September). Advocacy takes a new tack. *NASW News, 44*(8).

Ostertag, H. C. (1946). Our legislative responsibility for the aged. In *Proceedings of the National Conference of Social Work: Selected papers, Seventy-third annual meeting, Buffalo, New York, May 19–23, 1946.* New York: Columbia University Press.

Oxford English Dictionary (2d ed.). (1989). Oxford: Clarendon Press.

Ozawa, M., & Kirk, S. A. (1996). Welfare reform. *Social Work Research, 20*(4), 194–195.

Pacey, L. M. (1950). *Readings in the development of settlement work.* New York: Knickerbocker.

Panitch, A. (1974). Advocacy in practice. *Social Work, 19*(3), 326–332.

Pardeck, J. T., & Meinert, R. (1994). Do social workers have a major impact on social policy? Yes or no? In H. J. Karger & J. Midgley. *Controversial issues in social policy* (pp. 93–106). Boston: Allyn & Bacon.

Patten, S. N. (1907). *The new basis of civilization.* New York: The Macmillan Company. In D. M. Fox (Ed.) (1968). Cambridge, MA: The Belknap Press of Harvard University Press.

Patti, R. J. (1974). Limitation and prospects of internal advocacy. *Social Casework, 55,* 537–545.

Patti, R. J. (1980). Internal advocacy and human service practitioners: An exploratory study. In H. Resnick & R. J. Patti (Eds.), *Change from within: Humanizing social welfare organizations.* Philadelphia: Temple University Press.

Patti, R. J., & Dear, R. B. (1975). Legislative advocacy: One path to social change. *Social Work, 20,* 108–114.

Paul, J. L. (1977). A framework for understanding advocacy. In J. L. Paul, G. R. Newfeld, & J. W. Pelosi, *Child advocacy within the system* (pp. 11–31). New York: Syracuse University Press.

Paull, J. E. (1971). Social action for a different decade. *Social Service Review, 45,* 30–36.

Pawlak, E. J., & Flynn, J. P. (1990). Executive directors' political activities. *Social Work, 35*(4), 307–312.

Payne, J. E., & Pezzoli, J. (1977). Citizen advocacy. *Arete, 4,* 153–159.

Pearl, G., & Barr, D. H. (1976). Agencies advocating together. *Social Casework, 56*(12), 611–618.

Pearlman, M. H., & Edwards, M. G. (1982). Enabling in the eighties: The client advocacy group. *Social Casework, 63*(9), 532–539.

Peled, E., & Edleson, J. L. (1994). Advocacy for battered women: A national survey. *Journal of Family Violence, 9*(3), 285–296.

Perlmutter, F. D., & Adams, C. T. (1994). Family service executives in a hostile environment. *The Journal of Contemporary Human Services, 75,* 439–446.

Perloff, J. D. (1996). Medicaid managed care and urban poor people: Implications for social work. *Health & Social Work, 21*(8), 196–201.

Peterson, M. S., & Urquiza, A. J. (1993). *The role of mental health professionals in the prevention and treatment of child abuse and neglect: National Center on Child Abuse and Neglect; The user manual series.* McLean, VA: U.S. Department of Health and Human Services, Administration for Children and Families.

Petr, C. G., & Spano, R. N. (1990, May). Evolution of social services for children with emotional disorders. *Social Work,* 228–234.

Piven, F. F., & Cloward, R. A. (1975). Notes towards a radical social work. In R. Bailey & M. Brake (Eds.), *Radical social work.* New York: Pantheon.

Poole, D. L. (1996). Keeping managed care in balance. In P. L. Ewalt, E. M. Freeman, S. A. Kirk, & D. L. Poole (Eds.), *Social policy: Reform, research, and practice* (1997). Washington, DC: NASW Press.

Powell, J. Y., & Causby, V. D. (1994). From the classroom to the capitol—from MSW students to advocates: Learn by doing. *Journal of Teaching in Social Work, 9,* 141–154.

Pray, K. L. M. (1945). Social work and social action. In *Proceedings of the National Conference of Social Work: Selected papers, Seventy-second annual meeting, 1945.* New York: Columbia University Press.

Pritchard, L. (1997, October). Legal issues in the protection of consumer rights. In R. J. Gabriele (Ed.), *Healthcare reform: A consumer, family and advocate perspective* (pp. 26–30). Alexandria, VA: National Mental Health Association.

Prizant, B. M. (1999, August 3). *Enhancing communicative and socioemotional competence in young children with autism spectrum disorders.* Presented at the Third Annual S. Gail Mayfield Training Institute, August 2–5, 1999. Shenandoah University, Winchester, Virginia.

Proceedings of the National Conference of Charities and Corrections at the Thirty-fifth annual session held in the city of Richmond, VA, May 6th to 13th, 1908. Fort Wayne, IN: Fort Wayne Printing Co.

Pumphrey, R. E., & Pumphrey, M. W. (Eds.). (1961). *The heritage of American social work: Readings in its philosophical and institutional development.* New York: Columbia University Press.

Raider, M. (1982). Protecting the rights of clients: Michigan sets a model for other states. *Social Work, 27,* 160–163.

Reamer, F. G. (1998). The evolution of social work ethics. *Social Work, 43*(6), 488–500.

Regis, J. D. (1984). What every social worker needs to know about the law. *Practice Digest, 7*(2), 10–12.

Reid, I. D. (1955). Social change, social relations, and social work. In *The Social Welfare Forum, 1955: Official proceedings, 82nd annual forum, National Conference of Social Work, San Francisco, California, May 29–June 3, 1955.* New York: Columbia University Press.

Reid, W. J. (1977). Social work for social problems. *Social Work, 22*(5), 374–381.

Reisch, M. (1986). From cause to case and back again: The reemergence of advocacy in social work. *Urban and Social Change Review, 19,* 20–24.

Reisch, M. (1990). Organizational structure and client advocacy: Lessons from the 1980s. *Social Work, 35*(1), 73–74.

Richan, W. C. (1973). Dilemmas of the social work advocate. *Child Welfare, 52*(4), 220–226.

Richan, W. C. (1980). The administrator as advocate. In F. D. Perlmutter & S. Slavin (Eds.), *Leadership in social administration* (pp. 72–85). Philadelphia: Temple University Press.

Richan, W. C. (1983). Social work administration under assault. *Administration in Social Work, 7,* 9–19.

Richan, W. C. (1996). *Lobbying for social change.* New York: Haworth Press.

Richmond, M. E. (1906). The retail method of reform. In M. E. Richmond, *The Long View: Papers and Addresses.* New York: Russell Sage Foundation.

Richmond, M. E. (1907). The family in distress. In M. E. Richmond, *The good neighbor in the modern city.* Philadelphia: J. P. Lippincott.

Richmond, M. E. (1910). The interrelationship of social movements. In M. E. Richmond, *The long view: Papers and addresses.* New York: Russell Sage Foundation.

Richmond, M. E. (1917). *Social diagnosis.* New York: Russell Sage Foundation.

Richmond, M. E. (1920). What are you thinking? In M. E. Richmond, *The long view: Papers and addresses* (1930). New York: Russell Sage Foundation.

Richmond, M. E. (1922). *What is social case work?* New York: Russell Sage Foundation.

Richmond, M. E. (1923). Sir Charles Stewart Loch. In M. E. Richmond, *The long view: Papers and addresses* (1930). New York: Russell Sage Foundation.

Rickards, L. D. (1992). Professional and organized provider associations. *Administration and Policy in Mental Health, 20,* 11–25.

Riddle, J. I., & King, L. (1977). Advocacy in an institution. In J. L. Paul, G. R. Neufeld, & J. W. Pelosi. *Child advocacy within the system.* New York: Syracuse University Press.

Riley, P. V. (1971). Family advocacy: Case to cause and back to case. *Child Welfare, 50*(7), 374–383.

Roberts, M. (1983). Political advocacy: An alternative strategy of administrative practice. *Social Development Issues, 7,* 2–31.

Roberts-DeGennaro, M. (1986a). Building coalitions for political advocacy. *Social Work, 31,* 308–311.

Roberts-DeGennaro, M. (1986b). Factors contributing to coalition maintenance. *Journal of Sociology and Social Welfare, 13*(2), 248–264.

Rock, B., & Congress, E. (1999). The new confidentiality for the 21st century in a managed care environment. *Social Work, 44*(3), 253–262.

Ronnau, J. (1995). Family advocacy services: A strengths model of case management. In B. J. Friesen & J. Poertner (Eds.), *From case management to service coordination for children with emotional, behavioral, or mental disorders: Building on family strengths.* Baltimore: Paul H. Brookes.

Rosenthal, E., & Rubenstein, L. S. (1993). International human rights advocacy under the "principles for the protection of persons with mental illness." *International Journal of Law and Psychiatry, 16,* 257–300.

Ross, E. C. (1985). Coalition development in legislative advocacy. *Exceptional Children, 51,* 342–344.

Ross, E. C. (1992). Success and failure of advocacy groups: A legislative perspective. *Administration and Policy in Mental Health, 20,* 57–66.

Ross, R. J. S. (1977a). The new left and the human service professions. *Journal of Sociology and Social Welfare, 4*(5), 694–706.

Ross, R. J. S. (1977b). Problems of advocacy. *Journal of Sociology and Social Welfare, 4*(8), 1246–1259.

Rothman, J., Erlich, J., & Teresa, J. (1977). Adding something new: Innovation. In F. Cox, J. Erlich, J. Rothman, & J. Tropman (Eds.), *Tactics and techniques of community practice.* Itasca, IL: F. E. Peacock.

Rothman, J., Erlich, J. L., Tropman, J. E., & Cox, F. M. (Eds.). (1995). *Strategies of community intervention* (5th ed., pp. 26–53). Itasca, IL: F. E. Peacock.

Ruffolo, M. C., & Miller, P. (1994). An advocacy/empowerment model of organizing: Developing university-agency partnerships. *Journal of Social Work Education, 30*(3), 310–316.

Russell, H. M. (1994). *A child's advocate guide to the Virginia General Assembly.* Richmond, VA: Virginia Department of Mental Health, Mental Retardation, and Substance Abuse Services.

Saleebey, D. (1990). Philosophical disputes in social work: Social justice denied. *Journal of Sociology and Social Welfare, 17,* 29–40.

Saltzman, A., & Proch, K. (1990). *Law in social work practice.* Chicago: Nelson-Hall.

Sanborn, F. B. (1887). Regulation of emigration: Report of the standing committee on alien papers and criminals. In I. C. Barrows (Ed.), *Proceedings of the National Conference of Charities and Corrections, at the Fourteenth annual session held in Omaha, Neb., August 25–31, 1887.* Boston: George H. Ellis.

Sancier, B. (1984). Social work and the law. *Practice Digest, 7*(2) (entire issue).

Sands, R. G. (1991). *Clinical social work practice in community mental health.* New York: Macmillan.

Schlager, E. (1995). Policy making and collective action: Defining coalitions within the advocacy coalition framework. *Policy Sciences, 28*(3), 243–270.

Schloss, C. N., & Jayne, D. (1994). Models and methods of advocacy. In S. Alper, P. J. Schloss, & C. N. Schloss (Eds.), *Families of students with disabilities: Consultation and advocacy.* Needham Heights, MA: Allyn & Bacon.

Schlozman, K. W., & Tierney, J. T. (1986). *Organized interests and American democracy.* New York: Harper Collins.

Schneider, R. L., & Netting, F. E. (1999). Influencing social policy in a time of devolution: Upholding social work's great tradition. *Social Work, 44,* 349–357.

Schneider, R. L., & Sharon, N. (1982). Representation of social work agencies: New definition, special issues, and practice models. *Administration in Social Work, 6,* 59–68.

Schopler, J. H., Abell, M. D., & Galinsky, M. J. (1998). Technology-based groups: A review and conceptual framework for practice. *Social Work, 43*(3), 254–268.

Schottland, C. I. (1953). Social work issues in the political arena. In *The Social Welfare Forum, 1953: Official proceedings, 80th annual meeting, National Conference of Social Work, Cleveland, Ohio, May 31–June 5, 1953.* New York: Columbia University Press.

Schwartz, W. (1969). Private troubles and public issues: One social work job or two? In *Social Welfare Forum* (pp. 34–38). New York: Columbia University Press.

Scotch, C. B., & Lane, L. (1972, June). *The organizational context of client advocacy.* Unpublished paper delivered at the annual meeting of the National Conference of Social Welfare, Chicago, IL.

Segal, E. A., & Brzuzy, S. (1998). *Social welfare policy, programs and practice.* Itasca, IL: F. E. Peacock.

Shanker, R. (1983). Occupational disease, workers' compensation, and the social work advocate. *Social Work, 28*(1), 24–27.

Sharwell, G. R. (1978). How to testify before a legislative committee. In J. W. Hanks (Ed.), *Toward human dignity.* New York: National Association of Social Workers.

Shaw, R. (1996). *The activist's handbook: A primer for the 1990s and beyond.* Berkeley, CA: University of California Press.

Sheafor, B. W., Horejsi, C. R., & Horejsi, G. A. (1994). *Techniques and guidelines for social work practice* (3d ed.). Boston: Allyn & Bacon.

Shera, W. (1996). Managed care and people with severe mental illness: Challenges and opportunities for social work. In P. L. Ewalt, E. M. Freeman, S. A. Kirk, & D. L. Poole (Eds.), *Social policy: Reform, research, and practice* (1997). Washington, DC: NASW Press.

Sherman, T. A., & Johnson, S. S. (1975). *Modern technical writing.* Englewood Cliffs, NJ: Prentice-Hall.

Shiffman, B. M. (1958). Effecting change through social group work. In *The Social Welfare Forum, 1958: Official proceedings, 85th annual forum, National Conference on Social Welfare, Chicago, Illinois, May 11–16, 1958.* New York: Columbia University Press.

Simons, R. L. (1982). Strategies for exercising influence. *Social Work, 27*(3), 268–273.

Simons, R. L. (1988). Generic social work skills in social administration: The example of persuasion. *Administration in Social Work, 11,* 241–254.

Slavin, P. (1999, April). Clinton hears pitch for patients' rights bill. *NASW News, 44*(4).

Smith, V. T. (1887). The Economy of the state in the care of dependent and neglected children. In I. C. Barrows (Ed.), *Proceedings of the National Conference of Charities and Corrections, at the Fourteenth annual session held in Omaha, Neb., August 25–31, 1887.* Boston: George H. Ellis.

Smith, V. W. (1979). How interest groups influence legislators. *Social Work, 24,* 234–239.

Smucker, B. (1999). *The nonprofit lobbying guide* (2d ed.). Washington, DC: Independent Sector.

Sommer, R. (1990). Family advocacy and the mental health system: The recent rise of the Alliance for the Mentally Ill. *Psychiatric Quarterly, 61*(3), 205–221.

Sonnichsen, R. C. (1988). Advocacy evaluation: A model for internal evaluation offices. *Evaluation and Program Planning, 11,* 141–148.

Sonnichsen, R. C. (1989). Advocacy evaluation. *Knowledge: Creation, Diffusion, Utilization, 10,* 243–259.

Sosin, M., & Caulum, S. (1983). Advocacy: A conceptualization for social work practice. *Social Work, 28*(1), 12–17.

Spakes, P. (1987). Social workers and the courts: Education, practice, and research needs. *Journal of Social Work Education, 23*(2), 30–39.

Spano, R. (1982). *The rank and file movement in social work.* Washington, DC: The University Press.

Spencer, A. G. (1923, November 28). Letter to Jane Addams. Swarthmore College Peace Collection; WILPF Papers.

Steele, H. W. (1908). Press and publicity report of the committee: Publicity in social work. In *Proceedings of the National Conference of Charities and Corrections at the Thirty-fifth annual session held in the city of Richmond, VA, May 6th to 13th, 1908.* Fort Wayne, IN: Fort Wayne Printing Co.

Stern, L. W., & Gibelman, M. (1990). Voluntary social welfare agencies: Trends, issues, and prospects. *Families in Society: The Journal of Contemporary Human Services, 71*(1), 13–23.

Stewart, C. J., Smith, C. A., & Denton, R. E. (1989). *Persuasion and social movements.* Prospect Heights, IL: Waveland Press.

Stockdill, J. W. (1992). A government manager's view of mental health advocacy groups. *Administration and Policy in Mental Health, 20*(1), 45–55.

Strom-Gottfried, K. (1998). Applying a conflict resolution framework to disputes in managed care. *Social Work, 43*(5), 393–401.

Stroul, B. A. (1995). Case management in a system of care. In B. J. Friesen & J. Poertner (Eds.), *From case management to service coordination for children with emotional, behavioral, or mental disorders: Building on family strengths.* Baltimore: Paul H. Brookes.

Strunk, W., & White, E. B. (1959). *The elements of style.* New York: Macmillan.

Sunley, R. (1970). Family advocacy: From case to cause. *Social Casework, 51*(6), 347–357.

Taebel, D. A. (1972). Strategies to make bureaucrats responsive. *Social Work, 17,* 38–43.

Takanishi, R. (1978). Childhood as a social issue: Historical roots of contemporary child advocacy movements. *Journal of Social Issues, 34*(2), 8–28.

Talmage, W. H. (1915, October 18). Letter to Jane Addams. Swarthmore College Peace Collections, WILPF Papers.

Talmage, W. H., & Flandreau, S. D. (1915). *Ethical economics: A strong paper read before the state bar association on September 1st by Rev. William Henry Talmage, Flandreau, S. D., Chairman of Social Service Commission of South Dakota, and Secretary of the Other Economic Leagues of America.* Attached to Talmage (Oct. 18, 1915) letter to Jane Addams.

Taylor, E. D. (1987). *From issue to action: An advocacy program model.* Lancaster, PA: Family Service.

Taylor, E. D. (1991). The role of structure in effective agency advocacy. *Social Work with Groups, 14,* 141–151.

Taylor, G. R. (1922, June 12). Letter to Jane Addams. Rockford College Archives.

Taylor, G. R. (1922, June 12). Letter to Julia C. Lathrop. Rockford College Archives.

Taylor, G. R. (1932, April). Julia C. Lathrop: 1858–1932. *The Compass, 6.*

Teare, R. J., & McPheeters, H. L. (1970). *Manpower utilization in social welfare.* Atlanta, GA: Southern Regional Education Board.

Tefft, B. (1987). Advocacy coalitions as a vehicle for mental health system reform. In E. M. Bennett (Ed.), *Social intervention: Theory and practice: Vol. 11. Studies in health and human services* (pp. 155–185). Lewiston, NY: Edwin Mellen Press.

Terrell, P. (1967). The social worker as radical: Roles of advocacy. *New Perspectives: The Berkeley Journal of Social Welfare, 1*(1), 83–88.

Thompson, J. J. (1994). Social workers and politics: Beyond the Hatch Act. *Social Work, 39,* 457–465.

Thursz, D. (1971). Social action. In R. Morris (Ed.-in-Chief), *Encyclopedia of Social Work* (Vol. II, 16th issue). New York: National Association of Social Workers.

Tourigney, A., Bongiorno, P. A., & Acquavita, R. J. (1993). *Handbook for rehabilitative advocacy.* Washington, DC: National Rehabilitation Association.

Traczek, B. (1987). *Domestic violence: The all-American crime: A collaborative model for a community response.* Milwaukee, WI: Task Force on Battered Women.

Trattner, W. I. (1994). *From poor law to welfare state: A history of social welfare in America* (5th ed.). New York: Free Press.

Tropman, J. E. (1997). *Successful community leadership: A skills guide for volunteers and professionals.* Washington, DC: NASW Press.

Tropman, J. E., Lauffer, A., & Lawrence, W. (1977). A guide to advocacy. In F. M. Cox, J. L. Erlich, J. Rothman, & J. E. Tropman, *Tactics and techniques of community practice* (pp. 199–207). Itasca, IL: F. E. Peacock Press.

Tucker, T. (1913). Social justice. In *Proceedings of the National Conference of Charities and Corrections at the Fortieth annual session held in Seattle, Washington, July 5–12, 1913.* Fort Wayne, IN: Fort Wayne Printing Company.

Uehara, E. S., Sohng, S. S. L., Bending, R. L., Seyfried, S., Richey, C. A., Morelli, P., Spencer, M., Ortega, D., Keenan, L., & Kanuha, V. (1996). Toward a values-based approach to multicultural social work research. *Social Work, 41*(6), 613–623.

Van Gheluwe, B., & Barber, J. K. (1986). Legislative advocacy in action. *Social Work, 31*(5), 393–395.

Villone, P. (1983). Staff planning groups: Internal advocates of permanency planning for children in foster care. *Social Work with Groups, 5,* 81–93.

Vosburgh, W. W., & Hyman, D. (1973). Advocacy and bureaucracy: The life and times of a decentralized citizen's advocacy program. *Administrative Science Quarterly, 18,* 433–448.

Wade, A. D. (1966). The social worker in the political process. In *The Social Welfare Forum, 1996, Proceedings, 93rd annual forum, National Conference on Social Welfare, Chicago, IL, May 29–June 3, 1966* (pp. 52–67). New York: Columbia University Press.

Wales, J. C. (1915, October 1). Letter to Jane Addams, with attachment *Continuous mediation without armistice.*

Wales, J. C. (1915, October 22). Letter from J. G. Wales to J. Addams. State Historical Society of Wisconsin, Julia Grace Wales Papers. From University of Illinois at Chicago: The University Library, Jane Addams Memorial Collection.

Wallach, L. (1994). Media advocacy: A strategy for empowering people and communities. *Journal of Public Health Policy, 15*(4), 420–436.

Ward, M. (1995). A place for advocacy in child welfare systems: The case of adoption. *Child Welfare, 74,* 619–632.

Warner, A. G. (1889). Notes on the statistical determination of the causes of poverty: *Publication,* American Statistical Association, New Series I, No. 5. In R. E. Pumphrey & M. W. Pumphrey (Eds.), *The heritage of American social work: Readings in its philosophical and institutional development* (1961, pp. 183–201). New York: Columbia University Press.

Warner, A. G. (1894). The causes of poverty further considered: *Publication,* American Statistical Association, New Series, IV, No. 27. In R. E. Pumphrey & M. W. Pumphrey (Eds.), *The heritage of American social work: Readings in its philosophical and institutional development* (1961, pp. 49–68). New York: Columbia University Press.

Warren, R. L. (1971). *Truth, love, and social change.* Chicago: Rand-McNally.

Weaver, H. N. (1999). Indigenous people and the social work profession: Defining culturally competent services. *Social Work, 44*(3), 217–227.

Webster's New World College Dictionary (3d ed.). (1996). New York: Simon & Schuster.

Weil, M. O. (1996). Community building: Building community practice. In P. L. Ewalt, E. M. Freeman, S. A. Kirk, & D. L. Poole (Eds.), *Social policy: Reform, research, and practice* (1997). Washington, DC: NASW Press.

Weil, M. O., & Gamble, D. N. (1995). Community practice models. In *Social Work Encyclopedia* (19th ed., pp. 577–593). Washington, DC: NASW Press.

Weil, M. O., Zipper, I. N., & Dedmon, S. R. (1995). Issues and principles of training for case management in child mental health. In B. J. Friesen & J. Poertner (Eds.), *From case management to service coordination for children with emotional, behavioral, or mental disorders: Building on family strengths.* Baltimore: Paul H. Brookes.

Weiner, L. S. (1998). Telephone support groups for HIV-positive mothers whose children have died of AIDS. *Social Work, 43*(3), 279–285.

Weiss, J. O. (1992). Genetic disorders: Support groups and advocacy. *Families in Society, 74*(4), 213–220.

Weissbrodt, D. (1989). *Immigration law and procedure in a nutshell* (2d ed.). St. Paul, MN: West Publishing Co.

Wilensky, H. L., & Lebeaux, C. N. (1958). *Industrial society and social welfare.* New York: Russell Sage Foundation.

Williams, A. W. (1931). Wanted—an effective spur for social values. *Social Forces, X,* 53–61.

Williams, C. (1986). Improving care in nursing homes using community advocacy. *Social Scientific Medicine, 23*(12), 1297–1303.

Wineman, D. (1968). Captors, captives and social workers in a civil society: A position statement. Unpublished manuscript.

Wineman, D., & James, A. (1969). The advocacy challenge to schools of social work. *Social Work, 14,* 23–32.

Wirth, L. (1949). Social goals for America. In *The Social Welfare Forum: Official proceedings, 76th annual meeting, National Conference of Social Work, Cleveland, Ohio, June 12–17, 1949.* New York: Columbia University Press.

Witkin, S. L. (1998). Human rights and social work. *Social Work, 43*(3), 197–201.

Wittenberg, E., & Wittenberg, E. (1989). *How to win in Washington.* Oxford: Basis Blackwell.

Wolfensberger, W. (1977). A model for a balanced multicomponent advocacy/protective services schema. In L. E. Kopolow & H. Bloom (Eds.), *Mental health advocacy: An emerging force in consumers' rights.* Rockville, MD: U.S. Department of Health, Education, and Welfare; Public Health Service.

Wolk, J. L. (1981). Are social workers politically active? *Social Work, 26,* 283–288.

Woods, M. E., & Hollis, F. (1990). *Casework: A psychosocial therapy.* New York: McGraw-Hill.

Woodside, M. R., & Legg, B. H. (1990). Patient advocacy: A mental health perspective. *Journal of Mental Health Counseling, 12,* 38–50.

Yep, R. K. (1992). Advocating in the public policy arena. In C. Solomon & P. Jackson-Jobe (Eds.), *Helping homeless people: Unique challenges and solutions* (pp. 29–40). Alexandria, VA: American Association for Counseling and Development.

Yoo, J. (1999, May). The supreme court rediscovers an old clause. *The Wall Street Journal,* p. A31.

Young, D. R. (1992). Organising principles for international advocacy associations. *Journal of Social Policy, 3,* 1–28.

Index